The publisher gratefully acknowledges the generous support of the Classical Literature Endowment Fund of the University of California Press Foundation, which was established by a major gift from Joan Palevsky.

Caesar in the USA

Caesar in the USA

Maria Wyke

UNIVERSITY OF CALIFORNIA PRESS
Berkeley · Los Angeles · London

University of California Press, one of the most distinguished
university presses in the United States, enriches lives around
the world by advancing scholarship in the humanities, social
sciences, and natural sciences. Its activities are supported by
the UC Press Foundation and by philanthropic contributions
from individuals and institutions. For more information,
visit www.ucpress.edu.

University of California Press
Berkeley and Los Angeles, California

University of California Press, Ltd.
London, England

Library of Congress Cataloging-in-Publication Data

Wyke, Maria.
    Caesar in the USA / Maria Wyke.
        p.   cm.
    Includes bibliographical references and index.
    ISBN 978-0-520-27391-7 (cloth, alk. paper)
        1. Caesar, Julius—Influence.   2. United States—
    Civilization—Classical influences.   3. Political culture—
    United States—History.   I. Title.
    DG262.W96   2012
    306.20973—dc23   2012005217

Manufactured in the United States of America

21   20   19   18   17   16   15   14   13   12
10   9   8   7   6   5   4   3   2   1

The paper used in this publication meets the minimum
requirements of ANSI/NISO Z39.48–1992 (R 2002)
(Permanence of Paper).

Contents

List of Illustrations   *vii*
Acknowledgments   *xi*

Introduction   *1*

PART ONE. EDUCATION

1. Maturation   *21*

2. Americanization   *47*

3. Militarism   *68*

PART TWO. POLITICAL CULTURE

4. Dictatorship   *101*

5. Totalitarianism   *130*

6. Presidential Power   *167*

7. Empire   *203*

Notes   *239*
References   *277*
Index   *297*

Illustrations

1. The official Virginia state seal / 3
2. An early variant of the Virginia state seal / 3
3. President Lincoln caricatured in the British press as an assassinated Caesar (1865) / 5
4. "Officers, Standard-Bearers, and Musicians," color plate, from F.W. Kelsey, *Caesar's Commentaries* (1918) / 31
5. Caesar decides to bridge the Rhine, from *Caesar in Gaul,* edited by B.L. D'Ooge and F.C. Eastman (1917) / 34
6. "The Assassination of Caesar, 44 BC," from the painting by C. Rochegrosse, in *Caesar in Gaul,* edited by B.L. D'Ooge and F.C. Eastman (1917) / 39
7. "The Shepherd Meets a Proconsul," from A.C. Whitehead's *The Standard Bearer* (1914) / 42
8. Caesar presents Caius with his bride, from A.C. Whitehead's *The Standard Bearer* (1914) / 43
9. Richard Mansfield as Brutus, in Shakespeare's *Julius Caesar* (1902–3) / 57
10. Scene 8 (the assassination of Caesar), from Vitagraph's *Julius Caesar* (1908) / 61
11. A few moments later in scene 8 (the assassination of Caesar), from Vitagraph's *Julius Caesar* (1908) / 61

12. Advertisement for the United Cigar Stores, from the program for a revival of Shakespeare's *Julius Caesar,* New Amsterdam Theatre, New York (1927) / 66

13. *Vercingétorix jette ses armes aux pieds de César,* Lionel Royer (1899) / 77

14. Wolf-holes at the siege of Alesia, 52 B.C.E., from F.W. Kelsey, *Caesar's Commentaries* (1918) / 79

15. Wolf-holes along the German line near Ypres, 1914, from F.W. Kelsey, *Caesar's Commentaries* (1918) / 79

16. "The End of a Perfect Year," cartoon by Marcus, *New York Times* (c. August 1916) / 82

17. Caesar accepts the surrender of Vercingetorix, still, from Enrico Guazzoni's *Cajus Julius Caesar* (1914) / 85

18. Caesar and Mussolini, from *Reincarnazione di Cesare: Il predestinato* by Rosavita (1936) / 106

19. "Mussolini, the New Colossus of Rhodes," *Travaso* (New Orleans), cartoon by Albert T. Reid for the Bell Syndicate (c. 1936) / 113

20. Brutus (Orson Welles) salutes Caesar (Joseph Holland), in Orson Welles's *Julius Caesar* (1937) / 116

21. Antony (George Coulouris) harangues the mob over Caesar's body, in Orson Welles's *Julius Caesar* (1937) / 118

22. The cast of characters for *Julius Caesar, Classics Illustrated,* no. 68 (February 1950) / 142

23. The cover of *Julius Caesar, Classics Illustrated,* no. 68 (February 1950) / 144

24. Caesar arrives for the ceremony of the Lupercal, in MGM's *Julius Caesar* (1953) / 149

25. Antony emerges from the Capitol with the body of Caesar, in MGM's *Julius Caesar* (1953) / 153

26. Paul Newman as Brutus, in *You Are There*'s "The Assassination of Julius Caesar" (8 March 1953) / 161

27. Ed Murrow, in *See It Now*'s "A Report on Senator Joseph R. McCarthy" (9 March 1954) / 163

28. First page of *Caesar's Conquests, Classics Illustrated,* no. 130 (January 1956) / 172

29. "Ev Tu?" Herblock cartoon, *Washington Post* (10 June 1966) / 182

30. Poster advertising the film adaptation of Shakespeare's *Julius Caesar* directed by Stuart Burge (1970) / 193

31. Roscoe Orman (Brutus), Sonny Jim Gaines (Caesar), and Gylan Kain (Cassius), in a scene from Shakespeare's *Julius Caesar,* Public Theater, New York (1979) / *199*

32. Cartoon by JAS to accompany the article "The Last Emperor," *The Guardian* (13 September 2002) / *212*

33. "Hail, Bush," photomontage by Steve Caplin, front cover of G2, *The Guardian* (18 September 2002) / *213*

34. Doonesbury's first representation of George W. Bush as a Roman soldier's helmet (13 April 2003) / *218*

35. Screenshot of Julius Caesar (Ciarán Hinds) accepting the surrender of Vercingetorix, in HBO's *Rome,* season 1, ep. 1 (2005) / *229*

36. Screenshot of the conspirators encircling Brutus and Cassius after the assassination, in HBO's *Rome,* season 1, ep. 12 (2005) / *231*

Acknowledgments

My investigations of the reception of Julius Caesar in Western culture have taken place over the course of more than a decade. The research project fully came to life thanks to the generosity of the Leverhulme Trust, whose award of a Major Research Fellowship in 2000 allowed me an initial expanse of time to concentrate fully on the afterlife of the Roman dictator. I am also extremely grateful to the Arts and Humanities Research Council (AHRC) for the award of a second period of research leave to study Caesar in 2006, and to the Department of Greek & Latin at University College London for providing me with more than matching leave. *Caesar in the USA* is the final product of those investigations, following on two exploratory articles on Caesar in anti-Fascist American theater (1999) and Cold War cinema (2004), the contributed volume *Julius Caesar in Western Culture* (2006), and the monograph *Caesar: A Life in Western Culture* (2007). At various points across the chapters of the present work (as indicated in the notes), I draw on, adapt, and substantially expand selected parts of that earlier material in order to construct a larger, continuous narrative focused on Julius Caesar's shifting place and function in the popular culture of the United States of America, from the start of the twentieth century into the first decade of the twenty-first.

University College London (both through its Dean's Research Fund and its Futures Fund) generously made a substantial contribution toward the costs of obtaining images for this book and permissions to publish them. This work would not have seen the light of day without the consideration of a number of librarians and archivists in Los Angeles (in the libraries of the University of California, Los Angeles, the University of Southern California, the Academy of Motion Picture Arts and Sciences' Margaret Herrick Library, and the Research Library at the Getty Research Institute), Washington (in the Library of Congress and the Folger Shakespeare Library), New York (in the New York Public Library, the New York Public Library for the Performing Arts, and the Museum of Modern Art), Rome (in the British School at Rome, the Biblioteca Nazionale Centrale, the libraries of La Sapienza, and the American Academy), and London (in the British Library and the libraries of UCL and the University of London). And, specifically, Ned Comstock of the Cinematic Arts Library at USC continued kindly to draw my attention to—and supply me with materials on—American films and television programs that feature Julius Caesar.

I have also been lucky enough to receive diverse types of help from a number of other quarters, which I acknowledge at the relevant points in this book. I would like here to express my special thanks to Amy Richlin and Margaret Malamud for their warm and vitalizing hospitality, and their intellectual support, curiosity, and friendship, across the years of my project on Caesar and throughout my academic life. In the course of the years in which I have been working on *Caesar in the USA*, audiences at talks I have delivered in Dublin, Madrid, Rome, Los Angeles, Anaheim, and London have also offered much useful comment on its detail and its purpose. The readers for the University of California Press undertook to provide a number of thoughtful corrections and detailed observations. Bridget Wright produced the index with energy and enthusiasm. Any errors or seeming partialities that remain are entirely my own.

Finally, I would like to express great admiration for the intellectual patience of my husband, David Oswell, who discussed this project with me many times over the years and, in so doing, helped me perceive the broader point of what I was trying to achieve. My daughter and stepdaughters—Beatrix, Matilda, and Amelia—have again put up with my distraction gracefully and provided me with much happy distraction of their own. At least as far as my family is concerned, Caesar has now most fortunately met his end.

Introduction

The thirteen colonies of the New World fought their war of independence as American Brutus against British Caesar. The design that the Constitutional Convention of Virginia adopted on 5 July 1776 as the seal of their newly independent commonwealth graphically encapsulates the importance of Julius Caesar to the very foundation of the new nation. The first seal of the royal colony of Virginia had displayed the portrait of the British king James I on the obverse, and on the reverse a crown atop the heraldic coat of arms of the Stuarts. But, in the revolutionary period, British monarchy and its heraldic symbols were roundly rejected, and in their stead the Roman republic was embraced as the highest model of civic virtue. A number of variants of the Great Seal of Virginia came in and out of favor over the course of the next century, but the obverse of the version finally settled on by the General Assembly may be described thus: the Roman goddess Virtus, representing the spirit of the commonwealth, leaning on a downward-pointing spear and holding a sheathed sword, treads on Tyranny, represented by a man prostrate, a crown fallen from his head, a broken chain in his left hand, a limp whip in his right. The motto underneath this contrasting couple reads in Latin *Sic Semper Tyrannis* (Thus Always to Tyrants).[1] The victorious goddess wears Amazonian costume; the prostrate male is clothed in a Roman soldier's uniform and sandals. The man's identity is fixed by the Latin motto inscribed beneath him, since that motto is traditionally held to have been the words spoken by Brutus as he slew Julius Caesar in 44 B.C.E.[2]

Juxtaposition of the official seal with an early variant in which Virtus treads on the body of the British king George III (figs. 1 and 2) clarifies how, at the moment of the formation of the United States of America, the Roman dictator and aspirant to kingship was displayed as an icon of what needed to be overcome in order for the new republic to emerge.

Julius Caesar arrived in the cultural landscape of North America's colonial settlements from Britain, as part of the classical education of their elite. Privately and in institutions like the Boston Latin School, the languages, literatures, histories, and material culture of ancient Greece and Rome were taught and studied as an Old World defense against the perceived savagery of the American wilderness and as the essence of "learning" or "civility." Despite lively suspicion that classics was of no use to the New World, reading Greek and reading, writing, and speaking Latin opened up a path for the children of the elite straight into college and then positions of rank in the state or the church. For a minority of settlers, classics (and, therefore, Caesar) was also relived daily through their domestic architecture and furnishings, rituals and symbols, and even in the naming of their slaves.[3] A thorough education in Greek and Latin, as well as a broader engagement with the rich cultural traditions of antiquity, supplied colonial statesmen with models for government, but the Roman republic in particular was idealized as capable of delivering the New World from imperial domination. As American resistance developed into revolution and then into open war, the royal government of Great Britain was troped in political debate as Caesar to the newly emergent Rome of the Continental Congress (a corrupting, pernicious tyrant assaulting the autonomy of a republic).[4] If Julius Caesar was their villain, patriots found their heroes and their Roman virtue in Cato the Younger, Brutus, Cassius, and Cicero—all statesmen who had courageously martyred themselves in order to protect the liberty of their republic. Thus, transplanted to America from the London stage, Joseph Addison's tragedy Cato was performed in many cities along the northeastern coast from 1735 as an incitement to rebellion. Set in the North African city of Utica, the play indulges stirring declamations by noble Cato and his fellow senators as they plan their patriotic defense against Julius Caesar, the ruthless autocrat outside the walls. As many historians have noted, on 11 May 1778, when war was still being waged against the forces of the British king, the commander in chief of the American army, George Washington, chose to witness a rousing performance of Cato enacted by his own soldiers in their military encampment.[5]

Yet as a threat to the British crown, Brutus was a more useful model.

FIGURE 1. *(left)* The official Virginia state seal. Virginia State Board of Elections. www .sbe.virginia.gov.

FIGURE 2. *(right)* An early variant of the Virginia state seal. From the title page of Henry Howe, *Historical Collections of Virginia* (Charleston, SC, 1845).

When the British government proposed to tax the American colonies directly, without the prior agreement of their assemblies, the famed orator Patrick Henry protested eloquently against what he saw as the degeneration of George III's rule into tyranny. Before the delegates to the colony of Virginia's House of Burgesses, on 30 May 1765, he declared that the British king might profit from the knowledge that "Tarquin and Caesar had each his Brutus." Leaders of the American Revolution admired Cato and Cicero for their bold struggle against the Roman dictator but passionately identified with Brutus and Cassius as the Roman statesmen who had managed heroically to prostrate the destroyer of their country's liberties.[6] Alongside Addison's *Cato*, Shakespeare's *Julius Caesar* had also been transplanted to the colonies, and patriots noted and memorized from it aphorisms spoken by the conspirators—such as "Cassius from bondage will deliver Cassius" (*JC* 1.3.90)—to circulate in letters and political pamphlets as adornments of their revolutionary rhetoric.[7] In performance, severe alterations were made to acting scripts so that the Elizabethan tragedy could call on American audiences to play the part of a Brutus who, conveyed to this new land, might now long outlive the overthrow of Caesarean tyranny.[8]

Once independence was won, colonial memory of the hated Julius Caesar lived on in expressions of anxiety that, having expelled tyranny, the new nation might be inviting it back in. At the time of the constitutional debates of 1787–88, for example, many American statesmen and intellectuals expressed their alarm that a presidential Caesar could be created by the structures of government now being put into place. Opponents of federalism's centripetal and hierarchical organization criticized the scope it gave the executive branch to abuse power, and, in particular, warned that the joint office of president and commander in chief constituted an accumulation of powers comparable to that of a monarch or a military despot. Federalists, in turn, accused their opponents of an antirepublican demagoguery that would ignite civil war between the states, reduce the nation to anarchy, and unleash the dictatorship of an American Caesar.[9]

The Virginia state seal had bestowed the identity of patriotic Brutus on the whole commonwealth as it fought for autonomy against Britain's royal Caesar (although the identification was mediated, and the murder carefully ennobled, by use of the goddess Virtus and a narrative pose displaying the calm that ensues after a tyrant is slain). Yet, almost one hundred years later, Virginia's motto was proclaimed by an American Brutus in the act of murdering his home-grown Caesar. After John Wilkes Booth shot President Abraham Lincoln from the stage of a Washington theater, on the evening of 14 April 1865, he waved his pistol (obedient to the command of Shakespeare's Brutus that the conspirators wave "our red weapons o'er our heads," *JC* 3.1.109) and cried out to the audience "*Sic semper tyrannis*. The South is avenged." Booth's grandfather, father, and brothers had all been touched by the persistent American practice of celebrating resistance to tyranny through the invocation of the name of Roman Brutus (both Lucius Junius, who led the revolt against the Roman kings, and Marcus Junius, who assassinated the aspirant king, Caesar). Grandfather Booth had written about himself as a Brutus when he left Britain to participate in the American Revolution, and John Wilkes's father and one of his brothers were given the name of Junius Brutus at birth. All three brothers had also frequently performed on the American stage in Shakespeare's rendition of the Roman assassination.[10] Yet, at one time a serving soldier in the Virginia militia and a star of the southern stage, John Wilkes Booth felt himself called on to play in particular the Brutus of the American South against the North's Caesar. Lincoln had attracted accusations of Caesarism since he had become the sixteenth president of the United States in 1861. In the eyes of his opponents, he had increasingly centralized government, accrued despotic powers, violated civil liberties and the Constitution, provoked civil war and the secession of southern states, and destroyed the republic. Consequently, calls had been issued

FIGURE 3. President Lincoln caricatured in the British press as an assassinated Caesar. "Attained," *London Fun,* 6 May 1865. From R.R. Wilson, *Lincoln in Caricature* (New York, 1945), pl. 163, pp. 326–27.

to follow Roman history, to resist Lincoln's usurpations of power, even to assassinate him.[11]

In the aftermath of the assassination, the northern press could conveniently add extra drama to an already-dramatic deed by enveloping its shocked reports in the language of Shakespearean tragedy, for the deed had occurred in a theater and had been undertaken by an actor of Shakespeare against a president whose noble ambitions (including the preservation of the Union and the emancipation of slaves) had been cruelly cut down. Across the Atlantic, where the British press had savagely caricatured Abraham Lincoln and his leadership throughout the Civil War, the magazine of political satire, *London Fun,* appeared to offer a belated tribute to the American president as a political martyr in a Roman republic (fig. 3). Yet an observant reader would note that the cup of Victory that Lincoln is tragically prevented from fully grasping stands on the plinth of *Vanitas* (Vanity), while his incongruous Caesarean costume of wreath, short tunic, sandals, sword, and starry mantle demean rather than augment his dignity and the gravity of his death.[12]

During the eighteenth and nineteenth centuries, however, Julius Caesar did not function in the culture of the United States only as dictator and destroyer of republics—an "Other" in need of patriotic eradication. Many of the patriots who fought against the armies of the British king, and the founders who established a new republic, were also students of Caesar. He was routinely feared by pupils in the private lesson or the grammar-school classroom for the punishment that might follow errors of translation, but admired in the personal library and the university for the purity and lucidity of his Latin and the easy access it gave his adult readers to the culture of antiquity.[13] By the 1830s, education in the dictator's war commentaries was sufficiently widespread among the American male elite for a professor at a southern university, bemoaning the inadequacies of the schoolmasters who taught Latin, to remark that visitors to their private grammar schools might well suffer the misfortune of hearing "a class of little marble-players recite a lesson in Caesar, giving poor Julius, alas!, more stabs than he received from the daggers of all the conspirators in the Senate-house, and avenging the Gauls upon him for all his murders."[14]

The Roman general was also valued in the military academy for the content of his commentaries *De bello Gallico* and *De bello civili* and the training they might provide in the art of war. At the end of the nineteenth century (just before the point where this book will begin), the decorated Civil War veteran Theodore Ayrault Dodge published a detailed account of Caesar's campaigns dedicated "to the American soldier," whom he regarded as better than the Roman legionary for his dedication to his country rather than his general.[15] Dodge had visited the theater of the Roman general's campaigns in Europe, drawn on the ancient authorities, utilized the data that had emerged from the excavations and military studies funded by Napoleon III, and read the French emperor's own history of Julius Caesar. Across forty chapters analyzing the Gallic and Civil wars, the lieutenant colonel offers a guarded appraisal of Caesar as general: he has an ambition for power akin to that of Napoleon I; he does not exercise the patriotism of a Hannibal or Washington; he is decisive, energetic, clear-sighted, and skillful; he calls for admiration but not human sympathy. Dodge makes it clear at the opening and the close of his book that he writes for students of war as an American military historian exercising vigilant "hypercriticism" against the rising tide of Caesar worship flowing from France. Nonetheless, he still waxes lyrical about the extraordinary virtues of Julius Caesar in the round:

> Had he been nothing but a soldier, Caesar would still be the equal of the other great captains. Taking him as the statesman who built on the ruins of the Republic the foundations of the Empire, as the patron of learning who founded libraries in all the great towns, and filled Rome with men of science, culture and letters, as the legislator who drafted laws which still control the jurisdiction of the world, as the profound scholar who dictated the correction of the calendar, as the thinker, for the grasp of whose mind nothing was too intricate, nothing too broad, Caesar was, indeed, "the foremost man in [sic] all this world" [slightly misquoting Brutus's judgment in JC 4.3.22]. (1892, 736)

These brief examples of the operation of Julius Caesar in the culture of the United States before the twentieth century demonstrate the importance, and some of the diversity and the workings, of his reception. Caesar is called on both to foment American rebellion and to teach its soldiers military strategy and heroism, to distinguish the new nation from monarchic Britain, and republican America from imperial France, but also to set Anti-Federalist against Federalist and the South against the North. Significant facilitators of that reception are dramas (especially Shakespeare's Elizabethan tragedy) and the Roman general's own war commentaries. War (the American War of Independence and the Civil War) and political debate (about the proper constitution for a republic, the necessary limitations on the power of a president, and the dangers of demagoguery or of Napoleonic absolutism) operate as spurs to cultural uses of Caesar. Yet despite the importance of the Roman dictator's reception, at the level even of the initial and continuing formation of American national and local identity, there is as yet no full-length study of Caesar in the United States. There are now a number of works on the reception of ancient Greece and Rome in America, especially but not exclusively during the eighteenth and nineteenth centuries;[16] this book, however, is distinguished both by its focus on a single historical figure (and his persistent circulation also as an Elizabethan tragic character) and by its concern with more recent, popular culture.

AMERICAN IDENTITY, POPULAR CULTURE, CLASSICAL RECEPTION

Many critics have speculated as to why Julius Caesar has been favored with an afterlife in Western culture that has been so extraordinarily rich and enduring.[17] His exceptional talents, put to use in military and political actions on an astonishing scale, mark him out from most of his peers. The survival of his own lucid yet partisan voice in his commentaries on the wars he fought turns him into an immediate presence for his readers. He lived his life already with an eye to its future reception, promoting his *fama* (or lasting recognition) even to the point of seeking divine status. The drama of his murder at the center of imperial government touches him with tragedy and at least some humanity. Immediately thereafter, his assassination is narrated as an immensely important ethical and political problem: should such a life be extinguished? The place and the time of that life also render it momentous, for in retrospect it is understood to have occurred in the most powerful city of classical antiquity, at the point of its historic transformation from an imperial republic to a monarchic empire, and (more imprecisely) from paganism to Christianity. Having risen to the position of "perpetual dictator" at that time and place, Julius Caesar is retrospectively turned in narrative and visual shorthand into the primary *agent* of the Western world's transformation—for good or ill. His very name becomes the sign of Rome, of the end of republics and the rise of empires. Reenvisioned in this posthumous context, Julius Caesar's life provides a whole vocabulary with which to articulate or to challenge conquest, imperialism, usurpation, dictatorship, tyranny, and assassination.[18] Alexander the Great has likewise been analyzed as having become a cultural myth of enduring relevance, and a flexible signifier in later discourses of power and government.[19] Yet this book makes clear that the flexibility of such historical figures has interesting limits. Neither Alexander nor Caesar is so pliable that the story of the former's reception in the United States would match that of the latter's. No matter how distant or distorted, the afterlife of Julius Caesar in modern America is still tied to the life the Roman dictator lived in the last days of the Roman republic. Julius Caesar brings with him from antiquity, and from his earlier receptions, certain preconditions that affect his re-presentations (if he is to remain recognizably and usefully Caesar).

Caesar in the USA is concerned to explore not only the distinctiveness of Julius Caesar as a mode of reception of classical antiquity but also the distinctiveness of that reception in modern America—that is across the twentieth and the beginning of the twenty-first centuries. One of the distinctive features of that reception (as at the time of the War of Independence and the Civil War) is the extent to which the Roman dictator is utilized in cultural forms and practices that openly seek to create or interrogate a sense of nationhood and of American identity. For a significant part of the twentieth century, for example, the study of Latin is the study of Caesar's *Gallic War,* and the study of Shakespeare is dominated by *Julius Caesar.* Knowledge of Caesar as both Roman text and Elizabethan play is manipulated and transformed better for it to participate in the pedagogic process of socializing young people and acculturating them into an ideal American citizenship. Yet the partisanship of the former and the equivocations of the latter also work to bring that ideal into question. The originary operations of Caesar as the new republic's Other—tyrant, destroyer of republics, prostrate monarch—mutate across the 110 years this book traverses broadly in line with mutations in America's political perceptions of itself and its role in the world. Not all the cultural forms under scrutiny here are overtly engaged with the politics of national life, such as the rise of dictatorships, of totalitarianism, of excessive presidential power, of American empire. Yet those forms (political, pedagogic, theatrical, cinematic, televisual, historiographic) intersect with each other and converge in ways that always connect America's Caesar back to discourses of the nation. The fractures that emerge in the representations of the Roman dictator across these cultural forms also match fractures that have occurred in the process of creating multiple subcategories of American identity (such as those of ethnicity, gender, political allegiance, or location). Analysis of Caesar's complex and varied receptions in modern America thus exposes the continuity of his use in identity formation from the eighteenth and nineteenth centuries through to the twenty-first, not just at the level of nationhood but also at the level of the person—from the president of the United States to the Italian-American school student.

This book is concerned with modern popular cultural representations of Julius Caesar. In the course of the twentieth century, classics and the classical tradition were regularly deployed to defend elite culture against the assaults of mass culture. In recent years, however, there has been a proliferation of works by classical scholars that have explored the relationship between antiquity and mass culture, especially with regard to the reconstruction of ancient Greece and Rome in Hollywood cinema, but also in comic books, on television, and in computer games.[20] Such classicists have come to value the study of popular culture: often the initial or the principal point of access to antiquity for its many consumers, its practices of representation can have wide-reaching and intense effects (given their appropriations of antiquity to address modernity's concerns about politics, gender, race, class, religion, or sexuality) and frequently draw on, democratize, or challenge the representations of "high" culture. *Caesar in the USA,* however, embarks on sustained analysis of popular cultural forms (as they have been conventionally understood) only in its last three chapters, where it investigates in detail representations of the Roman statesman in the modern media of film, television drama and documentaries, the detective novel, the comic book, print journalism, and across the Internet. Julius Caesar is omnipresent in modern American culture. With Caesar, like Shakespeare, cultural hierarchies of high and low, popular and elite, concertina and collapse.[21] Thus a loose definition of the "popular" has been employed here that can accommodate a broad array of cultural forms, including state education,[22] and the "popular" is regularly analyzed as it overlaps or merges with representations of the Roman dictator considered more authoritative. Examination of the convergences and mergers of "highbrow" and "lowbrow" Caesars in American culture brings into sharp focus the specific determinants of Caesar's popular cultural production (the drive for financial profit as well as political topicality, educational uplift, or gripping entertainment), and the mechanisms specific to each medium for his reproduction and consumption.

Scholars who have explored the relationship of antiquity to modernity in the realm of the political observe that the classical past is not passively received into modern political thought but "mobilized to enact a new future."[23] "Reception" of Julius Caesar into the popular political commentary of (and about) the modern United States frequently consists in an explicit, and at times angry, claim that the Roman past will be America's future. Investigation of that reception across time demonstrates the extent to which visions of America's future have changed. In 1776, Julius Caesar lay prostrate and beaten beneath the foot of the state of Virginia's Roman virtue. During the twentieth and at the start of the twenty-first century, commentators on the governance of the United States of America argue not that Caesar is dead but that Caesar is coming.

CAESAR IN THE USA

I began this project in 1997, undertaking intermittently over the course of almost a decade preliminary surveys of archival materials on the reception of Julius Caesar in modern America. I completed two other projects on the Roman dictator's reception in the same period that aided my understanding of the American materials coming to light: an edited collection of essays on representations and uses of Caesar in Italy, France, Germany, Britain, and the United States from antiquity to the twenty-first century (*Julius Caesar in Western Culture*, 2006); and a "metabiographic" monograph that explored the appropriation in different periods and societies of canonic episodes in his life, from capture by pirates to apotheosis (*Caesar: A Life in Western Culture*, 2007). During that time and subsequently, I visited—sometimes repeatedly—archives, libraries and special collections in Washington (the Library of Congress, the Folger Shakespeare Library), New York (the New York Public Library, the New York Library of the Performing Arts, the Museum of Modern Art), Los Angeles (the various libraries of the University of California at Los Angeles and the University of Southern California, the Academy of Motion Picture Arts and Sciences' Margaret Herrick Library, the Getty Research Institute's Research Library), Rome (the Biblioteca Nazionale Centrale, the library of the University of Rome at La Sapienza, the American Academy in Rome, and the British School at Rome), and London (the British Library, the Institute of Classical Studies, the Warburg Institute, the British Film Institute, and the libraries of University College London and the University of London). I also made use of a wide array of Internet resources, such as the American newspaper archives available via ProQuest.

In more recent years, I proceeded to select for closer examination case studies from across the twentieth and the beginning of the twenty-first centuries that constituted some of the most influential, culturally significant or widely disseminated receptions of Julius Caesar in modern America. These were also chosen as exemplary of broad thematic shifts in Caesar's use that emerged in the course of my compilation of the initial materials, as illustrative of how that use intersected with political and social developments in the United States and abroad, and as demonstrative of the diversity of media within which Caesar has been appropriated and represented (such as school texts of Caesar's own writings, editions of Shakespeare's *Julius Caesar*, teachers' handbooks and journals, juvenile and adult historical novels, detective fiction, popular historiography and classical scholarship, play productions, films and television dramas, comic books, advertising, and political commentary in the print and digital media). The story of Julius Caesar's reception in the United States that emerges here as a result, in particular the twinning of themes and time periods across the next seven chapters, is designed to be suggestive rather than definitive. For example, the years 1956 to 1989 were not the only ones in the history of the United States that witnessed the deployment of the Roman dictator as an instrument with which to attack presidents who were thought to have accrued excessive power (see chapter 6). However, those years do bear witness to a special intensity or persistence of Caesar's use in that manner, a use that is distinguishable from his deployment to interrogate totalitarianism during the Cold War (chapter 5) or empire at the beginning of the twenty-first century (chapter 7). It is also the case, to offer another type of example, that this story could have been more nuanced if I had had the opportunity to visit archives in other parts of the United States, especially some of those in the South. However, while I investigate some of the specific and highly developed sets of associations that have broadly determined the trajectory of Julius Caesar's American reception in modern times, I also attempt as much as is practicable throughout this book to draw attention to the astonishing plurality of Caesars that have circulated concurrently, and continue to circulate, in the culture of the United States.

One striking realization in the course of this research has been the extent to which Julius Caesar's reception in modern American culture has been driven by or intersects with his strong presence in the American education system and, therefore, in the process of making American citizens. Consequently the first two chapters proper are concerned with Julius Caesar in high-school classrooms and the public spaces that were linked to the teaching of Caesar, such as those in which Shakespeare's tragedy was performed and films starring Caesar were projected. During the 1900s and 1910s, the Roman general encroached directly on the lives of many young Americans as one in every two high-school students submitted to the rituals of learning Latin and, in their second year of its study, routinely read sections of Caesar's war commentary *De bello Gallico* (chapter 1). School education was recognized as a technology of government and an agent in the socialization of the child, while Latin was perceived and presented by its advocates as a gateway to full participation and advancement in national life for those willing to study it. A whole pedagogic industry of textbooks, commentaries, biographies, historical novels, and even practical activities (such as model making and playacting) worked to direct the assumed boy-readers of Caesar's perfect Latinity to their general's lessons for the creation of an ideal masculine virtue that they were supposed to enact in their adult American life. In the day-to-day practice of schoolteachers, however, Caesar's text was susceptible to transgressions of its conventional gendering and an intricate splintering of judgments on his literary, military, and ethical activities.

Julius Caesar often encroached on the lives of young Americans from two directions simultaneously, as many students studied Shakespeare's dramatization of his assassination as dictator at the same time as they read his own accounts of his preceding victories as general in Gaul (chapter 2). Despite their distinction from each other as direct Roman history and mediated Elizabethan drama, each of these texts was often drawn on to elucidate the other. And despite their foreign origins, both Shakespeare's *Julius Caesar* and Caesar's *Gallic War* were taught to students as a mechanism for assimilation into modern American life, and as a moral mirror in which they might glimpse relevant ethical and political lessons. But it was Shakespeare's tragedy that came to dominate the child's impression of Julius Caesar and propelled the Roman dictator's circulation beyond the classroom far into American culture more broadly. Often performed in the late eighteenth and nineteenth centuries as a patriotic replay of the New World's noble rebellion against the tyranny of the Old World, in the early twentieth century Shakespeare's *Julius Caesar* was more often explored in the classroom and acted on the stage in terms of the criminality of political assassination and the ethical failure of the conspirators' shadowy struggle for republican liberty. Interpretation of an Elizabethan play whose concerns appeared so closely to match those of American political debate frequently embraced reflection by teachers, students, directors, actors, reviewers, and spectators on their own investments in liberty or in Caesarism. Piggybacking on the cultural standing and the familiarity of Shakespeare's play, the American film industry attempted to sell to a mass audience its mute rendition of *Julius Caesar* as both uplifting education and gripping entertainment. The Roman dictator entered into American popular culture as both a play and a man and was even enlisted into the corpus of advertising signs (signifying education, sophistication, power, and success) that modern marketing deployed to render its products desirable.

Julius Caesar flourished in twentieth-century American mass culture not least because two key texts intimately associated with him had taken root in American state education. But momentous events (like assassinations, wars, or the rise of dictatorships and empires) could stimulate a sudden escalation of interest in and topical use for the Roman statesman. Chapters 3 and 4 effectively bridge the analysis of Caesar in

American education and in popular culture. Chapter 3 explores the tremendous impact of the First World War on the perception and the use of the Roman general in, and beyond, the curricula of American high schools. Soon after the terrain of northwestern Europe became a battleground in the summer of 1914, Latin teachers and even education commissioners began to claim that ancient history was repeating itself. On that basis, they pressed the value of teaching and reading Caesar's *Gallic War* for the light it could cast on present military strategy and tactics. Roman Caesar is coupled with the German Kaiser (or set against him) to support the case for the utility of the Roman commander's superbly clear Latin commentaries, for the durability of his military genius, for American engagement in combat on foreign soil. But, at the same time, war in Europe led other American educators to question whether the study of classics was the best method for inculcating the fundamental values and needs of modern national life (such as a feeling for justice or vocational knowledge of science). By war's end, many American school commentaries on the *Gallic War* had adopted aspects of the French nationalistic discourse of Celtic origins and Gallic heroism and were beginning to transfer their sentimental allegiance from the Roman author to his enemy Vercingetorix, even though teachers had the opportunity to draw on other representations of a heroic Caesar currently in circulation (such as that of the Italian film industry) to support their call to attend to the Latin text. But, by the late 1920s, when enthusiasm for war was long dead and Caesarean militarism was taking on an unpleasant Italian flavor, few high-school practitioners of classics now looked on Julius Caesar as the best author to educate America's future citizens.

From Chapter 4, *Caesar in the USA* no longer orients its perspective to hold American classrooms at the center of its focus. Concern turns from the institution of the high school, and pedagogic preoccupations with how to teach the *Gallic War* to students at a time of world war, and toward the institution of radical, populist theater and its staging of Shakespeare's *Julius Caesar* as political instruction for American adults in the dangerous attractions of demagogues. The shaping of Julius Caesar as a glorious paradigm for an idealized Mussolini in the ideology of Italian Fascism gave impetus to the creation of revisionist narratives of the Mussolini-Caesar coupling within the discourses of American anti-Fascism. In that context, an unremittingly visceral revival of Shakespeare's Roman tragedy was performed on the New York stage in the late 1930s. Subtitled in its publicity "Death of a Dictator," its modernist style enacted the demagogic processes whereby dictatorships had been established in Europe and might yet emerge within the United States itself (the former achieved partly through the use of a Mussolini lookalike for Caesar and the utilization of quasi-Fascist uniforms and "Nuremberg-style" lighting; the latter through a familiarly dark and spare urban set and a dress code for the conspirators that spoke of Italian-American gangsterism). Directed by Orson Welles, who also played Brutus as a liberal bewildered by the resilience of the masses' desire for dictatorship, this modern-dress production became the most celebrated and influential revival of Shakespeare's *Julius Caesar* on the American stage in the twentieth century. For decades to come, teachers across the United States would utilize the production's striking interpretative stratagems to demonstrate to students the political topicality of the Elizabethan drama, until readings of Shakespeare's Caesar as stand-in for Fascist dictatorship and its dangers became cliché.

The Roman past of Julius Caesar has repeatedly been represented and consumed in the culture of the United States as what the nation is not—or what it has, or may, become. In chapter 5, this history of the Roman dictator's American reception reaches the period of the Cold War and observes that reception's new embrace of fears about totalitarianism both abroad and at home. At the same time, its perspective shifts yet further from mass education and populist theater to popular culture as it has been conventionally understood, exploring the Caesar of Hollywood cinema, television drama and documentary, and the comic book. This wider-ranging analysis exposes some of the characteristics and determinants specific to the Caesar of American popular culture. The modern mass media of film, television, and the comic book all attempt to gain a share in the cultural legitimacy and aesthetic weight that attaches to the Roman general, not least because of his association with a classical education and the Elizabethan Bard. While use of Caesar offers them the look of high culture, they in turn offer their consumers the promise that they will democratize that culture and render it more accessible. Mass media producers also construct a close relationship for their Caesars with those of scholarship and of high-school education: a film's technical adviser draws on recent scholarly understanding that Julius Caesar's political ambition was directed toward the establishment of a one-party, totalitarian state; study guides are produced by the film studio for use in American classrooms that further attempt to endorse the medium as a gateway to both knowledge of Caesar and cultural citizenship. The commercial need to maximize audiences and income drives the promise of not only educational uplift and political topicality but also entertainment, and that promise is in part fulfilled by highly distinctive strategies of representation (such as the camera close-up, the star system, or the color coding of comic strips) and of marketing (such as publicity posters, publication patterns, or television scheduling). Separately and in combination, those strategies can generate a complex and ideologically contradictory Caesar (a Stalinist leader of a police state, a McCarthyite demagogue, a conquering hero fighting communist conspirators), but one that is responsive to the contradictions of Cold War ideology and the fine line it drew between patriotism and subversion.

Receptions of Julius Caesar in modern America do not always turn exclusively for their material to the triumphant general of Caesar's *Gallic War* or the ailing tyrant of Shakespeare's *Julius Caesar.* And the lessons drawn from Roman republican history and the broader life of the dictator have been not just predictive for America's future but also downright apocalyptic. From the late 1950s, popular historiography and political commentary coalesced to produce the menacing prospect of a new Caesar arriving in the White House (chapter 6). The United States would in the near future repeat on an even larger scale an inexorable sequence of terrible errors already experienced in the Roman past (so it was argued): democratic growth, imperial expansion, loss of liberty, executive autocracy, urban overgrowth, social and moral decay, the disintegration of the republic, and, finally, Caesarism followed by nuclear holocaust. In the alarmist discourse of postwar American conservatism, Julius Caesar became a stick with which to beat the perceived excesses of liberal democracy as it was practiced under the administrations of John F. Kennedy and Lyndon B. Johnson. Evidence emerges at this point of a moment of neat symbiosis between political criticism (this time from the left-liberal perspective) and classical scholarship. A journalist looks to Roman party politics and its manipulations of the electorate to understand American presidential campaigns, and a classical historian looks to American nominating conventions to understand Roman party politics and its electoral procedures; each feeds off the work of the other for elucidation. Having flourished in the late 1950s and throughout the 1960s, the rhetorical convention by which Julius Caesar and Roman republican history are deployed as admonitory topoi for America's grim future gradually fades in the early 1970s. Yet scattered throughout this chapter are salutary reminders that representations of Julius Caesar then (as at other times) are not confined to the overtly political. The tobacco manufacturer Philip Morris exploited a

Caesarean tag to persuade customers that with a packet of Marlboro cigarettes they could also buy a muscular, conquering masculinity. Caesars Palace exploited an image of the Roman dictator as extravagant spender, gambler, womanizer, and refined consumer to attract guests to stay at its casino resort. Even Shakespeare's play could provide a platform to act out other concerns, such as a struggle against Britain for American cultural independence, or against white Anglo-America for a more radical and inclusive conception of cultural (and national) identity. Ventriloquating Shakespeare's Caesar might even constitute a form of psychotherapy—an elemental route to understanding not just the dangers of dictatorship but also the damaging excesses of self-love.

Caesar in the USA begins in the American high school and ends on the global stage. It opens in the relatively confined spaces of the American classroom with close scrutiny of the repetitive reading, rewriting, and declamation of selections from Julius Caesar's original war commentary *De bello Gallico*. There it brings into the light the changing social, political, and ethical lessons American students were required to extract from the small rituals of the study of the Latin text. It closes in the global expanse of twenty-first-century popular political discourse with analysis of the more blatantly manipulative rhetoric of New Rome and a new Caesar. To operate effectively as a vital mechanism by which to critique the presidency of George W. Bush, that rhetoric requires the breakdown of the Roman republic to be situated within a few short years between 49 B.C.E., when Julius Caesar crossed the river Rubicon with his legion into Italy, and 44 B.C.E., when he was assassinated on account of his aspirations to divinity and kingship. The destruction of the Roman republic's institutions must be imputed to the agency of the dictator alone. The river Rubicon must mark the boundary between republican liberty and imperial tyranny. Caesar must be identified as the first emperor of Rome who placed his country on a path that led straight to imperial overstretch and final, ignominious fall. These simplifications of Roman history enabled political commentators nationally and internationally to articulate a vigorous assault on the Bush administration that seemed credible even despite its extremity. It achieved authority by virtue of the long American tradition on which it drew that, throughout the nineteenth and twentieth centuries, has taken Julius Caesar as index and embodiment of the collapse of republics and the rise of empires. It gained further force from its convergence with other discursive fields for the representation of Julius Caesar in the United States (such as the pedagogic, theatrical, televisual, or historiographic), and they in turn gained a sense of urgent political relevance. While, in this way, the Roman past and its first Caesar have been made to speak to the American present, some critics have argued that this imperial present can now speak to the Roman past. That is, situated in our new imperial context and utilizing modern models of empire, we can turn to reevaluate the structures of the empires of the past and gain renewed understanding of some of the actors in their rise and fall, including Julius Caesar.

As *Caesar in the USA* works outward from the investigation of close readings of Julius Caesar's *De bello Gallico* to seemingly superficial journalistic exploitations of his name, and moves across American cultural history from the beginning of the twentieth century to the start of the twenty-first, a range of interesting issues emerge that deserve further exploration. As author, general and dictator, Caesar has had an intriguing role to play in the making of modern American identities and in their splintering (I have mainly engaged with differentiation by political allegiance and partly with differentiation by gender and ethnicity but have been unable to consider geography, such as a North/South divide). He has also had an important function in debates about the value to Americans of a classical education and, in particular, the study of Latin. His reception has exhibited bursts of intensity in periods of political crisis, when the occurrence of assassination, war, dictatorship, totalitarianism, or empire appears to give him fresh relevance. Exploration of Julius Caesar's modern reception in the United States also draws our attention to the processes of classical reception itself as a distance that separates us from antiquity but also a tie that draws us back to it—as source of differentiation, explanation, prediction, acculturation, or entertainment.

PART ONE

Education

CHAPTER I

Maturation

1900–1914

In the early years of the twentieth century, Julius Caesar encroached on the lives of many young Americans. Public high schools experienced exceptional growth between 1900 and 1910, and Latin was regularly included as an option in their curricula. As working-class and immigrant children started to enter secondary education in substantial numbers, they (or their parents on their behalf) chose the study of Latin as a gateway to full participation in American life and a path to social advancement, not least because Latin was still compulsory for admission to American colleges. By 1910, only U.S. history and algebra were recruiting more high-school students, and one in every two students was enrolled in a Latin program and was reading Caesar. The first decade of the twentieth century was among Caesar's finest times in the United States.[1]

Young Americans began their study of the Latin language and their memorization of its grammatical rules in their first year in high school. Their second year of Latin was commonly known as "the Caesar grade" or "the Caesar year" because in that year (when they were approximately fifteen years old) students were first introduced to Latin literature through Julius Caesar's commentary on his conquest of Gaul, *De bello Gallico* (or *The Gallic War*).[2] In a classical canon that reached back as far as the Renaissance, Caesar's writings held a "time-honoured place as the first Latin classic to be placed in the hands of the beginner."[3] In the American curriculum, Caesar had been selected as the second-year text because of the near-perfect regularity of his syntax and the simplicity of his linguistic form. The latter comprised a limited, repetitive vocabulary of between 1,200 and 1,300 words, and that vocabulary was concrete more often than abstract and abounded in verbs of action. Thus, translating Caesar allowed a constant review of the basic principles of Latin grammar and syntax. Yet, in the schoolrooms of the United States, the Roman general's commentaries on his war against fellow Romans—the three books of De bello civili (or The Civil War)—received scant attention. It was almost always only De bello Gallico whose content was perceived to reward the labor students were required to bestow on its linguistic forms. Offering a story featuring rapid narrative, vivid character-sketching, and seemingly heroic adventures (some even on Anglo-Saxon terrain), the Gallic War was thought to be far more appealing and wholesome for the readership with whom educators seemed most concerned—boys.[4] Study of the Gallic War also nicely balanced study in second-year English of Shakespeare's bloody tragedy Julius Caesar.[5] Together the two works framed and shaped the rise and the fall of the greatest of Roman statesmen.

Consequently, how to teach Caesar's commentary on his military campaigns in Gaul became a matter of fundamental concern and extensive debate among schoolteachers, academics, and other professionals who advocated a classical education for young people in the United States. If the nation's young people could not be persuaded of the merits of the Roman general's text, then they might give up Latin at only the second-year hurdle. Without Julius Caesar, classics might just fade away.

THE VALUE OF A CLASSICAL EDUCATION

The pervasive presence of Julius Caesar in the classrooms of American high schools and in the everyday lives of students during the early twentieth century deserves close scrutiny. It was at the turn of the century that education came to be recognized as a technology of government, and schools as institutions of the nation and agents of child socialization. Although the cultural norms laid down by school curricula were always vulnerable to reinterpretation, transgression, or rejection in the day-to-day practice of both students and teachers, in theory they were set in place to instruct young people in moral maturity and national character and to shape them into adults who would become good citizens.[6] Moreover, in this same period, the United States witnessed social change of such rapidity and intensity that the new system of mass education increasingly became the object of explicit anxiety and intervention by state boards. As the nation changed from a largely agrarian to an industrial and commercial economy, as its population doubled, cities grew, and urban high schools filled up with the children of immigrants of mostly southern European rather than Anglo-Saxon origin, "Americanization" became a fundamental mission of educators.[7] Paradoxically, they thought that (alongside other high-school subjects) Caesar's Latin could eradicate the foreignness from these new arrivals on American soil.[8]

In the long history of European pedagogy, both the Latin language and the culture it embodied had traditionally been cast as masculine, imperial, and uniquely civilizing, while classics had been tightly interwoven with ecclesiastical, intellectual, and political institutions.[9] In the United States, however, the value of a classical education had been questioned from the foundation of the nation, and ever since the classical curriculum had constantly been subjected to challenge (even, and especially, when Latin enrollments were at their highest) as elitist, irrelevant, useless, obsolete, dead, Old World.[10] Consequently, in the first two decades of the twentieth century, buoyed by the increase in high-school enrollments, American advocates of a classical education fought to restore to the public the belief that the study of Latin would mold noble characters and good citizens.[11]

Textbooks for students, practical manuals for teachers, and public lectures at universities often contained quasi-religious witness to the importance of classics, and of Latin in particular. For example, in 1911 Professor of Latin Language and Literature at the University of Michigan, Francis Willey Kelsey (author of one of the most enduring and widely used school commentaries on Caesar, recently the president of the American Philological Association, and, at this juncture, president of the Archaeological Institute of America), collated into one volume a series of papers on Latin and Greek in American education. Kelsey included talks he had originally delivered at meetings of the Michigan Classical Conference and the Michigan Schoolmasters' Club, followed by an extensive list of testimonials from medics, engineers, lawyers, theologians, ambassadors, newspaper editors, and other academics as to the value of "humanistic studies," and buttressed these various arguments with encouraging statistical data on classics enrollments drawn from reports of the Commission for Education in Washington. Kelsey began with a summary of seven ways in which Greek and Latin are valuable as educational instruments (a summary much cited in later literature of this kind). Access to the ancient languages (1) brings the boyish mind under control by virtue of translation's scientific method of observation, comparison, and generalization; (2) makes our own language intelligible (including its technical vocabulary) and develops powers of expression; (3) brings the mind into contact with literature in elemental forms; (4) gives insight into a basic civilization; (5) cultivates the constructive imagination; (6) clarifies moral ideals and stimulates to right conduct (because the natural sciences are devoid of moral illustrations); and (7) furnishes means of recreation (1927, 15–33).

Professor Kelsey here flavored the discipline of classics with ethics and the science of modernity. Elsewhere he added race and gender. In his view, classics succeeds because "there is a readier sympathy, a closer affinity between an Englishman or American and a cultivated pagan of Athens or Rome than seems possible between Anglo-Saxon and oriental stock" (1927, 28). Yet classics is also in danger of failing, in Kelsey's misogynistic view, because "our secondary teaching is in no inconsiderable degree in the hands of young women without adequate preparation for their work, who engage in teaching as a makeshift, and either grace the schoolroom with their presence briefly on the way from the commencement stage to the altar or, if they remain for a period of years, continue to teach without an ambition for self-improvement" (46–47). More inclusively (given his likely readership), Professor of Classics and General Literature at Florida State College for Women, Josiah B. Game, produced a handbook of Latin for high-school teachers, which was first published as a bulletin of the Missouri State Normal School in 1907 and then revised and republished in 1916 and 1925 (both moments of crisis for classics in schools). In it, he boasted: "To those who believe that our country's future is intimately bound up with the kind of education offered in the schools of today, it is very gratifying to know that more young men and young women are now studying Latin than at any other time in our history."[12] But for academics and teachers alike, a key question emerged: could the text selected for the second year of high school—Julius Caesar's *Gallic War*—live up to these bold advocacies of Latin?

ENLIVENING CAESAR'S COMMENTARIES

The crucial concern for advocates of a classical education was how to get students beyond a painful struggle with the *Gallic War* as a tortuous catalogue of grammatical constructions to an appreciation of the value of Latin as one of their school subjects. Even the future president, Woodrow Wilson, had set his mind to the problem when teaching ancient and modern history at the undergraduate women's college Bryn Mawr. In a personal letter to the college's departing professor of Latin dated 2 August 1888, Wilson (himself on the verge of leaving for higher pay and an all-male college) followed up a discussion they had previously held face-to-face on the matter of how to teach Caesar to boys:

> My dear Mr. Slaughter
> . . . The whole matter stands in my mind thus: Boys like generals, like fighting, like accounts of battles: if, therefore, they could be given a just conception of the reality of this man Caesar—could see him as a sure-enough man (who in his youth, for instance, a fop and a lady-killer, was yet in his full age an incomparable commander and a compeller of liking, nay, of devotion, on the part of the rudest soldier—was himself a lover to strategy and force); if they could be made to realize that these. Commentaries were written, in many parts probably, in the camp (on some rude stool, perhaps—the noises or the silence of the camp outside) when the deeds of which they tell were fresh in the mind—perhaps also heavy on the muscles—of the man who was their author as well as author of their history—if, in short, they could be given a fellow-feeling, an enthusiasm, or even a wonder for this versatile fellow-man of theirs, reading the Commentaries would be easy, would be fun—and their contents would never be forgotten, I should say. Maps help to give pictures of the fight; if the boys could be gotten to play at the campaigns it would be a capital help; anything to dispel the idea that Caesar wrote grammatical exercises in hard words!
> *Cordially yours,* WOODROW WILSON[13]

As an academic, Wilson held research interests in the history of government and, more specifically, in the concept of successful political leadership.[14] As an educator, he would soon be attempting to shape the ideal university at Princeton, and to establish the liberal arts (especially literature) as an appropriate training for classes of graduates whom he expected to lead America's national life.[15] Small wonder, then, that he might once have reflected on how to enliven the Latin of Julius Caesar for fifteen-year-old boys laboring over it at high school. This he does, as many schoolteachers would also do, by placing dramatic emphasis on content, context, and author over form (and all in a rhetorical style that recalls Cicero's love of the tricolon crescendo). For the future president, the content of the *Gallic War* is enjoyably military, and its author attractively frivolous in his youth while developing in maturity into a leader of manly robustness. The potentially fraught relationship of student to textbook is translated into the certain devotion of the soldier to his general. The circumstances of composition are given a raw physicality—the uncomfortable stool, the sound of silence, the aching muscles. Caesar is the empathetic agent of action, the writer of his own recent story, not just the nominative subject of verbs. If teachers could communicate this message through visualization and enactment as well as routine translation, then it would be hard for boys to drop the text of second-year Latin, as well as, by implication, the study of classics. Years later, when the widow of the addressee found Wilson's letter among her deceased husband's papers, she offered it for publication to the editor of a classics journal. The now-widened readership of these recommendations may only have regretted that they had been sent originally to a man named Slaughter.

Among schoolteachers of Latin, such concerns and recommendations were expressed regularly and publicly in the pages of their magazines and journals, and at meetings of their classical associations. In January 1909, for example, in the *Classical Weekly,* Mary Harwood of The Girls' Latin School in Baltimore wrote with equal passion:

> Yet if our boys and girls are ever to come out victorious from grappling with Caesar's ablatives absolute, laying siege to his gerundives, and fighting the barbarian subjunctive to a finish, they must be given, somehow or other, a little of the courage and enthusiasm that Caesar inspired in his soldiers. How easily this could be accomplished if the pupils could only see in the text what the old Roman saw—a moving picture of thrilling dramatic action, where the tramp of soldiers' feet, the cry of battle and the shout of victory could almost be heard! But they seem to think there is nothing to be evolved but an endless confusion of camps, marches and grammatical constructions.[16]

The teacher neatly borrows from the content of Caesar's commentary to treat learning Latin as a thrilling war. The rhetorical ploy transforms her into an inspirational general and her pupils into courageous and enthusiastic legionaries. Reading the *Gallic War* is an exciting battle (involving "grappling," "laying siege," and "fighting to the finish"), and the act of understanding its Latin positions the students with its author, turning them almost into miniature Caesars: seeing the action, hearing the tramp of soldiers' feet, the cry of battle, and the shout of victory.

From the late nineteenth century through the first decades of the twentieth, classics teachers, university professors, and other educators in the United States developed and advertised a whole array of pedagogic strategies to present Caesar's *Gallic War* (and, therefore, Latin and the whole discipline of classical study) as engaging, relevant, and topical for

American students and, frequently, even to infuse them with a love for the Roman general. Everywhere they placed emphasis not just on aids to comprehension of Caesar's linguistic form but also on the practical, ethical, and topical opportunities provided by Caesar's content.

BEGINNER'S CAESAR

Even in the twentieth century, juvenile instruction in Latin (as in Greek) followed a pattern that had originally been laid down in the Renaissance. Through recitation and written exercise, young people put to memory the grammatical rules of the classical language (its parts of speech, accidence, and syntax) and a portion of its lexicon, and then utilized this linguistic code to decipher texts of increasing difficulty. In the first year of high school, reading the original language was often confined to relatively mechanical translating, and where such schooling in Latin operated as a strict, ritualized practice of rewards and punishments applied rigorously to boys, it has since been understood as akin to a puberty rite, a testing passage from youth to manhood.[17]

American high-school students often encountered Julius Caesar's Latin and his war in Gaul almost as soon as they began their study of the language, when they were about fourteen years old. A popular school textbook for beginners bore the title *Bellum Helveticum,* because it took as a structuring Latin text Caesar's account of his opening campaign in 58 B.C.E., when he opposed the migration of the Helvetian tribe west through the Roman province of Transalpine Gaul (*Gallic War* 1.1–29).[18] After ten preliminary lessons, it is the vocabulary and the syntax of Caesar's narrative that guide the student's advance through the forms and grammatical rules of the Latin language. First published in 1889, and revised and reprinted over the course of more than twenty years, this beginner's guide to Latin based on reading a small segment of Caesar was highly successful. The two teachers from a boys' high school in Brooklyn, New York, who revised the 1906 edition (Arthur Lee Janes and Paul Rockwell Jenks) identified what they saw as the primary cause of the book's pedagogic excellence: the first twenty-nine sections of Julius Caesar's *Gallic War* were "a model of perfect Latinity" and "an illustration of the most important principles of the language."[19]

At *Gallic War* 1.2, for example, the episode proper begins with Caesar imputing to the Helvetian chieftain Orgetorix the highest aristocracy (*longe nobilissimus*) and the greatest wealth (*ditissimus*), a greed for kingship (*regni cupiditate*), the instigation of a conspiracy among his fellow nobles (*coniurationem nobilitatis*), powers of political persuasion (*civitati persuasit*), the urge to march with all his people's forces beyond their borders (*ut de finibus suis cum omnibus copiis exirent*), and the ambition to gain sovereignty over the whole of Gaul (*totius Galliae imperio potiri*). Some of these characteristics, abilities, and ambitions look suspiciously like a projection elsewhere of Julius Caesar's own— an early manifestation of the artful representation, the propaganda, or *Tendenz* that critics now commonly disclose in Caesar's commentaries on his military achievements.[20] In the classroom recitations and drills laid out in the 1906 edition of the textbook *Bellum Helveticum,* however, this first glimpse of Orgetorix extends across lessons 30 to 35, where it provides illumination for young readers on Latin's simple and compound verbs, verbs governing the dative, adjectives with a genitive ending in –*ius,* and the use of the ablative. And, in anticipation of translating Caesar's exact words, students are required to translate repetitively, from English into Latin and from Latin into English, starker versions of these sentiments, often utilizing the future tense: "Orgetorix will make these conspiracies" (lesson 30.278.1) or *ab Orgetorige imperium totius Galliae occupabitur* (in translation, perhaps, "control of all Gaul will be won by Orgetorix": lesson 31.287.2). In the second decade of the twentieth century, some classical scholars, like the Italian Guglielmo Ferrero, were challenging the credibility of the motivation for migration that, as narrator of the event, Caesar attributes to the Helvetians.[21] In the day-to-day life of American high schools, by contrast, students were attempting to attain linguistic skill in Latin by repetitively mimicking and confirming the Roman general's controlling narrative voice, along with his certainty about events and his urgency about responding to them.

Yet, if Latin was Caesar, and Caesar was Latin, critics of a classical education might assimilate the attributes of one to the attributes of the other. The manipulation of readers, deceit, propaganda, cruelty, and aggression do not sit comfortably with the advocacy of a subject for study in high school. Hence the accuracy and thoroughness that American teachers and their textbooks demanded from the translations of first-year students were frequently merged with the qualities of the Latin text the students were obliged to translate. And its author, Julius Caesar, was identified as a great general and the founder of lasting empire better to secure Latin as a great language and its study as a vigorous discipline deserving to endure in the curricula of schools throughout the United States.[22]

To redress the otherwise mechanistic pedagogy for first-year Latin and to anticipate the start made on the narrative of the *Gallic War* proper in the second year, many educators advocated the orchestration of the kind of child's play that Woodrow Wilson had once recommended to Mr. Slaughter. In his handbook for Latin teachers, the abovementioned Professor Game advised organizing a number of practical activities to accompany the introduction to the language in the first year of high school:

> When you begin Caesar, call attention to the various implements of war used by Romans and Gauls and invite pupils to make models. The response will be immediate. Get one to make a *hasta* [long spear], full size, another a *pilum* [javelin], then a *gladius* [sword], and so on. A little paint or wood stain will give the color needed. The *vinea* [movable shelter], *scorpio* [catapult], *aries* [battering ram], and Caesar's bridge will appeal to boys. Girls can make a *vexillum* [military banner], or dress a doll like a *legatus* [officer], or a *miles* [soldier], an *imperator* [commander in chief] etc . . . If business moves slowly, offer to accept a good piece of work of this kind in place of all or part of the term's examination, and a scene of unrivaled activity will delight you. It is really worth more to a boy to get into direct touch with the Roman army by making models of some of the weapons used by the soldiery than it is to go through an examination.[23]

Even as late as the 1920s edition of his handbook, and despite his employment at the Florida State College for Women, the professor of classics perpetuates in his advice to teachers on classroom play a traditional conception of gender division: boys make weapons, construct model siege-craft, build bridges; girls sew flags or dress dolls as toy soldiers.[24] The Latin language, the world of Julius Caesar, *and* the practices for studying them are all conceived as inherently masculine—girls are omitted from Professor Game's concluding remarks about the value of engaging the Latin learner closely with the Roman army.

That gendered pedagogy is reinforced visually by the images of Roman and Gallic military ranks that regularly interspersed the pages of the first- and second-year textbooks for reading Caesar. An American girl at high school in the 1900s or 1910s would be hard put to see herself, for example, in the taxonomies of masculinity employed to illustrate her beginner's textbook *Bellum Helveticum*. The *imperator* himself, a Gallic chieftain, and some of their respective officers line up opposite her lesson 25 (based on a simplified fragment of *Gallic War* 1.1 and containing drills on the present, imperfect, and future indicative passive of the third and fourth conjugations), while ranks of Roman soldiers parade opposite her lesson 64 (based on a fragment of *Gallic War* 1.7 and concerning the conjugation of the verbs *volo, nolo,* and *malo*). If that girl proceeded to second-year Latin, she would again find often quite colorful illustrations of the Roman author alongside his loyal legions taking up whole pages of her copy of the high-school commentaries on Caesar's *Gallic War* (see fig. 4).

In the *Classical Weekly* for 23 January 1909, Mary Harwood (the enterprising teacher from The Girls' Latin School in Baltimore) outlines a very carefully tiered strategy that she recommends for juvenile play-acting with the Roman dictator and his army. Students' interest should be aroused, she says, right from the start. Care should be taken not to confine the first year of Latin to potentially tedious labor over grammar. So, in the first semester of the first year, for fifteen minutes every Wednesday afternoon, she prepares the ground for second-year Caesar by reading to her girls a story about Roman daily life (the girls realize to their surprise that, like us, the Romans ate, drank, and were happy or sad). On the first Wednesday of the second semester, she explains the politics of the Roman republic ("much condensed and in one-syllable English"), and on the second Wednesday the "wonderful personality" of Caesar (described here as one day a fashionable elegant in the city and the next a hardy soldier in the field of war; one moment farsightedly planning the kingship of the Roman Empire, the next rushing into the thick of the fight).[25] By the third week of the second semester, the teacher has reached the Roman army and the parallel formation of a Saturday morning Latin Club. There, with great enthusiasm, her pupils make pinewood swords and broomstick spears, sugar-barrel shields embossed with gold-paper thunderbolts, canvas helmets decorated with feather crests, battle flags of red silk topped by cardboard eagles that are coated in silver paper, and—most important of all, she observes—a real knapsack packed with real wheat, a real blanket, two stakes, and a cooking pan. After all this practical work, her girls can "almost hear the trumpet order to march."[26]

This moment of gender transgression, when young American girls almost imagine themselves to be serving soldiers summoned to battle, is short-lived. From the end of the nineteenth century, the profession of Latin studies gradually became more feminized—the proportion of women substantially increased among high-school and college students and teachers of classics (as Professor Kelsey complained in 1925).[27] Yet continuing constraints on gender put a sudden brake on Harwood's gusto at this point in her report. The account of the Saturday morn-

1. Commander, *imperator*. 2. Lieutenant-general, *legatus*.
3. Centurion, *centurio*. 4. *Lictor*. 5. Standard-bearers, *signiferi*.
6. Eagle-bearer, *aquilifer*. 7. Trumpeter, *tubicen*. 8. Hornblower, *cornicen*.
9. Eagle, *aquila*. 10. Banner, *vexillum*.

FIGURE 4. "Officers, Standard-Bearers, and Musicians."
Color plate between pp. 70 and 71 of F.W. Kelsey's *Caesar's
Commentaries* (Boston, 1918), taken from the designs of
H. Reinhard.

ing club is largely given over to a lively description of the girls dressing
themselves up as Roman soldiers and picking up with relish the "real"
paraphernalia of war (knapsacks, rations, blankets, and weapons). It
ends briefly, however, with what the girls enjoy "best"—to dress dolls
like Roman soldiers. The scale of practical activity is diminished, its
materials become cheaper and more flimsy (colored paper and book
straps), the setting more comfortably feminine and domestic (the girls

borrow from their mothers' sewing bags), and, as a consequence, the girls' engagement with the Roman army is infantilized.

As they approach and then embark on their "Caesar year," the Baltimore girls prepare further by listening to their teacher's character-driven stories of the Helvetian migration (the treachery of the chieftain Orgetorix, the jealousy of Dumnorix toward his brother, and the devotion to Caesar of his lieutenant Labienus, *GW* 1.2–29). They are asked to envision the alarming prospect of the whole population of Washington swarming down on their own city, and to pace the Roman mile on their local walks. Finally, when they begin to read the first books of the *Gallic War* as continuous narratives, their practical activities are resumed with the constant construction of appropriate military models: such as a clay-and-cardboard camp to quarter the Roman general (inclusive of small trenches, ramparts, and stakes, tiny brown-paper tents and match-stick soldiers); a sand battlefield, powdered-chalk river, and woods of hemlock twigs for combat against the fierce Nervii (*GW* 2.15–32); and toy boats equipped with tiny boat hooks and boarding bridges that float in pans for the sea fights in which Caesar outwits the Veneti (*GW* 3.7–16). In the account Harwood provides for the *Classical Weekly*, the teacher and her students do not reach the fourth book of the *Gallic War* and, therefore, do not have the opportunity to construct the model that, elsewhere, is most frequently recommended for students learning Latin in high school—Caesar's ingenious bridge over the river Rhine (*GW* 4.17, and see the schoolbook illustration in fig. 5).[28] Building a small-scale replica of the Rhine bridge (with its rapidly assembled balks, piles, transoms, crossbeams, poles, and wattle work) operates as a tangible metonymy for overcoming the greater complexity and narrative flow of second-year Latin: it demonstrates physically that a wondrous edifice can be constructed out of interlinked parts, provides a visceral sense of direction and purpose, and offers the excitement clearly absent from drills in accidence and syntax. In Professor Game's handbook for schoolteachers, that pleasurable outcome is proffered to boys. He suggests girls can sew little articles of Roman clothing.[29]

THE CAESAR YEAR

During the late nineteenth century and the first few decades of the twentieth, a small cottage industry of school commentaries on the *Gallic War* took root in the United States. The commentaries were designed to support the teaching of Latin in the second year of high school—the crucial

Caesar grade. For school use, to begin with, the Roman general's commentaries on his campaigns in Gaul were usually delimited to the complete narratives of the first four books, from the Helvetian migration in 58 B.C.E. to the first expedition on British soil in 55. By the 1920s, high-school Caesar had often been whittled down even further to just the first two books in their entirety followed by excerpts from the other five.[30] While the amount of original Latin text shrank, its explanatory baggage grew. In 1907, for example, a professor of Latin at the University of Kansas, Arthur Tappan Walker, brought out a much-revised edition of a school commentary that had originally appeared in 1891. Already in the case of Professor Walker's *Gallic War* (1907), as in so many other commentaries on Caesar, vocabularies, notes on linguistic constructions, illustrations, maps, and other explanatory matter are positioned across the same pages as Caesar's own words, in order to save students from endless page-turning in their search for clarification. Often such illustrations and annotations overwhelm the Latin text itself: as when a small fragment of Caesar's detailed description of the bridge over the river Rhine at *Gallic War* 4.17 squats in a corner above and beside the editor's fulsome linguistic exposition, neat diagrams, and advocacy of model making. Similarly, in the 1918 edition of *Caesar in Gaul* edited by Professors Benjamin L. D'Ooge and Frederick C. Eastman, a diagram of the bridge built by Caesar's soldiers takes up far more space on the page than the Roman general's original description of it (fig. 5), while the commentary includes, along with Caesar's Latin, an introduction (on Caesar's life, the countries in or against which he campaigned, and the organization of Roman military affairs), a review of first-year syntax, notes, a grammar, prose composition exercises, word lists, and vocabularies from Latin into English and English into Latin.

Before the young American readers of second-year Caesar arrive at the Rhine frontier and the Roman general's magnificent feat of engineering, however, they have had to negotiate not just the dreaded conditional construction and the seemingly boundless obstacle of indirect discourse, but also a catalogue of Caesarean slaughters—and the one they have most recently encountered in book 4 is also the most controversial. After two Germanic tribes, the Usipetes and the Tencteri, had crossed over the Rhine near the coast into Gaul in 55 B.C.E., Caesar had detained their envoys, attacked their camp, hunted down their women and children as they fled, and massacred on the riverbank all the surviving men who had not drowned in terror first (*GW* 4.14–15). Even at the time, opponents of Caesar at Rome argued that he should be surrendered into

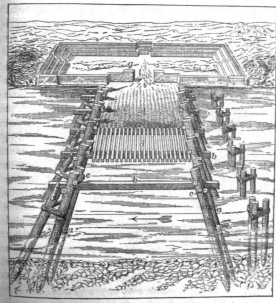

FIRST INVASION OF GERMANY   113

He decides to bridge the river

17. Caesar hīs de causīs quās commemorāvī Rhēnum trānsīre dēcrēverat; sed nāvibus trānsīre neque satis tūtum

PONS A CAESARE IN RHENO FACTUS

aa, tigna bina sesquipedalia; *bb*, trabes bipedales; *cc*, fibulae; *dd*, derecta materia longuriis cratibusque constrata; *ee*, sublicae ad inferiorem partem flumīnis pro ariete oblique actae; *ff*, sublicae supra pontem immissae; *g*, castellum ad caput pontis positum

esse arbitrābātur, neque suae neque populī Rōmānī dignitātis esse statuēbat. Itaque, etsī summa difficultās faciendī pontis prōpōnēbātur propter lātitūdinem, rapiditātem, 5

FIGURE 5. Caesar decides to bridge the Rhine. From *Caesar in Gaul*, edited by B.L. D'Ooge and F.C. Eastman (Boston, 1917), 113.

the hands of the enemy, since he had violated the truce that had preceded these terrible events.[31] Many American handbooks for second-year Latin, in consequence, do not cast high-school students in relation to their text of the *Gallic War* as adoring and disciplined soldiers in the army of Caesar's Latin learners. After the first year, the greater maturity of the students (now mostly fifteen years old), their increased command of linguistic forms, and, chiefly, the necessities of content drive classical scholars to introduce their commentaries with a more balanced attitude to the Roman general and his achievements. A degree of ethical separation must now obtain between Caesar's acts and his telling of them; so long as the Latin remains pure and simple, its author may be temporarily besmirched.

Concessions to the cruelty of the content, nevertheless, remain slight. In the preface to his edition of the *Gallic War* (1907), for example, Arthur T. Walker argues that the warfare was indeed bloody but greatly justified by its result: "The one means of safety for both Gauls and Romans was that the Romans should govern all the country west of the Rhine and should hold the Germans at bay on the other side of that great river" (10). The Gallic campaigns are to the benefit of the Roman state, not just to the political career of the ambitious proconsul (9–10). He was admittedly cruel, but only "sometimes" and "from policy"; by nature he was clement (18). His narrative was hastily written for selfish political purpose, but there is no proof that it contains at any point a single intentionally false statement (20). Similarly, when introducing *Gallic War* book 4, the professor from Kansas admits emphatically that when the Roman general slew a whole host of German men, women, and children in 55 B.C.E., he "made himself guilty of the most treacherous and indefensible act in his whole career" (252). Yet defense immediately follows on the same page: it was imperative to teach other German tribes never to cross the Rhine and invade Gaul (252). After the ruthless massacre, Caesar's narrative moves smoothly on to the rapid creation of his bridge over the river Rhine, a bridge that permitted brief forays into the territory of the Germans themselves. Commentary on the construction of the bridge, in all its marvelous complexity and apparent purpose, must have come as some relief to Walker.

More evasive, and yet also more equivocal, are the high-school manuals for the composition of Latin prose that also worked to structure students' moral understanding of Caesar's Gallic campaigns.[32] In 1910, William Gardner Hale, professor of Latin at the University of Chicago, published in the *School Review* a survey of thirty-two such books for high-school use at the same time as the first volume of his own contribution to the genre appeared.[33] Teaching composition, he argued, is especially difficult during the second year of Latin at high school. The English sentences assigned are disconnected and mostly meaningless or absurd and render the business of writing Latin dull and artificial. It is far better to design a composition book as a companion to the second-year text. The lessons should be on a scale and in an order to match each week's sequential reading from book 1 to book 4 of the *Gallic War*.[34] Such was the strategy adopted by Charles M. Baker and Alexander J. Inglis one year earlier, for their *High School Course in Latin Composition* (1909). At the time, the authors were employed at the Horace Mann School, originally founded for teacher observations and educational experimentation, and attached to Columbia University in New York.[35] The section of their course dedicated to second-year Latin contains a series of twenty-eight lessons based on Caesar's war commentaries. Each lesson focuses on one principle of syntax and includes one set of English sentences for written translation into Latin (half to be completed at home and half in the classroom), followed by another set for oral translation into Latin to reinforce rapidly the earlier drills. In lesson 26, "The Passive Periphrastic," the first ten sentences assigned for homework read as follows (Baker and Inglis 1909, 160–61):

1. Caesar said to the ambassadors of the Usipetes, "Your tribe must not remain in Gaul."
2. I ought not to grant, especially to so great a multitude, the privilege of settling in Gaul.
3. Therefore you must return to the lands whence you have come.
4. The ambassadors themselves made no promises, but said that they had to report Caesar's orders to their (countrymen).
5. Meanwhile you, Caesar, ought not to come (any) nearer with your army.
6. You ought to remain here; in this place you ought to await our answer.
7. Caesar decided that not even this (request) ought to be granted.
8. If I delay here, I shall afterward have to contend with an enemy (that is) better prepared.
9. For these Germans will not think that they must return to Germany at my command.
10. Caesar therefore decided that he ought to fight-it-out with the Germans as soon as possible.

So that American high-school students will not yet have to face the ordeal of reproducing Latin's syntax for indirect speech in only their second year of study, the authors on a number of occasions change the indirect construction in Caesar's original text into direct speech. As students labor over their compositions at home, therefore, they are being asked to speak as if they were the delegation from the German tribes (5 and 6). The momentary breach is more than counteracted by the opportunity provided to both speak (1, 2, and 3) and *think* (8 and 9) as Caesar. The "passive periphrastic" conjugation, knowledge of which these sentences are designed to test, constitutes a verbal formation that signifies necessity or obligation. The exploitation of the Usipetes episode to put the construction to use transforms that brutal episode into a list of what Caesar and the Germans "must" do or "ought" to do. Such exercises in prose composition manage to extract from the Latin the cruelties of Julius Caesar (there are no sentences to translate concerning ruthless massacre), and to inject a much-needed tone of right conduct.

SUPPORTING MATERIALS

For background information, the American community of classics teachers and academics suggested to each other a range of writers on Julius Caesar from Napoleon Bonaparte to Theodor Mommsen, but, in the first decades of the twentieth century, over and above all others they advocated the British classical scholar T. Rice Holmes and his magisterial study of *Caesar's Conquest of Gaul* (1899). Rice Holmes, they argued, discusses with such "impartiality" and "thoroughness" both the geographical and the military issues raised by the *Gallic War* that a copy "should be in the hands of every teacher of Caesar"[36] and "in the library of every secondary school throughout the land."[37] Originally published in 1899 as a monumental volume almost nine hundred pages long, *Caesar's Conquest of Gaul* had been divided between a historical narrative of the campaigns and an exhaustive series of scholarly articles intended to elucidate the Roman general's commentaries on matters textual, geographic, topographic, military, ethnological, social, political, and religious. In 1903, the first part was republished separately, by demand, as a more manageable little book.

Rice Holmes found favor as an aid to the teaching of second-year Latin in American high schools because he argued that Caesar's text should be read "not merely as a lesson in construing but also as history."[38] In the preface to his abridged 1903 edition, he also disclosed that when he originally began his research on the *Gallic War* his purpose had been to help schoolboys "realise that those pages were not written for the purpose of inflicting mental torture, but were the story of events which really did happen, and many of which rival in interest the exploits of Cortes or Clive."[39] Furthermore, it was noted,[40] Rice Holmes was a man of military experience and considerable scholarly acumen, a voice then of considerable authority that could refute (and did, over seventy pages of his original edition) the well-known charges that Caesar's commentaries on his campaigns were tendentious—composed in order to put the general's unconstitutional or inhuman acts in the best possible light, to magnify his achievements and to conceal his mistakes, and thus further his self-regarding political ambitions back home in Rome. Once the boys understood (thanks to the labors of the British scholar) that their second-year Latin text was a fine document composed in a terse and vigorous style, their minds should fill with "living, throbbing interest" in its historic events: the melancholy practice of western migration, the first recorded interview between Roman and Teuton, and the first crossing of the British Channel by a Roman army.[41]

In American classrooms (heavily armed with the approach and the meticulous investigations of Rice Holmes), teachers impressed on students in a number of ways the historicity of Caesar's narrative. In 1906, for example, an article in one of the teachers' weeklies by Professor Walter Dennison of the University of Michigan advertised that the principal of the local Bay City school had visited the most important Caesarean localities in France, catalogued the photographs he had taken according to the movements through Gaul of Caesar's troops, and kindly made them available as slides for distribution and display to any high school possessing a stereopticon lantern.[42] Put Caesar's battle plans neatly on the blackboard every day, Dennison also advised, with opposing forces indicated by different colored chalk (red, say, for the Romans, and yellow for the Gauls). Explain troop movements as if they were a game on a checkerboard. Draw parallels between ancient and modern warfare and expose the differences (such as artillery, transport facilities, or the spyglass). Study strategy. Bring students' attention to the text's lessons for life: making the most of one's resources, exercising caution, valuing a defensive attitude.[43] In sum: teach the *Gallic War* as military history, and you will succeed in both awakening and sustaining the interest of schoolboys in Latin.

Less weighty (in every sense), more accessible, and more entertaining than Rice Holmes's scholarly monograph were the many historical biographies of Julius Caesar produced expressly for young Americans in this period. Unconstrained by the limits of the second-year Latin curriculum, such books told the Roman dictator's whole life story in suitably stirring terms. Michael Clarke's *Story of Caesar* (1898), for example, works its way past the protagonist's very kindly treatment of the surrendering Helvetians (54), the contemptuousness of the German chieftain Ariovistus (55), the wonderful feat of bridge building across the Rhine (68), and the remarkable invasion of Britain (67) through the civil war to conclude its biography dramatically in the ninth chapter with the murderous conspiracy set in motion by Roman senators jealous of their

FIGURE 6. "The Assassination of Caesar, 44 BC." From the
painting by C. Rochegrosse. Color plate between pp. 8 and 9
of *Caesar in Gaul,* edited by B.L. D'Ooge and F.C. Eastman
(Boston, 1917).

erstwhile friend's great powers (113).[44] As with the school commentaries, the early chapters of Clarke's account are interspersed with fine line-drawings of the ranks of Caesar's soldiers and the clever weaponry with which they defeat their exotic enemies, whereas only a single, small battering ram provides illustration for the chapters where Caesar engages in his great struggle with Pompey.

Toward the end of this particular juvenile biography, however, the author suddenly inserts the denser, more violent contours of a full-page painting to accompany his more emotive narrative of the murderous events of the Ides of March. Facing Clarke's description of how Caesar reacted when he saw Brutus among the murderers (1898, 117), the painting—*Death of Caesar* (1887) by the popular French artist Georges Antoine Rochegrosse—colors the assassination in terms of the collective savagery of the conspirators and the disorder that ensued in the seat of government (fig. 6). In *Story of Caesar,* Clarke also looks to a famed literary source to help confirm that the death is a bloody murder (he never applies to it the less critical term "assassination"). A quotation appears at the bottom of page 117, abruptly rounding off Clarke's description:

Then burst his mighty heart,
And in his mantle, muffling up his face,
Even at the base of Pompey's statue,
Which all the while ran blood, great Caesar fell.
(SHAKESPEARE)

Clarke treats this passage from act 3, scene 2 of the tragedy *Julius Caesar* as if it were almost the personal testimony of the great dramatist. He fails to note that he has extracted the words from the cunning oration delivered by Antony to the plebeians in order to stir them up to mutiny.[45] As he draws near to his concluding comments in this final chapter of Caesar's story, Clarke also informs his young readers that thus died "the greatest of all the Romans" (1898, 118). He then turns that Roman into a role model for American students when he compares the dictator explicitly to the first president of the United States: each, he states, was honored as "the father of his country" (118). Then, above a drawing of a wreath, he ends (119):

> Many eminent authors have written about Caesar, and nearly all in words of the highest praise and admiration. Truly his name is
>
> > "One of the few, the immortal names
> > That were not born to die."

Here Clarke evokes the sixteenth president of the United States, Abraham Lincoln.[46] He quotes, this time, from a famous American poem by Fitz-Greene Halleck that originally concerned a freedom fighter active in the war for the independence of Greece. Lincoln had used these same lines in 1852 to eulogize the statesman Henry Clay as a voice also calling for the liberty of Greece and as another unforgettable patriot,[47] but, on Lincoln's death thirteen years later, the verses were regularly transposed yet again this time to eulogize the assassinated president himself.[48] Thus the juvenile biography (through explicit parallel with the first president and implicit parallel with the sixteenth) doubly confirms Caesar as a hero fit for liberty-loving Americans.

High-school Latin teachers also recommended historical novels to their students, of which more were written about Julius Caesar and the Gallic War than any other part of Roman history.[49] One enduring favorite was A. C. Whitehead's *The Standard Bearer: A Story of Army Life in the Time of Caesar,* which was first published by the American Book Company in 1914, after which it enjoyed many subsequent editions.[50] The author was a Latin instructor in a boys' high school in Atlanta, Georgia, and his historical fiction takes as its focal point a crucial moment from *Gallic War* 4.25 when, during the campaigns of 55 B.C.E., Caesar's soldiers are hesitating to jump from their ships and wade onto the shores of Britain. At that moment, two very important things happen: first, a valiant standard-bearer of the tenth legion plunges forward into the surf to lead the way; and second, in the Latin, Caesar's text turns for the very first time in four books of commentary on the war (and for maximum dramatic effect) to the use of direct speech. In this way, American students are forced to confront Latin's imperative mood:

> Meanwhile our soldiers were hesitating, chiefly because the sea was so deep; then the man who carried the Eagle of the Tenth legion appealed to the gods to see that his action turned out well for the legion, and said: 'Jump down, soldiers, unless you want to betray our Eagle to the enemy—I at least shall have done my duty to the republic and to my commander'. He cried these words in a loud voice, then flung himself away from the ship and began to carry the Eagle towards the enemy. Then our men urged each other to prevent such a disgrace and all together jumped down from the ship. (GW 4.25; trans. Hammond 1996, 82)[51]

Whitehead turns Caesar's nameless standard-bearer into the novel's fictive hero, Caius. Caius first encounters Caesar when, while still a boy, he has successfully fought off some robbers attempting to steal his sheep. The shepherd is impressed by the stranger who just then passes by in a chariot and inquires kindly about what has happened (Whitehead 1972, 19–20 and illustrated on 10; see fig. 7):

> His face was rather pale. A large nose, full firm lips, and dark piercing eyes were overhung by a forehead, broad and high. There were lines and seams, too, of power and set purpose. All together he was a man whose quick and vivid energy, bold determined will, and masterful intelligence caused Caius to feel at once that he would love and respect this man friendly to him, and would hate and fear him hostile. The young shepherd knew by instinct that he was in the presence of one who would spare none of his vast energy in executing the far-reaching plans which his august and massive intellect might conceive and his inflexible will determine.

Inspired by this encounter with the general, Caius becomes a soldier in the Roman army on service in Gaul. Meeting his *imperator* from time to time, Caius fights the Germans and the Nervii. Rising up the ranks to become a standard-bearer, he propels Caesar's hesitant legions onto British shores, and, promoted higher still to the rank of commander, our hero is taken prisoner by the Gauls and almost sacrificed to their gods. In this way, Julius Caesar's war commentary is translated into the story of a young boy's steady growth from shepherd to soldier to standard-bearer to commander. Caius's progress is clearly displayed in the novel's division into five books, the first four of which are entitled *Pastor, Miles, Aquilifer,* and *Dux*.

In the final book of the novel, *Vir,* Caius becomes a mature man of

FIGURE 7. "The Shepherd Meets a Proconsul." From A.C.
Whitehead's *The Standard Bearer* (New York, 1914), 10.

twenty-four who witnesses with his own eyes the surrender of the Gallic
chieftain Vercingetorix. *The Standard Bearer* closes with the hero's
union in marriage to a Nervian princess, gifted to him by Caesar himself (Whitehead 1972, 293 and illustrated on 294; see fig. 8):

> "Here, fellow soldiers, is a rare jewel which I would bestow in marriage
> upon our young soldier and officer, Caius Volcatius Tullus. She is a Nervian
> princess, and he is a Roman patrician. They have been true to each other in
> the greatest danger, and have in turn saved each the other's life. Now may
> you all join me in wishing them long happiness in their mutual love." And
> there among the sights and sounds of war they were married in accordance
> with the good old Roman customs.

FIGURE 8. Caesar presents Caius with his bride. From A.C. Whitehead's *The Standard Bearer* (New York, 1914), 294.

The novel concludes thereafter with the appointment of Caius as governor of Gaul, which he then rules with justice and moderation, spreading civilization to the new Roman province.

Following the nineteenth-century tradition of didacticism in children's literature, and the narrative structures that shaped the genre as both entertaining and instructive,[52] the young characters and the young readers of *The Standard Bearer* are placed under the command of and trained according to the paternal adult voice of the book (whether that of Caesar or the author). The "real business" of such literature—whether about school or, as here, the army and empire—was to develop and socialize their boy heroes and their readers by putting on display and testing the foundations of an ideal masculine virtue.[53] But, in the second decade of the twentieth century, this particular brand of juvenile historical novel works on three, rather than two, levels: it entertains, it instructs, *and* it enlivens second-year Latin. The fictional character learns and develops thanks to campaigning with Julius Caesar; the young reader will mature thanks to the adult author's depiction of that fictional sequence of events; and, by implication, the second-year student at high school will become a better person by means of the exercises and drills their Latin teacher assigns them based on the *Gallic War*. Now Latin is rendered highly relevant to American schoolboys (and, again, less directly so to American schoolgirls), because, in the novel, their set text has been converted into a story of growth from childhood to maturity, a rite of passage into society (here represented by the army and Roman government) and up into its highest levels of responsibility. The lessons of *The Standard Bearer* are loud and clear: reading Caesar's war commentaries will make you a man, virile, courageous, highly successful, civilized (and fully heterosexual).

DENIGRATING CAESAR

Yet even a relatively imperceptive student in second-year Latin at high school might notice that, at times, they held in their hands quite different judgments on Julius Caesar, and that the lessons to be learned from the author, his works, and his Latin syntax might be of a darker, more subversive kind. In *The Standard Bearer*, for example, masculine virtue can conveniently take root and blossom in the person of the young hero, Caesar's namesake Caius, and remain there unsullied, for, soon after he enters the Roman army, the boy begins to walk a separate moral path from his commander. In the first book of the *Gallic War* (the Latin commentary from which the novel takes its inspiration), Caesar says that, after he laid down terms of surrender for the Helvetians, during that same night, 6,000 men who belonged to their canton of Verbigene broke out of the camp and made a break for German territories. Once they had been brought back, the general says of himself that he categorized them as enemies (*reductos in hostium numero habuit*, GW 1.28), while the Helvetians who had obediently remained behind in camp he permitted to surrender. Whitehead expands vividly on Caesar's original phrasing when he recounts how young Caius first took to soldiery (1972, 77):

> The next morning Caius beheld a horror which he had not imagined possible. At the command of Caesar, unarmed, the Verbigenians were marched up to a line of legionaries, who stabbed them as they came, until rows and heaps of the huge stripe-clad bodies lay stiff and silent in great pools of their own blood.
>
> And then pity awoke in the heart of the young Roman for his hated enemies, even the Gauls.

By the time Caius becomes a man and a Roman officer, after six years in the army of his ruthless commander, he realizes that "he had hated bloodshed and carnage more and more with each great battle he had seen. He heartily wished it could all be ended" (255–56). And, when the war finally does end, it is Caius (not Caesar) who is to be found ruling Gaul "with justness and moderation" (295).

Similarly, in *Story of Caesar*, Clarke insists that eminent authors have written with such admiration about the Roman general that he has entered the company of "the few, the immortal names." After narrating the death of his hero, in an appended chapter Clarke assembles substantial quotations from some of the most familiar idolaters of the nineteenth century: De Quincey ("Without Caesar there would have been no perfect Rome," 1898, 162), Mommsen ("He appeared to desire nothing but to be first among his equals," 166), and Froude ("He fought his battles to establish some degree of justice in the government of this world, and he succeeded, though he was murdered for it," 164). Yet littered throughout the same chapter are borrowings from other nineteenth-century authors whose vision of immortal Caesar turns out to be, in places, wholly antithetical to the biographer's own.[54] For example, Clarke also cites a judgment of Julius Caesar's standing against two other statesmen of recent times:

> Washington, who established and administered honestly a new government, was far inferior as a general to Caesar, who only lived long enough to destroy an old constitution. As a man, the American was immeasurably superior to the Roman, whose career may be better compared with that of the first Napoleon, not Caesar's superior in military ability, and greatly below him in nobleness of character.[55]

Reading this, a student in second-year Latin might note that, whereas Caesar comes out tops in military matters, ethically he ranks a very poor second to noble Washington. Many much more damaging remarks are permitted to appear within the pages of *Story of Caesar*, including those of the headmaster of Rugby school, Thomas Arnold, on the appalling criminality of Caesar's slaughters during the Gallic and the civil wars (159–60): "If from the intellectual we turn to the moral character of Caesar, the whole range of history can hardly furnish a picture of greater deformity. Never did any man occasion so large an amount of human misery, with so little provocation."[56]

Even in the classrooms of American high schools, the Latin teacher might occasionally speak out frankly against the author of the set text their second-year students were required to study. In the preface to his sermonizing work *Caesar's Character or In Defense of the Standard of Mankind* (1907), William Waddell recalls the occasion that spurred him to write it: "One day at high school, the instructor in Latin, speaking of Caesar, said: 'Caesar's character has never been satisfactorily explained, but undoubtedly he was one of the greatest monsters that ever lived.'"[57] Encouraged by this memory of his teacher's contemptuous assessment, the writer then develops a counterattack against what he perceives to be the growing army of worshippers of Caesar and his modern counterpart, Napoleon. The author's stated purpose is to explain why the "standard of mankind" (what a man should be) must be maintained against the degenerate tastes of the failing nation, led down into luxury and pleasure by its ambition to make money (Waddell 1907, 26).[58] We must conclude anew against the modern world's Caesarists, Waddell argues, that the character of their false hero stands, in fact, for the lowest type of man (169) and that he "owes the world a debt that only centuries in Hades could pay" (240).

Thus, in the early years of the twentieth century, many young Americans routinely encountered Julius Caesar as author of perfect Latin, maker of men, and civilizer of nations (both ancient and modern). Yet, at the same time, love of Caesar could be presented in many quarters—and even in American classrooms—as modern man's undoing and as a sign of the nation's social and moral decline from the purity of its simple republican beginnings.

CHAPTER 2

Americanization

1900–1914

In the early years of the twentieth century, Julius Caesar often encroached on the lives of young Americans from two directions simultaneously. When aged about fifteen, many students read Caesar's commentaries on his campaigns in Gaul in their second-year Latin classes and Shakespeare's dramatization of his assassination and its consequences in their second-year English classes. The relationship between these two experiences could be quite intimate. While Shakespeare's play was drawn on to provide tragic color and a conclusion to the Latin narrative of the victorious general, Roman history and Caesar's writings were used to provide historical background and a prologue for the drama of the murdered dictator. Shakespeare's tragedy dominated the American student's impression of Caesar as statesman and had long been a driving force behind the Roman's circulation beyond the book and the classroom, out on the stage and in American culture more broadly.[1]

Julius Caesar's war in Gaul had constituted an originary moment in the birth of the French nation, and from the mid-nineteenth century his opponent Vercingetorix had been transformed into a model of Gallic heroism fit to inspire all the nation's students;[2] in the twentieth century, material traces of the Roman general's campaigns still littered the landscape of France, and his troop movements could be pinpointed on modern maps of the country. Although more tentative, Caesar's invasion of Britain nevertheless also belonged in the initial pages of school textbooks on the history of England. But Caesar's feet had never trod on American soil, and the specifics of the Gallic War had no obvious place in school narratives of the formation of the American nation. Consequently, much ingenious work had to be done by high-school Latin teachers to make the Roman general's writings on military matters seem relevant to their students. Teachers of Shakespeare's *Julius Caesar,* however, found their set text much easier to manage, since the Elizabethan tragedy "deals with characters and events belonging to a period in Roman history perhaps better known and more interesting to us as American republicans than any other epoch in the life of the world," as Robert R. Raymond, principal of the Boston School of Oratory, proclaimed in 1881.[3]

The drama's interrogation of the danger of tyranny, the benefit of republicanism and political liberty, the legitimacy of assassination, and the nature of genuine patriotism could easily translate into the familiar language of American political debate. Both time and place are already out of joint in Shakespeare's tragedy, in which the streets, houses, and bodies of ancient Romans display the chimney tops, striking clocks, and doublets of Elizabethan England.[4] The cross-temporal and cross-spatial migration of Shakespeare's Caesar to the United States was first driven by the private reading and public performance of the play in revolutionary mode during and after the War of Independence; and, in the twentieth century, Caesar's claim to cultural territory in the United States was confirmed by the strategies of analysis that became customary in American scholarship. Reflecting in the late 1930s on the differences between nineteenth- and twentieth-century studies of Shakespeare, Esther Cloudman Dunn, professor of English at Smith College, stated: "The genius of Shakespeare is extraordinarily sensitive to the hour and the age. Into his book, each age has peered, as into a mirror, to see its own face. The images in that mirror fade and are replaced as the decades go by. But the mirror is not discarded."[5]

SHAKESPEARE'S *JULIUS CAESAR* IN THE CLASSROOM

There are a number of "ages" or focal points in the history of the American reception of Shakespeare's *Julius Caesar* on the stage and in the classroom, as well as at the university.[6] The first (or almost the first), and one of the most influential, belongs to the revolutionary era, when the tragedy was read and performed as a call to fight for the liberty of the New World against the tyranny of the Old.[7] As late as October 1990, the founder and president of The Shakespeare Guild, John F. Andrews, commented in the press on how *Julius Caesar* had persistently been Americanized in this way for more than two hundred years:

> If you're like a lot of Americans, your school days included a class in which you recited orations from *Julius Caesar.* You may have been taught that the title character in Shakespeare's tragedy was a forerunner of the King that Britain's New World colonies felt driven to defy in 1776. And you may have learned that the Patrick Henrys and Nathan Hales who took arms against George III were following in the steps of honourable patriots who had done what they'd had to do during the most soul-trying days of republican Rome.[8]

In the late nineteenth century, the play was adapted into prose for the benefit of the very youngest of readers. Two volumes of *Tales from Shakespeare* (1893 and 1894) were published in Philadelphia as an American supplement to the hugely successful prose abridgments of Shakespeare's plays produced much earlier in England by Charles and Mary Lamb. In the additional American *Tales,* Harrison S. Morris (a writer, businessman, and philanthropist) rendered as prose stories those sixteen plays of Shakespeare that the Lambs had chosen to omit, including *Julius Caesar.* Morris makes no explicit reference to the American Revolution or the War of Independence within his simplified narration of the tragedy's plot, yet it is notable that the title character is introduced as a man who would be king, and as a danger to the liberties of Rome (167). Cassius and Brutus are figured as honorable patriots, sad at heart, who cannot countenance the dictator's ambition. Although the text of act 1, scene 2 of Shakespeare's play clearly presents an envious Cassius luring his friend into murderous conspiracy,[9] in the American *Tales from Shakespeare* political seduction is rewritten for the nation's young people as brave patriotism: Cassius and Brutus talk "together," they are "both" aware of the dangers for Rome, they tell "each other" their thoughts, find themselves "at one" in their resolve, and thus enter into "an agreement" to prevent Caesar's assumption of kingship (168). The tragedy's original staging of ethical unease about conspiracy and assassination vanishes, and the American prose synopsis replaces it with a heroic camaraderie that better matches the idealized national history of colonial revolution. The War of Independence gains prestigious cultural antecedents (both Roman and Shakespearean), and the Elizabethan drama relevance for young Americans.

Yet, despite the comments of Andrews in 1990, Shakespeare's *Julius Caesar* was by no means always taught in high school as a dramatization elsewhere and else when of heroic American rebellion against cruel

British tyranny. The apparently clear parallel between the senators' conspiracy against the Roman dictator and the colonists' revolt against the British king had been muddied by the events of the Civil War. When John Wilkes Booth shot President Lincoln, in the view of many, a mad Brutus had felled a mighty leader.[10] Roman history and Elizabethan drama were now internalized, not as a noble revolt by the New World against the tyranny of the Old, but as the tragic struggle of the South against the authority of the North. And by the turn of the century, moreover, the United States now possessed its own admirers of Caesar and Caesarism,[11] and its own lovers of empire.[12]

Earlier in the nineteenth century, Shakespeare had begun life in America's schools as fragments, quarried for noble tags that were then collated in readers to teach elocution and to be used in declamation exercises. By the beginning of the twentieth century, the readers had largely been replaced by texts of whole plays selected from a juvenile canon in which *Julius Caesar* almost invariably appeared.[13] Introductions and annotations invited high-school students to read Shakespearean plot and scene analytically and ethically and were utilized by teachers to inculcate in their heterogeneous charges notions of American civility, gentility, and nobility (and, in the case of *Julius Caesar,* patriotism).[14] In a teachers' manual published in 1915, *Teaching Literature in the Grammar Grades and High School*, Emma Miller Bolenius vividly recalls an English period on Shakespeare at her school in Newark: "It was eleven o'clock. In the sunny English room the class had assembled. A Chinese boy sat in front of the teacher's desk; here and there a Russian with eager face waited for the work; a Greek boy's dark eyes glowed in expectation; the rest were more or less American. They had 'finished' *Julius Caesar*" (180). Bolenius then goes on to advocate to other English teachers that, for this type of keen but diverse audience, they should extract from Shakespeare's tragedy suitable lessons for life—the bard should take on a civilizing and assimilating authority. Talk intimately with your pupils, she advises, about such issues as real patriotism, high ideals, and the standards by which to judge them, civic duties and conflicts between them, honor, and "the contemptible side of conspiracies" (185). Here recognition in the Elizabethan tragedy of both political ambiguity (the *contemptible* aspect of conspiracies) and ethical complexity (*conflicts* between duties) works at least partially to sully the patriotism of Brutus. By implication, Caesar is cleansed of his late eighteenth- and early nineteenth-century villainy.

Few juvenile texts of Shakespeare's *Julius Caesar* went as far in their ethical and political reappraisal of the protagonists as that published by Henry Norman Hudson in 1874. In his youth a farm boy, then southern schoolteacher, churchman, and literary critic, by the 1870s Reverend Hudson had become a professional editor of Shakespeare, disseminating his conservative interpretation of the Bard's plays across the United States in lectures of considerable popularity.[15] His edition of the Roman tragedy formed part of a widely distributed series he had designed in order to present the plays of Shakespeare to students as a "school of virtuous discipline."[16] In his introduction, Hudson announces himself perplexed by Shakespeare's characterization of the Roman dictator as "a grand, strutting piece of puff-paste" (1874, 10). Rather, the historical Caesar is "the great sun of Rome" who had to be shorn of his beams to let Brutus's "ineffectual fire" catch the eye (13). Brutus is "a shallow idealist" (15–16) who murders the world's greatest statesman (18) just as that statesman was seeking with extraordinary clarity of vision to imperialize the state (20). Hudson's Bonapartism stands momentarily revealed when, in a note on Caesar's falling sickness (discussed by Brutus and Cassius at *JC* 1.2.252–54), he observes that Napoleon was also said to have suffered from epilepsy toward the end of his life (25).

More often, in the decades after the Civil War, editors of school Shakespeare elaborate not on the political greatness of Caesar but on the ethical failure of Brutus. In *Shakespeare for the Young Folk* (1881), the principal of Boston School of Oratory quoted above, Robert R. Raymond, finds *Julius Caesar* to be of great interest to Americans as both tragedy and history "because it shows us how a true and pure republican, so many centuries ago, was wrought upon to commit a great crime to save the liberties of his country, and teaches us, by the disastrous result of his effort, the vanity of expecting to do good by evil means."[17] Teaching Shakespeare's play to high-school students on these terms allowed some quite explicit and elaborate parallels to be drawn with the history of the United States.

In *The Ethical Element in Literature* (1891), a handbook for teachers, the author Richard D. Jones bases his pedagogical approach to Shakespeare's Caesar on the educational philosophy of Illinois State Normal University. The university had been founded in the Midwest to create a class of professional educators and to drive the notion of literary value away from a "rhetorics" of mechanical skill in reading, writing, and speaking to the "poetics" of spiritual appreciation of content.[18] Foreshadowing the comments of the Shakespeare scholar Esther Cloudman Dunn, the Illinois teacher argues ambitiously that literature is "a moral mirror wherein man may read the lesson of the past" (1891, 2) and, utilizing that powerful instrument, schoolteachers may determine the character and destiny of their students (5) and quicken their community toward a higher life (8). Tragedy exposes human weakness magnified in grander figures and more awful results (2), while Shakespeare in particular teaches us "the relative importance of apparently conflicting duties" (23). According to Jones, the decisions made by Shakespeare's Roman characters, and how they reach them, should educate young Americans in the ethics of their recent political struggles. At the commencement of the Civil War, General Robert E. Lee faced a conflict of loyalty between duty to his own state of Virginia and duty to the federal authority of the United States. The cause he chose was right (Jones claims), but, tragically, it was in conflict with a higher cause, so "Robert E. Lee was the Brutus of the nineteenth century. Every one respected his personal integrity. 'Oh, he sits high in all the people's hearts!' as a man and a soldier. And yet he marched under the black flag of treason. His motives were right, his judgement wrong, his life a tragedy" (26). Similarly, American history should help us understand Shakespeare's Roman characters politically: "Brutus was the Robert E. Lee of the first century B.C. Both stood for the maintenance of the old order of things. Both were resisting a change in the government—Brutus a change toward centralization of power in the form of imperialism, Lee the same tendency toward centralization in the form of a stronger Federal government, a Nation instead of a nation" (35).

Taking as one of his two central examples of ethical literature the Shakespearean play "most largely read" (29) in Illinois's public schools, Jones demonstrates to his readership of teachers how best to draw out the play's ethical lessons for students. He does this by domesticating Shakespeare and relating *Julius Caesar* closely to local state history. Illinois had provided a large number of troops for the Union army. It was the birthplace of President Lincoln and had been home to the Union general Ulysses S. Grant.[19] Jones shapes Brutus as a Roman Robert E. Lee to render Shakespeare's lessons more vividly immediate and uses Shakespeare pointedly to prick the growing reputation of the defeated commander as the preeminent hero of the South.[20] The Caesar who emerges from all this is not coupled with the North's Abraham Lincoln (that association had been made adversely, after all, by the president's southern opponents and his assassin),[21] yet the Roman dictator is here given positive qualities that match turn-of-the-century support for the prospect of American *imperium*.[22] According to the analysis of Jones,

Shakespeare misrepresents the historical man Caesar as arrogant and pompous but at least lets his spirit triumph in the play as it did in the world, for his spirit is "the imperial idea" (31).

Similarly, in his illustrated school edition of *Shakespeare's Tragedy of Julius Caesar*, first published in 1872 and then revised and reprinted at regular intervals into the twentieth century, William J. Rolfe (the former headmaster of the High School, Cambridge, Massachusetts) prefaces his text and notes with approval of the play's second half—the half relatively neglected when the tragedy is read or staged in the "revolutionary" key. Here, he argues, we can see the "ruling spirit" of the historical Caesar powerfully at work once he has become a ghost and a memory (1903, 13–17). Rolfe also includes an appendix in which he concludes that Brutus "is one of the noblest and purest of men, but is implicated in a conspiracy which, though nominally patriotic in its purpose, is utterly base and execrable in the means it proposes for carrying out that purpose" (218–19). There follows in the 1903 edition a new section on the "moral" of the play, in which the editor of school Shakespeare declares: "Assassination is no legitimate means of political reform. . . . Thrice has this been most impressively illustrated in our own national history; but anarchists and assassins are slow to learn the lesson of Caesar's murder almost two thousand years ago . . . ; but the truth remains true, as when Christ first enunciated it, 'They that take the sword shall perish with the sword!'" (233).

By the time Rolfe produced this particular juvenile edition of Shakespeare's *Julius Caesar*, America had suffered the assassination of three of its presidents: Abraham Lincoln in 1865, James A. Garfield in 1881, and, most recently of all, William McKinley in September 1901 (at the Pan-American Exposition held in Buffalo). McKinley's assassin, in the popular view, had been motivated by a monstrous anarchist credo, even though subsequently he proved to be scarcely familiar with anarchy's political philosophy.[23] Although the turn-of-the-century president could claim the status of founder of a colonial empire, given that the United States had annexed the Philippines during his first term of office, his fatal shooting was not performed or troped in the press as the murder of a Caesar in the way President Lincoln's had been. Nevertheless, swift inclusion of reference to this third presidential assassination in the final pages of Rolfe's revised school text gives Shakespeare's *Julius Caesar* a fresh and shocking topicality at the beginning of the twentieth century. Thus, for second-year high-school students, the colossal statesman of the Elizabethan tragedy they study in English classes is brought closer into line with the conquering general whose war commentaries they parse in Latin: while the robust and self-aggrandizing Caesar of the *Gallic War* is partially diminished, the aged and frail Caesar of Shakespeare's play is partially rejuvenated.

SHAKESPEARE'S *JULIUS CAESAR* ON THE STAGE

In the first two decades of the twentieth century, criticism of staid methods of teaching Shakespeare's *Julius Caesar* in the high-school classroom grew in tandem with criticism of methods of teaching Julius Caesar's *Gallic War*. In association conferences, professional periodicals, and books on pedagogy, many teachers of English, university academics, and other educators urged a shift away from rhetorical and ethical instruction to the dramaturgic and interpretative. In the late nineteenth century, American students had been required to study in silence heavily annotated texts of selected plays. Critics perceived this approach to ape inappropriately the philological technique of line-by-line analysis that had traditionally been favored for the reading of classical texts and to aim, equally inappropriately, at the same outcome—better grammar. Teachers of English protested that this took the drama out of Shakespeare and advocated instead regular employment in the classroom of oral reading, debate, and student performance. As an article in the *English Journal* in 1914 put it with memorable concision, "If we are to teach a boy *Julius Caesar* aright, we must let him hear Cassius plot and see Caesar stabbed."[24]

English teachers in American high schools organized practical, socialized projects on Shakespeare's *Julius Caesar* similar to those Latin teachers advocated in second-year study of Caesar's *Gallic War*. But the origins of the English set text in the promptbooks of the Elizabethan playwright provided much easier justification for physical activities. Get students to build a miniature theater, costume their dolls, and stage a tragic puppet show, educators recommended. Solve play-related problems in discussion or in a mock trial, or, best of all, encourage students to perform the play in their own classrooms. In *Teaching Literature in the Grammar Grades and High School* (1915), Bolenius continues her reminiscences of teaching *Julius Caesar* in the English classes she gave in Newark:

> The writer will never forget that day when the eleven o'clock class "finished" *Julius Caesar* by giving in concert the great speeches of Brutus and Antony, which they had memorized.

"We'll act it," exclaimed the teacher. "Impromptu! Who will be Antony?"

The very soul stood out in the face of Theophanes, the Greek boy. A firm pressure came into the lips of a Jewish boy, a student with a keen, logical mind.

Quick as a flash, the teacher pointed: "You, Antony," she said; "you, Brutus. The whole class will be the mob, with you as first citizen, you as second citizen," etc. Then she withdrew to the back of the room, and turned the responsibility over to the class.

. . . Under the inspiration of a living, glowing Antony pleading for his friend, boys forgot that they were just boys. They cried their parts of disgust or approval, not waiting one for the other, but spontaneously. The young Greek spoke of Caesar's triumphs, of his will, of how he loved the commons. He worked upon their emotions, stirring them up to denunciation of the "honourable men" as traitors. He drew them closer about the pitiful substitute for Caesar on the front seat [a folded overcoat]—the class acting the parts in spite of themselves—and showed them "dead Caesar's wounds," until many an eye glistened. Then skillfully the boy orator diverted the clamorous mob into definite action. How his voice rang out! (182–83)

The teacher's relative sympathies for the protagonists of *Julius Caesar* emerge from the racial taxonomy on which she bases her choice of classroom performers: the logical, nameless Jew to deliver the "logical, dispassionate words" (183) of Brutus; soulful, young Theophanes to inspire the citizens to action. The pity is for Caesar (and not just because his corpse is represented by an old overcoat). Just as, on a Saturday morning in 1909 in a Baltimore Latin club, young girls almost forgot themselves to become Caesar's legionnaires, here in 1915 in a Newark high-school English class, boys forget themselves long enough to become supporters of Caesar and Caesar's heir.

Not only did English teachers advise each other to have their students perform *Julius Caesar* in the classroom or on the school stage, they also recommended that students be taken to see revivals in professional theaters. Writing in the *English Journal* in 1913, Allan Abbott of the Horace Mann School and Teachers College in New York (the same combined institution that had issued a Caesar-led course in Latin composition in 1909) proffered a new, experimental program in drama for high schools, one that designedly brought the teaching of play texts closer to acting and the stage. For the most part, the syllabus (including Shakespeare's *Julius Caesar*) followed the New York theater season. Students were taken to see productions and were required afterward to write report cards evaluating them.[25] The first such American revival of Shakespeare's tragedy in the twentieth century was that by the actor-manager Richard Mansfield. It ran in Chicago's Grand Opera House from October 1902, then moved to New York in December 1902, where it had a run of fifty performances, and thereafter toured many cities until the end of the season.[26]

During the course of the nineteenth century, Shakespearean drama had dominated American theaters, and the nineteenth-century stage (rather than editions of the plays) had been the primary means by which Shakespeare had entered and remained in American culture, from the mining camps of the West to the large cities of the East.[27] Of all Shakespeare's oeuvre, *Julius Caesar* was the most favored for revival; in the last three decades of the century alone there had been thousands of performances of the play.[28] Yet Mansfield's production in 1902 was recognized as unique, a new version for the new century. The star had purchased from London the spectacular scenery devised by Sir Lawrence Alma-Tadema for a different Shakespearean revival in England, and then placed within it, on his American stage, hundreds of extras.[29] The subtle orchestration of lighting worked on the spaces in which the protagonists moved to give them signature moral atmospheres: a shadowy Brutus set against a radiant Caesar.[30] In the words of admiring reviewers, the orchard of Brutus (act 2, scene 1), for example, contained downstage two huge cypress trees that loomed over a couch draped in purple fabrics. The whole scene was immersed in the blue-gray light of a timid moon that veiled the face of Brutus and marked the place as sombre, mysterious, mournful—and fit for conspiracies. In contrast, the capitol (act 3, scene 1) held mighty Caesar center stage seated on a high throne hung with royal purple. Although graced on either side by Roman senators ranked in semicircular tiers, it was Caesar who drew the theater audience's eye, crowned with golden laurel leaves, costumed in robes of crimson, full in the light, a blazing imperial vision.

Mansfield's acting style and star persona further shaped his Brutus (fig. 9) as "the image of a noble person, fatally besieged by one sacrificial, delusive idea, and predestinate to ruin."[31] The actor-manager embodied the transition that was taking place in American theater from the visceral orations of the nineteenth century to the more naturalistic, psychological portraits of the twentieth.[32] And, when he came to play Brutus in 1902, Mansfield was already famed for the peculiar mannerisms, bizarreness, or eccentricity of his idiosyncratic stage portraits, including, fifteen years earlier, the emotionally complex split personality comprised by the title characters of *Strange Case of Dr Jekyll and Mr Hyde*.[33] During the theatrical season of 1902–3, journalists who attended Mansfield's production of *Julius Caesar* were particu-

FIGURE 9. Richard Mansfield as Brutus, in Shakespeare's *Julius Caesar* (1902–3). Photographed by Lutz. By permission of the Folger Shakespeare Library.

larly struck by the originality with which he had directed two scenes of Shakespeare's Roman tragedy. At the beginning of act 1, scene 2, when Caesar amid vast processional pomp makes his first entry onto the stage, Mansfield's Brutus is already there. In a shadowy corner, leaning against a fountain, costumed in a silver-embroidered black toga, dark and sinewy, he smiles sadly as, for several long minutes, he watches the freemen of Rome throw up their caps in joy for Caesar's triumphant return home.[34] More startling still, at the end of the quarrel scene with Cassius (act 4, scene 2), when Brutus is passing the night before battle reading a book, the stage is flooded with a green-blue light. But then, against all precedent, "the Ghost" of Caesar does not enter, speak, and exit. Instead a disembodied voice from the wings projects the ghost's words, and the theater audience is invited to understand "this monstrous apparition" (JC 4.2.327) as a figment of the assassin's mind, and to bear intimate witness to his diseased imagination and his spasms of terror.[35] Remorse displaces the zealous idealism of Brutus in act 5, scene 5.[36] Bathed in a twilight gloom, Mansfield played out the conspirator's despairing suicide quietly and without melodrama, posed on boulders that lay strewn before a broken pine tree. On the point of death, a critic recalled, "over the sad face and dreamy eye there passed the memory of the whole tragedy in one moment of immovable silence."[37]

This was a new, bizarre Brutus wholly suited to the disturbed political climate of the United States at the beginning of the twentieth century.[38] In the *New York Sun*, 2 December 1902, the art critic James Huneker appraised Mansfield's Brutus as

> the true *Anarch*, the dreamer of mad dreams, the regenerator of universal ills. . . . His *Brutus* is a study in exalted mania—a mania that has for its theme no craving after mortal pelf, but a utopia of justice. The slaying of *Caesar* has all the deliberateness of one hypnotized by cruel fate. After the act momentary remorse is soon crowded from his face by a rapt joy—the joy of a man who has fulfilled his mission. He is no mere regicide, but an arm selected by the gods to scourge the tyrannical, the unrighteous. Nevertheless he is a fanatic. Consecrated by history we only see the heroic side; transpose *Brutus* to the twentieth century and we would load him down with the opprobrious term of Anarchist and put him speedily out of existence.

In this review of the 1902 production of Shakespeare's *Julius Caesar,* like Rolfe in his revised school edition of the tragedy, the theater critic binds the deed of Brutus to the murder a year earlier of President McKinley and the swift execution of his assassin, Leon Czolgosz. Mansfield's focus in performance on the tormented interiority of the Roman conspirator speaks to the interrogation and trial of Czolgosz, whose motivation was debated feverishly in the press in terms of his dangerous devotion to anarchism or his tragic derangement.[39]

Not all critics were grateful to Mansfield for his topical diagnosis of Brutus as "a monomaniac suffering with melancholia which has intervals of hysteria," as Barrett Eastman so described it in Chicago's

Evening Journal for 15 October 1902. The paper's theater critic protested strongly:

> Caesar, like Napoleon, was an enemy of his country, and a tyrant, whom all the interests of the human race demanded should be overthrown. But the genius of both Caesar and Napoleon was so nearly superhuman that the world, by common consent, has agreed that they shall not be judged by the standards that apply to all other men who have ever lived. . . .
>
> And yet—strange anomaly!—in the play of "Julius Caesar," while Caesar himself is never vilified for a single instant, we are shocked and grieved and pained by the wanton murder of the effigy that represents him; and, though Shakespeare intended us to sympathize with Brutus and Cassius and the rest, we detest them thoroughly, however sincere we think they are.
>
> We feel that were Caesar twenty times an enemy of liberty and a thousand times a murderous tyrant, yet these pygmy men who prate of liberty and weary us with the recital of their own petty wrongs should have gone down upon their knees and thanked God, fasting, that they were privileged to be the playthings of such a man as Caesar.
>
> To such a height has hero worship risen in the worship of Julius Caesar and Napoleon Bonaparte!
>
> For this reason the play of "Julius Caesar" has never been convincing and never will be, though every actor in it were Richard Mansfield.

For this writer, as for many commentators on Shakespeare's play at the beginning of the twentieth century, disparagement of Brutus carries huge significance because it would seem to contain, by implication and for dramatic cohesion, a politically insidious praise of Caesar.[40] Judgment on Shakespeare's original representation of the assassination of the Roman dictator and the play's revivals on the American stage in the early twentieth century very often trespasses beyond questions of literary interpretation and aesthetic value. Editor, teacher, student, director, actor, reviewer, and spectator all find themselves invited to address the relationship of the play to the historical figure, the modern cult and consequences of Caesar worship, and their own investments in the slogans of liberty and tyranny.

SHAKESPEARE'S *JULIUS CAESAR* IN THE NICKELODEON

In the pages of the *Classical Weekly* for 23 January 1909, Mary Harwood of The Girls' Latin School in Baltimore offered her fellow teachers some advice: their second-year students might acquire some of the enthusiasm of Julius Caesar's legionaries for the Gallic War if only they could see in their text "a moving picture of thrilling dramatic action."[41] At the start of the preceding month, just such a motion picture had been released by the Vitagraph Company of America. Recommendations for students to see it, however, came not from teachers but from the fledgling film industry and its supporters, and for obvious reasons those recommendations were directed at students not of Caesar's *Gallic War* but of Shakespeare's *Julius Caesar.*

Julius Caesar (1908) constituted an adaptation of Shakespeare's play to screen, overseen by J. Stuart Blackton and directed by the actor William V. Ranous, who here played Antony. But, in this "transitional" period for cinema (as it developed away from the initial production of brief visual attractions toward feature-length narratives), authorship of the film was clearly advertised as in the possession of the company.[42] At this time, Vitagraph was one of the largest of the American film production companies and a powerful force in the pre-Hollywood industry both at home and abroad. Systematically, it packaged itself and its products as patriotically American, not least through use of an eagle as its logo, whose raised wings simultaneously formed a V shape and evoked the eagle that was the symbol of the United States.[43] In the period 1907 to 1913, adaptations to screen of the plays of Shakespeare were one of Vitagraph's most plentiful outputs. And, around these adaptations, the company organized elaborate marketing campaigns that utilized the familiarity and cultural prestige of the Elizabethan playwright to sell its brand of film as both quality entertainment and an improving education.[44] Wherever *Julius Caesar* was shown, Vitagraph's logo was ubiquitous on screen. The emblematic eagle was both stamped on the explanatory intertitles and ingeniously embedded into the action—whether decorating the arch beneath which the conspirators stab Caesar and exult over his corpse (figs. 10 and 11) or carried as a standard by the Roman armies struggling over his succession. Shakespeare's dramatization of Roman political assassination and its aftermath was rebranded as a thrilling tale in moving images created by an all-American company.[45]

Vitagraph's *Julius Caesar* follows the standard format of the period for film adaptation of a literary classic. The text is compressed into one short reel of fifteen scenes that take up a little less than fifteen minutes of running time.[46] From the film's opening, where Rome's tribunes "upbraid the citizens for praising Caesar" (act 1, scene 1) to the suicide of Brutus (act 5, scene 5), it narrates the drama speechlessly. Some of the most celebrated scenes of the tragedy are selected and then mutely reproduced as brief tableaux that (in both theatrical and painterly style) are frontally framed and shot almost exclusively at mid-range with an

FIGURE 10. *(top)* Scene 8 (the assassination of Caesar). From Vitagraph's *Julius Caesar* (1908). Courtesy of the Library of Congress.

FIGURE 11. *(bottom)* A few moments later in scene 8 (the assassination of Caesar). From Vitagraph's *Julius Caesar* (1908). Courtesy of the Academy of Motion Picture Arts and Sciences.

immobile camera.[47] Quite often, however, the film ventures away from such techniques into a more cinematic mode, as when (in scene 10) it utilizes Prospect Park in Brooklyn for location shooting,[48] deploys the special effect of superimposition to manifest Caesar's ghost (scene 11), and continues beyond the conclusion of Shakespeare's play (in its final scene 15) to show Brutus laid out on his funeral pyre. Through a camera that, unusually, is positioned on high we are invited to witness Mark Antony ceremoniously setting light to the wood stacked neatly under "the noblest Roman of them all" (as the intertitle that precedes the scene proclaims). While the javelins and swords of the Roman armies are raised in salute, the screen is enveloped in flames. Such narrative innovation complicates any attempt Vitagraph may otherwise have made to appropriate Shakespeare's *Julius Caesar* as an authoritative drama with contemporary political resonance for Americans. So soon after the murder of President McKinley, the cinematic celebration of an assassin scarcely works as a patriotic act in the past tense.[49]

If the Vitagraph film *Julius Caesar* intermittently innovates in relation to its Shakespearean source, it also plays with its debts to nineteenth-century theater and the visual arts. At the very moment the film imparts decorum to Caesar's murder by composing its architecture, props, and choreography as a movement-image of Jean-Léon Gérôme's neoclassical painting *The Death of Caesar* (1867), it also displays some humor.[50] In the painting, a senator is captured asleep at the moment the conspirators have turned away from the bloodied corpse and are leaving through the arch to pronounce the death of tyranny (matched most closely by the still in figure 11). In the moving picture, the senator's sleep has a long duration (and he is only temporarily obscured in figure 10). While in very close proximity, he remains nevertheless undisturbed by the conspirators' petitioning of Caesar, the dictator's murder, the assassins' hasty departure, and Mark Antony's arrival and outpouring of grief.[51] Similarly, despite drawing on the spectacular pictorial realism and performance conventions of turn-of-the-century theater (such as the elaborate sets, antiquarian props, and crowd choreography of Mansfield's revival of the Elizabethan tragedy in 1902–3),[52] Vitagraph cleverly expresses a preference for cinematic action over theatrical verbiage within its own Shakespearean adaptation. In act 5, scene 1 of the play, before the battle of Philippi, the leaders of the opposing Roman armies meet. Brutus recommends "words before blows" (5.1.27), but their parley swiftly descends into an exchange of verbal abuse.[53] Reproduced momentarily without attribution in the intertitle that leads into Vitagraph's comparable scene, the tag "Words before blows!" takes on the tone of a complaint against the many speeches Shakespeare's Romans proclaim when they perform his text on stage.[54]

The American trade paper *Moving Picture World* reviewed Vitagraph's *Julius Caesar* on 5 December 1908. The review's author, W. Stephen Bush, had repeatedly written with enthusiasm about the new medium, protesting its aesthetic and moral worth.[55] On this occasion, his specific comments on the film were preceded by articles on "the influence of the pictures" and "Shakespeare in moving pictures." Manufacturers, he warned, must watch the quality of their pictures carefully; otherwise better-class patrons will turn against them, and profits will be seriously reduced; prejudice against motion pictures is now so serious a factor in the world of instruction and amusement that it may even stand in the way of film versions of Shakespeare. Between the years 1907 and 1913, the American film industry was systematically seeking new audiences among the higher-paying middle classes through the creation of dedicated movie theaters across the nation and the production of adaptations of "quality" literature.[56] Shakespeare fitted the bill admirably—his plays were extraordinarily well-known, gripping, and neither lewd nor in copyright.[57] But, toward the end of the first decade of the twentieth century, Shakespearean adaptations like *Julius Caesar* were also being shown in the storefront nickelodeons of the big cities, venues against which clergy and civic reformers railed as moral sinkholes and physical death traps.[58] As a countermove, and better to distinguish film exhibition from other apparently sordid urban entertainments, members of the film industry attempted to defend nickelodeons as "places necessary for the amusement of the poor and for their moral and educational uplifting."[59]

"Uplift" became the industry's catchphrase, uplift for the untutored minds that attended urban nickelodeons—namely, immigrants without English, the illiterate working class, and children. And who better to acculturate, edify, and Americanize these social groups (in the nickelodeon as in the high-school classroom) than the most celebrated poet of the English language?[60] In imitation of the pedagogic strategies of social reformers who organized immensely popular, free recitals of excerpts from Shakespeare's plays, film venues began to provide live lectures to accompany the projection of their silent versions of Shakespeare (although, paradoxically, only the better venues could afford them). As Bush explained in *Moving Picture World,* he himself had delivered such talks in film theaters across the country and had witnessed with his own eyes the hold of the Bard on audiences.[61] So, if lectures on Shakespeare's plays could attract thousands, the critic ventured, then why not moving pictures tens of thousands?

A moving-picture enthusiast, Bush saw plainly the value to schools of Shakespeare films (and of Julius Caesar in moving images). Religious groups and civic activists were far less convinced about the benefits to the nation's young people (and its immigrants and laborers) of watching films, even ones adapted from Shakespeare. The storefront nickelodeons seemed to operate outside adequate social controls and had been derided as schools for scandal—schools teaching delinquency to boys and promiscuity to girls.[62] By the end of the month in which Vitagraph released Julius Caesar, the social reformers had temporarily succeeded in shutting down all the nickelodeons in New York (where there were over five hundred).[63] Although the nickelodeons were soon reopened, Vitagraph's Julius Caesar was specifically targeted at the municipal proceedings, and the film became notorious subsequently for its alleged immorality. According to the chief who was responsible for the provision of licenses to entertainment venues in New York City, "Scenes of crimes and depravity on the stage, which are witnessed by the most respectable people in the land, seem to be too violent and harmful in their effects upon the minds of the young to be permitted in show houses. . . . Brutus must not murder Caesar in the presence of our children."[64] Consequently, the assassination scene was cut for the Chicago exhibition of the film,[65] even though, five years earlier, it had been spectacularly enacted there by Richard Mansfield in the Grand Opera House. Until this point in the early twentieth century, film had escaped social control. Brutus could stab Caesar at will in the highschool classroom and on the professional stage, because school textbooks and teachers, directors, actors, and press reviews all worked to shape the reception of Julius Caesar's assassination in suitably uplifting terms. But in the urban storefront nickelodeons, without the interpretative guidance of a live lecture, America's youth, immigrants, and laborers could make whatever they liked out of the murder in moving pictures of the Roman statesman.[66]

Vitagraph's Julius Caesar (1908) was criticized not only for immorality but also for inadequacy as a version of Shakespeare. Even W. Stephen Bush acknowledged in his review that this film did not match up to Vitagraph's other quality Shakespearean fare, because mute rendition of the Roman tragedy into moving pictures was an especially grave and difficult problem: "Of course, none of these plays without a lecture are more than a bewildering mass of moving figures to the majority of patrons of electric theatres, but none stands more emphatically in need of a good lecture than 'Julius Caesar'" (447). Furthermore, he observed, there were too many moments of burlesque at which audiences became tired or laughed: Mark Antony looks like an old "waiter in a French restaurant"; Brutus performs "Roman harikari by proxy"; the funeral finale bears "a fatal resemblance to a Rhode Island clambake" (447). The discomfort of the critic and the weary laughter of film spectators constitute responses to the relative failure of the interlocked objectives of the Vitagraph film—highbrow instruction and lowbrow amusement.

JULIUS CAESAR IN POPULAR CULTURE

Despite its homage to the nineteenth-century high cultural Caesars of neoclassical art and the legitimate theater, Vitagraph's *Julius Caesar* also conforms to the "key scene, key image, key phrase" circulation of Shakespeare and his Roman play in American popular culture of the nineteenth and early twentieth centuries.[67] The pervasive integration of Shakespeare's cultural authority and his dramatic characters into American mass culture of this period, and their thoroughgoing domestication, have long been acknowledged.[68] "Shakespop,"[69] and a vernacular Julius Caesar in particular, were then ubiquitous—in school curricula and cheap editions, variety theater and vaudeville sketches, and even in ephemera such as advertising cards.[70]

Key phrases from Shakespeare's Roman play are scattered through the intertitles of the Vitagraph film, just as direct quotations or paraphrases littered the everyday speech of turn-of-the-century Americans.[71] In anticipation of his review of *Julius Caesar*, the moving-picture commentator W. Stephen Bush himself noted: "Pick up any book or newspaper, listen to any conversation, and you will be astonished how often, consciously or unconsciously, the words of the great poet are quoted. They have indeed in the most literal sense become household words" (446).[72] Although Vitagraph did not utilize them, two such phrases spoken by Shakespeare's Julius Caesar became advertising favorites: "Let me have men about me that are fat" and "Yon Cassius has a lean and hungry look" (*JC* 1.2.192 and 194, respectively). During the 1880s and 1890s, for example, the lard refiners N. K. Fairbanks and Company issued a series of trade cards that included the image of a pig in a rendering vat accompanied by the words "Let me have those about me that are fat, sleek headed chaps, and such as sleep o'nights." Lean and

"He Hath a Lean and Hungry Look—"

FIGURE 12. Advertisement for the United Cigar Stores. From
the program for a revival of Shakespeare's *Julius Caesar,* New
Amsterdam Theatre, New York (1927). By permission of the Billy
Rose Theatre Division, The New York Public Library for the
Performing Arts, Astor, Lenox and Tilden Foundations.

hungry Cassius was often set apart from a fat Caesar made content by
the product he was being exploited to advertise—as in trade cards for
Libby, McNeill and Libby's cooked corned beef.[73]

Even when Shakespeare had been elevated above the culture of
American everyday life later in the twentieth century, and revivals of his
plays were confined to "superior" theaters,[74] advertisements were often
reproduced (and thus kept in circulation) within the pages of the programs that were sold to accompany such performances. In this new context, lard and corned beef were replaced by more refined and expensive
products better suited to the wealthier and more discerning consumers who might be reading such material when watching a revival of the
Elizabethan play. In June 1927, for example, while the Roman tragedy
was playing at the New Amsterdam Theatre on Broadway, the theater
program contained an advertisement from United Cigar Stores, which
at the time operated the largest chain of cigar stores in America. A cartoon depicts a thin, miserable Cassius standing far apart from a rotund,
contented Caesar, who, in the conspiratorial embrace of his good friend
Antony, pronounces: "He Hath a Lean and Hungry Look—" (see fig. 12).
Underneath the quotation from Shakespeare's *Julius Caesar* a lengthy
caption contains this proclamation: "Poor Cassius! Had there only been

a United Cigar Store on a near-by corner, where he might have found in a box of United cigars the true secret of contentment, there is no telling how far Julius would have gone in making the world a better place to live in." Shakespeare's *Julius Caesar* gives added value to the company's brand of "choice Hundred Dollar Cigars" (10¢ each, $100 per thousand). As a play and a man, Caesar enters into the corpus of advertising signs deployed by modern marketing to make products seem desirable. This Americanized Caesar signifies the education, sophistication, sociability, and happiness (as well as the humor evident in overturning the tragedy's plotline) that theater patrons can buy along with their UCS cigars. And reference here to the capacity of Julius to make the world a better place to live in also works to connect the UCS company and smokers of its products with such global ambition.[75]

Julius Caesar rode into American popular culture on the back of Bardolatry, but it was not just Shakespeare who propelled and kept him there. As this book demonstrates on numerous occasions, there was much more to the Roman dictator than the celebrated Elizabethan play that bore his name, and much more to his cultural significance than the manner in which he died and the pleasures he enjoyed while he was alive.[76]

CHAPTER 3

Militarism

1914–1920s

Julius Caesar came to flourish in twentieth-century American mass culture not least because two key texts that were intimately associated with him—his own *Gallic War* and Shakespeare's *Julius Caesar*—had taken root in American state education. But historic events (like assassinations and war, whether civil or foreign) could stimulate a sudden escalation of interest in and topical use for the Roman statesman, both in and outside the high-school classroom. Soon after war broke out in Europe in the summer of 1914, the pages of newspapers and magazines, as well as the professional journals of classics teachers, began to fill with shocked acknowledgment that ancient history was now repeating itself.

From across the Atlantic, observation of the war taking place on the terrain of northwestern Europe could only be distant, clouded by strict censorship of dispatches and newspaper reports, and obscured by partisan pleas either for American neutrality or for intervention.[1] Once again, American high-school teachers swiftly demonstrated their enterprise by re-presenting the currency of second-year Latin and, especially, Caesar's *Gallic War*: the school text now made urgent reading for present times. Latin teachers even began to claim that close scrutiny of Caesar's commentaries on his war in Gaul would provide for Americans a better understanding of the present war than any newspaper report. Caesar's campaigns, they observed, engaged with the same battlefields and similarly aggressive leaders. Furthermore, they noted, this present war was to be distinguished from other modern wars and was developing, instead, a military strategy and tactics similar to those Caesar deployed with his

Roman legions (such as forced marches and close formations, short-range combat with either sword or bayonet, cavalry screens, use of the flank, fortified ditches for artillery, and rivers as rear protection).

A few months after the commencement of war in Europe, for example, Arthur L. Keith (a teacher from Northfield, Minnesota) submitted to the *Classical Weekly* an article entitled "Two Wars in Gaul." In it, he observed that recent movements around Mülhausen had crossed the same terrain that Caesar had covered in his battles against the German chieftain Ariovistus, with the same strategic opportunities utilized then, as now, of the Vosges Mountains and the river Rhine. And, more recently still, near the slopes of Craonne, fierce fighting had been going on right in the vicinity of Caesar's camp, and the river had been choked now as then with the bodies of the slain. Keith's piece opens with this claim:

> It is the tritest of sayings that history repeats itself, but in the events of the past few weeks the truth of this saying has been unusually well illustrated. The war occupying the northwestern part of Europe is in many features the repetition of a conflict held in those parts nearly two thousand years ago. Then a Caesar was regarded as the aggressor; now, no matter how much justification may lie back of the act, a German Kaiser is accounted the aggressor. Caesar represented the toga-clad nation which felt it its peculiar destiny to extend its dominions to the end of the world. The Germans, in like manner, are no doubt influenced by their firm conviction that they are about to find their place "in the sun." . . . As the Roman conquest was big with portent for the future, so now a German victory may alter the whole course of future history. (1914, 42–43)

Thus, at the beginning of his account, the classics teacher Keith couples Roman Caesar with the German Kaiser, and the Roman ideology of military conquest with modern German imperialism (the latter through reference to the notorious phrase "a place in the sun" that had been regularly deployed by Kaiser Wilhelm II of Germany to demand for the Second Reich maritime power and a colonial empire).

The title Deutscher Kaiser had been assumed by Wilhelm's grandfather following the unification of Germany in order to bestow on himself and his new empire the legitimacy, grandeur, and political supremacy associated with ancient Rome and its Caesars. After the accession of Wilhelm II in 1888 and in the years leading up to the Great War, however, the official coupling of the Kaiser and Caesar was often exploited in sectors of the British and American press as one of many rhetorical devices through which to criticize Germany's growing bellicosity.[2] At first the young emperor's evident passion for things military was construed as mere posturing: "The style is that of a school-boy masquerading in a charade as the God Mars."[3] Almost ten years later, in a British article reprinted in the popular New York journal *The Eclectic Magazine of Foreign Literature,* the Kaiser's delight "in posing as the great Caesar" was now understood as a manifestation of his alarmingly absolute constitutional authority; for this journalist, he was a modern embodiment of divine right, and a despot whose will was the real law of the land.[4] In accounts of the Kaiser published in the American press at the outbreak of war, he had ceased to be a mere masquerader; now he had categorically become both "this Caesar of the Germans" and "a real war lord."[5] In the week before the publication of Keith's article "Two Wars in Gaul," however, a letter to the editor of the *New York Times* (headlined "Belgian Resistance to Caesar") claimed the existence of a vast difference between the Caesar of ancient Rome and the Kaiser of modern Germany. Although they had invaded the same territory, fought against the same peoples, and achieved the same overwhelming victory, Julius Caesar (the writer claimed) had shown mercy to the few survivors of his conquest of the Nervii, giving them freedom, exemption from taxation, and the title of allies. The Kaiser, in stark contrast, was now levying enormous war taxes on the devastated cities of Belgium, refusing even to feed its people, and imposing wholesale Germanization on the prostrated country.[6] Keith might have read such a report with some relief, for it whitewashed Julius Caesar better to blacken the character of the Kaiser. In his own article, Keith managed to wash from Caesar any taint that the customary association with the Kaiser might generate (and any aversion to Caesar's text it might encourage) by suggesting that the current repetition of conflict in northwestern Europe constituted evidence for Caesar's military genius, the durability of his strategy and tactics, the reliability of his war commentaries, and the urgency now attached to reading them.[7] Conveniently then, it was not necessary to reconstitute the Roman *imperator* better to match Wilhelm II as a demonic *Kriegsherr* (warlord) with aspirations to world domination.[8] Rather, Julius Caesar's superbly clear Latin narrative could be said to illuminate the present war in Europe, and the present war could even attest to his enduring greatness as an extraordinarily accomplished general.

A CRISIS FOR CLASSICS

At the same time as this new currency for the Roman general and his war commentaries emerged, however, classics found itself in the throes of a renewed crisis. When Josiah B. Game of Florida State College for Women reflected back on this period some ten years later, in the third edition of his handbook for high-school teachers of Latin, he recalled that the war in Europe had led Americans forcefully to question their educational system.[9] In sum: if the purpose of education was to furnish the fundamental ideals of national life (such as a sense of justice), then it had singularly failed. The anti-Latinists, according to Game, were crying that, in time of war, the sciences should be better developed within the curriculum in order to teach the mechanisms necessary for the protection of the nation against other nations. One such "anti-Latinist" (although himself a major in classics) was the progressive educator Abraham Flexner.[10] In autumn 1916, while working for the philanthropic General Education Board, Flexner published a pamphlet entitled "A Modern School." To subsequent storms of protest from classicists, he proposed that "neither Latin nor Greek would be contained in the curriculum of the Modern School,— not, of course, because their literatures are less wonderful than they are reputed to be, but because their present position in the curriculum rests upon tradition and assumption. A positive case can be made out of neither."[11] Classicists coordinated a series of countermoves against this proposition, including letters of protest to the General Education Board, irate articles in the popular press and professional journals, and hundreds of moving testimonials from some of the most senior members of America's social elite.

Some of these testimonials were delivered in person at a conference held at Princeton University on 2 June 1917, just two months after the United States finally entered the war in Europe. The conference determined that, in fact, current times demanded the continuation of the study of classics in America's schools. The published proceedings, entitled *Value of the Classics,* were edited by Andrew F. West (dean of the graduate school at Princeton), who concluded his own introductory appeal to save Greek and Latin for Americans with a striking evocation of community, patriotic duty, endurance, tradition, and virility: "We are called anew to duty in the time of trial and may well listen to voices of the past which bid us prepare well to play our part like men. We shall need their help" (1917, 33). Gone here is the pedagogic emphasis of the high-school classroom on the discipline of drills in grammar, or the construction of a student's relationship to the text as a soldier to their commander. Now, at this supremely critical juncture and for an adult audience, West treats Greek and Latin as guiding voices, kindly voices that can offer to us the soundest of advice in this our most terrible hour if we would only listen. *Value of the Classics* also contained supportive testimony from the serving American president Woodrow Wilson and from all three living ex-presidents: Cleveland, Roosevelt, and Taft. They, together with business leaders, bankers, lawyers, physicians, ministers, engineers, and even scientists, concurred in the view that Latin (and ancient Greek) helped forge courage, wisdom, and a faith in freedom.[12]

In the view of Professor Game, looking back from the perspective of the 1920s, these emphatic endorsements of Latin as necessary for making the "best type of man," pronounced with authority by "many of our country's noblest and best men," built up a stone wall around the discipline against which the charges of the anti-Latinists thankfully fell down flat.[13] Despite such positive recollections, Latin did experience a significant decline during the Great War. During this period, the proportion of high-school students choosing it as a subject dropped by more than 10 percent.[14] Moreover, as the second-year set text, Julius Caesar's *Gallic War* did not fit that easily on any American moral map, especially one that charted Latin as a journey of learning leading to courage, wisdom, faith in freedom, and a robust masculinity.

AMERICAN HERO

Even as military history was repeating itself in Europe, some teachers and educators had no difficulty attributing the most noble and historic goals to the Roman general during his Gallic campaigns. Thus, in 1917 Benjamin L. D'Ooge and Frederick C. Eastman (professors of Latin at Michigan State Normal College and the State University of Iowa, respectively) produced a second-year textbook for use in American schools during the nation's military engagement in the Great War.[15] The authors describe their new text, *Caesar in Gaul*, excitedly to young readers as "a book of exploration, adventure, and conquest. It tells the story of some of the most thrilling events in the life of one of the greatest men in history—Caius Julius Caesar, the Roman. . . . The curtain of centuries is drawn aside and we see as in a moving picture the dawn of civilization in Europe two thousand years ago" (1917, ix). If this rosy portrayal of war in ancient Europe as the harbinger of civilization does not offer sufficient reassurance to young Americans of Caesar's virtue, a short biography of its commander in chief provides further moral certainty. Written in simple Latin, it concludes: *omnino Caesar erat vir quem hostes timerent, amici amarent, omnes admirarentur* (10). Dutiful users of the text might practice use of the subjunctive in descriptive clauses by translating this summary of the man as follows: "Caesar was entirely the kind of man whom enemies feared, friends loved, and everyone admired."

The following year, another such admirable Caesar was even brought back to life in a lighthearted fantasy written for high-school Latin teachers and published in the *Classical Journal*. "Caesar redivivus" by A.P. McKinlay, a Latin teacher from Portland, Oregon, begins on a houseboat by the river Styx. There, in the afterlife, the Roman general muses over the attacks made on him by proponents of the "new education." Thus invigorated, Julius Caesar can now defend himself against twentieth-century assaults with the full authority of his own voice. He describes himself as a linguistic necessity, because "I furnish the key that unlocks the haunts of many spelling demons, such as 'separate', 'necessity', and 'absence'" (McKinlay 1918, 103).[16] He also stakes a claim to being a political necessity, because his *Gallic War* provides the answer to "the Teutonic question" (104). After this double defense, the Latin teacher brings Caesar up from the underworld to provide a running commentary on various bulletins that arrive from the field of operations in modern Europe. The catalogue of "I told you sos' that follows is suitably impressive: the need to establish a strong buffer state against Germanic pressure; the importance of preserving the legal freedoms of allies (*GW* 1.45); Belgian bravery; German faithlessness and military efficiency; the Germanic "will to power"; the Germans' mistreatment of hostages (*GW* 1.36). Thus the Roman general himself, in direct response to news from the present front, confirms the currency and the prescience of the second-year set text for Latin and is positioned on the side of the Allies.

In a grand finale, McKinlay broadens out the function Caesar here serves as embodiment and defender of classical studies, and now promotes him to the rank of protector of all Western culture against Germanic assault. At the end of the fantasy, Caesar produces a bulletin of his own on the current crisis:

> On all sides is heard the hue and cry, "See what Germany's system of education has done for her. We too must be vocationalized or lose in the battle of life. Hence get away from the past; set your eyes on the future; teach everybody a trade; throw Latin to the dogs and the classics on the junk pile."
>
> "Let me plead," concluded Caesar, "that the trustee nations of Graeco-Roman culture turn a deaf ear to these siren tones and, remembering how essential the classics are to the understanding of the language and the history of the Occident, highly resolve to maintain the trust put in their keeping, for what would it profit them to gain the guerdon of a specious victory and yet finally, yielding to the allurements of a seductive imitation, fall down and worship before the golden calf of Teutonic *Kultur!*" (110)

This teacher from Oregon neatly constructs current educational debates as another front in the war that must be fought against Germany and won. War in Europe was not (as Game claimed above) the only reason a growing body of professional educators had begun to call for urgent transformation of the high-school curriculum. By the end of the second decade of the twentieth century, high schools had changed from serving only a small minority to serving most of the nation's age cohort. Progressives such as Flexner argued for a radical transformation of these institutions better to support America's growing democracy. Guided by a utilitarian conception of a curriculum that prepared students for their adult lives as workers, citizens, or homemakers, they campaigned against liberal arts training as both elitist and irrelevant.[17] "New" educators and government officials had looked to the German educational system as a model for how schools could better support the nation's industrial and technological competitiveness on world markets, and had written back favorably on Germany's technical and trade schools.[18] By 1918, the year in which McKinlay's Caesar spoke out against the injunction to "teach everyone a trade," the National Education Association had published a report fully endorsing vocational education (such as agriculture, home economics, or business) against academic education (such as Latin and, therefore, Caesar).[19] Ingeniously (and conservatively), McKinlay nationalizes America's educational debate as a second cultural campaign of the Greco-Roman West against Germany and gives revivified Caesar command of the defense for which he has such excellent prior experience.

Further endorsement of Caesar as the wholly admirable general who brought France into the civilized world and courageously withstood the onslaught of German barbarity also appeared outside the classroom and the community of America's high-school Latin teachers. The current affairs magazine *The World's Work* dedicated an issue in October 1917 to the contribution France had made to Western culture. The theme was clearly designed to counter any unpatriotic dissent regarding the United States' decision (taken just a few months before) to enter the European war. The magazine's circulation had already been boosted substantially over recent years by its policy of publishing numerous editorials, features, supplements, and special issues on hostilities in Europe in which it pressed ever more vociferously for Americans to break their neutrality.[20] In the October 1917 issue, John H. Finley (then commissioner of education for the state of New York and responsible for overseeing the commitment of the state's teachers to the war effort) opened his piece, titled

"France, Battleground of Civilization," by pointing out Julius Caesar's importance in the present crisis:

> There is probably no production of the ancient world that has such an emphatic modern ring as Caesar's description of his Gallic wars. Most of us remember Julius Caesar as a gentleman who spent the larger part of his existence composing Latin histories that have since vexed the lives of millions of schoolboys. Yet no work deserves more careful reading at this present hour. The very first page of the "Gallic Wars" might almost have been written by a correspondent in the present war. (1917, 629)[21]

The account in *Gallic War* 1.31–54 of Caesar's campaign against the German king Ariovistus confirms, for Finley, the innateness of national character.[22] The Roman commander, he claims, betrayed a fondness for the Gauls as brave, impulsive, lighthearted, gay, and adventurous, whereas he detested the Germans then (as the world did now) for being harsh, uncivilized, violent, militaristic, and treacherous. Throughout Caesar's narrative, ancient explanation can be found for the modern Germans' mania for devastation, their constant craving to reach the Kaiser's "place in the sun," and their disinclination to observe treaties and agreements (630). The cruelty and insolence of their ancient king have also resurfaced in the behavior of their modern Kaiser (631). Here *The World's Work* calls up Julius Caesar and his *Gallic War* to combat the propaganda campaigns of those members of the German-American community who had been attempting to garner support for the cause of the Central Powers.[23] Read Caesar, and we immediately see (implies Finley) that German perfidy is a seam running thousands of years deep.

Ingeniously, the New York commissioner for education also twins the military strategy of the Roman commander with the foreign policy of the American president.[24] Woodrow Wilson's ambition for "peace with honor" in the years leading up to spring 1917 is repackaged as a heroic failure also suffered by one of the most illustrious generals in history: "Caesar's policy at first somewhat resembled that of our own President Wilson. He wished to avoid war if that were humanly possible. So he resorted to negotiation" (Finley 1917, 631). A summary follows of Julius Caesar's preliminary encounters with Ariovistus in *Gallic War* book 1 that has been shaped by Finley to recall America's relations with Germany before military intervention: a series of attempts to bring the German king to terms, the delivery of ultimatums, the extraction of pledges, and the discovery of Germanic treachery. When Woodrow Wilson finally committed the United States to conscription and the provision of money, ships, and soldiers for combat in Europe, a significant proportion of the American population still favored nonintervention. Consequently, opinion needed to be mobilized in many quarters in support of this radical step into combat on foreign soil.[25] In the pages of *The World's Work,* readers are informed that the valiant peace offensives of both the Roman general and the American president had the same sad outcome. Yet the modern turn to war will have (we may, on the basis of this historical comparison, comfortably presume) the same happy outcome, for, after Caesar's campaigns in Gaul, "this part of France was freed of Germans for many centuries" (632). Caesar and his campaign against Ariovistus are Americanized better to predict victory for the president and his new policy of military intervention.

SUBJUGATOR OF FRANCE

Yet such inventive pairings, which attempted to sustain the emotional alignment of Americans with the author and protagonist of the *Gallic War,* could scarcely match up to those that had operated far longer and more commonly in the national discourses of Europe. Ever since the mid-nineteenth century, and even more feverishly during the current years of conflict on French soil against Germany, France had shaped itself (and been shaped by others) as a valiant Vercingetorix resistant to the encroachments of Germany's Caesar.[26] This nationalistic discourse of Celtic origins and Gallic heroism even infiltrates the American textbook *Caesar in Gaul* that Professors D'Ooge and Eastman had designed to fulfill the requirements of the New York syllabus for second-year Latin and to represent the Roman general's conquest as Gaul's cultural salvation.

In a departure from nineteenth-century pedagogic conventions, the syllabus for New York comprises the first four books of the *Gallic War* in full, followed (for added adventure and conquest) by selections from books 5 to 7, and even from book 3 of the *Civil War.* Although students encounter the climactic siege of Alesia and the surrender of Vercingetorix (commander of all Gallic tribes) in only two brief paragraphs of English summary, nevertheless the frontispiece of *Caesar in Gaul* displays in full color a reproduction of Lionel Royer's celebrated tableau of the Gallic chieftain's surrender outside Alesia's burning ramparts (fig. 13). The painting, exhibited from 1899 and soon acquired for public display in a museum of French national heritage, presents a defiant Vercingetorix tossing his weapons at the feet of a vicious-look-

FIGURE 13. *Vercingétorix jette ses armes aux pieds de César*, Lionel Royer (1899).
© Musée Crozatier, Le Puy-en-Velay, France / Giraudon / The Bridgeman Art Library.

ing Caesar who is surrounded by a thuggish pack of legates. To suit the national myth of French resistance, the chieftain sits high on his white horse gazing down at his conqueror cloaked in red. It was (and still is) a standard source for the illustration of noble Gallic capitulation to cruel Roman onslaught in French primary-school histories on the origins of the nation, such as that by Ernest Lavisse (first published in 1913).[27] Similarly, the American schoolbook *Caesar in Gaul* juxtaposes its Latin account of how Vercingetorix took the lead in the struggle for Gallic independence with a photograph of a bronze memorial to the chieftain designed by the sculptor Aimé Millet in 1867 (176). The monument celebrating national self-sacrifice bears the features of Louis Napoleon and stands at the site of Alesia whose excavation had been financed by the emperor himself.[28] Finally, the section of the textbook dedicated to the Latin narrative of the *Gallic War* concludes with a description of Vercingetorix as "a gallant patriot, who lacked only success to be hailed as the savior of his country" (192). These Francophile features of the American high-school text do not mesh well with its opening characterization of the Roman commander as "one of the greatest men in history" (ix).

Similarly ambivalent was the revised edition of Francis Willey

Kelsey's popular high-school text *Caesar's Commentaries,* which was published in 1918 to suit the new conditions of American intervention in the Great War. (See chapter 1 for more on Kelsey, who was a professor of Latin language and literature at the University of Michigan and an energetic advocate of the value of Latin and Greek as educational instruments.) The revised edition had been designed, its author explained in his preface, to interest the high-school student anew in Caesar as well as to assist him [*sic*] with second-year Latin:

> America's entrance into the world conflict has aroused universal interest in warfare. Viewed in the light of the great struggle, Caesar's Commentaries take on a new interest. Modern armies have clashed on the battlefields of the Great War; modern camps are laid out in a way to suggest the manner of the Romans. The strategy of Joffre and of Hindenburg finds its prototype in that of Caesar, and modern armor, especially in types of helmet and breastplate, strikingly resembles that of ancient times. In countless ways—even to Caesar's statement "Of all these the bravest are the Belgians"—the World War reproduces on a larger scale the campaigns of Caesar. (iii)

Kelsey then continues to renew schoolboy interest in the Roman dictator by laying out disparate parallels between the Gallic War and the Great War throughout his introduction. Comparisons link Julius Caesar to the generals of both the French and the German armies, while his Roman legionnaires share features with soldiers and sailors of the United States armed forces. Thus, in the first introductory section, "Warfare Ancient and Modern" (ix-xx), Kelsey describes and illustrates the wolf-holes that were made by Caesar's troops when besieging Alesia in 52 B.C.E. (these consisted of round holes with sloping sides in the center of which strong pointed stakes were firmly planted). Enemy soldiers advancing across ground so prepared, he notes, risked slipping and impaling themselves on the projecting points. The editor then compares these defense works to the wolf-holes that had been positioned by the Germany army along its line near Ypres in Belgium in 1914. He also includes a photograph of the modern defense works (fig. 15) adjacent to an illustration of the ancient ones (fig. 14) to help his schoolboy readers to make their own visual comparison between Roman and German tactics. Immediately after, and in stark contrast, Kelsey compares the Roman legionary with American soldiers and sailors (in terms of trenching tools, average marching distances, and weaponry) and positions adjacent to each other illustrations of a Roman legionary and a United States sailor, both in marching order (xiv and xv).

In the second introductory section, "Caesar's Commentaries and the

FIGURE 14. *(top)* Wolf-holes at the siege of Alesia, 52 B.C.E.
From F.W. Kelsey, *Caesar's Commentaries* (Boston, 1918), ix.

FIGURE 15. *(bottom)* Wolf-holes along the German line near
Ypres, 1914. From F.W. Kelsey, *Caesar's Commentaries* (Boston,
1918), x.

Great War," Kelsey compares Caesar's march into Gallic territory with that of the German army into Belgium in September 1914—both, he admits, were unmotivated (xxiv). Much later in the schoolbook, he also recognizes Vercingetorix as "the greatest of the Gauls, the first national hero of France" (424), though this is in passing and in small print. When he reaches his conclusion, however, Kelsey shows no compunction in eulogizing Julius Caesar fulsomely: "Of all the Romans, Caesar was without doubt the greatest.... His genius was transcendent in three directions—in politics, in war, and in literature" (601). At the end, Caesar's dictatorship at Rome and his massacres in Gaul are cast into the shade by his third and greatest gift: the lucidity of his narrative technique. After some six hundred pages explaining to American schoolboys the clarity of Julius Caesar's writing style, such an aesthetic judgment may seem to void the troubling ethical implications of the text's opening comparisons between Caesar's military strategy and that of the Kaiser.

GERMANIC VILLAIN

As the Great War progressed, Julius Caesar acquired more and more villainous features in the classrooms of American high schools. In May 1918, when American troops were beginning to be involved in checking and pushing back the last-ditch German offensive in France, and all American schools were undertaking war activities with their students, Margaret T. Englar of Western High School in Baltimore reported to the Classical Association of the Atlantic States what she saw as the contribution a teacher of second-year Latin could make to the war effort: "When we think war, hear war, eat war, and know that some of our pupils are already feeling the hardships of it, how can we refrain from the discussions that are naturally precipitated by the text we are reading?"[29] When she talks with her students, however, about the relationship of Caesar's campaign reports to those from the current front, the Gauls and their descendants become "our" inspiration to fight for the preservation of freedom:

> Again and again, particularly in Book 7, the Gauls urge the preservation of liberty as one of their chief duties, and the struggle for independence culminates in the courageous work of Vercingetorix. It is this same love of freedom, which has seemed to live in the land of France, that has made possible for the French people their great Republic and enables them now to furnish inspiration to us and to other nations in our fight for democracy.[30]

Vercingetorix is then aligned with the American government, commandeering food, drafting all men of arms-bearing age, distrusting the enemy's offers of peace.

Both Ariovistus and Julius Caesar, in these classroom discussions, are closely aligned with Germany's leader "William II" (as they had been only in passing in Keith's article of 1914). The Kaiser's treatment of small nations, Englar argues, so closely resembles Caesar's treatment of the tribe that students ask her: "Has the Kaiser read Caesar's account of the Gallic Wars?"[31] Englar's class is not surprised by the resemblance because, she says, they know that the Kaiser has taken Julius Caesar as a model. Wilhelm II did actively promulgate Germany's stake in the Roman Empire. He ordered the reconstruction of the Roman fortified camp that had been excavated at Saalburg, and, even though it dated to a period later than Caesar's campaigns of the 50s B.C.E., the purpose of the reconstruction announced in the American press was to illuminate schoolboys' research into Caesar's *Gallic War*.[32] A special cable from Berlin on the archaeological project, published in the *New York Times* on 22 April 1913, carried the headline "Kaiser Helps Out Caesar." That the Kaiser had not only studied Caesar's text but also identified closely with its author finds support in an anecdote from the German statesman Friedrich August von Holstein. In his published diaries, he recalls that once, in summer 1889, Wilhelm II stood in silent contemplation before a statue of the Roman general that was on display in the Museo Borbonico in Naples. Afterward the Kaiser confided: "I think I have a mission to destroy Gaul, like Julius Caesar."[33] The Kaiser here, as elsewhere, represented himself as the powerful Caesarean enemy of modern France.

A cartoon by Marcus in the *New York Times* in early August 1916, in counterpoint to this imperial self-fashioning, utilized the Greco-Roman god of war to highlight German butchery.[34] With Death as his right-hand companion, Mars surveys with grim pleasure from on high the carnage he has accomplished across the fields of northern Europe and, like the Roman general in his war commentaries, expresses satisfaction with a perfect end to a second year of campaigning (fig. 16). The newspaper also reported that on 1 August 1916, in celebration of the end of the second year of war in Europe, the Kaiser had proclaimed to German forces on land and sea: "Comrades: The second year of the world war has elapsed. Like the first year, it was for Germany's arms a year of glory. On all fronts you inflicted new and heavy blows on the enemy." Paradoxically (but presumably in order to reinforce the cou-

FIGURE 16. "The End of a Perfect
Year," *New York Times*, c. August
1916. From *The New York Times
Current History: The European War*,
vol. 8 (New York, 1917), 1164.

pling of the classical with the modern), the caricature in the *New York Times* appears to give its Greco-Roman deity some Teutonic features. The full beard in particular evokes the monumental statue of Hermann (or, in Latin, Arminius) set up in the Teutoburg Forest in the late nineteenth century to celebrate the German chieftain's victory there over three Roman legions in 9 C.E. The statue became so popular that a replica of it was erected by the Germanic-American community in New Ulm, Minnesota, in 1890 to laud its cultural heritage and foster a sense of ethnic unity.[35] But, in 1916, the caricature worked to decry the cruelty of Germany's modern commanders and the sons of Hermann. Almost two years after the publication of the political cartoon, when the United States had now entered the war, American high-school teachers and their students replicated these identifications between the Greco-Roman and the Teutonic military machines, the classical and the modern. And, in order to oppose the Kaiser and his armies, they resurrected Vercingetorix as both a French and an American hero.

A CAESAR FOR ITALIAN AMERICANS

Help was at hand for the high-school Latin teacher who might be concerned that Julius Caesar would fall from grace, if the United States were embroiled in the Great War as a modern-day Vercingetorix resisting the Kaiser. A month after the American film company Vitagraph had released their mute rendition of Shakespeare's *Julius Caesar* (1908), Baltimore Latin teacher Mary Harwood wished that her high-school students might see in their text of the *Gallic War* "a moving picture of thrilling dramatic action."[36] Similarly, when Professors D'Ooge and Eastman introduced their wartime edition of *Caesar in Gaul* (1917) to second-year Latin students, they envisaged the experience of translating Caesar's war commentaries in terms of the visual pleasures of film spectatorship: "The curtain of centuries is drawn aside and we see as in a moving picture the dawn of civilization in Europe two thousand years ago" (ix). The film that thus represented the war in Gaul as a victory for Roman civilization over Gallic barbarity was a silent epic made by the Italian director Enrico Guazzoni, *Cajus Julius Caesar* (1914). It had been imported to the United States in late 1914 for distribution and exhibition across the country's movie theaters but continued to circulate, especially among universities and schools, well into the next decade.[37]

This triumphant Italian Caesar emerged from a very different context of early twentieth-century nationalism than had the resistant French Vercingetorix. The classicist Guglielmo Ferrero, looking back at this period from an exile imposed on him by the Fascist regime, noted that the First World War had reawakened in Italy romantic, Napoleonic illusions about the Roman dictator as "the hero-usurper and the saviour-tyrant."[38] During the 1900s, Italy's new-right nationalists had begun to demand a more authoritarian regime and to elaborate fantasies of national regeneration built on grand imperial ambitions; Italy must have dictatorship and war to triumph once again among Western nations as it had in its glorious Roman past. In support of the idea that war was the most effective means of rebuilding the nation, the nationalists pressed for seizure from the Ottoman Empire of its provinces in North Africa and, buoyed by victory in Libya in 1912, proceeded to campaign vociferously against the Liberal government's policy of neutrality in the Great War.[39] The release in Italy of Guazzoni's cinematic biography of Julius Caesar fell precisely within the crucial period of the *intervento* (the ten months between the declaration of Italian neutrality in April 1914 and military intervention on its northern frontier in May 1915). By now, moreover, epic films set in the Roman past had already been conscripted into the Italian campaign for wars of national aggrandisement; their spectacular sets, vast crowd choreography, and imperialist narratives were designed to mobilize popular support for Italian empire among film spectators.[40]

Initially, *Cajus Julius Caesar* is more romantic melodrama than triumph followed by tragedy. In a gesture of linguistic affection, Caesar is named Caio in the Italian intertitles. We learn that young Caio secretly loves Servilia, sister of the strict moralist and political schemer Catone. Forced into marriage with Marco Bruto in order to save her lover's life, Servilia has to confess to her husband that she carries an illegitimate child. Born unaware of his origins, little Bruto is taught by his uncle to hate his true father and grows up unwittingly to plot and perform his father's murder. This domestic drama of young love cruelly crossed—the house of Cato is set against the house of Julius—and unknowing parricide establishes an engagingly humane rather than a superhuman dimension for Caesar.[41] Otherwise, in keeping with the increasingly bellicose climate of the *intervento,* the film largely represents its protagonist as a military chief and the embodiment of conquering Italy.

The Roman campaigns in Gaul are magnified and drawn out on screen into a struggle between civilization and barbarity. In long shot, a sea of cheering senators and plebeians part to allow the Roman commander to ride off screen into war at the head of his cavalry, followed by standard-bearers who raise aloft Rome's spread-winged eagles, and neatly armored Roman foot soldiers who parade slowly in disciplined formations out of a magnificently metropolitan Forum set and head off into the wilderness of Gaul. There the undisciplined enemy, dressed in bulky furs and wearing spiked helmets, run and lurch headlong out of dark woodlands like savage animals. The film's spectators could marvel at the spectacular battle sequences that follow and the siege works so skillfully assembled by the Roman soldiers at Alesia. Then, after the Roman troops have broken "the undisciplined impetuosity of the savage hordes," another intertitle boasts poetically: "The irresistible claws of the gilded Eagle have crushed the savage and obstinate resistance of the wild boar of the Gauls."[42] In contrast to the disposition of the scene in Royer's painting, we now observe Caesar ("the gilded Eagle") sitting magisterially aloft on his judgment seat to receive the surrender of the humbled, horseless chieftain Vercingetorix ("the wild boar") (fig. 17). At last, news of Caesar's magnificent victory is brought to the senators waiting apprehensively back in Rome. Here, in this crucial sequence, at the moment of Caesar's greatest glory, the film narrative cleverly places its spectators in a position superior even to Rome's senators and to contemporary Roman readers of Caesar's commentaries, for, by virtue of their status as film spectators, they have all just been in Gaul and witnessed

FIGURE 17. Caesar accepts the surrender of Vercingetorix. Still, from Enrico
Guazzoni's *Cajus Julius Caesar* (1914). Courtesy of the Library of Congress.

with their own eyes the deeds that, tantalizingly, the senators at Rome
can only hear reported to them.

When this cinematic Caesar matures and is made aware of the impending danger to his life, he is shown courageously refusing to insult the dignity of the Senate by taking about with him an escort of armed guards.
Informed by the soothsayer on the Ides that the hand that first touches
him will kill him, Caesar (against the historical record) is approached by
Brutus. Given the film's earlier, melodramatic concern with this frustrated
father-son relationship, and with Caesar's continual efforts throughout
the narrative to protect or save the life of his unknowing boy (both at
Ravenna and at Pharsalia), his last words let slip the final tragic betrayal:
"And thou, Brutus, my son?" And so we reach the funeral of the film's
incarnation of Italian empire: the extraordinary man (according to an
intertitle) "who, immortalized and consecrated in history, will ever represent the Imperial dominion of Rome which civilised the entire world."

In Italy, during the *intervento*, spectators well understood the jingois-
tic characterization of the dictator offered up by Guazzoni's spectacular
film, and reviewers correspondingly reveled in its militant Caesar and
his masterful conquest of other nations:

Caesar the conqueror, the invincible, is here shown not as the tyrannical man Cicero tried to make him appear as, in all the ostentation of his eloquence, but as the magnanimous man, and the contrasts between these two natures of Caesar which are put into higher relief, enthralling the spirit of the spectator, transport him to the glorious times of the Republic, of the Consulate, of the Empire; from the opening curtain, it thus seems the grand Roman age lives again, lives again in all the splendour of its past.[43]

In this form, replete with the poetics of warmongering, *Cajus Julius Caesar* would also have been seen by many Italian immigrants in New York. Three million Italians had arrived in the United States from the beginning of the twentieth century to the time of the film's American release, and the vast majority had settled in New York City. There, in *la colonia* or the Italian community, immigrants could watch reenactments in moving pictures of the glorious imperial past of their homeland, at very low prices, in dedicated movie theaters or communal meeting spaces that offered Italian films as one of many ethnic attractions. While Italian high-school students would have had Caesar's *Gallic War* or Shakespeare's *Julius Caesar* taught to them as part of a curriculum for Americanization, their encounter (and that of their parents) with Guazzoni's invincible Caio instead drew them into an Italian national identity. These immigrants mainly came from Southern Italian peasant stock and brought with them to the United States diverse, parochial identities. Now, through historical films imported from "home," they might develop a novel, national attachment and a broad-brush patriotism.[44] Enthusiastic reviews in ethnic newspapers such as *Il Progresso Italo-Americano* also endorsed the films' nationalistic ideology, encouraging spectators to applaud—as Italians—the "glories of Rome's eagles everywhere triumphant."[45]

Watching *Cajus Julius Caesar* in New York City, such spectators might also have acquired a consciousness of their distinct ethnicity as Italian Americans and even a temporary cultural pride in their supposed racial difference from the original "core" of Americans, who possessed an Anglo-Saxon or Teutonic ancestry.[46] Such an awareness of their ethnicity might have been vividly brought to their attention had any of these Italian Americans paid the higher prices to see Guazzoni's film during its first run in more upmarket, middle-class theaters, where it bore the shortened title *Julius Caesar* and was supplied with English intertitles. Had they been able to join the invited audience that turned up, for example, at Forty-Second Street's new Candler Theater on the evening of Tuesday, 10 November 1914, they would have been confronted with a rather different film.[47] For English-speaking American audiences, characters' names had been changed, whole scenes abridged, deleted, or repositioned, Shakespearean quotations added, and the jingoism of the original radically diminished.

A CAESAR FOR ANGLO-AMERICANS

Understanding the market value of spectacular, feature-length historical films that could appeal to notions of high art and uplift, the motion-picture entrepreneur George Kleine imported Guazzoni's film, along with many other Italian historical epics, for wide distribution and exhibition across the United States.[48] He also collated and retained in a series of scrapbooks an extraordinary set of documents about *Julius Caesar* (the English-language version), including distributors' publicity and sample programs, newspaper reviews, letters from exhibitors, and comments by individual consumers, all of which provide extraordinary and vivid testimony to the many ways in which the Italian Caesar was "denationalized" and rendered more palatable for Anglo-American consumers and for educational institutions.[49]

One immediately apparent and striking difference between the Italian and the Anglo-American Caesars is that the former's sexual immorality has been very carefully erased. In the original film, we observe a secret ritual in the Temple of Eros where the youthful affair between Caio and his mistress Servilia is consecrated. This very same scene, in the Anglo-American version, is transformed by the intertitles that precede it into a secret but genuine marriage to Cornelia. Similarly, a later Italian sequence in which another veiled, cloaked, and conniving mistress (Tertullia, wife of wealthy Crasso) donates money toward Caio's election bid for the consulship is transformed for Anglo-American screens into a demonstration of the devoted love of Caesar's wife-to-be Calpurnia. For Anglo-American spectators, moreover, there is no melodrama of paternity, no illegitimate son, no familial betrayal. Brutus always remains just the nephew of Cato and in origin Caesar's good friend. And, at the close of the English-language version, the most sincere mourner at Caesar's funeral is not identified as his one true love and first mistress, Servilia (as in the Italian version), but his loyal ex-wife Cornelia. The motivation for these substantial moral improvements to Caesar's sexual behavior (which would have been made by the George Kleine Motion Pictures distribution company) can most probably be attributed to the necessity of meeting the currently stringent requirements of American film censorship. Within just a few months of the arrival of *Cajus Julius Caesar* in the United States, in early 1915, the Supreme Court unanimously agreed to deny motion pictures the constitutional protection of freedom of speech. The decision crowned the numerous efforts at local and state levels to control the content and the exhibition of films that had begun with the attack on the immorality of Vitagraph's *Julius Caesar* in 1908.[50] In mainstream American cinema of the second decade of the twentieth century, the Roman dictator would be permitted to sully neither the sanctity of marriage nor the dignity of paternity.

Perhaps less surprisingly, much of the bellicose imagery in the original intertitles of Guazzoni's film—designed to stir Italian specta-tors (wherever they lived) to thoughts of war, conquest, and imperial dominion—were also toned down or altogether removed from Kleine's *Julius Caesar*. When the Roman troops march so spectacularly out of the Forum and off screen to instigate war in Gaul, an Italian intertitle declares excitedly: "The Triumphant Eagles proudly spread their wings, happy presage of the laurels to decorate the brow of Caesar." No inter-title has been inserted at this same point in the Anglo-American version of the film. Later, when Vercingetorix surrenders, *Julius Caesar* includes no reference to the irresistible claws of the gilded Eagle crushing the resistance of the wild boar. Instead the comparable English intertitle observes more modestly that "Gaul bows before the victorious Roman eagles." For Italian-speaking audiences, the good news subsequently delivered from Gaul to the waiting Roman Senate is that "the gilded Roman Eagle has stayed its triumphant flight, spreading beyond the seas the majesty and might of the name of Rome." For English-speaking viewers, the Roman senators merely learn that "all Gaul is at the feet of mighty Caesar." Thus, across the Atlantic and outside the Italian-American *colonia,* in the process of translation into English, much of the nationalist rhetoric embedded in the original Italian intertitles of Julius Caesar's cinematic biography (all those soaring, crushing, trium-phant Eagles) has disappeared.

What has been inserted instead, to provide an alternative to Italian nationalism as cultural anchor for this cinematic Caesar, is a large num-ber of quotations from Shakespeare's play, especially (and inevitably) in the last reel, where the narrative finally reaches 44 B.C.E. and the Ides of March. The very first English intertitle of the reedited film cites Cassius's often-repeated words as he stoops to wash his hands symbolically in his friend's blood: "How many ages hence / Shall this our lofty scene be acted over, / In states unborn, and accents yet unknown!" (*JC* 3.1.111–

13). Divorced from their original context and transposed to open the film, the words can apply self-referentially to the cinematic reenactment that is about to follow, and reassuringly suggest to spectators that this version of Caesar will be authentic, because familiarly Shakespearean. Reformulated in Shakespearean terms, the closing moments of Kleine's *Julius Caesar* distinguish it subtly from Guazzoni's original. In the Italian version, the multitude is stirred by Mark Antony's single piece of direct speech (a brief address to Caesar's corpse described as once the victor in every battle, felled now by the hand of a traitor). But it is the sight of their hero's toga clotted with blood that ultimately drives the Roman people to sack and burn the palaces of the conspirators. In contrast, at this point, the English-language version includes a rush of four quotations from Mark Antony's celebrated speech to the plebeians in Shakespeare's play, inserted between the long shots of increasing crowd agitation. The dispersal of the mob to loot and murder is then immediately preceded by Mark Antony's final aside: "Mischief, thou art afoot, / Take thou what course thou wilt" (*JC* 3.252–53). Revised to suit an Anglo-American cultural context, it is Antony's rhetorical deceits, not the great Caesar's victories and generosity, his betrayal and gruesome murder, that cause riot.[51]

CLASSICS, CINEMA, AND CAESAR

From the end of 1914, Guazzoni's *Julius Caesar* (once it had been reedited and provided with English intertitles) began to be exhibited in numerous movie theaters coast to coast across the United States. As it was projected, it was accompanied by a suitably affecting score. Kleine's company recommended, for example, that the "half reel furioso" by the Chicago-based photoplay music composer Sol P. Levy be played under the title "Mischief thou art afoot," thus accentuating a sense of mayhem rather than majestic tragedy at the film's close.[52]

The numerous reviews of this new English-language *Caesar* that George Kleine diligently pasted into his scrapbooks repeatedly indicate that what mattered above all else was not any contemporary political resonance in the cinematic biography of "the conqueror, the invincible," but the educational value for students of seeing it enacted realistically on screen. For American newspaper reviewers, watching Caesar in moving images was a far more enjoyable experience than their remembered classroom reading of his commentaries. In the *Chicago Herald* for 21 November 1914, a journalist observed: "To the thousands of students who have poured over the more or less dry old histories it should be quite refreshing to sit in a comfortable chair and see the immortally famous deeds of the conqueror enacted by living figures amid environments, indoor and out, which lend to it so keen a sense of realism." While, more expressively, a reviewer commented in the *Boston Transcript* for 3 November 1914:

> The pity was not for Caesar's fate, though it was portrayed in finely tragic pantomime, but pity for ourselves—that we should have been a generation of school children who would not read Caesar's Commentaries by day and then see these motion-pictures by night. How much more the dull reading would have meant to us, could we have been thus admitted into the councils of the Senate Chamber and watched the brute reality of the fighting which Caesar described.

And when New Mexico's *Clayton Citizen* noted that on the Ides of March 1915 "the assassination of this great man in pantomime will be one of the scenes on the canvas at the Dixie," it also urged that all the high-school students in the district should attend the afternoon matinee even if it was at the district's expense, for "they will get more history in two hours here than in school in a year."

From the moment Guazzoni's *Julius Caesar* was released, university academics and teachers in colleges and schools across the country also took note of the enormous pedagogic potential of moving pictures of such startling visual realism that they seemed to bring Caesar and ancient Rome back to life.[53] In November 1914, the San Francisco press reported that, after witnessing a private viewing of the film, and on his own initiative, Professor William Dallam Armes of the University of California arranged its presentation by invitation to three hundred "society and university folk" (including representatives of the Pacific Coast branch of the American Philological Association and the American Historical Association, high-school teachers, artists, musicians, business men, and society women). The audience, the newspapers reported, "swept from the frescoed ballroom of the St Francis Hotel into the wide halls and vast spaces of the great Roman civilization." After a short talk by the professor promising a real historical and educational treat, they applauded scene after scene thunderously.[54] Scholars of Roman history or of Shakespeare were swiftly engaged to provide lectures in the movie theaters wherever Kleine's film was showing.[55] Journals of the classical community pronounced that historical films were "the finest kind of publicity for the Classics," and *Julius Caesar* "perhaps the most interesting as an aid to high-school Latin" (*Classical Weekly*, 8 May 1915). Seven years after the film's original release, it continued to be screened regularly at the local professional conferences of American classics teachers, such as the Third Annual Conference of the Latin Teachers of Iowa (held over 4–5 March 1921) and the Classical Association Conference in Richmond (held in April 1921). And, in 1922, the chair of Latin at one high school on Long Island declared *Julius Caesar* to be "the finest educational moving picture I have ever witnessed. It is historically accurate and is a most wonderful visual lesson. It should be shown in every high school in the country."[56]

The lessons teachers and academics hoped spectators would learn from viewing the film evidently concern not just wars in Gaul, dictatorship, and assassination. Endorsements displayed in George Kleine's publicity during these years are quite explicit about the film's pedagogic achievements: *Julius Caesar* is "of great value in helping High School girls and boys to visualize the setting for the Latin texts" (Francis E. Sabin, assistant professor of Latin, University of Wisconsin); "I am writing you to express to you my appreciation for the excellent work which you are doing, not only for the classics but for a liberal education" (Alexander L. Bondurant, Department of Latin, University of Mississippi). Filmed Caesar was entertaining, accessible, and popular. Filmed Caesar appeared capable of giving the lie to any hostile conception of classics as an instrument of the elite wielded only to hammer out gentlemen, generals, and presidents. Thus Guazzoni's film was eagerly taken up as another weapon in the arsenal of classicists who were battling in precisely this same period to defend their discipline from the assaults made on it by progressive educators.

Between 1914 and the mid-1920s, the relationship between Caesar, cinema, and classical education became intimate and mutually beneficial, because the motion picture industry was as quick as the educational establishment to see what filmed Caesar could do for it and as eager to take that advantage. While Guazzoni's *Julius Caesar* seemed capable of conferring popularity on classics, it could in turn confer on the motion picture industry the sheen of cultural authority and utility that it so eagerly sought. Ever since the debacle of 1908, when all the nickleodeons in New York had been temporarily closed down, the industry had begun to regulate and standardize its processes of production, distribution, exhibition, and consumption, including the preemptive creation of its own board of censorship. From that same period, Italian historical films were regularly imported by Kleine and other distributors for sale to middle-class markets. The stylistic attraction of this genre lay in its ever-increasing length, narrative sophistication, and spectacular sets, while its thematic staging of the Roman past in particular seemed to bring to moving pictures both aesthetic respectability and educational value.[57] More immediately, *Julius Caesar* seemed capable of meeting the growing demands of film reform organizations such as the Better Films Movement. Formed in the same year in which the Italian film arrived in the United States, its members sought to promote the production of "better" films through organized patronage (such as publication of local reviews and the generation of community interest) of those that met the criteria of narrative coherence, realism, and uplift. Those that passed muster were usually adaptations of literary classics, biographies, and instructive documentaries.[58]

As *Julius Caesar*'s run in movie theaters came to an end, George Kleine selected it for inclusion in a package of twenty features that seemed to meet the Better Films criteria and that he entitled "Cycle of Film Classics." He then offered this privileged group of supposedly "educational" moving pictures for additional nontheatrical distribution nationwide, through the agency of state university and other institutional film exchanges, to local schools, colleges, churches, and civic associations.[59] In a neat doubling of the pedagogic rhetoric of classicists (and drawing often on their enthusiastic endorsement), the publicity of Kleine's own company began to bill *Julius Caesar* as "the greatest educational subject on film," and the trade papers talked of how silver-screen Caesar could support or even spice up college and high-school curricula:

> Students of the classics will be entirely satisfied with the reproductions of buildings, furniture, dress, armor, accessories; and who knows but that many of the participants in the picture may not be lineal descendants of the very Romans whose part they play?
>
> Children going to school, to whom Caesar is the awful author of involved sentences and grammar-crammed paragraphs, will with keener zest sharpen their wits trying to find out how the very human lover of Cornelia and Calpurnia captured the gigantic wily Gaul, and won the love of every soldier under his command.
>
> And then, besides, many of the English subtitles are direct quotations from Shakespeare's play. (*Exhibitors Trade Review*, 18 February 1922)

Alongside Kleine's special distribution system, exhibitors were strongly encouraged by the company to take advantage of the "tremendous pedagogic powers" of *Caesar* and advertise it locally in novel ways; suggestions included offering prizes to young spectators (such as a set of Shakespeare's plays or Plutarch's *Lives,* or, perhaps more attractively, gifts of money) for the best essay on the life of the Roman dictator.[60]

George Kleine's surviving scrapbooks contain vivid testimony to the success of this symbiosis between Caesar, classics, and cinema, which seems to have lasted almost ten years. Guazzoni's *Julius Caesar* was endorsed enthusiastically by the National Better Films Committee, teachers organized screenings for their entire school, and permission was even sought for stills from the film to be reproduced in a first-year Latin grammar.[61] The scrapbooks also contain many letters sent to university film exchanges or to Kleine directly from grateful teachers, academics, and local exhibitors describing the extraordinary enthusiasm with which *Julius Caesar* was consumed by its young American audiences. On 19 January 1922, for example, the State University of Montana Film Exchange wrote to Kleine quoting a school principal, who (as the letter noted) was undertaking to bring moving pictures for the first time to the little town of Southern Cross:

> The picture exceeded my expectations in a number of ways and it certainly pleased the spectators. Even yet the children drape themselves in rugs and blankets, in toga style, carry wash-boiler lids for shields and relive the scenes of the film. Julius Caesar is the first film to have been exhibited here and was the first "movie" for many of the youngsters. I wish to thank you for having secured a production of such high class for our initial exhibition.

And, in another letter to Kleine two months later, the same university exchange noted that "when [the film] makes a figure such as that of Caesar so living that children impersonate him in their play, it must be of vast importance from an educational point of view."

Not all teachers, exhibitors, and reviewers were as enthusiastic about Guazzoni's moving picture biography. In the view of the film's critics, this Italian Caesar had been insufficiently domesticated and anglicized. In April 1922, one teacher from Barringer High School, Newark, submitted a list of historical defects, such as "Cato is represented as the chief instigator of the murder of Caesar in 44 B.C., Cato died in 46 B.C., and Shakespeare is no doubt right in assigning that role to Cassius." Worse still, and far more disappointing, the Gallic scenes did not match the syllabus in American high schools for second-year Latin: Where was the landing in Britain? Or the day Caesar overcame the Nervii?[62] Nor did the film's plotline match the syllabus for second-year English, as the *Boston Morning Globe* for 3 November 1914 observed: "The play in no way resembles the Shaksperian [*sic*] tragedy. It has a genuine Italian flavor in introducing Caesar in the earlier scenes as a lover, decidedly of the Romeo order." Thus, even as the cinematic portrayal of the Roman general was utilized to support an American classical education and the American motion picture industry, it was simultaneously recognized as essentially foreign. Trade and press reviews, taking up an Anglo-American perspective, variously commented on the *Italian* flavor of *Julius Caesar* in its landscapes, its plotline, its spectacle, its actors, their emotive acting style, and even (as in the *Exhibitors Trade Review* above) their genealogical connection with the Roman past.[63]

Curiously, though, among all the documents contained in Kleine's scrapbooks for almost a decade of exhibition, only one expresses any disquiet over the evident militarism of the film's hero or wonders whether playing at Caesar might have a detrimental impact on the political outlook of young Americans. On 12 February 1922, the critic James O. Spearing reported in the *New York Times* on audience reaction to the film when it was shown in a Broadway theater to a house half full of schoolboys. Uniquely, he did not appreciate that Caesar was the man of the hour:

> The boys took no time at all in making up their minds that Caesar was a satisfactory hero for them, and throughout the showing of the photoplay they were his ardent partisans. They cheered his victories and his triumphal entry into Rome, they booed the Gauls and hissed Pompey off the screen . . . and they accorded Antony Novelli, in the role of Caesar, the same honor they customarily give to Tom Mix, Harry Carey and William S. Hart. He was their man of the hour. All of which may provoke reflections by the thoughtful. Of course, the study of Shakespeare's play and Roman history has introduced Caesar to some, if not all, of the boys, but it is doubtful whether he has ever evoked half the enthusiasm as a textbook figure that he enjoyed in his screen embodiment. Does this then mean anything to the advocates, or the opponents, of visual education? And should the alacrity with which Young America gave their heart to a purely military and political hero be taken as an indictment of an educational method which still makes heroes of the favourites of Mars, or as a manifestation of the congenital bellicosity of man against which the Conference for the Limitations of Armament can be of no avail?

Film spectatorship is dangerous, according to Spearing's observation, if young people are going to confuse the quintessentially American genre of the Western with the Italian historical epic, their love of the cowboy with love of a conqueror. Nor, in his view, should American visual or textual education make a hero out of the Roman general when delicate negotiations were currently under way to reduce the scale of national armed forces and expenditure on arms from the vast levels that had been required to service the Great War. Perhaps the *New York Times* critic had an inkling of what was soon to come. Days before his protest against glorifying Julius Caesar on screen, a treaty had been signed in Washington by the United States, Britain, France, Italy, and Japan intended to limit battleships and maintain international peace.[64] Yet within a matter of months Mussolini would be marching on Rome to launch a new quest for Italian empire and, in his own words, "a new Caesarian epoch."[65]

THE PROBLEM WITH SCHOOL CAESAR

In 1910 half of all high-school students studied Latin (and, therefore, Caesar's *Gallic War*). By the 1920s that proportion had been reduced to approximately one-quarter.[66] The progressive education movement and world war had together made Julius Caesar problematic as a gateway to the study of Latin and advocate for a classical education. The American Classical League commissioned a nationwide survey of instruction in Latin in 1924 that involved the participation of thousands of schoolteachers. The "Report of the Classical Investigation," published by Princeton University, found that Latin's crucial purpose as a preparation and a requirement for entry into college had by now disappeared. Its authors concluded that more than two-thirds of school students must secure educational returns on their study of Latin during the first or second year of high school, as they were no longer pursuing the subject beyond that point. A new syllabus for Latin was needed to develop the power of students to read the language, and to provide them with some understanding of the "historical-cultural" values of ancient Rome.[67] Many teachers (as well as the report's authors) now thought Caesar not entirely fit for either function.

After the report's recommendation that study of Caesar's war commentaries be postponed in American high schools until the second half of the second year, Josiah B. Game (the professor of classics at Florida State College for Women whom we have had cause to meet several times before) complained bitterly about earlier first-year Latin schoolbooks:

> Most of the texts are dull and heavy from the first to the last page. Many start with Caesar, stay with Caesar, and end with Caesar. Pupils are "Caesared" day in and out, for a whole year. Not a bright or amusing thing appears from cover to cover. In order to learn Latin, pupils simply must study; but they will work joyfully and gladly over something that is of human interest, whereas they grow weary of persistent drudgery. (1925, 70)

Pedagogic and ethical considerations have here removed from Caesar's Latin narratives their traditional status as "a model of perfect Latinity."[68] Game was equally damning about the syllabus for the second year:

> This is the critical year in Latin classes throughout the country. The mortality rate in this year is fearfully high. . . . It is nothing short of barbarous cruelty to force faithful, trusting students of the ordinary second-year type into Caesar at the very opening of this year. Any other subject under similar circumstances would have been driven out of the schools long ago, impedimenta and all, and rightly so. Much of the bitter opposition to Latin has not been due to any lack of value in the Latin but the stupid pedagogical guidance which has stubbornly kept this rock of destruction where it could do its deadly work. (84)

As a result of the "Classical Investigation" and such forceful comments as these from classics teachers and academics, the study of Caesar's Latin text was postponed later and later into the second year of high school, and the amount to be read in the original gradually diminished, while the illustrations (of Roman soldiers, weapons, camps, siege engines, ships, bridges, Gauls, and Germans) became more frequent and more colorful. By the late 1920s, teachers were able to claim that students could grasp in their hand, in a single volume, everything they needed for a rewarding second year of Latin, Caesar included.

Jared W. Scudder's *Second Year Latin,* published in 1927 and utilized in American classrooms for decades thereafter, provides a convenient example of the new schoolbooks, in which the Latin text of the *Gallic War* only emerges after 260 pages of other material.[69] Preceding Caesar's text, the second-year student finds chapters and exercises on such matters as the fourth and fifth declensions, irregular adjectives, the infinitive, and the use of the subjunctive, and a short history of Rome and of the life of Julius Caesar, both composed in simple Latin for easy translation. Following Caesar's text, a further 200 pages supply exercises in Latin composition, a summary of forms and explanations of Caesarean syntax, and, finally, word lists and vocabularies both from Latin into English and from English into Latin. In the middle of the work, selections from the *Gallic War* are often interspersed with so many illustrative maps of battle maneuvers and photographs of the terrain, guiding questions about individual sections, explanations of constructions or technical terminology, and cross-references to other parts of the commentary that sometimes Scudder scarcely squeezes more than a few of Caesar's words onto a single page. Yet embedded in this new textbook for the postwar period is a biography of Caesar in Latin whose introduction still harbors nineteenth-century Bonapartist tones of admiration:

> The Republic, which had begun so promisingly, had proved to be a failure,— not because it was a republic, but because the governing body, the Senate, had become utterly weak and corrupt. If Rome was to survive at all, it could only be through a different form of government, with absolute power centred in the hands of a single strong man.
>
> In the Latin that follows we have an account of the remarkable life and achievements of the great Roman statesman who was destined to effect this change and establish an *imperial government,* under which Rome was to endure for four hundred years longer. (Scudder 1927, 210)

For many practitioners of a classical education in American high schools in the 1920s, teaching Caesar's *Gallic War* in this way was too big a risk. Lauding Caesar would only provide progressive educators with further evidence that the study of Latin was more likely to destroy than to build faith in democratic freedoms, and more likely to break than to make the best type of man.

Game's despairing description in 1925 of second-year Caesar as "this rock of destruction" stands in stark contrast to the comments of teacher Mary Harwood reproduced in chapter 1. During Julius Caesar's educational and ethical heyday in the United States, in the latter part of the first decade of the twentieth century, teachers talk of their students fighting a thrilling war and winning a victory with the Roman general as they clutch his words like weapons in their hands. Now, in the 1920s, when war is no longer thrilling and Caesarean militarism is taking on a nasty Italian flavor, the talk among American teachers is of the defeat, destruction, and even death of the poor young reader swept onto the hazardous rocks of Caesar's *Gallic War.* Shakespeare's *Julius Caesar* has remained a staple of the American high-school curriculum throughout the course of the twentieth century and on into the twenty-first.[70] But Caesar's *De bello Gallico* has never regained the extraordinary degree of attention and sheer admiration that it commanded in the United States in the early years of the twentieth century.

PART TWO

Political Culture

CHAPTER 4

Dictatorship

1920s–1945

During the third decade of the twentieth century, concern about the centrality of Julius Caesar's war commentaries to the American high-school curriculum for Latin developed rapidly. Nevertheless, whole books of the Roman general's *Gallic War* and selections from his *Civil War* continued to be taught in classrooms across the United States, and Latin teachers continued to present to each other strategies for maintaining their students' interest in this now somewhat problematic second-year set text. Writing in the *Classical Journal* for April 1929, for example, Fanny Howell of Lake City, Iowa, asked her readers to picture the scene taking place in almost any Latin classroom in the Midwest in September or February each year (depending on the dictates of school curricula). Involved are three characters: "*Discipulus Americanus,*" "C.J. Caesar," and—their mutual friend—the teacher.[1] As in the enthusiastic first decade of the century, the action is presented not as regimented drills in Latin grammar and the routine translation of Caesar, but as extraordinary frontline combat.[2] For weeks, she observes, these three characters are to meet "in daily conference" to fight thrilling battles against the Helvetii and the Nervii, to throw a bridge across the river Rhine, to outsmart the Veneti at sea, to navigate the Channel and fill the savage Britons with fear, and, finally, to force brave Vercingetorix from his stronghold and lead him in captivity back to Rome as tribute to the genius of Caesar and the efficacy of ancient Rome's armies.

In this busy scenario, the American student is once again envisaged as a boy: fifteen years old, a high-school sophomore and an athlete, eager for adventure and inclined to worship "men who dare and do" (Howell 1929, 509). Before he holds his second-year summit armed with Caesar's war commentaries, this boy (as Howell imagines him) already has in his possession a favorite story of masculine derring-do that she leads us to believe Caesar's narrative will match or even supplant. The book in question is *We*, the best-selling autobiography of the American aviator Charles A. Lindbergh. It had been published in 1927 and recounted the author's solo flight that same year across the Atlantic from New York to Paris. This is how the teacher recommends that young Americans come to know "C.J."—by domesticating her Latin text as an airplane flight across space and time and attributing to its author the traits of an adventure-seeking Roman Lindbergh. Immediately upon the aviator's historic flight, he was lauded in the popular press as an inspiring incarnation of ideal American masculinity.[3] The constituent parts of that masculinity are those Howell now claims Caesar can encourage in "the boy of today": "industry, efficiency, ingenuity, fairness, cooperation, and leadership" (514). In this novel context, even the customary recommendation that American students build model Rhine bridges, catapults, and ballistas matches and draws ethical value from the contemporary promotion of model airplane kits as vehicles for juvenile self-improvement.[4] In contrast to the urgent, serious, and sustained analogies created between the Gallic War and the Great War over a decade earlier, these connections between ancient and modern tales of derring-do are evidently superficial, light-hearted, and ephemeral. Thus, for good measure, Howell immediately introduces a second, more mundane set of parallels: between the strategies of the Roman general and those of a good basketball captain. Both think, signal, and act at speed. Both block and guard their opponents and keep them from their goal.

In the 1920s and early 1930s, similarly topical yet insubstantial connections between past and present were imposed on the other key text for the promulgation of Julius Caesar to his American "disciples." In the *English Journal* for December 1931, for example, Kathleen Brady (a teacher from Aberdeen, South Dakota) outlined a project on Shakespeare's Roman tragedy that she had set her eleventh-grade journalism class during April and May of that year. In order to review and implement the techniques of journalistic writing that her students had learned that semester, they were required at its close to produce a complete newspaper following the acts of the play, from an opening editorial expressing patrician views on Caesar's triumph to a news feature on the supernatural events preceding the murder, from a correspondent's account of the civil war that ensued to a closing appreciation of Brutus. At the center of these amateur newspapers (on which were bestowed such grand titles as *The Roman Herald* or *The Roman Tribune*), the South Dakota students were ordered to place a news article describing Caesar's murder in detail from the perspective of an eyewitness, summaries of the speeches made over the corpse, and an intimate obituary. Ironically, a real newspaper reporter had published just such a project in a real newspaper some sixty years earlier—but as an entertaining assault on the clichés and the parochialism of the worst kind of sensational journalism. Utilizing the pen name "Mark Twain," Samuel L. Clemens published a humorous sketch in the *Californian* on 12 November 1864 entitled "The Killing of Julius Caesar 'localized'" in which he claimed to be translating from the Latin "the only true and reliable account" of the bloody murder, an account that had purportedly appeared in the second edition of the *Daily Evening Fasces* on the Ides of March 44 B.C.E. The "translation" concludes:

> We learn that the coat deceased had on when he was killed was the same he wore in his tent on the afternoon of the day he overcame the Nervii, and that when it was removed from the corpse it was found to be cut and gashed in no less than seven different places. There was nothing in the pockets. It will be exhibited at the Coroner's inquest, and will be damning proof of the fact of the killing. These latter facts may be relied on, as we get them from Mark Antony, whose position enables him to learn every item of news connected with the one subject of absorbing interest of to-day.[5]

Here, in an early satirical experiment, Twain modernizes act 3 of Shakespeare's play to report Caesar's assassination as a contemporary murder in a big American city, a corrupt city controlled by unscrupulous politicians who hold self-serving hacks in their pay.[6] Nonetheless, the conversion of act 3 into modern banner headlines became a regular assignment set in English classes across the United States throughout the twentieth century and on into the twenty-first, aimed at the development of students' writing skills and their interest in the play as perennially relevant. In 1931, in her version of such a journalistic project, teacher Kathleen Brady recommends to her students as good models for their obituary of the Roman dictator recent press reports on the tragic deaths of Knute Rockne and Nicholas Longworth. For a few weeks in spring 1931, then, Julius Caesar simultaneously took on the heroic features of a celebrated college football coach and the Speaker of the U.S. House of Representatives.

A FASCIST EDUCATION

During this same period, in stark contrast, Julius Caesar was taking shape in the Italian education system as a quintessentially Fascist hero, and was being aligned systematically with a Caesarean Mussolini as matching revolutionary dictators of past and present. From 1923, the year after the Fascist Party's "March on Rome" and its acquisition of power, the newly installed regime began a series of modifications to first the second-ary- and then the elementary-school systems in Italy. The party sought to secure its long-term future in government through the education and training of Italy's youth in Fascist beliefs and values. The "fascistization" of Italian schools was organized at the level of the state with a relatively light touch at first, but the political indoctrination of students was car-ried out more aggressively and regulated more vigorously after the dec-laration of Italian empire in 1936.[7]

While some Americans were bemoaning the progressive disappearance of ancient Greece and Rome from the high-school history syllabus,[8] and the classical languages from the requirements for entry into Ivy League universities,[9] the Fascist government was insinuating its core myth or doctrine of *romanità* (the "Romanness" of modern Italy) into the history textbooks of Italian children, as well as into the rituals and the routines of adult daily life. In the course of the regime, Roman history poached a larger and larger share of the curriculum and the life of *Cesare* was taught according to Fascism's ideological script: the importance of valor and military discipline, the strength and omniscience of the leader, his will to power, the necessity of revolution, the ideal of dictatorship, war's cleansing properties, the grandeur of empire.[10] And while enrollments in Latin programs were declining radically in the United States from a high of 49 percent of all high-school students in 1910 to 16 percent in 1934 (on its way to a 7.8 percent low in 1949),[11] the Fascist regime was launching "Pan-Latinism," or Latin for all, as a central pedagogic instru-ment in the promotion of Italian racial superiority.[12] Latin, according to the *Duce*, was the language of soldiers, conquerors, and constructors and lay at the root of Italian. Speaking Latin would give voice to the genea-logical connection of the ancient with the modern tongue and, therefore, manifest the purity of the race.[13] And while American teachers plucked at whim contemporary parallels for Julius Caesar from among the nation's celebrities, the school textbooks published by the Fascist state all worked painstakingly to conjoin him with Benito Mussolini alone.

The Roman general now showed up earlier in the educational life of an Italian child than in that of an American, with more emotional intensity, with a far stronger invitation to hero worship, and with an emphasis not on the battlefields of Gaul or the political assassination in the Senate but on Caesar's crossing of the river Rubicon in 49 B.C.E. and his overthrow of the Roman republic. The popular state textbook *Centostelle*, an anthology published by Piero Bargellini in 1941 and targeted at nineyear-olds, praised Mussolini on the grounds that, like Caesar, he "has marched on Rome, not to sack it or punish it, but to liberate it from incapable leaders. . . . He too has conquered the world. He sees . . . whole regions to be colonized; countries waiting for law; people who want to work. He wants justice done, injustice set right. He sees there are wounds to heal, sadness to console, treason to punish, and heroism to exalt."[14] Italian children also confronted this amalgamation of Roman *dux* and Italian *Duce* outside their classrooms, in the paramilitary youth groups into which they were enlisted at every stage of their school career. Starting out as Sons of the She-Wolf and ending up conscripted into the Fascist army, boys passed through cohorts, centuries, and legions, wore Roman emblems, carried Roman banners, and gave the "Roman" salute. While individual American teachers had organized Saturday morning clubs to stimulate and entertain young readers of Caesar's *Gallic War* with cardboard model-making and military dress-up, now Italian children were being groomed through *romanità* and Caesar for real combat.[15] A state handbook for commanders of these juvenile centuries contained a resonant address directed to the ten-year-old boys who were in their charge: "If you listen carefully . . . you may still hear the terrible tread of the Roman legions . . . Caesar has come to life again in the Duce; he rides at the head of numberless cohorts, treading down all cowardice and all impurities to reestablish the culture and the new might of Rome. Step into the ranks of his army and be the best soldiers."[16] Even beyond the classroom and children's military training grounds, in everyday adult life throughout Italy and the course of the Fascist *ventennio*, the regime systematically cast Mussolini as a modern reincarnation of Julius Caesar—a dramatic role for the *Duce* that he chose heartily to endorse.

The two dictators were effectively fused in school textbooks, propagandist pamphlets, and classical scholarship produced by Fascist historians. Together *dux* and *Duce* become impulsive and virile generals, strong of mind, superior in intellect, exceptionally energetic, hawkeyed, and good-looking. They each initiate forceful political revolutions, march on Rome, violently uproot a rotten republic, establish a new order, found an empire, and rescue Italy and its people from the corrup-

FIGURE 18. The linked profiles of Caesar and Mussolini. From *Reincarnazione di Cesare: Il predestinato* by Rosavita (Milan, 1936). Reproduced from Gillo Dorfles, *Kitsch: An Anthology of Bad Taste* (New York, 1969).

tion of the privileged classes.[17] During the second decade of the regime, Mussolini was even lauded as having surpassed the achievements of his predecessor. An illustration in the volume *Reincarnazione di Cesare— Il predestinato* (published in 1936 by Rosavita; see fig. 18) sets a battered, blind-eyed portrait bust of the Roman dictator behind the fully formed, sharp-eyed profile of his modern reincarnation and remarks: "Caesar outlined, initiated, dreamed; Mussolini perfected, fortified, created, achieved."[18] Such couplings established a distinct and direct Roman heritage for the Fascist regime, in order to legitimate historically its violent beginnings, stimulate enthusiasm for present-day dictatorship, unify culturally the disparate masses participating in its ceremonies, and predict a glorious imperial future. Thus Mussolini himself instituted spectacular public rituals of veneration for the Roman dictator on every Ides of March and on every anniversary of the March on Rome, and his autobiography, newspaper columns, interviews, public speeches, radio broadcasts, and filmed newsreels frequently presented Julius Caesar as his favorite Roman exemplar.[19]

AMERICAN PRO- AND ANTI-FASCISM

In the United States, the *Duce* achieved extraordinary publicity and wide acclaim until news broke in 1935 of the Italian invasion of Ethio-

pia. Expert in the tactics of popular journalism and the strategic manipulation of modern media, Mussolini granted innumerable interviews to
journalists who worked for American newspapers in order to dissemi-
nate within the United States a favorable image of his leadership. And,
by 1927, his government had established a highly effective press service
in America better to secure and sustain that image. Mass circulation
dailies and weeklies published enthusiastic endorsements of Italian Fascism and its *Duce* throughout the 1920s and a good part of the 1930s.
In this same period, the Italian-American press, such as *Il Progresso
Italo-Americano,* demonstrated its overwhelmingly pro-Fascist sympathies. Although anti-Fascist individuals and groups quickly emerged,
their anxieties and criticisms were opposed and overpowered by the
strength of the pro-Fascist press and of organizations such as the Fascist League of North America (later reformed as the Lictor Federation). Holding patriotic parades, celebrations, and demonstrations in
the streets of American cities, many members of the Italian-American
community saw in the regime a welcome spur to racial pride. No other
Western nation gave greater support to Italian Fascism nor sponsored a
personality cult for Mussolini so forcefully in its press.[20]

The *Saturday Evening Post* (a popular weekly magazine boasting
almost three million subscribers) took the lead in the production of articles commending Mussolini as Italy's redeemer. From May to October
1928, for example, it serialized in ten parts *My Autobiography*—a work
that, purportedly, Mussolini had just completed in order to describe his
background and catalogue his achievements after five years in power.
Within its pages, Richard Washburn Child (the former U.S. ambassa-
dor to Italy) had contributed an effusive foreword: "It is one thing to
administer a state. The one who does this well is called a statesman. It is
quite another thing to make a state. Mussolini has made a state. That is
superstatesmanship."[21] Although Child is identified as the text's editor
and translator, he appears to have ghostwritten the entire book (with
the *Duce*'s closest aides) in order to manufacture a Mussolini suitable
for consumption by the broadest possible American readership.[22]

Alongside his talk of discipline, work, and the corporate state, the
modern dictator's Caesarean rhetoric and rituals also became a political discourse familiar to many Americans. An early presentation to an
American readership of Mussolini's love for Caesar came from an interview that Lady Grace Drummond Hay (correspondent for the London
Daily Express) had held with the *Duce* in Rome in August 1925. Under
the headline "Mussolini as Julius Caesar," her chat with the Fascist

leader was reproduced in the weekly magazine the *Literary Digest* (New York) on 26 September of that year:

> "Why do you work with Julius Caesar looking over your shoulder all the time?" came my somewhat irrelevant question as I caught sight of a bust of the great Caesar in a niche over the desk. Mussolini's face took on an inspired expression, his eyes a curious, dreamy look, and his voice sounded strangely moved as he replied, almost reverently: "He—he is my ideal, my master—Julius Caesar, the greatest man that ever was!"

The *Digest* packages this account with noticeable disapproval. It acknowledges at the start that Mussolini's Caesarism has been sharply criticized elsewhere in the British press; the *Duce* has "owned up" to love of Caesar while also making the (un-American) claim that "there is no such thing as liberty." After details of Hay's interview, it adds adverse comments plucked from the London *Chronicle* and the *Evening Standard,* in the latter case including the following: "The great trouble . . . is the supply of Caesars. If a Caesar fails to breed a Caesar, there is the certainty of a breakdown in the system. If a Caesar, on the other hand, breeds several Caesars, there is the certainty of civil war." The whole piece is illustrated by a cartoon from Amsterdam's Socialist newspaper *De Notenkraker* in which readers see Mussolini perched absurdly high on a throne that is precariously supported on sticks tied one above the other. Peering down anxiously, he cannot make out that the men below him are sawing his whole edifice down.[23]

Elsewhere in the American press during the 1920s and early 1930s, journalists regularly twinned Mussolini with Caesar. In particular, the *New York Times,* following a largely (but not exclusively) pro-Fascist line until the mid-1930s,[24] published a special cable from Rome on 18 August 1925 detailing the Hay interview without adverse comment. The banner headline read: "Caesar Is His Ideal, Mussolini Declares."[25] At the start of the following year, an article in the same newspaper by Henry W. Bunn carried the dramatic title "An Age of Dictators Impends: Julius Caesar Depicted as the Arch-type for All Time—Mussolini and Others of the Increasing Modern Breed are Imitators of the Boldness and Capacity of the Ancient Roman" (*New York Times,* 24 January 1926). In the article, Bunn argued that dictators emerge when states are in acute crisis. The genuine dictator is a supreme hero, whose function after usurpation is purgative and reconstructive. Caesar was the greatest of these because he scrapped a tyrannical constitution and curbed both privilege and communism through the institution of a military monarchy. Writing in the

New York Times, the journalist thus replicates Fascist rhetorical strategies, shaping and praising Caesar (while eliding his political failure and his own bloody end) in order to provide for Mussolini a seemingly legitimate and grandiose model in the past for present action:[26]

> In an airplane view the problem confronting Mussolini is very like the Caesarian problem—a Constitution broken down and become an instrument of tyranny in the hands of a selfish, purblind oligarchy, weekly temporizing (as in old Rome) with the Bolshevist menace. To reform or to scrap is the question which Mussolini (as with Caesar, as indeed with all dictators) [*sic*], whose solution we are watching so intently. The old polity reformed to the want of the time or a new one, belike a Caesarian military monarchy (whereof the instrument is at hand)?

By 1935, however, even *New York Times* reporters were pursuing the weaknesses or the darker implications of the historical analogy in order to express concern about Fascism's aggressively imperialist agenda. An article by Shepard Stone in the *New York Times* for 13 October 1935 begins: "Stirred by their modern Caesar and his soldiers marching into battle, Italians are once again dreaming of empire."[27] Yet, however much *il Duce* plays the tune of Roman grandeur to lure Italians on (the reporter warns), the empire he is creating covers nowhere near the extent of the Roman Empire under the Caesars, and even that empire was weakened and ultimately destroyed by slavery and corruption.[28] Similarly, a few months earlier, an article entitled "Duce Wants to Be a Modern Julius Caesar" in the *Chicago Defender* (27 July 1935) cautioned that Mussolini's imperial ambitions did not stop at Ethiopia but were spreading to Africa's Mediterranean coast and the regions in which Julius Caesar had once exercised command. Here connection with Caesar is utilized not to offer Mussolini political motivation but, rather, to expose it.

During this period, the newsreels produced by the Hearst Corporation captured most completely for American viewers the laudatory identification of the *Duce* with Julius Caesar that the Fascist regime had initiated, and Mussolini himself had nurtured. To newsprint versions of the identification, newsreels added sound, vision, and action. Now, in cinemas across the nation, American audiences could witness with their own eyes Mussolini's spectacular performance of his Caesarean rituals surrounded by Rome's ancient monuments and applauded by swarming crowds of supporters. From the advent of sound newsreels in 1929, Americans could also hear with their own ears snatches of the modern dictator's powerful oratory and the immense cheers it engendered, listen to the pompous voice-overs that tried to guide their understanding of such Fascist political theater, and take in the vibrant music that attempted to set an appropriate tone and stimulate a sympathetic reaction.[29] Hearst Metrotone News for 21 November 1934, for example, included among its stories one entitled "All Rome Hails City's Rebirth." The news story documents one of the major ceremonies that had taken place in the preceding month to mark the twelfth anniversary of the Fascist Party's March on Rome.[30] In long aerial shots and in close-ups, the camera pans along the Circus Maximus, picking out parading athletes, celebrating crowds, and a uniformed and smiling Mussolini who delivers a Fascist salute. The camera then relocates to a packed Piazza Venezia and offers a close-up of Mussolini puffing out his chest on the balcony of party headquarters as he begins to declaim on the rebirth ·of ancient Rome. Over these two scenes, accompanied intermittently by martial music, an off-screen voice declares bombastically (and in an American accent):

> Over the rebuilt street of the Circus Maximus, where centuries ago chariots rolled and gladiators fought, twenty-five thousand fascist athletes pass and salute their miracle man Mussolini. They celebrate the rejuvenation of ancient Rome dug from its ruins under the direction of Italy's modern Caesar.
>
> Countless thousands assemble in the new square of Romulus and Remus to cheer their leader who twelve short years ago marched his Blackshirts into the eternal City. Like an emperor of old, il Duce holds the multitude spellbound as he expounds the glories of reborn Rome.[31]

AMERICA'S SAWDUST CAESAR

Although an anti-Fascist movement was slow to develop in the United States and was hampered by ideological divisions, during the 1930s individuals did launch increasingly bitter attacks against the growing threat of Fascism both abroad and at home.[32] Such attacks included revisionist histories of the Mussolini-Caesar coupling.

In 1925, the American journalist George Seldes (covering Italy for the *Chicago Tribune*) smuggled out reports on the murder of the Socialist Giacomo Matteotti and was punished by the regime with immediate expulsion.[33] Once back in the United States, Seldes compiled a systematic deconstruction of Fascism's histories and myths. He completed a first draft of the manuscript by 1931, but only after considerable difficulty and some years of delay was he able to get it published. The first influential discreditation in America of Italian Fascism, the book was entitled *Sawdust Caesar: The Untold History of Mussolini and*

Fascism (1935). The denunciation begins with a quote from the journalism of William Bolitho, who had published an unusually early and sustained series of assaults on Mussolini in the American daily the *New York World*. Three years after the establishment of the regime, Bolitho declared that Italian Fascists were inventing their own history: they had created, and were serving up in every language with illustrative photographs, a false epic about a romantic hero (Seldes, 1935, xi). In a passionate opening address to American readers that follows the quote from Bolitho, Seldes argues that Fascism has now become a formidable political force in America and will become an even more powerful threat to the Republic if it gains its own homegrown *Duce*. So, if we are to put a stop to American Fascism, he continues, we must understand Italian Fascism and its spiritual father better. And we must counter the chorus of unmitigated hero worship that has been sung by the majority of America's journalists and biographers while down on their knees before Benito Mussolini (xiii-xv).

According to the account provided by Seldes, Fascism is an inchoate movement in search of a programme, and Mussolini an opportunist in search of an image.[34] And, because one image to which Mussolini has become particularly attached is that of the Roman dictator, Seldes dedicates part of his final chapter, "Ave Caesar!" to a catalogue of numerous occasions, over the course of years and years, on which *il Duce* has posed as a Roman hero:

> Julius, the divider of Gaul, shines over Mussolini; the Duce looks into those cold pupil-less eyes every day while his press reminds him that he is the pure Roman emperor type in face and will, the true successor to the thrice-crown-refusing political ancestor. Even the textbooks of Italy have been changed so that today all the Caesars are unblemished heroes and the tyranny, corruption, and weaknesses of that ruler "who fell an easy victim to the cheap devices of the lewd Cleopatra" have been eliminated by the censor. To make their own hero greater, the idol of comparison has been cleaned and polished. (1935, 370)

Seldes notes, for example, that when Mussolini lands on African soil in April 1926, he struts like a Roman emperor in front of the motion-picture operators and is hailed by obsequious journalists with the cry "Ave Caesar!" Keeping within hand's distance a portrait bust of his cleansed and polished hero, the *Duce* looks to restore Rome to the grandeur of the Caesars. In 1932, the year of the tenth anniversary of the March on Rome, Mussolini orders the prefect of his local region of Romagna to change the name of its river to Rubicon. And, in the following year, Caesar's Italian successor donates to the nearby city of Rimini (the approximate location of ancient Arminium, where Julius Caesar is said to have incited his troops to march on Rome) a statue of his Roman idol, whom he lauds as "the great patron of Fascism, the first Black Shirt." Moreover, at the time of mobilization for the invasion of Ethiopia, in the summer of 1935, the *Duce* reminds his grenadiers as they stand in the capital by the ruins of Caesar's temple to Venus that the Roman general once dominated the world—that yesterday's Roman destiny may become Italy's tomorrow (370–72).

Mussolini, Seldes also claims, is always looking to a future where statues will be erected of his likeness and his name will shine on a piece of deathless bronze. But, in the view of this American anti-Fascist, the Italian dictator steps into the role of a monumental Caesar "as an actor into his makeup" (Seldes 1935, 370). Mussolini is a mediocrity, a man of straw and sawdust, whose memorials ought therefore to be swept away, as the book's final paragraph proclaims:

> Everywhere new statues appear of Benito Mussolini today and more will be erected in his lifetime. The statues of Julius Caesar will probably remain forever in Eternal Rome—but the day will surely come when in all the noble cities of Italy there will arise the statue of Giacomo Matteotti. A free people will then decide if there will be room also for those of our Sawdust Caesar. (382)

This estimation of Mussolini as an insubstantial Caesar made of sawdust caught on at his downfall in 1943. The American press reported that he had been, after all, only an actor on a temporary stage or a floppy rag doll stuffed with pretentiousness, rather than a genuine world leader deserving to be memorialized in solid, lasting bronze. But an American caricature of the Fascist leader from 1936 already demonstrates a similar conception (fig. 19): the Duce's aspirations to empire for Italy are Caesarean; his desire to be reproduced in bronze overblown. Draw by Kansas cartoonist Albert T. Reid and syndicated to the Italian-language paper *Travaso* (published in New Orleans), it depicts Mussolini as a huge new colossus in the costume of a Roman general, bestriding Italy and Africa, sternly guarding the gateway to the Suez Canal.[35] The cartoon touches on the failure of Great Britain and the League of Nations to close the canal in 1936, and thus prevent Fascist troop carriers sailing through it to reach Ethiopia and, consequently, to annex the African state as part of a newly "restored" Roman Empire in and beyond the Mediterranean.[36] The cartoon also borrows for its humor and its political point from Shakespeare's *Julius Caesar*, where,

FIGURE 19. "Mussolini, the
New Colossus of Rhodes,"
Travaso (New Orleans).
Cartoon by Albert T. Reid for
the Bell Syndicate (c. 1936).
Reproduced from *Il cesare di
cartapesta: Mussolini nella
caricature* (Turin, 1945).

at 1.2.135–38, Cassius (the chief conspirator against the ancient dictator) complains:

> Why, man, he doth bestride the narrow world
> Like a colossus, and we petty men
> Walk under his huge legs and peep about
> To find ourselves dishonourable graves.

In the American cartoon, the tiny winged figure of Peace clearly knows her Shakespeare. As she is rowed dishonorably in Europe's boat toward the huge spread legs of the new imperial colossus, she cries out in dismay in the accompanying caption: "Let's clear off and quickly!!."[37]

SHAKESPEARE'S EUROPEAN DICTATOR

A year later, on 11 November 1937 (and for 157 performances thereafter), audiences in New York were invited to witness an unremittingly visceral presentation of Shakespeare's *Julius Caesar* as anti-Fascist theater. The modern-dress version directed by Orson Welles became the most celebrated and influential production of the Roman tragedy to appear on the American stage in the twentieth century.[38] Looking back on the revival, John Houseman (Welles's partner in the production) recalled that it had been conceived as a political melodrama with clear contemporary parallels. All over the Western world sophisticated democratic structures were breaking down; the issues of political violence and the moral duty of the individual in the face of tyranny had become urgent and inescapable. To emphasize the similarity between the last days of the Roman republic and the political climate of Europe in the midthirties, our Roman aristocrats wore military uniforms with black belts that suggested but did not exactly reproduce the current fashion of the fascist ruling class; our crowd wore the dark, nondescript street clothes of the big-city proletariat.[39]

Costumed in contemporary military uniforms and city-street clothes, bluntly staged without division into acts or scenes, Welles's production of the Elizabethan drama presented the death of the Roman dictator as a swift series of increasingly alarming events, punctuated by sharp contrasts of light and darkness and jarring sound effects. It thus replicated the format of a current affairs radio broadcast or a "living newspaper," and the visual appearance of documentary film footage.[40] Yet this was no piece of pro-Fascist adulation, in the manner of the *New York Times* or Hearst's Metrotone newsreels. Instead, the modernist style of this Shakespearean revival, its narrative drive, and the context of its performance at the Mercury Theater invited audiences to understand it as an urgent warning and a vital lesson about the dangers of European dictatorships.[41]

Welles's *Caesar* constituted the inaugural production of the Mercury, a new radical repertory company he had set up with his partner John Houseman. Both men had already been involved in the 1930s movement of reformist theater that had been initially subsidized by Roosevelt's government as part of his New Deal of social, political, economic, and cultural reform. Their new company was established similarly as a challenge to Broadway's commercial theaters. Supported by left-wing organizations that supplied both its funds and its audiences, the Mercury Theater deliberately targeted a working-class and African-American clientele. It charged low ticket prices and held to an agitprop manifesto of both entertaining and informing its audience through a socially conscious repertoire made up, predominantly, of plays of the past that had "an emotional or factual" bearing on contemporary life.[42] To that end, the original text of Shakespeare's *Julius Caesar* was profoundly cut and simplified; scenes were reorganized, the identity of speakers changed, and the last two acts of the play almost completely eliminated. The tragedy's second half (the vengeance of Caesar accomplished through the machinations of Antony, the appearance of the ghost, and the initiation of civil war) was especially condensed, not, as in the late eighteenth and nineteenth centuries, to buttress the otherwise fragile heroism of Brutus, but in order to sharpen the focus on three of the protagonists in the tragedy that flows from dictatorship: Caesar, Brutus, and the mob.[43]

Under the direction of Orson Welles, this populist *Julius Caesar* also subordinated Shakespeare's text to experimental and bruising performance strategies better to bind the Roman (and Tudor) past to Europe's Fascist present. Rejecting the vastly elaborate scenography and stately choreography expected of productions of Shakespeare in the nineteenth century, Welles created a set that was bare and urban in design. A series of platforms covered the entire stage floor and rose gently up to a narrow ridge before falling back down steeply to the bloodred brick wall of the theater itself, whose pipes, hoses, and radiators were left fully in view.[44] Powerful shafts of light angling up from traps set in the steps and platforms, and streaming down from overhead, singled out or shadowed members of the cast in a manner that evoked for reviewers the spectacular staging of nighttime Nazi rallies.[45] The original score composed by Marc Blitzstein for trumpet, horn, percussion, and organ (including bugle calls and drumbeats) was composed to evoke "the pounding march of Hitler's storm troopers that we were hearing with increasing frequency over the radio and in the newsreels;"[46] while the constant flow of crowds across the unpadded platforms generated a dramatic drumbeat to accompany the scenes of angry mob disorder.[47]

Until 1937, Shakespeare's tragedy had never been staged in modern dress.[48] Now the contemporary dress code (the green shirts, epaulettes, belts, and boots of the military) and the choreography of Fascism (with its salutes, processions, and massed ranks of spectators) all reproduced on stage the magazine illustrations or the newsreel footage of 1930s Italy and Germany with which Americans were so familiar (see fig. 20). Out of Welles's revival, Julius Caesar emerged as a ranting European dictator surrounded by uniformed henchmen and rowdy workers, while Antony became his rabble-rousing replacement, and Brutus a liberal politician perplexed by how best he should oppose them.[49]

Yet Welles claimed in the program notes that no precise political analogy was intended, despite the modern dress code of the production. According to its director, the ambition of *Death of a Dictator* (as the Shakespearean revival was pointedly subtitled in some of its publicity) was not to "caricature any existing dictator, would-be dictator, or dictatorships."[50] The military uniforms and civilian costumes appear to be of relatively imprecise origin better to stimulate in audiences a range of correlations.

FIGURE 20. Brutus (Orson Welles) salutes Caesar (Joseph
Holland), in Orson Welles's *Julius Caesar* (1937). Photograph by
Cecil Beaton. © Conde Nast Archive / CORBIS.

The first and dominant correlation that reviewers who witnessed the
Mercury revival explicitly constructed was between this modern-dress,
militaristic Julius Caesar and Benito Mussolini. The identification was
brought most vividly to the attention of audiences at the start of the performance. Shakespeare's opening scene, in which the Roman tribunes
berate the commoners for celebrating Caesar's triumph and forgetting
Pompey's, was both postponed and abbreviated. Instead, the utter darkness and the marching throb of an overture were abruptly interrupted
by a voice crying "Caesar," a shaft of light, and the sudden presence on
the New York stage of the Roman dictator dressed in military attire,
head arrogantly thrown back, surrounded by uniformed subordinates,
saluting an admiring crowd of civilians. Poaching Casca's line from
Julius Caesar 1.2.14, this Caesar shouts "Bid every noise be still!" only
to hear from offstage the soothsayer's sinister warning. He disappears
back into the dark accompanied by Fascist salutes and cries of "Hail,
Caesar!" from the crowd on stage.[51] So successful was the reproduction of Mussolini's look and gesture that journalists frequently noted
in their subsequent reviews a remarkable physical resemblance between
the "sawdust" Caesar (who was played by Joseph Holland) and the
Italian dictator—the large brow, the staring eyes, the jutting chin, the
surly fixed expression, the harsh voice, the spare gestures.[52] In the con

text of this insistently anti-Fascist production of Shakespeare's *Julius Caesar,* Welles was adamant that there was no place for the Elizabethan playwright's equivocations about the Roman general: "Caesar is almost a cartoon dictator; he doesn't have to be played that way, but he can never be played sympathetically. He can either be full of pompous boast or ice-cold genius, but there's no love between him and Brutus. There's nothing that makes it a story of betrayal at all."[53] The Caesar of Welles is played as an emblematic tyrant of few frailties, little indecision, and no human warmth, whose accelerating accumulation of powers is fast destroying the traditional freedoms of the republican state.

If the opening of *Death of a Dictator* strongly brought to mind Mussolini and Fascist Italy, its Forum scene prompted comparisons principally with Hitler and Nazi Germany. A ten-foot-high pulpit covered in black velour had been wheeled up the back ramp in the dark. From it, first Brutus and then Antony orated directly outward above the crowds who had assembled below them and around Caesar's open coffin. Disconcertingly, therefore, they were also speaking directly to the theater audience. Caesar's heir Antony, in particular, raised his arm in a Fascist salute and, behind and above him, the powerful shafts of up light cast menacing shadows on the back wall while he harangued the plebeians (see fig. 21). Their transformation into a vengeful, frenzied mob was signaled aurally by the gradual escalation of their utterances from whispers and murmurs to shouts, chants, and screams. The memoirs of production staff indicate that all this stage business had been inspired by photographs and newsreel footage of the annual Nazi Party rallies, the most recent of which had been held at Nuremberg just two months before the opening of Welles's *Caesar.*[54]

The way Welles played out the huddled conspirators and the variously scuffling or thundering mob in his modern-dress revival of Shakespeare's *Julius Caesar,* however, stimulated quite different *homegrown* parallels in the contemporary reviews and, later, the histories of the production. According to the trade journal *Variety* (17 November 1937), the conspirators were portrayed as modern racketeers and affected "the turned-up collar" and "hand-in-the-pocket-on-the-trigger" look. They met as if they were in an alley beside the Mercury Theater and looked like a strike committee from a taxi-drivers' union, according to the *New York Daily News* (13 November 1937). And, in the words of a reporter from the *Washington Times,* with their pulled-down hats and assorted overcoats, the rabble appeared more like "'Little Caesar's' henchmen than Romans." Racketeers, labor unionists, and gangsters on the prowl in

FIGURE 21. Antony (George Coulouris) harangues the mob over Caesar's body, in Orson Welles's *Julius Caesar* (1937). Photograph by Alfredo Valente. By permission of the Special Collections of the New York Public Library.

America's city streets—these analogies demonstrate that Welles's *Julius Caesar* also addressed contemporary anxieties about the rise of Fascism within (as well as outside) the United States of America.[55]

LITTLE CAESARS IN THEIR LITTLE ITALYS

The warning contained within Welles's revival of Shakespeare's *Julius Caesar* could be understood in domestic terms because from the 1920s a strong bond had developed in American culture between Julius Caesar, Italian Americans, and gangsterism. One important contributing factor was the behavior of Italian-American gangsters themselves.[56] In 1925, Salvatore Maranzano left Castellammare del Golfo on the northwest coast of Sicily to take up residence illegally in New York's Little Italy. The city's ethnic enclave was fast becoming home to many such immigrants as a result of the Fascist government's policy to purge Italy of the Mafia. Already a firmly established mafioso in his mother country, Maranzano entered the bootlegging business that Prohibition had stimulated and achieved a formidable influence over other Sicilian criminals in New York City. A well-educated former seminarian, Maranzano kept a substantial library of books about ancient Rome and nurtured a strong fascination for Julius Caesar. The frequency with which he drew on the organization of the Roman Empire and the strategy and tactics of the Roman dictator to push for changes in the structure of New York's criminal gangs earned him the nickname "Little Caesar." According to the memoirs of an eyewitness, at a banquet held in May 1931 for hundreds of Italian criminals from all over the United States, Maranzano laid out his vision of a military chain of command from soldiers and crews, rising through captains, underbosses, and bosses, to himself as the *capo dei tutti capi* (or "boss of all bosses"). In a somewhat ironic mirroring of the role of *romanità* in the ideology of the Fascist regime, and of the Roman general in the personality cult of Mussolini, Maranzano desired to become "the Caesar of organized crime."[57] Although the quasi-military hierarchy Maranzano proposed was taken up and utilized by Italian-American criminals for decades to come, their self-proclaimed commander was shot and stabbed to death just a few months after the declaration of his Roman vision. Like the original Julius Caesar, this "Little Caesar" was brought down for his excessively autocratic ambitions.

The activities of Italian-American gangsters such as Salvatore "Little Caesar" Maranzano in New York or (and especially) Al Capone in

Chicago were widely disseminated during the 1920s and early 1930s through reports in broadcast, film, and print media. Those reports, in turn, inspired fictional literature and gave birth to the genre of the gangster film.[58] The heavily ironic title of the best-selling novel *Little Caesar* (1929) by W.R. Burnett referred not to Maranzano—for the author had taken Capone as his primary historical model in order to create the fictional gangster Cesare Bandello, known to other characters as Rico. Rico is only a "little" Caesar in the little Italy of an unspecified American metropolis because his power is all too transitory and feeble. The novel, and the film adaptation produced swiftly on the heels of its success, created a protagonist of immense appeal to its Depression-era consumers. Here was a tragic hero suited to modern times and spaces: a character who thrillingly rebels with extreme violence against the hardship and corruption of American society, but whose immorality is edifyingly punished by narrative close. So successful were the novel and the film that they spawned many copies in the early 1930s and confirmed a narrative structure for the American gangster of rise followed by fall, and a repetitive iconography of slick suits and dark urban alleyways.[59] The film *Little Caesar* (1930, dir. Mervyn LeRoy) gave an ethnicity, a story, and a look to organized crime in the United States, and a designation of such cultural power that "Caesar" far outlived its initial attachment to Italian-American gangsters of the 1920s and early 1930s. Thus, for example, by 1960 *High School Caesar* might refer not to a commentary on the *Gallic War* designed to support the second-year Latin curriculum but to a film about juvenile delinquency targeted at an emergent "teen" audience. Directed by O'Dale Ireland for Marathon Pictures, it displayed on its advertising posters the tagline "Mob rule in a high school." Played by a popular Anglo-American teen star, the lead character, Matt Stevens, extorts protection money from his fellow students, sells stolen test papers, and rigs the school-president elections. But he receives his comeuppance at the end, as the heavily moralizing but catchy title song warns him directly at the film's start: "You're playing a game that you never can win, High School Caesar, you're gonna get it in the end."[60]

SHAKESPEARE'S AMERICAN DEMAGOGUE

Two years before the production of Welles's modern-dress *Julius Caesar*, the Roman dictator had also been refigured in American political terms in a novel by the journalist Wallace Irwin. To produce a light and humorous social satire on the cynical reporters and crooked politicians of

America's big cities, *The Julius Caesar Murder Case* (1935) extensively domesticates both the history of the Roman republic and Shakespeare's tragic dramatization of Julius Caesar's assassination. Narrated from the perspective of Mannie Scribo, a star sports reporter for the *Evening Tibur,* the novel follows his efforts to solve yet another seemingly insignificant homicide in the city only to uncover instead a conspiracy to assassinate its dictator. Julius Caesar is here variously called "CJC" or "the Big Fella" (a nickname applied regularly elsewhere to Capone)[61] and is configured as a gangsterish politician whose corrupt administration the *Tibur*'s editor is too scared to expose.

The novel neatly betrays its allegiance to the relatively new American genre of hard-boiled crime fiction, utilizing a tough protagonist who matter-of-factly detects society's squalid secrets.[62] The investigative reporter Mannie observes how the citizens of a supposedly free republic wildly celebrate the arrival at the gladiatorial games of the man who tyrannizes them, "a wreath of bays sitting on his bald head like parsley on a hard-boiled egg" (Irwin 1935, 69). Mannie overhears the pathetic pretensions of the conspirators (a bloc of social-climbing, mealy-mouthed progressives in the Senate) to free Rome from tyranny. He catches Cassius in the act of berating Brutus in a low voice:

> "Now this is what you're supposed to do. Wait till he's just inside the lobby, then stick him and yell the slogan. You remember it?" "*Sic Semper Tyrannis*", repeated Brutus faintly. "Don't say it in that sick-cat voice", demanded Cassius. "Remember you are freeing Rome from a tyrant. And the object of this is to gather the Senate around us and start the Big Parade." (127)

While the conspirators are revving themselves up for the kill by repeating the patriotic motto of the state of Virginia (the very motto that John Wilkes Booth had uttered as he shot President Abraham Lincoln),[63] the novel's Caesar is unexpectedly brought down before he can reach the Senate house, in an alley by a butcher's knife in the back. Irwin doubly undercuts the tragic register traditionally cast over the assassination: it is not the work of friends driven to murder by their patriotic principles; nor, Mannie next discovers, did it even happen. CJC staged his death in order to retire safely from his life of crime. Mannie cannot report this terrible deceit in the newspaper because the administration's hand shaker, Antony, has bought it up and provided it with a "fanciful" account set in the Senate chamber of Democrats in political revolt, so instead Mannie writes himself as hero into this detective thriller. By the time the reader has confronted and absorbed these various plot twists, the irony of Irwin's opening dedication becomes clear: "To Benito Mussolini and Adolf Hitler. This book is affectionately dedicated with the author's feeling that in distance there is security." Throughout, the narrative style of *The Julius Caesar Murder Case* erodes the distance between European dictators and homegrown ones. The vocabulary of American politics during the Great Depression—Bonus Bills, Fresh Air Funds, Farm Relief, Progressives, Democrats, Fusionists, and third party movements—relocates tyranny and dictatorship within the heart of America's cities. Thus Americanized, Caesar can speak to contemporary fears within the United States that only a fine line separates the strong leadership of its president and some of its politicians from Fascist dictatorship.[64]

The Julius Caesar Murder Case was published in 1935, the same year as *Sawdust Caesar*, in which the journalist George Seldes had begun with the warning that Fascism within the United States would become much more threatening if the nation ever gained a homegrown dictator. Also in that year, Sinclair Lewis brought out a novel in which he envisaged in detail that America would indeed be transformed into a Fascist state by 1936. In the best-seller *It Can't Happen Here* (1935), despite the heroic denunciations of a newspaper reporter, the fictional politician Berzelius Windrup succeeds in being elected president on a populist platform and immediately becomes America's Fascist dictator. He establishes the "Corpo" regime and a private army. He changes the constitution to steal for himself all the powers of federal government but is eventually overthrown in a coup instigated by his own lieutenants. Here Lewis explicitly invoked Senator Huey P. Long, who had been branded by his right-wing opponents in the press "the despot of the delta" or the "Caesar of the bayous" for the tyrannical methods they claimed he was using to exercise power over the state of Louisiana.[65] In later interviews, the novelist declared that he had written and published his political fiction specifically to obstruct the left-wing senator's campaign for president.[66] In the event, Senator Long was assassinated in the Louisiana capital in September 1935, and a writer of a critical obituary somberly observed:

> He made himself an unquestioned dictator, though a State Legislature was still elected by a nominally free people, as was also a Governor, who was, however, nothing but a dummy for Huey Long. In reality, Senator Long set up a Fascist government in Louisiana. It was disguised, but only thinly. There was no outward appearance of a revolution, no march of Black Shirts upon Baton Rouge, but the effectual result was to lodge all the power of the State in the hands of one man.

If Fascism ever comes in the United States it will come in something like that way. No one will set himself up as an avowed dictator, but if he can succeed in dictating everything, the name does not matter. (*New York Times,* 11 September 1935)

Having seen a stage adaptation of Lewis's novel in 1936, it was also to Huey Long that Orson Welles turned in the publicity he released to explain the American dimension of his revival of Shakespeare's tragedy:

> Our Julius Caesar gives a picture of the same kind of hysteria that exists in certain dictator-ruled countries of today. We see the bitter resentment of free-born men against the imposition of a dictatorship. We see a political assassination, such as that of Huey Long. We see the hope on the part of Brutus for a more democratic government vanish with the rise of a demagogue (Antony) who succeeds the dictator. Our moral, if you will, is that not assassination, but education of the masses, permanently removes dictatorships.[67]

According to the theater director, then, what permanently removes dictatorship (whether it has occurred in a nation of Europe or in an American state) is not the act of assassination, but the education of the masses. And what might best make them come alive to its dangers is clearly political drama such as Welles's modern-dress production of Shakespeare's *Julius Caesar.*

One reviewer of *The Death of a Dictator* observed, disappointedly, that "all we get in the end is the new dictator praising Brutus martyr."[68] Such criticism misses the radicalism of Welles's production, since it took as its overriding theme not the necessity of eradicating dictatorship, but the ineffectiveness of liberalism in a world where the masses desire dictatorship and, therefore, are capable of generating and regenerating Fascism—a world of which the United States is an inseparable part.[69] In one of the weekly bulletins issued by the Mercury Theater company, the director provocatively described the chief conspirator against Julius Caesar as

> the eternal, impotent, ineffectual, fumbling liberal; the reformer who wants to do something about things but doesn't know how and gets it in the neck in the end. He's dead right all the time, and dead at the final curtain. He's Shakespeare's favourite hero—the fellow who thinks the times are out of joint but who is really out of joint with his time. He's the bourgeois intellectual, who, under a modern dictatorship, would be the first to be put up against a wall and shot.[70]

On stage, Welles substantiated the description by himself playing the noble Roman against the dominant tradition of previous American theater. This Brutus for the 1930s is no high-minded moralist and man of action, but a dreamer—tentative, self-conscious, and bewildered.[71] Now he is tragic rather than heroic because his idealism is misguided.[72] Assassination serves only to liberate the very forces he had been seeking to destroy.[73]

Hence the highlight of the New York production was a much adapted and extended version of the death of Cinna the Poet. In Shakespeare's tragedy, the scene in which Cinna the Poet is mistaken by a mob for Cinna the Conspirator and torn to pieces occurs immediately after Mark Antony has whipped the plebeians into a frenzy. As an echo or repetition in miniature of the conspirators' assassination of Julius Caesar, it uncomfortably connects the supposedly noble republican rationale of Brutus with the base passions of the mob (who are seeking instant revenge for the murder of their beloved leader), and the ritual sacrifice of a tyrant with the bestial onslaught on a man of letters.[74] Consequently, until this moment, *Julius Caesar* act 3, scene 3 was invariably omitted from American productions of Shakespeare's play as ill befitting a performance of the patriotic killing of kings.[75]

The memorably violent version of act 3, scene 3 staged by Welles opens calmly as Cinna saunters into a shaft of light. As he whistles a tune and muses on a dream he has just had, the poet observes figures emerge from the shadows and surround him. He begins to pull his verses out of his pockets thinking that the growing crowd wishes to hear them. But, instead, it presses closer in order to interrogate him. "I am Cinna the poet," he reiterates more and more loudly. The circle swells and tightens around Cinna when he attempts to move off, pushing him stage center. From offstage, chants can be heard of "Come. Kill. Ho. Slay." Then the mob swoops on their victim, daggers glinting, as he shies away and tries to plead with them. He is swallowed up in their midst save for one raised hand, and rushed away down the back ramp as if he were on the point of being devoured. In the ensuing blackout and silence, the audience at the Mercury hears one last frantic scream of "The POET!" and then the sudden crash of drum and organ struck at full volume.[76] In Welles's rendering of Shakespeare's play, the murder of Cinna the Poet is key.[77] The horrifying mob that appeared on stage in *The Death of a Dictator* was identified by the director explicitly with "the hoodlum element you find in any big city after a war, a mob that is without the stuff that makes them intelligently alive, a lynching mob, the kind of mob that gives you a Hitler or a Mussolini."[78] Danger comes from the people. Once enflamed by their demagogues, they will want yet more of them.

MODERNIZING CAESAR IN THE HIGH SCHOOL

The 1937 modern-dress production of *Julius Caesar: The Death of a Dictator* was a huge success and came to be much admired for its unconventional staging and its astonishing topicality. The *New York Journal-American* for 12 November 1937, for example, declared: "This is no genial condescending pat on Shakespeare's tolerant back. It has the startling impact of a slap in the face." For many reviewers, this extraordinary modernization of Shakespeare's Roman tragedy in a New York theater brought back to vigorous life a play that had long since been killed off in the high-school classroom. In an effusive appraisal published in the *New York Post* (12 November 1937), the theater critic John Mason Brown asserted: "The touch of genius is upon it. It liberates Shakespeare from the strait-jacket of tradition. Gone are the togas and all the schoolroom recollections of a plaster Julius. Blown away is the dust of antiquity. . . . Shakespeare ceases at the Mercury to be the darling of the College Board Examiners."[79] And throughout its long New York run, Orson Welles attempted fully to fulfill his company's promise to educate as well as entertain. Huge blocks of seats at the Mercury were made available at special rates for school and college bookings. Students from all over the state of New York were bussed in for the performances. Educational brochures were composed especially for these young audiences, as well as single-sheet mock-ups of tabloid newspapers carrying banner headlines such as "Dictator Slain, Rome Revolts" to demonstrate graphically the play's engagement with contemporary political concerns about Fascism. During the subsequent road tour across the eastern United States, a drama graduate would pave the way for the players by delivering lectures to students on the Roman tragedy and its contemporary significance. Over one-third of the theater tickets sold were purchased by educational institutions.[80] Although it was not the first American production to dress Shakespeare's *Julius Caesar* in modern trappings, *The Death of a Dictator* became extraordinarily influential throughout the rest of the twentieth century and into the twenty-first, both in terms of the modern-dress style of numerous theatrical productions of the Elizabethan play and of the strategies developed to teach it at American high schools. The identification of the plotline of Shakespeare's *Julius Caesar* with the rise and fall of Fascist dictatorship would eventually be reduced to cliché.[81]

In December 1931 (as we saw at the opening of this chapter), a teacher from South Dakota reported in the *English Journal* that she had engaged her eleventh-grade journalism class in a project on Shakespeare's *Julius Caesar* and had instructed them to write an obituary of the Roman dictator as if his murder were akin to the tragic death of an American sports star or a famed American statesman.[82] After the growth of anti-Fascism in the United States and the part the Roman dictator had been given to play in it (not least by George Seldes in 1935 and Orson Welles in 1937), strategies for teaching Shakespeare's *Julius Caesar* in the high-school classroom underwent a radical change. By December 1940, during another world war, a teacher from Lexington Junior High School in Kentucky recounted in the same journal how she had brought Shakespeare's *Julius Caesar* up to date. She began her students' study of the tragedy simply by emphasizing that Julius Caesar, Mark Antony, and Octavius Caesar were all dictators just as "Europe is full of dictators today."[83] After her Lexington ninth graders had read the play, one of their final assignments required them to substitute the names of living people for the Romans of act 4, scene 1 (where Caesar's heirs mark down those who must die): "One of the boys pictured the three dictators—Stalin, Hitler, and Mussolini—as gathered around a conference table dividing the map of Europe among themselves. Another had the same three dictators marking the statesmen of the world for execution. A quarrel resulted and John Bull and Uncle Sam had to step in and stop the fight" (Tolman 1940, 832). In what the teacher calls "the present world-situation," it is unsurprising that no student in her class comes up with an heir to Caesar living on American soil. The Soviet Union's alliance with Germany, its invasion of eastern Poland and annexation of the Baltic states, most likely stimulate the inclusion of Stalin among the triumvirate currently carving up Europe, and, after the shocking fall of France to German forces early in 1940, the students in Kentucky recognize Great Britain's role fighting courageously against the Nazi occupation of western Europe. But, while the students pick up on the "special association" currently developing between Britain and the United States (John Bull and Uncle Sam), they enthusiastically preempt American entry into the Second World War by a good twelve months.[84]

In April 1929, a teacher from Lake City, Iowa, still felt able to claim in the pages of the *Classical Journal* that reading the Roman general's war commentaries in Latin would instill in fifteen-year-old American boys the welcome virtues of "industry, efficiency, ingenuity, fairness, cooperation and leadership."[85] In the lead-up to and throughout the Second World War, however, the pages of the professional magazines of classics teachers remain very quiet on the matter of the social and ethical utility of the set text for second-year Latin. A lone voice recommends reading the war commentaries for the acquisition of virtue—but the particular virtue that can be acquired from such reading is strictly military, the voice is that of a soldier, and the readers proposed are college students rather than schoolboys. In the *Classical Weekly* for 2 May 1938, Donald Armstrong (at the time a lieutenant colonel in the United States Army and soon to serve as a general in World War II) describes "a new approach to Caesar" that has recently been designed for use at George Washington University. There, he argues, it is possible to overcome the schoolboy's distaste for Latin syntax and vocabulary and the soldier's lack of access to the spirit and clarity of the original narrative by teaching Caesar's commentaries to university students—in Latin and accompanied throughout by a professional soldier's experienced perspective on strategy and tactics.[86] In Armstrong's view, such a course properly discloses to civilians "the individuality and character of one of the world's few universal geniuses" (1938, 222).[87] However, and more often, publications aimed at young people or concerned with their education denounce the Roman general and link his villainy to that perceived to reside in the dictators of modern Europe. Thus, in *Living Biographies of Famous Rulers* (1940), written by Henry and Dana Lee Thomas as "the fate of Europe and of the world is in the balance" (299), Julius Caesar is described as born into "a country which for several generations had been engaged in the business of national aggrandizement through international slaughter" (31). Caesar develops the ambition "to wade into immortality through rivers of human blood" (33). And his *Gallic Wars* are an "indecent story of his robberies and his murders" and an "obscene and insidious poison" against which American youth should be protected (35). Correspondingly, Mussolini is "a hoodlum shrouded in a halo" who is "consciously, and (as history has proved) unwisely, trying to become another Caesar. He has apparently forgotten Caesar's unfortunate end" (290, 292).[88]

THE UNFORTUNATE END OF SAWDUST CAESAR

The events of Sunday, 25 July 1943, injected new life into the Caesarean rhetoric of anti-Fascism, since they provided the mass media in the United States with a welcome opportunity to represent Fascism as farce and Mussolini as a ham actor by whom the nation had been only temporarily duped. The coup that forced Mussolini's resignation on that Sunday instantly saw the *Duce* dismissed in American news reports as a "sawdust Caesar." Picking up on George Seldes's earlier anti-Fascist meta-phor, and elaborating on its theatrical implications extensively, America's press, radio, and newsreels now claimed to have understood its implications all along. Thus, on the following day, the *New York Herald Tribune* ran an editorial under the headline "The Sawdust Runs Out," which began: "The sawdust Caesar has collapsed in the ruins of his pasteboard empire. . . . Mussolini is out; his failure, and Fascism's, manifest to the world." Similarly, an editorial in the *Washington Evening Post* (under the headline "Sawdust Caesar") concluded: "Mussolini strutted a full 20 years on the world's stage. He leaves it ignominiously, having expanded till he exploded."

Hearst's News of the Day for Tuesday, 27 July 1943, was perhaps the most elaborate and inventive in its use of the theatrical metaphor. Over montage shots of the *Duce* (which even included extracts from the earlier newsreel of 1934 where Mussolini had been eulogized as a "miracle man" and a "modern Caesar"), the voice of John B. Kennedy gleefully proclaimed:

> Curtains for the sawdust Caesar. Boastful Mussolini, biggest ham of the age, has played his last balcony scene, shed his gaudy uniforms of which he had more than a monkey has fleas. Pompous, posturing Duce, who betrayed every cause he ever espoused, has strutted for the last time on the world's stage. Fate has at last overtaken the superclown whose vainglorious ambition plunged humanity into an abyss of blood and terror . . . So it's goodbye and good riddance to boastful Benito and his balcony empire, spouting the glory of war and fascism to the bitter end. The supreme, the tragic clown of the ages.[89]

For American journalists, it was more comforting to admit that they had been deceived by theatrical propaganda than to admit they had approved of the Fascist regime. Identifying that regime as a "pasteboard empire," and Mussolini as its "sawdust Caesar," was a necessary rhetorical ploy for journalists to emerge from the war in Italy with their political virtue intact.[90]

In the 1930s and early 1940s, "Caesar" came to be deployed regularly in the United States as shorthand for gangsterism, demagoguery, and dictatorship. Yet, as Lieutenant Colonel Armstrong demonstrated in the pages of the *Classical Weekly*, some readers of the war commentaries still managed to extricate from them a man of almost unsullied military virtue—a general "who showed an ability in strategy and engineering, in leadership and logistics that entitles him to a place among the world's great captains."[91] What better way, then, to demonstrate that you are entitled to a place among the world's captains than to believe yourself to be a modern reincarnation of Julius Caesar? Biographers of General George S. Patton regularly observe that in his youth he read a vast array of military histories, biographies, and memoirs and believed himself to be a reembodiment of great soldiers of the past, Julius Caesar and Napoleon included. Patton could see himself in a past life marching on campaign in Gaul in command of the Tenth Legion. Arriving at Langres in 1917, during his first command of the United States Tank Corps, Patton discovered that he was already familiar with the layout of the French city and could identify exactly where the Roman general had originally encamped. On the road to Trier in March 1945, he could smell the coppery sweat of Caesar's Roman soldiers. And when, soon after, he bridged and crossed the river Rhine (as the Roman general had done before him), it was the act of reading the *Gallic War* that gave him his sense of historic achievement and, even, military superiority to one of "the world's greatest captains."[92]

CHAPTER 5

Totalitarianism

1945–1955

As part of the prerelease publicity for its film adaptation of Shakespeare's *Julius Caesar,* the Hollywood studio Metro-Goldwyn-Mayer distributed a synopsis to the press in February 1953 prefaced by the following declaration:

> One of Shakespeare's most highly dramatic, universally popular and widely-quoted works, "Julius Caesar" is also his most topically modern play. It deals with realities of which present generations throughout the world are well, and sadly, aware—the jealous lust for power which breeds dictatorship and erupts in political violence; the twin tyrannies of autocratic government and mob rule, and the intense human conflict of those caught between such opposing forces. Letting present-day connotations of this great drama speak for themselves, in terms of recent and contemporary world events, M-G-M brings Shakespeare's "Julius Caesar" to the screen in its traditional and classic form.[1]

The advertising rhetoric of modern connotations, global tragedy, the rise of dictatorships and urban violence, and the brutal tension between autocratic government and mob rule binds this screen adaptation of Shakespeare's *Julius Caesar* to the modern-dress version staged by Orson Welles in 1937. At a time of financial crisis for Hollywood studios, MGM was seeking prestige and box-office success with the Bard,[2] and not just any of the Bard's plays but the first usually studied in high school.[3] It also brought in a director know to advocate film as a mode of theater (Joseph L. Mankiewicz),[4] and the very producer (John Houseman) who had worked with Welles on the creation of the staged *Julius Caesar* that was by now legendary for the political topicality it had once forced on astounded American audiences. In the later months of 1953, managers of the cinemas across the United States that were showing the film found themselves the beneficiaries of an MGM campaign book designed to offer advice on how to maximize audiences and income. The campaign book referred explicitly to Houseman's involvement in Welles's innovative revival of *Julius Caesar* and worked the Houseman connection in order to stress topicality as a central strategy by which to sell the film to the general moviegoer (as opposed to special-interest groups like school or university students). Fed the slogan of topicality by theater managers, it is no surprise that many newspaper and magazine reviewers were driven to read out of the film the anti-Fascist political vision of the prewar theatrical production.[5]

Yet the declaration MGM distributed to the American press also distinguishes Houseman's postwar filmed Caesar from his prewar staged Caesar. The Hollywood studio's version of the Elizabethan tragedy is "traditional" because it refrains from any radical cutting, simplification, or reorganization of the original play script.[6] It is "classic" because it utilizes neither modern nor Elizabethan sets, costumes, and props, but ancient Roman ones. It lets present-day connotations "speak for themselves" through a mode of cinematic conservatism,[7] rather than impose on them a voice through a brutally modernist theatrical style. And it engages not just with the events of the recent world war, but also with those of the contemporary Cold War.

"OLD ROME IN THE USA"

At the close of the Second World War and into the early 1950s, perceptions of the contemporary social and political relevance of Julius Caesar for the United States (in his military conquests, his mode of government, and his assassination) were especially full of paradoxes and contradictions. The Roman past has continually been represented and consumed as America's future, especially at times of political or social crisis. The broad sweep of Roman history—the rise and decline of empire—has been understood as a warning of what might happen to the United States. More occasionally, when Roman history's imagined momentum has been overlooked and periods of achievement isolated from the rest, an ancient outcome becomes a celebration of or even an encouragement for a modern initiative.[8] Thus, in 1944, Will Durant published the third volume of his monumental project *The Story of Civilization,* which bore as its title *Caesar and Christ.* The narrative at this stage in his vast project stretched from Romulus to Constantine and contained in its preface the pronouncement that "there, in the struggle of Roman civilization against barbarism within and without, is our own struggle . . . and the desperate effort of the Mediterranean soul to maintain some freedom against a despotic state is an augury of our coming task. *De nobis fabula narratur:* Of ourselves this Roman story is told" (Durant 1944, viii). In the judgment of Durant, the study of antiquity is worthless unless it is then written up as a "living" drama and made, in some way, to illuminate contemporary life (vii). Consequently, his popular history is littered with contemporary phrasing better to offer to the broad readership he (and his New York publishers Simon and Schuster) sought an illumination from the distant past on the wartime present—an illumination that, the author cautions, is mainly "menacing" (viii). However, in the year that the Allied forces landed in northern and southern France, and Paris was liberated from German occupation, Durant's chapter on Julius Caesar from youthful rake to mature statesman complicates the history lesson. For this Julius Caesar is not cast as a European dictator like Hitler (or Mussolini before he was removed from power), nor are his assassins shaped like modern Americans tasked to free the Mediterranean from barbaric despotism.

In *Caesar and Christ,* the Roman general grasps power because he hopes to establish a progressive leadership in a state where the aristocracy is selfish and narrow, the mob corrupt and ill informed, and the republic dead. Caesar regards dictatorship as unavoidable, if only to "lessen the abuses, inequities, and destitution which had degraded democracy" (Durant 1944, 180). As statesman, he attempts to bring all Italy and the provinces into some form of representational government shared with his constitutional monarchy, and, for that proposed attempt, the author labels him "one of the ablest, bravest, fairest, and most enlightened men in all the sorry annals of politics" (193–94). Caesar is, in sum, "the most complete man that antiquity produced" (197). Shortly before Durant recounts the dictator's assassination at the hands of ungrateful "bluebloods" who refuse to admit that liberty has "fattened their purses" and that order requires the curtailment of their own freedom (194–95), he claims that the general had dreamt of the capture of Parthia and its riches as a means to end economic depression and ensure world peace (194). While the summation of Julius Caesar recalls the eulogistic verdict of the nineteenth-century classical scholar Theodor Mommsen, the description of Caesar's social and political ambitions exhibits tinges of a glowing, liberal outlook on the presidency of Franklin D. Roosevelt and the strategies of his New Deal.

In contrast, the review of *Caesar and Christ* published in the weekly news magazine *Time* on 27 November 1944 saw only menacing illumination of life abroad and at home in Durant's account of Roman history and, specifically, in the rise of dictatorship in republican Rome. Under the title "Old Rome and the U.S.A.," the review declared that the fate of Rome was haunting the United States at a time when it had been unable to solve its own domestic and international problems. In the opinion of the journalist writing for *Time*, the perceived corruption of the late republic and the villainy of Julius Caesar serve to critique both dictatorship in Europe and totalitarianism at home. Written just twenty days after Roosevelt had won an unprecedented fourth term of office, the review noted that, with the rise of Sulla and Caesar, Rome forgot the secret of checks-and-balances republican government and broke with the old tradition of limited terms of office. So, by implication, the current American president and commander in chief had become a Caesar rather than a Cincinnatus, loving power too much, rather than retiring from it once he had served his country's purpose. From this conservative political perspective, Caesar should remain wholly uncelebrated and act as a warning against present-day demagogues and populist military leaders, against the growth of the state and the loss of individual moral hardihood. In this manner, the article continued by Roman proxy the assaults on Roosevelt that had begun in the 1930s, with the launch of his federal program of economic intervention, work relief, and social reform. Such assaults had grown in force when FDR attempted to reorganize the judiciary in 1937 and when, in 1940, he became the first American president to be reelected to a third term of office.[9] Political opponents, bankers, businessmen, and newspaper editors sniped at Roosevelt as an elected king or a twentieth-century Caesar.[10] Toward the end of the 1950s (as we shall see in chapter 6), popular histories of ancient Rome would begin regularly to construct much more sustained, direct, and derogatory parallels between the twentieth-century presidents of the United States and Julius Caesar. Often starting with a glance back at FDR, the postwar presidents began to be paired with the Roman dictator for their dangerous acquisition of extraordinary executive powers, and for the damage they were thereby accused of inflicting on their country and its republican origins.[11] For the authors of such works, America's future lay not in a rosy dawn of progressive leadership and state intervention, but in the dark night of homegrown tyranny and a corresponding loss of individual responsibility and moral fiber.

A POSTWAR EXISTENTIALIST

From the 1930s until the postwar period, however, the dominant mode of coupling the present and the Roman past conjoined Julius Caesar with Europe's dictators, Mussolini in particular. The Fascist ideology of *romanità* construed Roman history not as a detached political prediction but as a connected visceral inheritance: a revolutionary Roman general legitimates, glorifies, and engenders his virile Italian descendant. Simultaneously and in contrast, the American rhetoric of anti-Fascism cast Roman history as theater of horror: a modern clown postures bombastically in the military costume of Caesar. In January 1948, the Pulitzer Prize winner Thornton Wilder published *The Ides of March,* a historical novel that sought (like Seldes's *Sawdust Caesar*) to break the intimate bond Fascism had manufactured between the Roman dictator and the *Duce,* but also, experimentally, to reconfigure Caesar anew for America and the postwar world.[12]

The Ides of March opens with a dedication to two friends of the author, the first of whom is identified as "Lauro de Bosis, Roman poet, who lost his life marshalling a resistance against the absolute power of Mussolini; his aircraft pursued by those of the Duce plunged into the Tyrrhenian Sea" (5).[13] Wilder had spent the three years of direct American military engagement in the Second World War as an officer in the United States Army Air Force Intelligence and had been deployed in the United States, North Africa, and Italy to investigate internal resistance to dictatorship such as that so openly displayed by de Bosis. The author's biography combined with the book's dedication invites readers to suppose, as they embark on a novel set in and around March 44 B.C.E., that it will retroject the downfall of the *Duce* into the Roman past. And, at the outset, Wilder declares that the anti-Fascist leaflets that the Italian-American poet and pilot had dropped on Rome were his models for the fictive "broadsides of conspiracy" or chain letters that, in the pages of the *Ides,* the poet Catullus disseminates against "the Tyranny under which our Republic groans" (188). What de Bosis had been to Mussolini now Wilder's Catullus will be to Caesar.[14] Nevertheless, in *The Ides of March,* Wilder's Caesar is a tragic hero who resembles Mussolini only insofar as he too is a dictator at Rome who is resisted and, finally, overthrown.[15] Instead of constructing the Roman general as racial ancestor of the *Duce,* this postwar novel attempts to rescue Caesar from his Fascist self.[16] It rejects the strident and simplistic "inheritance" model of Roman history embedded in the political discourse and public ritual of *romanità* and replaces it with the complex ambiguities of a historical "fantasia" (7) composed in both a philosophic and a dramatic key.

The radically innovative structure of *The Ides of March* challenges the historical certainties about Julius Caesar that had been constructed and disseminated within the culture of Italian Fascism. The novel consists entirely of a collection of invented historical documents ostensibly composed in the period from September 45 to March 44 B.C.E.—official pronouncements, entries in journals and commonplace books, private letters, graffiti, and secret reports—save for the insertion of a few genuine poems by Catullus and a concluding excerpt from Suetonius's account of the assassination of Julius Caesar. Narrative is eliminated along with the presumption of an omniscient narrator able to reveal the truth about the Roman past and its people; rendered in epistolary mode, history gains the immediacy, the personal point of view, and the fragmentation of one of Wilder's many plays.[17] As an avowed fantasia rather than a reconstruction, the novel parades its historical contortions as purposeful literary tricks: Wilder explicitly chooses to push the supposed affair between the poet Catullus and the aristocrat Clodia, along with her brother's profanation of the rites of the Bona Dea, into the 40s B.C.E. in order for those events to collide with Caesar's assassination and to allow the novel's central character to ruminate in private correspondence, during the months leading to his death, on the nature of poetry and passion, religious belief and moral hypocrisy.[18] Furthermore, the novel's disparate documents are "authored" by a variety of individuals (from Clodia and Catullus to Cleopatra, Brutus, Caesar himself, and his wife's maid) and collated into four sections. Each of the sections in turn contains and expands the time frame of the one before, starting with just the month of September 45 B.C.E. and ending with the fullest phase, from August 45 to mid-March 44. Readers are thus required to crisscross the period preceding Caesar's assassination again and again, taking in ever-increasing blocks of time and fresh perspectives on (or from) the Roman dictator.[19] The combination of repetition and variation works to reveal history, and the life of Julius Caesar in particular, as multifocal, provisional, and always incomplete.[20]

Between them, the documents collated in the four sections of *The*

Ides of March also give shape to many Caesars or, at least, to multiple aspects of Caesar.[21] The novel's absolute ruler and those who interact with him in the months before his death do not only comment on issues of government but also reflect on love, poetry, religious belief, morality, free will, and destiny. Early on in the novel, for example, Julius Caesar speculates in a private letter to Turrinus (his reclusive friend and a disabled war veteran) on the many causes of Clodia's flagrant rejection of traditional Roman morality:

> Another excuse could be found for her and for those other women of her generation whose disorders are similarly calling attention to them. They were born into the great houses of wealth and privilege and were brought up in that atmosphere of noble sentiments and unceasing moralizing which we are now calling "the Old Roman way". The mothers of these girls were in many cases great women, but they had developed a series of qualities they could not transmit. . . . Their daughters, the more intelligent ones, on growing older became aware of this; they felt they had been lied to and they promptly flung themselves into a public demonstration of their liberation from hypocrisy. Imprisonment of the body is bitter; imprisonment of the mind is worse. (Document III, "Caesar's Journal-Letter to Lucius Mamilius Turrinus on the Island of Capri," *Ides*, 19)

Outside the novel, its author explains elsewhere how he had written this critique of sexual mores in a contemporary American key, since he identified Clodia with the scandalous actress and star Tallulah Bankhead, who, "brought up in the lying myths of Southern gentry," later "broke loose with a yell."[22] Such contemplative journal entries in *The Ides of March,* composed in the first person by Wilder's Caesar, are severely at odds with the dispassionate, third-person descriptions of military strategy and tactics in the Roman general's own war commentaries, and with the public orations of Shakespeare's Roman play. In its title, the novel echoes the warning delivered to the dictator by Shakespeare's soothsayer to "beware the Ides of March" (*JC* 1.2.18), yet the Elizabethan tragedy had given neither monologue nor interiority to its frail statesman.[23] Nor does Wilder's Caesar write the imperialist rhetoric of Mediterranean expansion mouthed by Fascism's Giulio Cesare. Instead the documents in the *Ides* reveal a ruler full of anxious introspection, concerned for the unpredictable vicissitudes of human existence.

Even in matters of politics and government, Thornton Wilder's Caesar is wholly disengaged from the point of view and the self-belief that had been imposed on Mussolini's *dux*. In *The Ides of March,* Julius Caesar rules Rome because (at least in his view) only he is sufficiently resolute to take on the heavy responsibilities such rule requires. Yet, in accepting the loneliness, the contingency, and the finitude of his existence as dictator at Rome, the novel's suffering Caesar stands revealed as an embodiment and extreme case of the dreadful condition of every human in an indifferent or hostile universe.[24] Wilder's autocrat has adopted the modes of thinking of an existentialist—a philosophical stance that had grown out of the French resistance and become especially fashionable among American intellectuals in the immediate postwar period.[25] The structure of the novel then presents the slow disintegration of this existentialist's Roman world. Each of the novel's first three sections ends with a calamity for Caesar that foreshadows his last: attempted assassination as he heads to a dinner party hosted by Clodia; erotic betrayal when he finds his beloved Cleopatra in the arms of Mark Antony; public humiliation as a Supreme Pontiff forced to deal with religious profanations.[26] Moreover, Wilder's Caesar (as well as his readers) knows that he is going to die, and as his inevitable death approaches he finds himself beset by philosophical crisis, as he explains in his private correspondence:

> These last weeks, not my dream, but my waking state has been the contemplation of futility and the collapse of all belief. Oh, worse than that: my dead call to me in mockery from their grave-clothes and generations still unborn cry out, asking to be spared the clownish parade of a mortal life. Yet even in my last bitterness I cannot disavow the memory of bliss.
>
> Life, life has this mystery that we dare not say the last word about it, that it is good or bad, that it is senseless, or that it is ordered. . . . This "life" in which we move has no color and it gives no sign. As you once said: the universe is not aware that we are here. (Document LXVII, "Caesar's Journal-Letter to Lucius Mamilius Turrinus on the Island of Capri," *Ides,* 206)

The tragedy of Wilder's postwar Caesar is that, for all his commitment to action, he dies with his work unfinished. And, in the end, he confesses himself unsure whether existence really is explicable completely in human terms. Is love instinct or passion? Is his epilepsy a physical disorder or spiritual revelation? Has he shaped Rome or merely been the instrument of its destiny?[27] For those who had only recently survived a second world war and witnessed the destructiveness of the atomic bomb, a crisis-ridden, doubting Caesar might have seemed entirely appropriate and instructive for their times.

Within a month of its publication early in 1948, *The Ides of March* had sold nearly fifty thousand copies in the United States, but its commercial success was only fleeting. It disappeared from best-seller lists just as quickly as it had arrived.[28] Although Wilder's novel depicts a tragic Caesar full of anguish and doubt, reviewers in the main saw only the dangerous reemergence of a flawless superman or *Übermensch*.[29] In newspaper and magazine articles, they often expressed puzzlement or discomfort over this step back to the heroization of dictatorship that had been manifest in earlier decades. The critic for the *New York Times* (22 February 1948) remarked with ironic restraint: "At the moment dictators are not very popular in the parts of the world Mr. Wilder knows best. People who are politically conscious may start looking for a cipher in this admiring portrait of a despot and may wonder what Mr. Wilder is up to."[30] Just a matter of weeks after the publication of Wilder's *The Ides of March* and its subsequent review in the *New York Times*, "the politically conscious" would hear President Harry Truman reinforce his declaration of the Truman Doctrine, which, a year earlier, had initiated the Cold War and cast the United States as the savior of the free world from Communist subversion or aggression.[31] Now, in March 1948, the president declared that the Soviet Union and its agents had destroyed the democratic independence of numerous nations in Eastern and Central Europe, including most recently the Republic of Czechoslovakia. With Mussolini and Hitler only recently removed from power in Europe, and Stalin still exercising supreme authority in and beyond the Soviet Union, many Americans could not warm to Wilder's Caesar as a humane dictator who presides with superhuman skill and charm over a society of malcontents.[32]

HERO OF THE NEW MEDIA

In contrast, in 1949 great admiration was expressed by journalists for a revival of Shakespeare's *Julius Caesar* that had been adapted for broadcast on television and visibly reunited the Roman general with his Fascist self. This revival was shaped by the early organization of television, as the new medium borrowed from radio the format of "quality" drama and developed into another hearth around which the postwar, newly insular family could gather.[33] In that year less than 10 percent of Americans had a television in their homes, and television programs were targeted at the only audience who could afford the relatively expensive sets—namely the affluent.[34] Thus the Elizabethan tragedy, produced by Worthington Miner for the Columbia Broadcasting System (CBS), appeared within the anthology series *Studio One* (1948–58), which presented a different televisual drama each week based on "classic" plays or novels.[35] These one-hour live-action performances were broadcast from New York City on Sunday evenings in three acts, interleaved with two commercial breaks advertising upmarket goods manufactured by the sponsor, Westinghouse. Miner's version of *Julius Caesar* was broadcast on 6 March 1949 and was applauded afterward for its innovative exploration of the young medium—together (critics declared) the Roman general, the Bard, and the television producer had raised the new technology of television to the status of art.[36]

Following the modernist style and the left-liberal spirit of the celebrated modern-dress staging by Orson Welles, Worthington Miner offered in his representation of Caesar's assassination a critique of the power of the state and the moral failure of many of its opponents.[37] His Caesar is Fascistic in uniform and gesture; his Cassius seduces Brutus into the conspiracy as the television camera moves relentlessly and disturbingly right into his conniving eyes; his Mark Antony mouths noble sentiments about dead Brutus, but the camera gives the lie to his words by closing in on his foot kicking the corpse into the street. In a review published in the *New York Times* (13 March 1949), Jack Gould (the paper's theater and radio critic) commented that Miner, like Welles, had edited Shakespeare's text into "a swiftly moving documentary on revolution." Yet, in labeling the Roman republican conspiracy and assassination a failed "revolution" and an ironic "implementation of idealism by violence," Gould also echoes the slogans of the ideological crusade that the United States government had launched in recent months against the Soviet Union. In the course of 1948 and early 1949, while Americans witnessed newsreel footage of the brutality attending the Communist coup in Czechoslovakia and the formation of the Soviet bloc in Eastern Europe, congressional committees fed to the press a menacing depiction of world Communism: its aim is world revolution; its means is violence; its driving force is the Soviet Union.[38] Thus, for the critic of the *New York Times,* all the innovations of the first televisual Caesar (the use of depth of field, mobile camera close-ups, movement, and lighting) worked to thrust American viewers abroad into the very turmoil of ancient Rome. Only at the end of the broadcast might they remember that they were in fact in their own homes—and, by implication, removed by both time and space from violent revolution, safe in the United States of America. The modernization of Shakespeare's Roman tragedy, in this more conservative rendition, offers an assault on only foreign, not domestic, politics.

The Roman general and his English Bard provided cultural legitimacy and aesthetic weight not only for the fledgling medium of American television but also for American comic books. On 9 March 1950, the *New York Times* carried an announcement that the tragedies of Shakespeare were about to become a "must" read for millions of comic-book fans.[39] Shakespeare had just appeared for the first time in comic-book format, and *Julius Caesar* was the first of his plays to have been chosen for abridgment into forty-eight pages of comic strip.[40] After the launch of the comic book in the 1930s (filled with miscellaneous stories of western adventure, romance, horror, comedy, or law and order), and the debut at the end of the decade of sustained narratives about superheroes (like Superman, Batman, and Captain Marvel), the president of the Gilberton publishing company in New York, Albert L. Kanter, developed the unique concept of producing comic-book versions of literary masterpieces, starting, in 1941, with *The Three Musketeers*. Carefully exploiting as sources the canon of great works of English literature in use at American high schools and colleges, or works familiar from their transformation into Hollywood films, *Classic Comics* (or *Classics Illustrated,* as the series was known from 1947) came to occupy a significant niche in the comic-book market, which, by the end of the 1940s, was selling sixty million copies per month from corner stores and newsstands across the United States.[41] From February 1950, readers could now buy for fifteen cents the *Classics Illustrated* adaptation of Shakespeare's *Julius Caesar* (and, for their money, also read within the pages of the same comic a much-abbreviated version of a famous opera, the story of a heroic dog and a pioneer of science, and the biography of the Elizabethan playwright as that edition's special author).[42] It would be followed in 1956 by *Caesar's Conquests*—a comic-strip abridgment of that other key text for the circulation of Julius Caesar in American culture, the Roman general's own commentaries on the Gallic War.[43]

Shakespeare and Caesar together lent legitimacy and integrity to a comic-book series that marked itself out as quite distinct from the other 150 or so titles then on the market. Each *Classics Illustrated* adaptation, including *Julius Caesar* as number 68 in the series, was sold according to the publishing pattern of book clubs. Unlike ephemeral magazines, the individual issues did not expire but were regularly reprinted and readvertised for purchase within later issues.[44] Together Shakespeare and Caesar could also appear to reinforce the promise of personal improvement suggested by this style of publication. Like the Caesar of silent cinema's moving images, comic-strip Caesar offered "uplift" to the masses.[45] Within the price range of young people, and ostensibly targeted at a juvenile readership, the *Classics Illustrated* comic books were presented by their New York publisher as a democratization of high culture and as a gateway through which its young readers could progress to mature literature and cultural citizenship. The publisher neglected to note, however, that a significant proportion of the readership for the *Classics Illustrated* Caesar was already adult and that young people were just as likely to substitute a comic book for their high-school set text as the other way around.[46]

In a competitive market for comic books dominated by boys' adventure fiction, the story of the Roman dictator's assassination could—if retold appropriately—even attract fans of that genre to the *Classics Illustrated* series. The events were familiar from the high-school curriculum, and they combined conspiracy, murder, battle, and suicide (and only the smallest of roles for romance and women) with colorful historical locations.[47] The interpretative strategies that *Classics Illustrated* adopted thus to market its comic-strip Caesar are disclosed by the way in which the edition condenses and accelerates its Shakespearean source text and substitutes explanatory captions, by the visual composition of its panels and speech balloons, and even by its color schemes.[48] Within the first few pages of the comic book, the cast of this abridged *Julius Caesar* are gathered together (fig. 22). At the center of the opening panel cluster emblems of empire, above them and to the right appears the title character, togate, garlanded, and clutching his staff of imperial power. The caption block beneath operates as a kind of objective dramatic prologue, to be distinguished from the subjective speech-balloons that issue from characters. At the outset, it identifies Caesar as a brilliant and popular general, victorious in wars abroad, returning home to wild acclaim.[49] This triumphant depiction carries allusions to the ticker-tape parade through the streets of New York held in June 1945, when millions of spectators celebrated the return to the United States of General Dwight Eisenhower, Supreme Commander of the Allied Forces and war hero victorious in Europe.[50] The plotline of a home-coming general brought down because of his political strength and popularity also presages and, in the comic-book's reprints of 1951 and 1953, overlaps with the biography of General Douglas MacArthur. After extraordinary victories in the Pacific campaigns of World War II, proconsular rule over the defeated Japanese, supreme command of the United Nations forces engaged in a counteroffensive against the North Korean invasion of South Korea, and belligerent advocacy of unlimited war against Communist China, MacArthur (known to some of his biographers as

FIGURE 22. The cast of characters for *Julius Caesar, Classics Illustrated*, no. 68 (February 1950). ©2010 First Classics Inc. All Rights Reserved. By permission of Jack Lake Productions Inc.

"American Caesar")[51] returned to a ticker-tape parade and a tumultuous reception in Congress in April 1951, although, by then, he had already been relieved of all his commands for insubordination and was soon to lose popular support as well.

Simultaneously, the stern, chisel-jawed features of the comic-strip Caesar in *Classics Illustrated* also cast him in the same mold as the more popular comic-book action heroes of the adventure-fiction genre, while, on his side of the panel and below him, Mark Antony's leopard-skin tunic and exposed muscular physique position him closer to the jungle and Tarzan than to the Roman rituals of the Lupercal. On the left of the panel, Brutus retains the handsome, chiseled features of the patriotic hero he had traditionally been on the American stage,[52] but already we see that he has been corrupted into the assassination plot by the wily Cassius, since they appear encircled together with Cassius pressing over Brutus's right shoulder. The brutal and scowling features of Cassius, Casca, and Cinna, depicted one above the other, reconstruct the assassins as typical comic-book villains, a depiction naturalized by increasing American anxiety during the early years of the Cold War about Communist expansion in Europe and Asia *and* Communist conspiracy at home.[53] From 1947 and the declaration of the Truman Doctrine, romance and anti-Communism had become central themes within the broader comic-book industry, not least because publishers could exploit such comic-strip plots to construct for their products a socially conscientious, even a patriotic, image. The exciting adventures of American soldiers and secret agents fighting Communists were targeted at boys; girls were offered the domestic pleasure of securing hearth and home for their heroes' return.[54] In the opening panel of the *Classics Illustrated* abridgment of Shakespeare's Roman play, Calpurnia and Portia figure at bottom left to suggest for female readers (however misleadingly) that the ensuing narrative contains a significant romantic dimension, while, at top right, Octavius Caesar, Julius Caesar, and Mark Antony between them embody a still militant and muscular postwar American masculinity now under threat from wily Communist conspirators.[55]

Within the condensed comic-strip version of Shakespeare's *Julius Caesar,* the tribunes only briefly reproach the plebeians for taking a holiday from their work to see the returning general, and they do not object, as they do in Shakespeare's play: "Wherefore rejoice?" (*J.C.* 1.1.32). The assassination is visualized as a savage and cowardly attack by Casca from behind our hero, aided by a cluster of swords that rise up to meet his from the bottom of the page. Noble Brutus is allocated one page of panels to explain briefly to the citizens, as they clamor for reasons for Caesar's murder, that he loved Rome more. Mark Antony, in contrast, is awarded three pages and three expansive speech-balloons in which to deliver part of the celebrated "Friends, Romans, countrymen" oration over "the piteous spectacle" of Caesar's corpse (*JC* 3.2). Some of the ethical complexity of the play is momentarily retained, as a caption provided to accompany scenes of rioting explains that "Antony made no effort to stop the frenzied mob that screamed for vengeance."

FIGURE 23. The cover of *Julius Caesar, Classics Illustrated*, no. 68 (February 1950). ©2010 First Classics Inc. All Rights Reserved. By permission of Jack Lake Productions Inc.

But then the narrative races away to the more satisfying terrain of battle action and the courageous suicide of soldiers in defeat.

Intriguingly, the line drawing designed by Henry C. Kiefer for the cover of this first Shakespearean *Classics Illustrated* does not correspond exactly to any panel contained therein (fig. 23). Here Antony is frozen imposingly in the foreground at the moment that he reveals the body of Julius Caesar to the Roman citizenry, whose tiny faces are crowded together in the distance.[56] There is no suggestion here that his action constitutes a manipulation of the mob: he is connected loyally to Caesar by virtue of their shared color-coding of strong reds (Caesar's roses and Antony's tunic), greens (Caesar's wreath and Antony's toga), and purples (Caesar's shroud and the mantle Antony pulls away from Caesar's corpse); the people are both tied to them by their pastel echoes of those colors and caught in neat array behind Caesar's body and beneath his heir's outstretched arm. Comic-book covers constitute a key visual condensation; they are designed simultaneously to catch the reader's eye, suggest content, and display editorial direction.[57] Here, it has been argued, *Classics Illustrated* plays cleverly with one of the thematics of Shakespeare's *Julius Caesar*—the relationship between elite patrician culture and a mass plebeian audience—to defend its own publishing mission.[58] Published in February 1950, this comic-book Caesar appeared just as mass culture became the focus of a debate in the United States that would develop by the mid-1950s into a widespread moral panic about the vulnerability of its youngest consumers. The comic-book form in particular was thought to nurture delinquency among juvenile readers. *Classics Illustrated* was not immune from such criticism, since the series appeared to debase texts as well as young people by converting sophisticated narratives incongruously into comic strips, poetry into speech balloons, the high into the low.[59] So now on the front cover of its sixty-eighth edition, we see the purpose of *Classics Illustrated*—to present literary masterpieces to the masses—embodied, justified, and elevated in the manly gesture of Mark Antony displaying dead Caesar to the people. Even the yellow color of his headband and the border of his tunic replicate the background on which is printed the title *Classics Illustrated*. Strategies such as these clearly met with considerable success, because (according to a history of the *Classics Illustrated* comic books) over time tens of thousands of American high schools bulk bought copies of those editions pertaining to their English set texts for use by less able students as aids to reading the original masterpieces.[60]

HOLLYWOOD'S TOTALITARIAN ROME

In the United States in the early 1950s, the twin pressures of pertinent contemporary events and the strategies of production, distribution, and consumption of popular media added further twists to the Roman tale of conspiracy and the death of a dictator. Like the comic-strip version of Shakespeare's *Julius Caesar* before it, Hollywood's moving-image version appeared to offer consumers liberation from the difficulty, the distaste, and even the physical discomfort of having to read a double dose of Caesar at school. On being invited by an MGM songwriter to see his studio's new film at the small but prestigious Booth Theater in New York, the Broadway theater publicist Richard Maney wrote about his own reaction in the *New York Times* the next day with evident pleasure in being able to repeat the errors of his adolescent education in Latin:

> His airy proposal all but shattered me. For Julius Caesar was the scourge of my youth, the pontifex maximus who poisoned my childhood. When just able to distinguish between puer and puella I had been pitchforked into Caesar's Commentaries. No sooner had I bludgeoned my way through "Omnis Gallia in partes tres devisa est," than I ran headlong into a semantic ambush. Everything turned black. For years my dreams were haunted by the brawl between the Gerunds and the Gerundives, the treachery of the Helvitii, the intrigue of the Ablatives and the Datives, the flight of the Nervii, the pursuit of the Usipates, the outlandish conduct of the Getorix boys, Orsin and Vercin. Too late I came upon a pony which unraveled this Latin foul-up.
>
> While still convalescing from the Commentaries, I was shuffled into Shakespeare, shortly learned to my horror that he had plundered Plutarch to further demoralize the schoolboys of the nation. Lives there a man who has not been threatened with the bastinado should he fail to memorize Antony's harangue over Caesar's bier? The anguish experienced in learning Antony's tirade was capped by the ordeal of reciting it to an audience of fellow martyrs. This was piling Helion on Ossa, if I may lapse into the Odyssey. (*New York Times,* 20 September 1953)

Freed from the classroom and projected onto a New York cinema screen, the story of Julius Caesar—at least for this theater publicist—at last possessed the crystal clarity and the relevance of newspaper headlines.

One crucial stylistic device MGM's *Julius Caesar* deployed to give its Roman-dress adaptation of Shakespeare a 1950s political feel was its use of black-and-white film stock. In an era of Technicolor superspectacles (such as the studio's *Quo Vadis* two years earlier), reviewers greeted with approval the "starkly appropriate blacks and whites and grays" of the photography.[61] Explanation for this choice was provided repeatedly by the producer John Houseman in studio publicity, press interviews, and magazine and journal articles. In *Films in Review* (April 1953), the producer claimed most fulsomely to associate color with shimmer, grandeur, and "irrelevant and spectacular show," and monochrome with intensity, simplicity, tragedy, and, most important of all, political analogy:

> *Julius Caesar,* when effectually performed before modern audiences, enjoys one clear advantage over most classic plays: the almost automatic emotion which this drama of political strife engenders in audiences, all of whom, in their time, directly or indirectly, by remote or immediate experience, have witnessed and suffered from analogous evils of political strife, demagoguery and mass violence. It was for us to encourage this empathy.

   While never deliberately exploiting the historic parallels, there were certain emotional patterns arising from political events of the immediate past that we were prepared to evoke—Hitler, Mussolini and Ciano at the Brenner Pass; the assemblage at Munich; Stalin and Ribbentrop signing the Pact; and similar smiling conference-table friendships that soon ripened into violence and death. Also Hitler at Nuremberg and Compiegne and later in the Berlin rubble; Mussolini on his balcony with that same docile mob massed below which later watched him hanging by his feet, dead. These sights are as much a part of our contemporary consciousness—in the *black and white* of newsreel and TV screens—as, to Elizabethan audiences, were the personal and political conflicts and tragedies of Essex, Bacon, Leicester and the Cecils. (185)[62]

For Houseman, as for subsequent commentators, black-and-white photography gave to filmed *Julius Caesar* the texture of newsreel or documentary footage on European dictatorships (especially the rise and the fall of Mussolini and Hitler). And to sustain the impression of breaking such a news story (in imitation of many high-school classroom assignments highlighting the relevance of Shakespeare's play),[63] the MGM studio published a mock newspaper called the *Daily Chariot*. Over a still of Louis Calhern as the mortally wounded Roman leader, the mock paper carried the following as its banner headline for 16 March 44 B.C.E.: "CAESAR SLAIN! Brutus, Cassius Head Plot In Stabbing of Dictator; Mobs Loot City, Many Die."

   Yet, from its inception, MGM's *Julius Caesar* was presented by its makers not just as an evocation in black and white of the fallen dictatorships of Italy and Germany, but also—and more urgently—as a commentary on the menacing continuation of Communist dictatorship in the Soviet Union.[64] In the preview program, the head of production, Dore Schary, introduced the screen adaptation in the following terms: "An audience which has witnessed the atrocities committed by modern police states in Germany, Italy and Russia finds nothing obscure about the playwright's observation that 'The abuse of greatness is when it disjoins remorse from power'. Shakespeare's lines on Roman tyranny, political ambition and the corruption bred by absolute power ring familiarly true today. They are as topical as yesterday's headlines." "Yesterday's headlines" had largely been concerned with neither Mussolini nor Hitler, but with Joseph Stalin—rumors of his physical decline and of conspiracies against him, propositions that he be assassinated, and in March 1953 (just three months before the film's American premiere) joyous confirmation of his death.[65] MGM's *Julius Caesar* is thus composed in a prophetic key, warning like Shakespeare's soothsayer that dictators are destined (and deserve) to die.

From the outset, Hollywood's monochrome Caesar is thus cast in a very different light from the comic-strip conquering hero who had graced the pages of *Classics Illustrated* three years earlier. Like the comic book, the film adaptation of Shakespeare's Roman tragedy opens with a form of dramatic prologue—the cinematic version is laid out over an imperial eagle embroidered on dark cloth that flutters and fills the film frame forebodingly. Laying claim to the historical authority of Plutarch's biography, the titles explain to spectators that the Roman general is returning from civil (not foreign) war, and that he has become "odious to moderate men" for the extravagance of his powers (not the object of jealousy for his political strength and popularity, as stated in the comic book's initial caption block).[66] Whereas the comic-book abridgment skips rapidly over Shakespeare's act 1, scene 1, MGM's screen adaptation makes considerable business out of the tribunes' protest that Caesar's triumph is paved with Roman blood and out of their attempt to "disrobe" his statuary of any honorific ornaments. Under the direction of Mankiewicz, the scene ends with the soaring wings of the dictator not yet plucked of their "growing feathers" (*JC* 1.1.72), for the tribunes are caught and marched off by Roman soldiers who bear their leader's spread-winged eagle insignia on their cloaks. The subsequent appearance of the dictator starts with a high-angled camera shot that captures the grand scale of the Lupercal ceremony, here conceived as a demonstration of people's susceptibility to demagoguery (or, as Shakespeare has the tribune Flavius put it, their containment through "servile fearfulness," *JC* 1.1.75). Neatly arrayed crowds cheer and salute as they are bisected by a long procession that enters from the bottom right of the screen and advances up and back through the monumental archways of a garlanded and bannered stadium (anachronistically replicating the structures of the imperial Colosseum). Trumpeters, petal throwers, fasces- and standard-bearers, helmeted and dark-cloaked soldiers all precede Caesar and his togate companions to the accompaniment of martial music (fig. 24). The camera then swoops down to focus in on the dictator and the first words of act 1, scene 2 of Shakespeare's play, while behind him we now see again a neat row of eagles embroidered across the cloaks of his military escort.[67] The colossal statuary and monumental architecture, the military pomp and hyperbolic adulation, the cult of personality, and the arrests and purges displayed in these opening sequences of Mankiewicz's *Julius Caesar* all constitute characteristics common to the European dictatorships of the 1930s and 1940s in Italy, Germany, and Russia.[68] But, in the eyes of contemporary specta-

FIGURE 24. Caesar arrives for the ceremony of the Lupercal, in MGM's *Julius Caesar* (1953). Courtesy of the Academy of Motion Picture Arts and Sciences, Margaret Herrick Library.

tors, the revelation in the remainder of the Lupercal scene of the physical frailty of the aged leader, a nascent conspiracy against him, and his own concern at the dangerous men who surround him would have tied the Roman dictator more closely to Stalin and the present tense of 1953.[69]

The technical adviser to the MGM film, Pier Maria Pasinetti, emphasized in many publications that he had drawn on his Italian origins and education (rather than expert knowledge of ancient history or archaeology) to help shape the reconstruction of ancient Rome on screen as a living, modern Italian city.[70] Yet, in the background notes he provided for the studio, he commented that the spectacle of Caesar's public appearances would recall for cinema audiences pictures of modern big shots in nonmilitary functions, such as the head of a totalitarian state, going to the laying of a cornerstone surrounded by bodyguards, hierarchs, and clients.[71] Pasinetti (a Venetian novelist and lecturer in the Italian Department at UCLA) declared himself to be more interested in advising on film sets, objects, and properties than on Roman political systems; nevertheless his choice of the phrase "head of a totalitarian state" discloses a broader ideological shift that had taken place in both the scholarly understanding and the popular use of Julius Caesar in postwar American culture.

One expert source Pasinetti stated that he drew on to help the MGM film studio reconstruct ancient Rome was the book *Party Politics in the Age of Caesar* (Berkeley, 1949) written by Professor Emeritus of Latin at Bryn Mawr College and ex-president of the American Philological Association Lily Ross Taylor.[72] In her seminal study, Taylor argued that the political struggles of the last years of the Roman republic showed remarkable parallels with those of the present: "Rival parties were striving by the use of arms for domination, and victory in the strife was to lead to the supremacy of a single party and the identification of that party under a totalitarian system with the whole state" (1949, 1). It was Julius Caesar who first attempted, and Augustus who succeeded, in reshaping the Roman republic and its personal parties of nobles and their clients into a single totalitarian party made up of all the citizens united in loyalty to their imperial ruler. At least that is the development Taylor describes, while claiming that it had never been properly understood until historians witnessed for themselves the modern domination of a leader and a party that became identified with the whole state (48–49, 162).

The American historian is here referring to European classical scholars of the 1930s who had interpreted the political conflicts of the late Roman republic in the light of National Socialism.[73] Yet, subsequently, the terminology of "totalitarianism" was brought into postwar political theory (most notably by Hannah Arendt) to describe both National Socialism and Stalinism, and to distinguish them more acutely from self-proclaimed "dictatorships" as unprecedented and more extreme twentieth-century modes of government involving a monolithic, highly policed state, a cult of the leader, a dogmatically held and imposed ideology including aspiration to world domination, permanent revolution, and a mass movement driven by perpetual terror.[74] As the Cold War continued and intensified, Nazi Germany and the Stalinist Soviet Union were frequently conflated as totalitarian regimes in academic and political discourse in order to place them polemically in opposition to the liberal, constitutional governments of the West. And in the Cold War culture of the United States, the concept of totalitarianism was then regularly and widely exploited to set the supposedly threatening and contagious Communist ideology of the Soviet Union against the freedoms and the democracy that were righteously portrayed as inherent in the American way of life.[75] Magazines such as *Life* supported the cultural campaign orchestrated by the U.S. government simultaneously to celebrate American freedom and to denounce Soviet Communism as subversive, conspiratorial, fraudulent, and brutal.[76] And a year after the release and distribution of MGM's *Julius Caesar,* the magazine also publicized further academic endorsement for the new interpretation of the Roman dictator as the instigator in the past of a turn to Soviet-style totalitarian government. A lengthy article in *Life* for 29 November 1954, on the publication of the final volumes of the monumental and sweeping *Study of History* by Arnold Toynbee, noted that, by virtue of the parallels the British scholar saw between phases of the Roman past and the West's present, "Julius Caesar and Josef Stalin are therefore, in one sense, contemporaries" (94).[77] Earlier that month, in an editorial on the completion of Toynbee's best-selling work and his extraordinary standing in America as "a scholar-prophet," *Life* presented the current phase of Western civilization alarmingly as at the edge of breakdown and in danger of replacement by a universal state like that introduced in the past at Rome.[78] Representing Caesar's Rome as totalitarian on screen in 1953 could thus claim the historical authority of current classical scholarship and the patriotism of the United States' anti-Communist cultural crusade.[79]

It was also *Life* magazine that forewarned American spectators very effectively to view MGM's reconstruction of Julius Caesar's Rome in the light of Soviet totalitarianism. The issue for 20 April 1953 carried on its cover a photograph of the actor Marlon Brando costumed as Mark Antony. Toward the back of the magazine, a series of captions printed next to stills from Mankiewicz's forthcoming adaptation of Shakespeare labeled its Roman characters according to the terminology of anti-Communism: the conspirators are "patriots"; Caesar and Antony are "dictator and disciple" (35–39). Only an advertisement for the security that family life insurance can provide separates the photographic preview from an article written by an ex-general of the NKVD (a Soviet secret police agency) describing how Stalin had employed the agency to charge, try, and execute his political enemies but, once his power was consolidated, removed them also as witnesses to his abuse of power. The article "Stalin's Secret Part III" (143–59) literally forms an intertext with the illustrations of the Hollywood film, and its subheading "He kills his friends, sets children adrift" appears on the front cover just above and to the right of Brando-as-Antony.

For many reviewers, MGM's *Julius Caesar,* on its release, fulfilled the patriotic, anti-Communist promise *Life* magazine had suggested for it. In particular, led by the pronouncements of the producer John Houseman himself,[80] attention was paid to the inventive manipulation of the camera in the film's version of the Forum sequence—act 3, scene 2 of Shakespeare's tragedy. The critic for the *New York Herald Tribune* (n.d.) even wrote admiringly of this bold use of the medium that "the bridegroom of poetry is propelled more forcibly toward the altar of the camera." Here, in the crucial Forum sequence, cinematography clearly works to fix the character of Mark Antony as an unscrupulous demagogue. As Brutus attempts, on the steps outside the Capitol, to render to the crowd "public reasons" for Caesar's death (*JC* 3.2.7–8), the camera focuses in on a woman whose terrified cry silences him. The camera then looks with him back and up higher at the cause of this howl: Mark Antony has emerged from within carrying the corpse hidden beneath its mantle, which, as Caesar's heir, he will soon utilize so shrewdly to stir the mob to violent revenge (fig. 25). The vertical composition on the steep steps and the fluidity of the camera movement looking up at Antony and down at Brutus disclose how the honorable conspirator has been tragically caught, in the producer's own terms, between "the twin tyrannies of totalitarian government and mob rule."[81]

When Brando, as Antony, begins the celebrated "Friends, Romans, countrymen" speech, the camera often looks down at the mob from his point of view positioned up high, or up at him from the point of view of the mob positioned down below, suggesting through his spatial dominance the skill of Caesar's successor at choreographing the masses. The camera also cuts intimately "from Marlon Brando, looking like a grieving young eagle, to the mirror-faces of the rabble reflecting each flash of indignation in Mark Antony's cleverly worded plea for vengeance" (*New York Herald Tribune,* n.d.). Most pointedly of all, at two moments in his rousing speech for retaliation against the assassins of Caesar, the camera focuses in on Antony's face when his back is turned from the crowd of Roman citizens, and thus reveals his expression exclusively to the film's spectators. In the first case, the camera discloses his calculating look when Antony has momentarily paused in his funeral oration, as if overwhelmed with grief. In the second, and closing the long Forum sequence, the camera fills the screen with the smirk of the departing Antony as behind and far below him tiny citizens, transformed into the gullible victims of a cunning demagogue, begin to loot and wreck the city.[82] Similarly, the proscription scene that follows, in

FIGURE 25. Antony emerges from the Capitol with the body of Caesar, in MGM's *Julius Caesar* (1953). Courtesy of the Academy of Motion Picture Arts and Sciences, Margaret Herrick Library.

which Antony, Octavius, and Lepidus condemn even their relatives to death (act 4, scene 1 of the Elizabethan drama), could be understood to offer to American spectators an intimate glimpse set in the Roman past of the multiple purges and executions that they knew to be "Stalin's secret."[83] At the end of the scene, the Hollywood director appends to Shakespeare's script a set of movements for Antony, now silent and alone after the departure of his allies. He gazes out over a balcony at the city of Rome, stretches with proprietary pleasure, notices a portrait bust of Caesar, turns it to confront him face-to-face, smiles boldly at his succession to dictatorship, and confirms his takeover by occupying Caesar's imposing, eagle-crested chair.[84]

Such cinematic strategies were both effective and influential. By the time of the wider distribution of MGM's *Julius Caesar,* for example, the *Cleveland Press* declared unequivocally in its review: "Today's world-wide struggle between the free nations and communism bears a striking resemblance to the events of 44 B.C., when Julius Caesar reigned over the Roman empire" (9 December 1953). Correspondingly, early in 1954, toward the end of the film's distribution, the organization Educational Consultants on Entertainment Films (ECEF) published a study guide emphasizing its value for discussion in American classrooms.[85] Written, it was claimed, by a committee of college professors, the guide appeared as part of a free newsletter estimating the worth of moving pictures. Their assessment clearly locates the narrative of the film—its exploration of the growth of conspiracy, the origin of revolution, the manipulation of public opinion, and the reaction of the masses to their leaders— comfortably outside the perimeters of the United States. In response to the film's representation of the mob, the guide encourages students to contrast "our own" responses to opinion-molding agents, and to decide whether "our safeguards" come from the Constitution, "our national character," or "our native sales-resistance." Of the representation of Caesar, it asks: Who is to blame for his transformation? How can people prevent such growth of personal power? "What safeguards do we have in our own country against such an eventuality?" Once students have viewed MGM's *Julius Caesar,* it finally pronounces, they should evaluate the appeals and the dangers of totalitarianism, and review—and, it implies, now have an answer to—the "challenge in the world today: democracy and totalitarianism, Iron curtain or freedom?" Sponsored indirectly by the film industry, ECEF mimics the strategies of high-school aids to the study of Caesar's *Gallic War* or Shakespeare's *Julius Caesar* and finds the filmed drama of Julius Caesar's assassination to be an excellent education in contemporary political systems and American patriotism.

Film critics have observed that close-ups constitute a spatial field unique to cinema and can be deployed either to supply or to specify sociopolitical meanings for Shakespeare's plays when transposed from theatrical performance to screen.[86] Close-ups continue to be used in the rest of MGM's *Julius Caesar* to fix the characterization of Antony as motivated by a calculating desire to succeed Caesar in the role of dictator at Rome: he sneers victoriously as he witnesses from a safe distance the defeat of his enemies in battle and, in the film's final moments, displays a "half-triumphant, half-admiring stare diagonally down the screen at the dead face of a Brutus who can no longer stare back" (*New York Herald Tribune,* n.d.). Thus, while the words of the Elizabethan play are supremely ambivalent on the ethics and the efficacy of tyrannicide, and represent Julius Caesar as simultaneously a vicious usurper and a good ruler (with Antony his match for both tyranny and loyalty), the Hollywood film's cinematography reduces that ambivalence to the topical matter of totalitarianism, its persuasive attractions, and the need to resist it.[87] The production of meaning for film, however, is achieved by many mechanisms, and those individual mechanisms do not necessarily build together a coherent political picture. The rich intertextuality and the complex construction of MGM's *Julius Caesar* open up the possibility of additional, even contradictory, readings of this film's Caesar.

AMERICAN CAESARS FOR COLD WAR CULTURE

Not all interpretations of MGM's *Julius Caesar* looked beyond the borders of the United States to find a contemporary equivalent of the film's Roman ruler. As we have seen thus far, America had long been a Roman nation, and Shakespeare's *Julius Caesar* an American play. Many commentators on the Cold War film adaptation were provoked to thoughts of American history, politics, and society by multiple aspects of the film's narrative and style, its casting, accents and acting, the machinery of the studio's publicity, the biographies of its producer and director, and a number of cinematic and televisual intertexts.

The classical sets and props of MGM's *Julius Caesar* could evoke for spectators not just the Europe of the wartime dictatorships but also the United States of America from its foundation to the present day. Like modern Rome, Berlin, and Moscow, Washington too was adorned with neoclassical public monuments.[88] Furthermore, in order to symbolize the national government of a modern republic, America's seat of power had also been named the Capitol and contained a chamber where its own senators met. Designed as a temple to liberty, the Capitol asserted architecturally (through its massive dome and rotunda, its vast porticoes and columns, its sweeping marble floors and array of portrait busts) the country's proud political inheritance of self-government from antiquity.[89] As a reviewer in the *Twentieth Century* for December 1953 observed of the film's Forum sets, "the steep stone steps of the Capitol might indeed have been in Washington." Caesar's totalitarian state was also projected onto a recognizably American landscape, as the film was partially shot on location in Bronson Canyon, a granite quarry in the vicinity of Hollywood Boulevard. There the battle on the plains of Philippi between the murderers and the avengers of the Roman dictator was choreographed to recall the kind of combat more familiar from the low-budget Westerns for which the quarry often provided a conveniently rugged setting.[90] Thus, the *New York Herald Tribune* (n.d.)

described MGM's representation of the fifth act of Shakespeare's tragedy as "an ambush in a gorge, staged like a skirmish between Apaches and United States Cavalry in a Western." The American landscape and the Western choreography also worked to fix the moral balance of the film in favor of the conspirators: they were identified by the film's makers, its consumers, and later critics with the U.S. Cavalry bravely riding through the pass, with Antony's men in the role of treacherous Indians perched high on the hill waiting to initiate their surprise attack.[91]

Similarly, MGM's casting of its leading character actor, Louis Calhern, as Julius Caesar led spectators back from his performance of the Roman dictator to his prior star persona as a player of smooth criminal gang leaders or paternalistic mobsters and, thus, to an interpretation of the studio's current film as "a sort of gangster picture with an ancient (44 B.C.) Roman setting" (Time, 1 June 1953).[92] Such generic interplay worked to create a domestic relevance for the film at the level not just of casting and acting but also of iconography and ideology.[93] Reflections of the topography of film noir emerge especially in Mankiewicz's direction of Shakespeare's act 1, scene 3, when the tempestuous night in which the senators meet and talk of drawing Brutus into their conspiracy manifests the prodigious power of the tyrant as well as a fearful premonition of his death. Dark, seedy streets glisten with rain. Chiaroscuro lighting casts the conspirators' faces in and out of deep, black shadows. Their windblown bodies are posed in unbalanced compositions in front of doorways and covered passages. Together these cinematographic strategies replicate those of the gangster film and mimic the appearance the genre gave to the violent world of crime that it depicted menacingly at work in America's cityscapes.[94] Generic interplay with the gangster genre also helped turn the anti-Communist narrative drive of MGM's Julius Caesar in a domestic direction. During the Cold War, Hollywood's explicitly anti-Communist films typically meshed organized crime and political corruption with totalitarianism and domestic espionage to double the paranoiac discourse of conspiratorial threats to postwar America from an enemy who lurked within, as well as outside, its borders.[95]

The studio's production and distribution of a mock tabloid—the final edition of the Daily Chariot for 16 March 44—also lent its Roman-dress version of Shakespeare's Julius Caesar the familiarity of events unfolding in an American capital city. The fabricated newspaper reported the death of the dictator in the "Capitol Rotunda" at the hands of various senators, claiming for its source numerous Capitol employees. It displayed an editorial asking where the cops were when the rioting began. It boasted an article detailing the various attempts made by the journalist Vittoria Sobbicus to obtain "the feminine angle" through exclusives extracted from the widow and the chief assassin's wife. And it mimicked the layout of contemporary newspapers by including a "Voce of the People" section, in which imaginary ancient correspondents complained about such modern topics as unemployment, spiraling national debt, tax hikes, and the difficulties of finding a parking space in town. Perhaps somewhat ill-advisedly, an MGM press book dated 1954 even suggested to its readership of regional theater managers that, as a publicity stunt, they should hire newsboys to distribute the tabloid around town while attracting customer attention with cries of "Assassination in the Senate!" Institutional marketing of this kind works to shape viewers' expectations and their experience of the film it publicizes, in this case exploiting the immediacy of journalistic discourse to create an intertextual relay between the Roman past, Shakespeare, and the American present.[96]

If aspects of the narrative style and institutional promotion of MGM's *Julius Caesar* stimulated contemporary commentators to think of American society generally, cautious pronouncements by its director and producer, combined with knowledge of their liberal credentials and experiences, provided further hints about how to read the film more immediately and specifically as a commentary on a current crisis in America's political scene—as an assault on the totalitarianism that lay *within*. Already by war's end, the United States had assumed a form of international interventionism previously associated with the European dictatorships, and totalitarianism had become identified by the liberal Left not only with Nazi Germany and the Stalinist Soviet Union but also with the growth of power within the United States itself of the military and the anti-Communist Right. That growth, in the liberal view, posed a severe threat both to American democratic values and to government by Democrats.[97] Thus, early on in the making of *Julius Caesar*, its director indicated an immediate political analogy for his Brutus in the contemporaneous presidential elections of 1952, when, despite the preceding twenty years of Democratic rule, the principled liberal and eloquent but aloof intellectual, Governor Adlai E. Stevenson, was overwhelmingly defeated by the crowd-pleasing, charismatic war hero, General Dwight D. Eisenhower.[98] Certainly, intimations of an American Brutus emerged from Stevenson's own rhetoric during his campaign speeches: he regularly identified Eisenhower simply as "the general" and defined patriotism as "the love of this Republic and of the ideal of liberty of man and mind in which it was born and to which this Republic is dedicated."[99]

Film critics, however, have connected the screen Brutus as played by James Mason more intimately with the liberal-democrat biographies of both the film's director and its producer, and read the noble Roman as constructed in their image. Between 1947 and 1953, the House Un-American Activities Committee (HUAC) focused some of its investigations and hearings specifically on the motion-picture and show-business industries, which led to the imprisonment, blacklisting, or boycott of many artists as Communists or sympathizers with Communism. Roughly in parallel, from 1950 to 1954, the Republican senator from Wisconsin and skilled demagogue, Joseph R. McCarthy, led a frenzied and sweeping drive to search out and eradicate any left-wing influence within the national institutions of the State Department, the army, and even the office of the presidency.[100] During this Cold War crisis, when the Red Scare was intensified by McCarthyism, John Houseman was frequently accused of being a Communist or fellow traveler by congressional witch hunters, while Joseph L. Mankiewicz suffered comparable accusations from fellow film directors, such as the right-wing Cecil B. DeMille.[101] In biographical readings of MGM's *Julius Caesar*, the producer and director are understood to have styled Caesar as dictatorial, Antony as demagogic, and gentle Brutus as an ideal version of themselves. Frequently shot against the looming shadows cast by massive Caesarean statuary or the tangled branches of barren trees, Brutus is displayed as a man of principle whose pure ideals are sullied by dirty politics. Caught in its dark web, he finds himself subjected to unjust accusations of treason by an unscrupulous, opportunistic demagogue who can manipulate the trusting masses all too easily.[102]

Significantly, however, no contemporary review that I have found of MGM's *Julius Caesar* suggests a reading of it as a defense of American liberalism or as an attack on McCarthyist repression until early 1954—some seven months after its premiere and while it was continuing its regional run. Even then the reviews mention no specific names when they connect the dictatorial Caesar and the demagogic Antony on-screen to present-day American politicians. After seeing the film on 25 January 1954, a journalist for the *Chicago Daily Sun-Times* declared:

> No textbook can impress the mind with the cynicism of a politician bent on inflaming the populace as the actual sight of such a man in action. Every generation has its share of such men. So has the present one. They pretend love of the people and profess their zeal for public service. But they are bent on

personal advancement and power. They arouse the crowd to hysteria today as well as in Shakespeare's time, by such similar tricks of the demagogue that the play "Julius Caesar" could seem as contemporary in spots as a TV program.

As the article in the Chicago newspaper intimates, this turn toward the nation's own demagogues in contemporary understanding of MGM's *Julius Caesar* can best be understood in terms of its relation to American television documentaries, and in particular to two that were broadcast almost exactly a year apart (three months before the release of the film and toward the very end of its run), and in both of which Julius Caesar figures.[103]

"The Assassination of Julius Caesar" was broadcast on Sunday, 8 March 1953, at 6:30 p.m. EST as part of an innovative, award-winning CBS network television series called *You Are There*.[104] Each half-hour play in the series recreated live a momentous event from the past, and each was designed to present its historical reconstruction as if it were a news story the network was breaking minute by minute. The teleplay about the murder of the Roman dictator began in the CBS studio, with one of its best-known news broadcasters as the anchor. Speaking straight to camera, he set the stage:

> Walter Cronkite reporting. March 15th, the 710th year after the founding of the city of Rome. And in Rome today an extraordinary political event is scheduled to take place here in the center of the world's economic and political power—the oldest living Republic is about to vote itself out of existence and become a monarchy. Instead of electing two consuls every year, there's a resolution before the Senate to make Julius Caesar king. . . . And Julius Caesar, who received every honor that the Republic legitimately can grant him, now awaits the offer of its dissolution and the imperial crown. But in the last few days, there has developed a very strong movement in the Senate to block—to head off—this monarchist movement.

By 1953 both the popularity of television and possession of a television set had increased very rapidly in the United States. Television had also become a newly important instrument for political display, debate, and electioneering.[105] Cronkite himself had only recently achieved celebrity as the CBS anchor who, in 1952, had sat in a makeshift television studio at the political conventions of the Democratic and Republican parties and summarized straight to the television camera his reports on the arcane processes whereby Stevenson and Eisenhower had been selected as the parties' respective presidential candidates. His presence framing each dramatic reconstruction of *You Are There* thus gave to the series the format, the authority, and the claim to dispassionate accuracy of a news bulletin.[106]

As befitted the overall title of the series and its format as a live news broadcast, "The Assassination of Julius Caesar" immediately plunged the American viewer into its dramatization of Roman history. The scene shifts from the studio to various locations in ancient Rome (the Capitoline Hill, the Senate chamber, and Caesar's palace) where the camera pries into the unfolding events of the Ides. On the spot (but always offscreen), other correspondents from the CBS news division often explain in a hushed voice-off what the television audience is seeing, and the actors who play their Roman interviewees speak in close-up directly to the camera and to the modern audience. Early on in the Senate chamber, for example, a voice identified as that of the journalist Winston Burdett announces excitedly: "Cassius is coming this way and I'll try to get him to say something about the main resolution before the senate today. Senator Cassius! Senator Cassius! Do you intend to try to block the motion today to make Caesar king?" Outside the garden of Caesar (played by Milton Selzer), and beyond the parameters of Shakespeare's tragedy, the camera spies through the latticework to witness the arrogant and cruel dictator reveal privately to his wife that he plans to kill tonight all those who speak out against him today. Again, after Caesar arrives at the Senate chamber, the camera at one point closes in from behind some columns to capture an intimate conversation between him and Brutus (played with passion by a young Paul Newman as the son whom Caesar publicly denies; see fig. 26). While Brutus acknowledges the corruption of senatorial politics that has driven Caesar pragmatically to grasp at absolute power, he protests idealistically: "I suggest that civil war, that anarchy, that ruin and struggle, are better than tyranny, that liberty is better than safety, and that death is better than slavery." The arguments in the chamber of the pro- and anti-Caesarean factions are filmed at much greater length than the assassination itself, which is played out briefly, as if the CBS correspondents and their viewers have suddenly become accidental witnesses to a murder that is now being broadcast live to the nation.

In addition to the program's journalistic style and the modernity of its script (in contrast to Elizabethan verse), the evident overlap between past and present in some of its political terminology also helped establish a domestic topicality for the news that was being broken of a tyrant's downfall. Politicians in a republic are overreaching their powers. There are Senate resolutions and bills, temporary recesses of the Senate, motions put forward to suspend constitutional rights, and a law

FIGURE 26. Paul Newman
as Brutus, in *You Are There*'s
"The Assassination of Julius
Caesar" (8 March 1953).
© CBS News Archive.

of national emergency already in place. In the studio-based epilogue
that concluded each docudrama, Cronkite signed off as anchor with the
show's tagline: "What sort of a day have we had? A day like all days,
filled with those events that alter and illuminate our times . . . And you
were there!" But, uniquely in the case of the teleplay about Julius Caesar,
Cronkite's presence locked the framework of America's nominating conventions around the reconstruction of Roman republican politics.[107] The
American television audience is brought face-to-face with Roman history in the making, and Roman history is relayed into the homes of
modern-day America rendered as a contemporary political event.

The CBS network, even in its studio-based opening and conclusion,
offered no explicit illumination of present times. It is the television audience, who, in the privacy of their own homes, have to take responsibility for seeing a historical analogy (and for making the implicit criticism
that the insight might entail). The series *You Are There* cleverly camouflaged its attacks on McCarthyism with the aesthetic cover of history.[108] Only retrospective analysis of the context in which the television series was produced and of the biographies of some of its makers
brings its political agenda completely out into the open. All three of the
chief scriptwriters for the series were on the blacklist and were therefore
writing under pseudonyms. One of them subsequently declared that the
series was probably the only place where any guerrilla warfare was conducted against McCarthy in a public medium, since its historical themes
were generally selected for their bearing on the terrors he perpetrated—
a serial historiography (the scriptwriter claimed) of losses of civil liberties and intellectual freedoms, investigations, witch hunts, trials, recan-
tations, and executions.[109]

MGM's *Julius Caesar*, however, began to be understood *explicitly* as an assault on McCarthyism only later, during the film's regional run, when the same network that had produced "The Assassination of Julius Caesar" aired a television documentary that openly attacked the junior senator from Wisconsin for being—among other things—America's modern-day Caesar. At 10:30 p.m. EST on Tuesday, 9 March 1954, CBS broadcast "A Report on Senator Joseph R. McCarthy" in its weekly half-hour news magazine series See It Now. Earlier programs in the series had already dissected examples of the abusive tactics McCarthy deployed to weed out Communists from American institutions, but this telecast was the most controversial. It retains a legendary status as the most courageous and influential documentary in television history (even though some critics now consider it to be a late follow-up by the otherwise timid medium on more rigorous critiques that had already appeared in the press).[110] Thus, in 2005, sequences from the telecast were reconstructed as the climax of a Hollywood film about television's exposé of McCarthy—Good Night, and Good Luck (dir. George Clooney)—and interpreted by spectators as part of a robust history lesson from the director on how contemporary broadcasters might be able to stand up courageously against the manipulations and repressions of the administration of George W. Bush.[111]

The telecast (as well as See It Now as a whole) was hosted by Edward R. Murrow, who was famous and much admired for his wartime radio reports from Europe. In the broadcast, McCarthy was presented as a shallow, sweaty, bullying demagogue tossing about wild and slapdash charges of treason and espionage. The unpleasant portrait was achieved by careful editing of newsreel footage and audiotapes of the senator's own outrageous public statements, a catalogue of increasingly scathing criticisms made against him by the highest members of the establishment, and censorious interventions throughout from Murrow live in the CBS studio. The anchorman observes at one point in the "Report," for example, that, in 1952, General Eisenhower had promised only conventional executive powers and trial by jury would be deployed in the fight against domestic Communism, but McCarthy had resorted to terrorizing Americans. Murrow also draws viewers' attention to an article by Truman published in the New York Times for 17 November 1953 (itself based on a speech that Truman had delivered on national television), in which the ex-president now defined McCarthyism as "the rise to power of a demagogue who lives on untruth." And, after newsreel footage shows McCarthy utilizing Cassius's question "Upon what meat doth this our Caesar feed?" (Shakespeare, JC 1.2.147) against a

FIGURE 27. Ed Murrow, in *See It Now*'s "A Report on Senator Joseph R. McCarthy" (9 March 1954). © CBS News Archive.

perceived abuse of power by the Secretary of the United States Army, Murrow counters in the studio by looking directly at the camera to ask his viewers: "And upon what meat does Senator McCarthy feed?" (see fig. 27). Murrow then produces a dramatic answer to his question for which the documentary goes on to supply the evidence: a diet of investigations and half-truths. This bandying of tags from Shakespeare's *Julius Caesar* continues into the documentary's tailpiece, before the program ends with Murrow's signature "Good night, and good luck." In the show's format, this was the moment when Murrow usually looked straight into the camera and provided resolution for or demanded action from his American television audience. On this crucial occasion, Murrow spoke boldly, at length, and with great eloquence:

> We proclaim ourselves—as indeed we are—the defenders of freedom, wherever it continues to exist in the world. But we cannot defend freedom abroad by deserting it at home. The actions of the junior Senator from Wisconsin have caused alarm and dismay among our allies abroad and given considerable comfort to our enemies. And whose fault is that? Not really his. He didn't create the situation of fear; he merely exploited it—and rather successfully. Cassius was right: "The fault, dear Brutus, is not in our stars, but in ourselves." Good night and good luck.

Three days later, this extraordinary televisual event was interlinked with the experience of seeing MGM's *Julius Caesar* on the cinema screen by a reviewer for the *Oklahoma City Advertiser* (12 March 1954). For her the film adaptation of Shakespeare's tragedy that she has just seen is the key to understanding the television documentary. On that basis, she argues, Murrow means that McCarthy is a Caesar whom the American people have themselves made and must, therefore, unmake: "He must have meant to imply that we have only ourselves to blame for the fears and the apathy by which freedoms are lost and dictators have their way." She then expresses pleasure that the fear of McCarthyism and its political repressions have now been shaken off by most commentators and newspapers, and looks forward to what will follow.[112] What did in fact follow, after the documentary had been broadcast in thirty-six cities across the United States, was a flood of enthusiastic responses to the young medium's heroic achievement. And, toward the end of 1954, some months after the televised Army-McCarthy hearings exposed the senator's cruelty and recklessness, McCarthy was formally condemned for working against the traditions of the Senate.[113] Television had been the tool that assisted Senator McCarthy's rise, and the weapon that accomplished his fall.[114] The American Caesar had finally been toppled, and the televisual medium freed from "servile fearfulness" (*JC* 1.2.75).

Yet the complexity of MGM's *Julius Caesar* (in the mechanisms of its production, distribution, and consumption) enabled its political meaning to shift and change not only across the early years of the 1950s but also at any one given moment. In studio publicity, trade reports, and press comments, the dominant topic for debate (apart from the difference between staged and screened Shakespeare) was how Mark Antony had been cast and performed. Before the film's release, newspapers and magazines speculated wildly on how Marlon Brando was going to match up to that daunting Shakespearean role. A reporter for the *New York Times* boasted that he had got onto the closed set with the express purpose of inquiring how Brando's performance was coming along (21 September 1952), while *This Week* (1 March 1953) claimed that, as far as the MGM studio was concerned, the success or failure of its production rested almost entirely on Brando's delivery of the key Forum speech. On the film's release, *Cue Magazine* (n.d.) recalled how news of the unusual casting had been met:

> Movie fans from the Bronx to Bangkok hooted derisively. What, their brawny boy, mouthing Shakespearean iambic pentameters! Critics expressed themselves as horrified at the prospect of "Streetcar's" Stanley Kowalski desecrating the King's English with his garbled growls. *Cinemonde* in Paris bannerlined the news with the French equivalent of "Brando learns English to Play Shakespeare!" And columnists cracked that critics would need a *Brando-Into-English* dictionary if they expected to cover "Julius Caesar."

The prospect of a loutish reading of "Friends, Romans, countrymen" even entered comic routines in nightclubs and skits on national television.[115]

Largely on the basis of his performance of Stanley Kowalski in *A Streetcar Named Desire* (on both stage and screen), and his deliberate adoption of the character's speech patterns and fashion style in his public life, Brando's star persona at the time embodied a virile American masculinity. That muscular, menacing masculinity found itself reinforced in MGM's *Julius Caesar* when set against the effete British intellectualism American viewers discerned in the performances of James Mason as Brutus and John Gielgud as Cassius.[116] The Shakespearean dialogue of the Forum scene conveniently sustained this opposition even further as Antony/Brando is required to reflect that he is "no orator" like Brutus/Mason, but only "a plain blunt man" (*JC* 3.2.210–11). On the release of *Julius Caesar,* the verdict of American critics on Brando's performance in the Forum scene was generally highly enthusiastic. *Variety* (3 June 1953) declared: "He turns in the performance of his career. His interpretation of the famous funeral oration will be a conversation piece. The entire speech takes on a new light as voiced by Brando." And *Boxoffice Magazine* (n.d.) noticed: "Gone is the nasal, word-slurring reading of lines which characterized many of his preceding film roles—to be replaced by a forceful, crisp, incisive performance that will crystallize the large fan following he has already established, and will win for him a legion of new and more discriminating admirers."[117]

Casting, star persona, accents, and acting style here all work against the political readings that had made of Mark Antony the disciple of a dictator (whether that dictator be a foreign or a domestic enemy). The producer, John Houseman, himself noted scornfully in one of his autobiographies that the casting of Brando as Antony effectively reversed the structure of the modern-dress *Julius Caesar* staged by Welles: "Now it was Marc Antony they were rooting for and the twelve hundred cheering bit players and extras massed on M.G.M.'s Stage 25 were merely reflecting the empathy of future audiences."[118] The studio furthered this dramatic political reversal when it took commercial advantage of Brando's immense popularity and acting success in the film and upgraded his performance retrospectively into that of the star role. A poster produced and distributed by MGM utilized the Cold War vocabulary of Communist conspiracy to label James Mason's Brutus a "gallant warrior seduced to a traitor's cause," John Gielgud's Cassius a "wicked conspirator in infamy," and Louis Calhern's Caesar a "mighty conqueror, victim of assassins." Marlon Brando's Antony achieves top billing as "the firebrand who set Rome aflame."[119] This billing procedure (in contrast to other types of intertextual relay instigated either by

MGM or by the director and producer) invited audiences to understand the film as an anti-Communist tract. It clearly touched a chord with some reviewers. In the *Saturday Review* (6 June 1953), for example, film critic Hollis Alpert expressed great admiration for the performance of Brando as Antony, while finding John Gielgud's Cassius the most topical performance of all: "I kept seeing in him (perhaps fancifully) the prototype of the Marxist intellectual. And it is Cassius, after all, who shows most knowledge of the revolutionist's handbook." All the virile masculinity that cannot reside in the frail and elderly Caesar borrowed from the Elizabethan play is transferred to Mark Antony, who takes up the mantle of his heroic leader, the politician-general. Thus, the presence of Brando as Antony in MGM's *Julius Caesar* restores the vision of the comic-strip adaptation of Shakespeare's tragedy seen earlier in *Classics Illustrated*.

Analysis of MGM's *Julius Caesar* demonstrates the richness of and the contradictions in the representation of the Roman dictator in Cold War American culture. The malleability of his screen image and the diversity of the political analogies it invites do not strip Julius Caesar of contemporary significance. Rather, they demonstrate that, when modern media like film and television construct their images of Caesar, those images can be as politically ambivalent or ethically uncertain as many others in Caesar's long tradition. Furthermore, their disjointed Caesars track and, therefore, capture the disjointed political ideologies of the Cold War era: pride in revolutionary beginnings and fear of revolutionary endings; revulsion from foreign dictators and attraction to general-presidents; support of both democratic government and demagogic illegality; distaste for imperialism and embrace of global dominance.[120]

CHAPTER 6

Presidential Power

1956–1989

At the Forty-Ninth Annual Meeting of the Classical Association of the Atlantic States (held in Baltimore, 27–28 April 1956), a Latin teacher from Walton High School in New York City held up a packet of cigarettes before his audience as he reached the end of his analysis of Julius Caesar's mesmeric "verbal magic." On the packet's face, he pointed out, were displayed the Roman general's three most famous words— *veni, vidi, vici*—which had been designed eloquently to relay back to Rome from Asia the ease, the speed, and the scale of Caesar's victory in 47 B.C.E. at the battle of Zela.[1] The teacher, Charles W. Siedler, catalogued the rhetorical devices of that famous phrase: a clever accumulation of three disyllables, a trimeter of spondees, triple alliteration and assonance, double asyndeton, a stirring crescendo, and a stunning climax ("I came, I saw, I CONQUERED"). Then he ended his talk with a suitably dramatic flourish: "And now, if you please, I'll smoke one of Caesar's own cigarettes!"[2] The Caesarean cigarette in question was a Marlboro, a luxury brand that had originally been targeted at women in the 1920s but, in 1954, had been repackaged and relaunched by its manufacturer Philip Morris better to attract male consumers and improve poor profits. On television and in magazines, the phenomenally successful advertising campaign downplayed the perceived effeminacy of Marlboro's new filter tips by repeatedly depicting the man who smokes Marlboros as a rugged, self-sufficient, and virile cowboy. Meanwhile the tobacco blend was strengthened, the original soft pack converted into a crushproof flip-top box, and at the tip of its bright red chevron a fake heraldic crest was positioned, under which a banner displayed the triumphant Latin motto borrowed from the Roman dictator. Caesar's "verbal magic" had become a merchandising metaphor that spoke eloquently of the tobacco manufacturer's aspirations to global dominance in a highly competitive market and persuasively invited male smokers to imagine they were only a packet of cigarettes away from some similarly stupendous victory (even, perhaps, the sexual conquest of their own modern Cleopatras).[3]

At the same conference, however, a teacher of genuine military combatants reflected more broadly and more seriously on the utility of Caesar for Cold War America. Participants at the 1956 Classical Association annual meeting were commemorating the bimillennium of the death of Julius Caesar. Stimulated by the importance of the occasion, W. H. Russell (professor of naval and military history at the United States Naval Academy) presented renewed understanding of the historical Caesar and the end of the Roman republic as an excellent means by which to understand the troubled American present, and to predict or even guide its future.[4] In tones of some urgency, the military historian claimed that the same form of transition that Rome had experienced in the 50s B.C.E—from an organized community of law to the illegality of competing arbitrary powers—was happening in the 1950s on a global scale. The author and his audience may not have contributed directly to that transition, as had Caesar (he conceded), nevertheless they shared with each other and with twentieth-century man more generally an obligation to understand it. An understanding of the modern transition, as well as guidance on how best to stave off a descent into complete anarchy, could come from consideration of the Roman general.

THE GENERAL-PRESIDENT

The credibility of Professor Russell's argument was facilitated by his overt formulation of Roman history in twentieth-century terms: Caesar had ended a deflationary depression through monetary policies that had foreshadowed the New Deal; he had brought to a close the hot phase of war against the Pompeians; immediately thereafter he had undertaken the cold war necessary to the fulfillment of his civil plans.[5] Reassessed just past the midcentury mark, this Julius Caesar subsumes into himself features of several recent American presidents. To draw a suitable lesson for the present from the history of the Roman dictator, however, requires him to be cast in particular as a precursor to the current president, General Dwight Eisenhower. While Eisenhower had his critics, for many Americans his military expertise and political authority provided much-needed comfort after the cumulative traumas of the Depression, the Second World War, and the initiation of the Cold War. Six months after the 1956 annual meeting of the Classical Association, Eisenhower would win reelection to the presidency in a landslide victory built in part on his reputation for having ended and prevented major wars, reduced defense spending, and demonstrated vigorous leadership in the containment of Communism during a series of international crises.[6] The otherwise curious and contrived depiction of Julius Caesar presented to an audience of classicists by an expert from the U.S. Naval Academy is best understood as the result of assimilation to the most positive of contemporary representations of President Eisenhower: a benign general who set ethical limits for his use of armed violence and used military force only to achieve civil goals. In the 1950s, however, the presence of a general in the White House made Julius Caesar especially apposite, not only as a military and political exemplar but also as a warning.[7] Through Caesar, Russell is not able to offer a straightforwardly optimistic endorsement of Eisenhower's foreign policy, for he acknowledges on several occasions in his paper that the brilliance of the Roman general was ultimately corroded by absolute power. Growth of government, ethical corrosion of the leader, and descent into chaos is what Russell indicates Americans will be forced to relive should they ever forget what happened to the Roman republic in the time of Julius Caesar.

The Roman dictator was not forgotten in the course of the 1950s and on into the 1960s. Just past midcentury, he achieved fresh relevance as a general-statesman made to match America's general-president.[8] He also continued to confront young Americans in high-school classrooms across the United States both as successful commander and as tragic tyrant. In April 1956, at the same bimillennial commemoration of Julius Caesar's death held by the Classical Association of the Atlantic States, Sylvia W. Gerber of Howard University reported to her colleagues with some concern that the Roman author now held a short-lived but pivotal position in the study of Latin at American secondary schools.[9] By now the second year of high-school Latin was less often labeled "the Caesar grade" or "the Caesar year" because study of De bello Gallico (the Gallic War) had been pushed back into the fourth semester to accommodate a year and a half of training in basic vocabulary and grammar and easy reading of made-up Latin.[10] Caesar, therefore, might kill off the study of the classical language, if students were insufficiently engaged by his war commentaries to continue with it into their third year of high school. One solution, Gerber argued, was very careful selection of the most interesting sections from the seven books of the *Gallic War*. Conveniently for Latin teachers (and their students), most of Gerber's roll call of inspiring passages—from battle with Ariovistus (1.39–54) to the surrender of Vercingetorix (7.1–4 and 68–90)—had already appeared at the beginning of the year in comic-strip format when *Classics Illustrated* published *Caesar's Conquests* (no. 130, January 1956) as another in its series of abridgments of literary masterpieces.

Julius Caesar's *Gallic War* proved very amenable to the interpretative strategies employed by the Gilberton publishing company to transform highbrow literary works into comic books capable of competing with the boys' adventure fiction that dominated the comic-book market, far more so than Shakespeare's tragedy (that other key text for the continued circulation of the Roman dictator in twentieth-century American culture). In contrast to the comic-strip Caesar of the earlier *Classics Illustrated* abridgment of Shakespeare's play (no. 68, February 1950), this Caesar is younger, more muscular, dynamic and triumphant, and wholly devoid of both female attachments and unhappy endings.[11] The Roman general is transformed into a virile caped commander and, in the manner of a superhero, sports a signature costume across most of the pages of the comic book of bright red cape and crest, golden-brown helmet, breastplate, and greaves (see the horse rider in the background of fig. 28). The first few frames of *Caesar's Conquests* literally authorize the war story that follows: readers see the general at night, dressed down in civilian tunic, writing this story by lamplight with a quill pen on a scroll (the labor of adaptation by Annette Rubinstein and illustration by Joe Orlando is nowhere mentioned). Yet, thereafter, the severe condensation of the Roman author's third-person narrative is presented in two visually distinct forms: as white speech-balloons issuing from the comic's characters, and as yellow caption blocks further distinguished by their italic font. A clear graphic distinction is created between seemingly subjective and objective narrative forms. The phrase "by Julius Caesar" printed on the cover and the first page, the opening depiction of the soldier composing his commentaries in camp, and the closing image of the wreathed conqueror clutching his completed scroll all work to imprint on the comic's unfolding series of conquests the mark of impartial, true history told by its chief protagonist.[12] The possibility that the general composed his campaign reports out of political self-interest is conveniently ignored.[13] Consequently, within the colorful pages of *Classics Illustrated*, Julius

Caesar is endorsed as a protector of Roman property and people, a savior of grateful Gallic tribes from their insolent and treacherous enemies, a fearless campaigner, and an inspiration to his troops.

At the comic's close, the Roman general's career is frozen at the point of having completed both his extraordinary conquests and his celebrated account of them; there is no prospect or hint of dictatorship and political deterioration.[14] Echoes here of President Eisenhower also work to hone this depiction of Caesar as a war hero turned mature statesman, for in 1948 the American general had published *Crusade in Europe*—a best-selling and critically acclaimed memoir of his military command in the Second World War.[15] Thus the title page of *Caesar's Conquests* can be understood in terms borrowed from the public image of America's popular general-president: the garlanded statesman in a red-bordered toga now posing statuesquely in the foreground has gained his expertise and authority from the military activities of his younger self, depicted in the background in his red-caped armor astride a rearing horse, his sword uplifted in a gesture of encouragement to the legionaries marching behind him (fig. 28).[16] The comic-strip abridgment of Caesar's *Gallic War* is also rounded off by a striking caption in white-on-black capitals addressed directly to its targeted, juvenile audience and positioned underneath the final frames: "Now that you have read the *Classics Illustrated* edition, don't miss the added enjoyment of reading the original, obtainable at your school or public library" (44). The Latin text has been transformed into a stirringly topical tale about a superhero on ancient battlefields better to attract schoolboy consumers of comics, and the comic book is then ostensibly sold to them as a preliminary to study of the original commentaries better to gain the support of high-school teachers.[17] To maximize sales, *Caesar's Conquests* was published in the year commemorating the bimillennium of the Roman general's death, at the start of a presidential election campaign that would return an American general once again to the White House, and at a time (more broadly) when Latin teachers were employing last-ditch tactics to make the second-year text attractive to their students. The commercial success of the issue and the scale of its circulation can be judged by the seven reprints published in the course of the next decade.[18]

While comic strips were shrewdly marketed to American young people and their teachers as spurs to the study of both Caesar's *Gallic War* and Shakespeare's *Julius Caesar*, motion pictures were promoted in high schools as enhancements of the study and the performance of the Elizabethan play. In 1957, William Lewin (formerly an English

FIGURE 28. First page of *Caesar's Conquests, Classics Illustrated,* no. 130 (January 1956). ©2010 First Classics Inc. All Rights Reserved. By permission of Jack Lake Productions Inc.

teacher in Newark and later editor of the film guide *Photoplay Studies*) reprinted in a textbook for use in American high schools his original guide to classroom discussion of MGM's *Julius Caesar* (1953), now repackaged as an experimental case study of the "photoplay approach" to Shakespeare.[19] With strong support from film exhibitors, Lewin had taken the lead over many years in advocacy of the film medium as a valuable educational resource and argued that American children should be taught to appreciate it.[20] Based largely on his initiative, the foreword of the textbook could report that schools were now showing films using 16mm projectors, and discussion of them had become part of the American curriculum. MGM's *Julius Caesar* was well chosen as a case study because it was available to schools from Films Incorporated (a subsidiary of Encyclopaedia Britannica Films) and was adapted from a Shakespeare play that, at midcentury, had held a central place in the American curriculum longer than any other work of English literature. Like other photoplay guides, this one treats film almost purely as a vehicle for understanding literary text. It contains little film critical discourse (such as that emerging on auteurism) or analysis of film form (other than brief references to star casting and performance).[21] Instead its concern is to announce the Cold War timeliness of Shakespeare's tragic representation of Caesar and to explore the historical inaccuracies of the play's eponymous protagonist. For Lewin, the historical Caesar was an extremely popular man of modesty, kindness, and generosity, "a genius in war and peace" sincerely devoted to the public interest, whereas Shakespeare's Caesar is played out as the conspirators' construct—"an overbearing, imperious, boastful tyrant."[22]

Other educators working within the much longer and more sophisticated tradition of Shakespearean critical practice acknowledged the Cold War topicality of the Roman tragedy and the crude impact such topicality could sometimes have on students performing the play. Addressing an audience of New England schoolteachers, Maynard Mack (professor of English literature at Yale) recalled a friend reporting to him that in 1953, when Joseph McCarthy was regularly berating his victims on American television, three boys were seen unconsciously to mimic the senator's mannerisms in their attempt to act out for their classmates the tyrannical ambition and intimidating oratory of Caesar's heir, Antony.[23] Now, that is, in 1960, the distinguished Shakespearean scholar ascribes a greater complexity and utility to the Elizabethan drama than had previously been attributed to it. Shakespeare's Caesar, he argues, is divided between human and superhuman selves. Modern embodiments of the superman of state are to be found all too frequently in the wider political world, but the split occurs psychologically within each one of us:

> The human Caesar who has human aliments and is a human friend is the Caesar that can be killed. The marmoreal Caesar, the everlasting Big Brother—the Napoleon, Mussolini, Hitler, Franco, Peron, Stalin, Kruschev [*sic*], to mention only a handful of his more recent incarnations—that Caesar is the one who must repeatedly be killed but never dies, because he is in you, and you, and me. Every classroom is a Rome, and there is no reason for any pupil, when he studies *Julius Caesar* to imagine that this is ancient history.[24]

Performance of the play, according to Mack, is a straight route to self-knowledge for students, who arrive at the realization that they too can grow colossal with self-love. In the professor's view, acting is elemental and instinctive, a kinetic and sensory experience, so when students speak and move as Caesar, they viscerally contemplate their own image in the play and the play's image in themselves.[25]

In the era of the Cold War, therefore, a multifaceted Julius Caesar was made available to high-school students and their teachers not just as a language lesson in Latin syntax and vocabulary or a history lesson about statecraft and the rise and fall of dictators, but also as a theatrical form of psychotherapy able to engage with troubled selves. Although the popular reception of Julius Caesar in the United States was most frequently and most densely social, political, and public, it could also be private and—if Professor Mack is to be believed—sometimes even therapeutic.

THE COMING CAESARS

If we do not confront the contradictions of Julius Caesar (his political failure and ethical corruption as well as his military success and civil reforms), we will be forced to live through the collapse of our own republic and the rise of our own dictator—the subtle suggestion that a military historian may have offered inadvertently to a gathering of classicists during a bimillennial commemoration of the Roman general's death soon became an impassioned assertion in postwar American political discourse. From the 1950s until 1974 (which saw the collapse of Richard Nixon's "Imperial Presidency" and the temporary resurgence of Congress), debates about the governance of the United States regularly considered whether the powers of the executive branch were escalating into a dictatorship. In such debates, ancient Rome (and its first "Caesar") often appeared as an admonitory topos.[26]

Most flamboyantly, in 1957 the French critic and sometime resident of the United States Amaury de Riencourt initiated substantial, alarmed debate that circulated well beyond the confines of the schoolroom, the university, or the naval academy when he revived the nineteenth-century concept of Caesarism and placed it (and its namesake) at the heart of a startling prediction about the future of the United States and its consequences for the whole world. In his succinctly titled book, *The Coming Caesars*, and in the summary of it published by the editors of the *National Review* (a recently founded and swiftly influential magazine of conservative opinion),[27] the author asserted that the United States of America now stood in the same relation to Europe as ancient Rome had once stood to Greece.[28] The adoption by modern America as well as ancient Rome of the twin strategies of democratic growth and imperial expansion proved decisive for their development, according to de Riencourt's cyclical vision of history. Just as Roman civilization had been fated to overcome Greek culture and master the world, so American civilization was now destined to triumph over a declining European culture and dominate the world of tomorrow. For the ancient and the modern civilizations the consequence was (or now would be) loss of liberty, centralization, and the arrival of Caesarism: "Our Western world, America and Europe, is threatened with Caesarism on a scale unknown since the dawn of the Roman empire" (de Riencourt 1957, 5). The argument borrowed its organic and biocyclical philosophy of history from Oswald Spengler and Arnold Toynbee:[29] civilizations trample over cultures and then ossify and decay into lethal tyrannies until the cycle begins again. However, at the same time as history is cyclical, in de Riencourt's confusing thesis it is also paradoxically apocalyptic: expanding democracy leads to imperialism, which in turn destroys republican institutions and concentrates absolute power in a single Caesarean ruler, leading to nuclear holocaust and the end of history.

In order to sustain a close and dense match over some 350 pages of text between the histories of Europe and ancient Greece and those of the United States of America and ancient Rome, de Riencourt is clearly constrained to twist and distort all four. And the achieved match is reinforced by the constant traffic of historical terminology across the centuries and the sea: the New Deal starts with the Gracchi in Rome, Roosevelt is the first real tribune of the people, while Julius Caesar establishes a permanent bureaucracy after the downfall of Roman big business. Such fiercely analogical and polemical historiography attributes to the Roman past causes and effects that its author considers a menace to the American present.[30] Drawing on the equally disputatious narratives of nineteenth- and early twentieth-century classical historians, de Riencourt molds a Caesar for the late 1950s. Theodor Mommsen's enthusiasm for a savior-king anointed with the oil of democracy is paradoxically meshed with Guglielmo Ferrero's distaste for an opportunistic and destructive dictator.[31] Julius Caesar now takes on the features of a "bold democrat" and a "great internationalist" who attempted to found an empire of equality and security at the same time as he deprived its citizens of their political freedom and accrued to himself powers greater than a king's (de Riencourt 1957, 334–35).

After running through his history of the failing Roman republic and its astonishing similarity to the history of the United States to date, de Riencourt asserts in striking terms:

> In truth, no mental effort is required to understand that the President of the United States is the most powerful single human being in the world today. Future crises will inevitably transform him into a full-fledged Caesar, if we do not beware. Today he wears ten hats — as Head of State, Chief Executive, Minister of Foreign Affairs, Chief Legislator, Head of Party, Tribune of the People, Ultimate Arbitrator of Social Justice, Guardian of Economic Prosperity, and World Leader of Western Civilization. Slowly and unobtrusively these hats are becoming crowns and this pyramid of hats is slowly metamorphosing itself into a tiara, the tiara of one man's world imperium. (1957, 330–31)

And (according to the author's dramatic conclusion) when this monstrous Caesar finally arrives in the United States, all that will be left for us is to cry despairingly, like Shakespeare's Brutus: "O Julius Caesar, thou art mighty yet!" (342). Nevertheless, within the pages of *The Coming Caesars,* de Riencourt concedes that it was not Julius Caesar who achieved Caesarism but Octavian, and that there is no sign of an impending American Rubicon. At both the opening and the close of his narrative, the author claims that the current president, General Eisenhower, has in fact been trying to restore dignity and responsibility to Congress (7, 331),[32] and that the president who most nearly established dictatorial rule was Franklin D. Roosevelt.[33] Caesarism and Caesar become shorthand in de Riencourt's apocalyptic rhetoric for an overarching historical trend rather than a specific mode of governance or man of action: "Caesarism is not dictatorship, not the result of one man's overriding ambition, not a brutal seizure of power through revolution. . . . It is a slow, often century-old, unconscious development that ends in a voluntary surrender of a free people escaping from freedom to one autocratic master" (5). American Caesarism, de Riencourt clarifies, will not be heralded abruptly by a military coup, nor will it initiate civil war or defy the Constitution. Instead it will emerge, or rather it is emerging, slowly from a gradual concentration of power in the office and the person of the chief executive (11). This process of concentration is already under way because democracy's drive toward war and foreign expansion has necessitated the enhancement of the powers of the executive over Congress. Moreover, the free people of the United States are surrendering their authority to one autocratic master voluntarily, for the masses (being democratic and egalitarian) are feminine and, therefore, positively seek out the masculine and paternal leadership of a Caesar.

Thus the Roman dictator is transformed into a conservative's stick with which he can beat the perceived excesses of liberal democracy.

In the alarmist context developed by de Riencourt his exaggerated parallels between the actions of the Caesars and the presidents of the United States provide warning beacons to shed light on the bleak destiny of the world. Or, a little more optimistically, the step back into Roman history on which the author leads his readers is, in his own metaphor, an opportunity to wake up and see properly the road we have all been traveling along like somnambulists (6), but also to adjust our path as best we can and before it is too late (356). Armed with our knowledge of the Roman past and historical cycles, we may be able to prevent or modify the worst features of American Caesarism and save ourselves from the holocaust.

Claims that the United States of America is becoming an empire and the president its Caesar have long been intertwined. During his period of office in the 1830s, General Andrew Jackson in particular was accused of both pursuing territorial expansion and augmenting the power of the president. To Jackson's opponents, he was America's Julius Caesar, that is to say an arrogant general turned demagogue who was now leading the Republic into domestic tyranny and a damaging imperialism.[34] Thus, the long familiarity of the Caesarean topos in American political discourse lends credibility to the French critic's thesis, as does its renewed, more urgent deployment after the Second World War. The prediction of presidential tyranny and political disintegration might well seem dangerously close to fulfillment at a time when the United States was growing in international stature,[35] and, in the view of some, too fast becoming heir to Europe's old colonial empires.[36] By using ancient Rome as an admonitory topos, the opponents of General Jackson were also able to stake a claim to moral guardianship of America's republican legacy—as noble Catos or Ciceros for the nineteenth century.[37] Here, as historiographer rather than politician, de Riencourt would appear to be staking a claim to the political and military expertise, the erudition and the aesthetic weight, of a twentieth-century Polybius. In a potential moment of self-reflection and aggrandisement, the French author describes the Greek historian as possessing the "keen eye of the outsider" (241) in his analysis of the rise of ancient Rome to empire.[38]

CAESAR IN THE WHITE HOUSE

Not surprisingly, the thesis that Julius Caesar was about to arrive in the White House immediately generated considerable debate. Some politi-

cal conservatives rejected the sustained Roman analogies contained in
The Coming Caesars (1957) as robustly as they denied its bold predictions of the damage America would do to the world. The same year
as the book's publication and summation in the *National Review,* the
political philosopher and libertarian Frank Meyer objected in a later
issue of the magazine (of which he was a cofounder) that the young
Frenchman's argument constituted a sinister European imposition on
the United States, designed to depict the latter speciously as the dull
Roman master of a Europe painted nostalgically as a once sparkling
Greece. According to Meyer (a convert to Catholicism), it also ignored
an essential characteristic of American political life, namely its Christian
vision of the innate value of the person and of his freedom under God.
Confident of the difference between Christian Americans and the iron,
soulless administrators of pagan Rome, Meyer boldly proclaimed that
Americans would indeed determine the fate of the West, but on their
own terms: any future American era of Western culture would be "not
Caesarist, but free" (1957, 233).[39] Additional (and more mundane)
objections to *The Coming Caesars* have included de Riencourt's inabil-
ity to count hats, as well as the extraordinary historical contortions,
contradictions, and contentions practiced by the author in order to turn
America into the new Rome and Caesarism into its destiny.[40] Other
contemporary commentators on the political right, however, supported
and even extended de Riencourt's claims. An essayist writing in the
anti-democratic monthly *Écrits de Paris* in 1958 added, as further proof
of the U.S. president's escalating Caesarean powers, the "autocratic"
decision of General Eisenhower the previous September to deploy federal paratroopers within the state of Arkansas (which he had made to
enforce the federal law of racial integration in the face of protesting seg-
regationists).[41] The current president, the author of the essay also proclaimed alarmingly, had at his disposal a force unavailable to any of his
Caesarean predecessors: nuclear energy.[42]

Until the twenty-first century, few political analysts have been prepared to readopt the kind of thoroughgoing historical coincidence
Amaury de Riencourt found between the Roman past and America's
future, or to return to a biocyclical understanding of history (as rise
and fall, ebb and flow, growth and decay). Yet, at moments of political
extremity or crisis in the 1950s and 1960s, commentators continued to
draw—though to varying degrees—both on Caesarism and on Julius
Caesar in order to paint disquieting pictures of the future of the presidency, of America, and of the world.[43] The monitory topos of the Roman

republic's fall suited the alarmist discourse of postwar American conservatism. Toward the end of the 1950s, an emerging ideological Right (as well as Left) began to attack the ascendancy of American liberalism and its commitment to an interventionist foreign policy and a regulatory and welfare state at home. In the tropes of conservative intellectuals: excessive democracy is a threat to freedom; the presidency is the agent of the will of the masses; Congress is collapsing; and, as a consequence, the ignorant citizens of the United States will soon submit to democratic despotism as their preferred mode of governance—unless, that is, they heed conservatism's clarion call to withstand the arrival (or, more dramatically, the presence) of their own American Caesar.[44]

On 3 May 1966, for example, the legend "Imperial America: A Look into the Future" appeared on the front cover of the *National Review,* by now the leading national magazine for conservative debate. Inside, Thomas Molnar (one of its regular contributors) accepted without hesitation that the United States had become an imperial power like Rome, and that Americans were the new Romans. Acknowledging national resistance to the idea of "Imperial America," Molnar counterclaimed that America's armed forces and foreign policy were the reluctant heirs to Europe's colonial conquests. From Saigon to Léopoldville, where the French, British, Belgians, and Dutch were once stationed, American GIs were now garrisoned. Guarding oceans and sea routes, air routes and space orbits, from "a great Asian power," they provide a new version of the old protective conquest—an atomic version of *pax Romana.* The Roman Catholic philosopher and political theorist then exploits the Roman analogy, however, not to ponder America's growth to empire but to pick apart what he perceives to be the tremendous and troubling domestic consequences of such growth. History demonstrates that empire *needs* a single power center (to permit quick decisions and fast action); imperial responsibility inevitably brings with it increased centralization. If, accordingly, the United States has grown like Rome from a small agrarian republic to world empire, then (Molnar asks his readers) "will the parallel hold and our Chief Executive become an Imperial Caesar?"[45]

In order to identify the inevitable domestic consequences of international growth, Molnar here catalogues a whole series of extraordinary correspondences between Julius Caesar (or, less specifically, the Caesars) and the "new-type" American presidents. Caesar and the modern president strip traditional institutions of their power (the Roman Senate, the American Congress). They both are commander in chief of the armed forces; it is they who decide troop movements (from Gaul to Egypt, from Germany to Vietnam). For their double role as chief administrator and military protector, they are compensated by considerable privileges (a crown for Julius, four mandates for Roosevelt). They are charismatic figures who promise but only partly deliver to the demands of the newly important masses. They curb the legislative arm of government, contain popular discontent (free grain distributions, antipoverty funds), and accrue a large staff who duplicate all forms of government and whose political existence is tied to their leader alone. Molnar's conclusion—where, in a rhetorical flourish, Caesar is put into the present tense and the here and now—demonstrates the predictive and apocalyptic functions the Roman equivalence is once again made to serve:

> Caesar leans on popular, radical elements, makes concessions, keeps the balance among pressure groups and grabbing hands. But on one point he cannot yield to the domestic left: on military matters, since the second chief support of his office is armed protection of the nation. Thus evolves the Deal: popular demands are satisfied, the poor and the proletariat are cared for by free grain and circuses; but the military budget is also approved, the foreign bases and allies are well supplied, the foreign potentates are flattered and kept in power, the legions and divisions splendidly equipped. The price is ever-climbing budgets, higher taxes, and built-in inflation.
>
> The end of the story? Caesar reaches for absolute power, and absolute power corrupts Caesar first, the public and its morality next. Priests or television screens divinize his Image. Eager, famished enemies appear at the gates.[46]

The author rounds off his essay by reassuring his presumably somewhat alarmed readers that these thoughts on a Caesarean presidency are merely an intellectual exercise and that none of his predictions might come true. This conclusion is scarcely meant to quell the alarm his preceding analysis was clearly designed to generate.

In his disturbing depiction of an "Imperial America," Molnar makes no direct reference to the current president of the United States, the Democrat Lyndon B. Johnson. Yet the date of his article is significant, as is his cynical reference to a demagogic president who keeps the poor sweet to gain their support both for his leadership and for costly military activity abroad (which further secures his position at home). Two years earlier, Johnson had called on his fellow Americans to help enrich and elevate their national life into "a Great Society" and, since then, had introduced a series of sweeping policy innovations to improve access to education, health care, and civil rights, to renew the urban landscape, and to protect children, consumers, and the environment. Yet, in the preceding year, the president had decided unilaterally to escalate the war against Communism in southeast Asia and had withheld from Congress his commitment of U.S. troops to ground combat in Vietnam at the same time that he had requested a huge increase in his military budget to pay for offensive operations. Criticism in particular of the president's policy in Vietnam (of his secretive military strategies and their cost in men and money) intensified in the early months of 1966 and was widely displayed in televised hearings of the Senate Foreign Relations Committee, in newspaper articles, and in nationwide demonstrations against the war.[47] An article in the *New York Times* for 2 March 1966, entitled "Caesarism in Democracy," had noted that such criticism was frequently expressed as the accusation that President Johnson had seized and now applies too much executive power. Its author, the newspaper's foreign correspondent C. L. Sulzberger, shrugs off this American example of Caesarism as a symptom of the times: it is absent, he argues, from failing democracies (like Belgium or Italy) but at work in successful ones (like those of the United States, Great Britain, and France).[48]

A month after the publication of Thomas Molnar's Roman speculations, however, a political cartoon appeared in the *Washington Post* for 10 June 1966 that graphically targeted President Johnson as a modern Caesar under attack by his own American Brutus (see fig. 29). Displayed on the left is a short, bespectacled senator dressed in a white Roman tunic and boots. He holds a cigar in one hand and raises up a scroll in the other on which is written "Dirksen·accuses administration of lack of candor on Vietnam." On the right, a tall President Johnson, swathed in a dark and enveloping toga and sporting Roman sandals and a laurel wreath, finds himself backed against a column. The caption over the President's head reads: "Ev Tu?." The Latin tag *et tu, Brute?* ("also you, Brutus?"), which Julius Caesar famously cries out in Shakespeare's play as he gives in to death at the hands of his closest companion, has been adjusted to become the despairing cry of an American president under attack by even his most trusted friend and ally, Everett (affectionately shortened to "Ev") Dirksen.[49] Leader of the Republican Party in the Senate and fully committed to both a civil rights bill and the war in Vietnam, Dirksen had remained until recently a staunch advocate of Johnson's supreme constitutional authority—as commander in chief and "holder of the sword" over and above Congress as "holder of the purse."[50] But, in May 1966, he finally called for a comprehensive debate about the situation in Vietnam and attacked Johnson's continued secrecy at a time when ground engagements and air strikes were

"Ev Tu?"

FIGURE 29. "Ev Tu?" Herblock cartoon, *Washington Post*,
10 June 1966. Copyright by *The Herb Block Foundation*.

both substantially on the increase.[51] The Herblock cartoon identifies
the modern confrontation as one between a bewildered Caesar and an
American Brutus who, though once loyal, has finally been pushed to
the brink.

CAESAR IN LAS VEGAS

The arrival of Caesar in the White House marks not only the political
disintegration of the American republic but also its social and moral
decay, according to the analogical strategies of conservative commentators. In his *National Review* article for 3 May 1966, for example,
Thomas Molnar proclaimed that, in "Imperial America," absolute

power corrupts Caesar first and the public thereafter. From World War II into the 1970s, levels of poverty in the United States diminished, while rapid and broad affluence effected many radical social changes. The majority of Americans experienced a substantial increase in their disposable income, access to extended education, and home ownership in newly constructed suburban developments. They achieved much higher standards of living (including more leisure time and paid vacations), were able to buy a wide array of consumer goods (including more, and more powerful, automobiles), and inhabited new spaces in which they could experience the "good life" (such as shopping malls and motels).[52] Many analysts viewed with profound distaste the massification of culture resulting from such economic growth and social prosperity. Frequently they drew on a historical model of moral decay as one of the fundamental causes of ancient Rome's decline and fall in order to construct in modern parallel a credible eschatological narrative of American civilization's own inevitable end.[53]

In Lewis Mumford's landmark study, *The City in History: Its Origins, Its Transformations, and Its Prospects* (1961), for example, the pathologically bloated megalopolis of imperial Rome rises up as a menacing lesson for the present to avoid at all costs. Tracking the evolution of urban forms (perceived as organic and corporeal) and linking them to particular social and cultural values, the American social theorist pauses in his eighth chapter to argue, from the example of ancient Rome, that a city's physical and economic expansion is not a testament to the genuine prosperity and humane culture of its citizens:

> Wherever crowds gather in suffocating numbers, wherever rents rise steeply and housing conditions deteriorate, wherever a one-sided exploitation of distant territories removes the pressure to achieve balance and harmony nearer at hand, there the precedents of Roman building almost automatically revive, as they have come back today: the arena, the tall tenement, the mass contests and exhibitions, the football matches, the international beauty contests, the strip-tease made ubiquitous by advertisement, the constant titillation of the senses by sex, liquor and violence—all in true Roman style. So, too, the multiplication of bathrooms and the over-expenditure on broadly paved motor roads and, above all, the massive collective concentration on glib ephemeralities of all kinds, performed with supreme technical audacity. These are symptoms of the end: magnifications of demoralized power, minifications of life. (Mumford 1966, 280–81)[54]

Today, Mumford claims, the pattern of imperial Rome's disintegration is being repeated "with exquisite mimicry" (278): imperial power and centralized control lead to urban overgrowth; overgrowth brings disorganization, unscrupulous exploitation, violence, decay, and breakdown. As life in the engorged city is coarsened and brutalized, so its population demands and obtains compensatory outlets—a purposeless materialism and barbaric mass entertainments.[55]

It was an equally exquisite irony, then, that the Roman metaphor for America's moral disintegration so frequently deployed in the 1950s and 1960s should be literalized in the Nevada desert as an enticing house of fun named Caesars Palace. The casino resort opened in 1966, the same year that Thomas Molnar proclaimed the impending corruption of the president and the people of "Imperial America." Located at the time in striking isolation at the head of the Vegas automobile strip, set back from the road by an ostentatious driveway, Caesars Palace was originally created as a hyperthemed architectural pastiche of imperial Rome in order to differentiate it from other roadside motels. A playfully kitsch classicism was everywhere manifest; its hotel suites, casinos, gardens, pools, nightclubs, restaurants, and bars were awash with columns, pediments, architraves, arches, colonnades, fountains, statuary, friezes, and mosaics. The complex was named Caesars—without an apostrophe—to suggest that, on entry, any gambler might become a powerful Caesar and this his palace of pleasure. Guests may well have experienced an added frisson of pleasure if aware that they were enjoying the very nightmare of conservative moralists and social theorists: the decadence of imperial Rome standing in microcosm on American soil.[56]

Both the name Caesars and the imperial Roman architectural theme were loosely conceived as an amalgamation of the most celebrated Roman emperors (including Augustus and Nero) and the whole age of empire. But the lives visitors were most encouraged to emulate during their stay were those recently envisioned by Hollywood for the Roman dictator and his Egyptian queen. This modern American palace was presented not as an authentic reconstruction of the ancient city's public architecture (whose monumental beauty Lewis Mumford had grudgingly admired) but as a collation of Hollywood's simulations, especially those of the recent and notorious film *Cleopatra,* which had been directed by Joseph Mankiewicz and released in 1963. According to the casino's original owner and chief designer, the gambler Jay Sarno, guests were supposed to feel that they had passed through a cinema screen to become stars in their very own Roman epic of high living. Every night for years and years thereafter, actors dressed as Julius Caesar (in greaves, tunic, breastplate, cloak, and laurel wreath) and Cleopatra (in a showgirl version of Ptolemaic royal costume) made an appearance to greet and entertain the patrons of the Palace. A visit to the Palace thus remained an invitation to become like Caesar or Cleopatra for the duration of one's stay. Even the signs on the restroom doors declared in Latinate script "Caesars" and "Cleopatras."[57]

In tandem with, and stimulated by, the local development of Caesars Palace, from the 1960s onward the Roman dictator increased his appearances in popular culture far more broadly as convenient shorthand in the language of advertising. The advertising industry appropriated the dictator's familiar biography as connoisseur and collector of high art, extravagant spender, refined consumer, virile womanizer, and risk taker (in addition to successful general, writer, orator, and commanding statesman) in order to associate Caesar-branded products—from cigarettes to cars and chocolates—with power, luxury, sophistication, sensuality, and a touch of imperial decadence.[58]

LIBERALISM'S RUBICON

The monitory topoi of Julius Caesar's rise to power and the ensuing fall of the Roman republic were not the exclusive property of conservative commentators in the United States during the 1950s and 1960s. When Theodore H. White published a melodrama entitled *Caesar at the Rubicon: A Play about Politics* (1968), it was widely understood—from White's reputation and the text's framing comments, structure, and content—to constitute a striking critical comment, by a sympathetic observer, on the direction in which the Democratic presidencies of John F. Kennedy and Lyndon B. Johnson were taking the nation.

Throughout his celebrated career as a reporter of the campaigns every four years for the American presidency, White turned to the Roman republic and to Julius Caesar for illumination. In his later autobiographical study, *In Search of History: A Personal Adventure* (1978), White noted the importance contribution made to his perception of American history and American electioneering by the classical education he had once received at the Boston Public Latin School. Although as a boy he responded poorly to the drudgery of drills in Latin grammar (he confessed), as an adult he realized how much his classroom lessons on Caesar and Cicero "had flaked off into the sediment" of his thinking.[59] In the same work, he demonstrated the analogical propensity of his political thought when he presented the period from the social reforms of the Gracchi to Julius Caesar's crossing of the Rubicon (133–

49 B.C.E.) as the only adequate eighty-odd-year parallel for the social changes that had so altered the political landscape of the United States from 1880 to 1960. In White's account, the United States had experienced demographic upheavals on a par with both the disappearance of a Roman republic of self-governing "farmers, yeomen, citizen soldiers and patrician leaders" and the emergence of newly enfranchised outsiders the manipulation of whose votes began disproportionately to influence the election of Rome's leaders. But, while Caesar put an end to the old republican system, because (White claims) it was incapable of governing an expanding population, the political journalist reassures his readers that "no such event is likely in the near future in America."[60]

Yet, in an interview with the New York Times, published in February 1971 to coincide with the first public staging of Caesar at the Rubicon, White insisted that—like Caesar—all American presidents confront the temptation to step beyond the law. He also noted that the three acts of his play leading Caesar across the Rubicon had originally been conceived while he was writing up an account of the 1960 presidential campaign. White won a Pulitzer Prize for that best-selling work, The Making of the President, 1960 (published in 1961), and with it he launched a new, behind-the-scenes, "insider" style of political commentary. Claiming for the political process of that year the shape of a three-act drama leading Kennedy to the White House (the primaries, the televised debates in Chicago, and, finally, the election itself),[61] White had produced a vivid depiction of the yearning for and achievement of the highest political office.

Some of the policies for which White came to exalt President Kennedy throughout his journalistic career reemerge in his dramatic presentation of Julius Caesar at Ravenna in the winter of 50–49 B.C.E., pondering whether to march on Rome and initiate civil war. For example, the reporter credits both leaders with radical political reforms: Kennedy shatters the old pattern of American government by a white Protestant elite and opens the door to participatory democracy for Catholics, African Americans, Jews, other ethnic minorities, women, and the young;[62] Julius Caesar enfranchises Rome's second-class citizens—Sicilians, Alpine Italians, Gauls, and Jews.[63] Like The Making of the President, 1960, so, a few years later, Caesar at the Rubicon demonstrates a concern with electoral procedures in a democracy. The prologue identifies Julius Caesar before he entered into dictatorship as a man of populist politics: "Rome was a Republic; the people were sovereign; their votes made power. To sway those votes was to sway power itself, and thus he invented, or developed, many of those techniques and devices so familiar to us in our manipulation of popular votes today" (White 1968, 9). And voting and its manipulation remain constant themes throughout the individual acts of the play, as when a young Antony returns from Rome to Gallic headquarters, accompanied by Caesar's chief political "bagman and briber" (Balbus),[64] to reveal the disquieting news that the Roman general has lost control of the people's votes in the Assembly to his enemy Pompey. Caesar's chief of staff (Labienus) responds with incredulity:

LABIENUS: When Caesar and I ran elections, that's where our vote always was.

ANTONY: (*Growing angry himself*) But that was nine years ago, I tell you. (*Pauses at far end of stage, clears his throat, then spits a gobbet of spit in an enormous arc.*) They spit! If they don't like the speakers, they spit. They have squads of spitters now. With a good back-wind, they can spray you at fifty feet. (*Wipes an imaginary spray of spit off his face.*)

BALBUS: Spit—and rocks, and knives, and gangs.

LABIENUS: Don't tell me about voters. Caesar and I *organized* them. The workingmen in *collegia*. The tribes through the bosses. Tickets for the games. Plenty of entertainment—

BALBUS: Plenty of entertainment—but the others have learned the tricks, too—

LABIENUS: (*Ignoring Balbus, for whom he has contempt*) I'm talking. And, on top of that, a few friendly troops in the Forum on election day, to quiet them, a nice orderly vote. (*Emphasizes*) *With troops.* (32)

But undoubtedly the most obvious tie that binds *Caesar at the Rubicon* to Kennedy's presidency is the role White gives within his historical melodrama to one of Julius Caesar's senior officers, Asinius Pollio. The historical Pollio's eyewitness account of the civil war that broke out after Caesar crossed the Rubicon has not survived. In White's script, however, Pollio takes on the role of both headquarters reporter and overall narrator: he engages in conversation with Caesar, constantly scribbles notes with a stylus on a waxed tablet for his forthcoming history, and explains the stage action to an imagined theater audience. In the final moments of act 3, scene 3, he even boasts to that audience of the "exclusive" he won as "the only reporter" to accompany the Roman general across the Rubicon River into Italy (142). In the American journalist's play, Pollio thus repeats for Caesar in the Roman past the role the author had played for John F. Kennedy in the early 1960s—as memorializer of the daring steps to and in political power.

Theodore H. White reported on John F. Kennedy's political ascent to the presidency and his leadership in an epic, triumphant key. He became a celebrated journalist of the new establishment and supporter of the administration, whose chief executive he often cast in the role of virtuous hero and savior of the nation. He also played an instrumental part in the manufacture of a mythic image for Kennedy immediately after the president's assassination on 22 November 1963.[65] A week later, for example, *Life* magazine published an exclusive and shocking series of pictures of the shooting in Dallas, its bloody aftermath, and the solemn return of the president's body to the White House. In an interleaved article, White mourned JFK with great eloquence as an incomparable leader of the United States: a man of memorable courage in his confrontations with Russia and memorable compassion in his attempts to legislate against "the ills of age, the troubles of youth, the hopelessness of the unskilled, the humiliation of its darker citizens."[66]

While Julius Caesar is also presented as a great social reformer in the epilogue to White's melodrama of 1968 (158–59), the Roman general's tragedy is here of altogether a different order. At the beginning of the first act, the character Pollio expresses sympathy but also critical distance from the man he will memorialize:

> POLLIO: (*As narrator*) Gaius Julius Caesar. (*Fondling each word of the name*) A man to make you wonder. And who's to say the right and wrong of what he did? Or what it cost him? I was twenty-five when he took me on, and he past fifty—and what's twenty-five to know how it aches when you've passed fifty? Whether the Republic had to die? Or whether he really had to break the law? (21)

The explicit ambition of *Caesar at the Rubicon* is to stage the process whereby the Roman general decided to disobey the Senate's order that he should lay down his military command and, instead, with his troops crossed the river that separated his Gallic province from Italy. Thus he broke the law, initiated civil war, and, in White's view, almost single-handedly destroyed Rome's republic. The American reporter depicts this momentous decision as the consequence of a tormented personality's breakdown—a breakdown made most manifest in the growing conviction of the *imperator* that he has become divine (148). Yet, in an extended prologue, White pronounces Julius Caesar to be "a man of our time," and modern history an echo of ancient Rome's (4): now, as then, a self-governing republic is beset by carnal indulgence, civil violence, protracted and destructive war on a distant frontier, and—by implication—a distrusted leader's abuse of the law. In these respects, White's historical play does not appear to reflect on the Kennedy years of the early 1960s in which it was originally conceived, but on the period of Lyndon B. Johnson's presidency, in which it was composed (during June 1966 and October 1967),[67] and the year 1968, in which it was published, for 1968 was a year that, in retrospect, White recognized as a watershed for American liberalism and the Democratic Party.[68]

From 1966 to 1968, the chorus of criticism of Lyndon B. Johnson's presidency coming from the right of the political spectrum was matched by increasingly violent criticism from the left. The death of tens of thousands of American soldiers in the protracted war in Vietnam, and the failure of the Great Society reforms to improve conditions for a large proportion of the African-American population, triggered explosive antiwar demonstrations and civil rights riots in many of the nation's cities. In the splintering Democratic Party, opponents of the president declared that prolonged war was corrupting democracy and creating an all-powerful chief executive. During the course of 1968, the United States suffered further staggering losses in Vietnam, the collapse of its economy under the weight of the war's expense, and the assassinations of both the civil rights leader Martin Luther King and the presidential candidate Robert F. Kennedy. Confronted by such signs of political and social disintegration, a sufficient number of the electorate voted for Richard Nixon and his promise to restore law and order to make the Republican candidate the next president of the United States.[69] Ancient Rome, therefore, was a place and a time sufficiently distant and more extreme—yet also recognizable enough—for the political commentator White to make it the setting for a dramatic critique of American liberalism's decline. In *Caesar at the Rubicon*, the Roman mob is more ferocious than today's, and their leader more barbaric and manipulative; murder is one of his political tactics (4–5), his conduct of war a strategy of total erasure (12), and dictatorship and divinity become his goals (9). Yet, as the *New York Times* reported in April 1968 on the publication of the script of the play, "Mr. White is concerned with analogy: his Caesar is a double impersonation; his Rome is as much Now as Then."[70]

The prologue of Theodore H. White's essay melodrama opens with the pronouncement that "every age has carved its own Caesar, dressing him with its own passions and fears" (1968, 3). Perhaps some part of the journalist's dramatization of Julius Caesar at the Rubicon functions as a mode of self-criticism—leaders may come dangerously to believe the myths of imperial grandeur and supreme power that the media construct around them.[71] Yet White also presents himself as a historian genuinely curious about the Roman general's decision to break Roman law, cause civil war, and jeopardize the institutions of the republic. It is scarcely surprising that, in this capacity, the political commentator's appended bibliography on Caesar should commence with two seminal works by Lily Ross Taylor, *Party Politics in the Age of Caesar* (Berkeley, 1949) and *Roman Voting Assemblies* (Ann Arbor, 1966). In the first of these "the greatest living American student of Caesar" (according to White)[72] had found analogies for Roman election campaigns in the maneuvering at American national nominating conventions, and in the second she listed her own close observance of American political meetings on a par with new excavations of Roman places of assembly and newly unearthed bronze tablets as the evidence on which she was basing her fresh interpretation of Roman voting procedures.[73] Between the reporter and the scholar, Roman history and American politics are positioned in perfect symbiosis—each feeds off the other for elucidation. Hints of this intimate relationship emerge early in the script of *Caesar at the Rubicon: A Play about Politics*, when one of the first gestures of the Roman general on stage entry is to sample grapes heaped in a silver bowl that are colored red, white, and blue (25 and 35).

THE "IMPERIAL PRESIDENCY"

During the course of the late 1960s and early 1970s, criticism of American imperial expansion and its association with executive autocracy in the White House grew in volume and intensity.[74] Yet the rhetorical convention that clothed critiques in hyperbolic Roman tropes appears, in contrast, to fade away. Even Amaury de Riencourt in his second examination of America's destiny failed to make concentrated and sustained use of ancient Rome as monitory historical equivalence, as he had done in *The Coming Caesars* (1957). Caesarism and ancient imperialism receive only passing reference in the introductory pages of his book *The American Empire* (1968), at the same time as its author boldly asserts that all his earlier predictions are now coming true.

Five years later, in *The Imperial Presidency* (1973), Arthur M. Schlesinger chronicled the gradual appropriation by the executive over the course of the twentieth century of three vital powers originally reserved to Congress by the Constitution. In the introduction to a later edition of his influential study (published in 2004), Schlesinger elaborated on his use of the term "imperial." The Cold War, he argued, had provided

American presidents with the opportunity routinely to exercise almost royal prerogatives in the field of foreign affairs: "What began as emergency powers temporarily confided to presidents soon hardened into authority claimed by presidents as constitutionally inherent in the presidential office: thus the Imperial Presidency" (x). In the new edition, the historian also reflected that, so conceived, the "Imperial Presidency" had reached its apogee in the twentieth century during Richard M. Nixon's administration. In his view, Congress had surrendered the power to make war to President Truman in 1950, while Nixon's mode of governance involved additionally the systematic restriction of the two other major powers held by Congress—the power of the purse, and of oversight and investigation.[75] The original edition of Schlesinger's presidential history was published in the wake of the Watergate scandal (but before Nixon's resignation in August 1974), when abuse of power, political corruption, obstruction of justice, systematic secrecy, and a populist manipulation of the television medium could all be added to a vigorously interventionist foreign policy and the aggrandizement of domestic powers as features of Nixon's "Imperial Presidency." Yet the author managed his analysis without mention of Julius Caesar and Roman Empire as either sustained analogy or even fleeting metaphor.[76]

Scandal, impeachment, and resignation made Richard Nixon the incessant object of media attention in the 1970s as an American president who had crossed over the line of legality.[77] Nevertheless, scarcely any of the coverage in the national newspapers of the United States sought in Roman history an explanation of his corruption or a prediction of his fall. It is unusual to find a brief column in the *New York Times* (published on 9 May 1972) discussing Nixon in Roman terms as "an American emperor" and "an unchecked Caesar," because, the journalist argues, the president made the decision to mine North Vietnamese harbors entirely on his own.[78] It appears that, as the political Right and Left moved from speculation and prediction to confirmation and description of the massive growth in presidential powers at home and the radical expansion of the United States' commitments overseas, the necessity of investigating the modernity, the distinctiveness, and the specifics of American imperialism became too pressing to embrace the Roman dictator within its terms.

Pedagogic and commercial pressures, however, as well as the traditions that govern the performance of Shakespeare's *Julius Caesar* on the American stage and its reading in American schools and universities,[79] continued in this period to propel opportunistic discoveries of modern relevance in the life and death of the Roman dictator. The first issue of the journal *Interpretations,* for example, was launched by the Department of English at Memphis State University in 1968—the year in which Nixon would be elected to the presidency. A member of the department's staff contributed an analysis of the "modernity" of *Julius Caesar* that concluded with a blunt claim: if you stress the play's modern relevance, you will attract the attention of your students and make them want to read it.[80] Writing his essay in late August 1968, Professor Harry C. Cotham exploits the equivocal characterizations contained in the Elizabethan tragedy in order to amass numerous instant parallels. So morally "good" but politically "inept" Brutus plays out in the Roman past the Democratic candidate vying at this moment for the presidential nomination in Chicago (a blundering Hubert Humphrey); Hitler, Mussolini, Castro, and Stalin are the modern world's Caesars, vain and proud dictators all; Antony sways the fickle and irrational Roman mob like a union leader inciting his fellow workers, and that mob erupts into violence like the Klu Klux Klan riding through black sections of an American town or Negroes looting and burning Detroit; the murder of Caesar destroys Rome's force for order just as the assassination of John F. Kennedy, Martin Luther King, and Robert Kennedy have brought turmoil to the nation's cities. The professor hooks Shakespeare's Julius Caesar to as many of the turbulent events of the last few years and months as possible, despite the radical contradictions his multiple parallels entail. He thus fragments Roman analogy into multiple, conflicting parts and draws it away from the coherent direction it had been taking in American political discourse during the 1960s—leading the United States into a dark future where Democratic liberalism has broken down and the presidency has disintegrated into dictatorship.

Similarly, in June 1970 the entertainment magazine *After Dark* predicted that a new British film adaptation of Shakespeare's *Julius Caesar* (directed by Stuart Burge) would need to be camouflaged behind a screen of contemporary American relevance in order to achieve good box-office results. Under the parodic headline "Extra! CJC Struck Down on Capital Steps!" the article speculated that in publicity for the film its studio (Commonwealth United) and its transatlantic backers (American International Pictures, or AIP) would construct links to the assassinations that had taken place in recent years on American soil. Just as expected, on the film's general release in the United States in February 1971, an advertising poster conflated the "treacherous" and "twisted" assassins of Julius Caesar with those of a roll call of

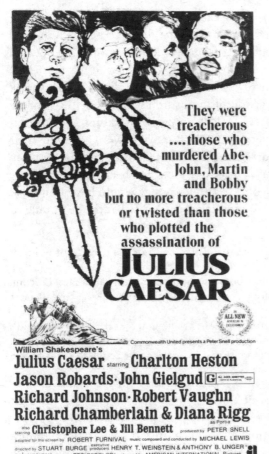

FIGURE 30. Poster advertising the film adaptation of Shakespeare's *Julius Caesar* directed by Stuart Burge (1970). Courtesy of the Academy of Motion Picture Arts and Sciences, Margaret Herrick Library.

American leaders who were both handsomely pictured and affectingly named Abe, John, Martin, and Bobby (see fig. 30). Equally predictably, AIP ran a major group sales campaign to attract the education market to the first version of the Elizabethan play to be produced in wide-screen Panavision and full Technicolor, with an all-star cast (but a relatively low budget). Among the exploitation strategies it recommended to theater managers were displays in public libraries, tie-ins at book stores, special screenings at local high schools, communiqués for English teacher associations and Shakespeare societies, and the distribution of a mocked-up newspaper—the *Roman Clarion* extra.[81] An article within the *Roman Clarion* stated explicitly that audiences viewing the AIP's new release would notice obvious parallels between the shocking headlines of the past decade and the murder of the Roman dictator. To aid that process and bridge the distance between ancient and modern political violence, the lead story on the front page opened: "Horror reigned in the Senate today when attending nobles witnessed the shocking assassination of the famed leader, Julius Caesar, struck down by the daggers of a group of opposition senators led by Marcus Brutus, Cassius and Casca."[82] AIP's campaign literature also recommended that when managers screened Burge's *Julius Caesar* in their local theaters they should dress their ushers in Roman costume and arm them with Roman weaponry. Once spectators had been ushered to their seats and back to ancient Rome in this way, they would have found yet further analogical guidance in the statement located at the beginning of their film program:

> Assassination is the tragedy of a demented mind or the outrage of political treachery.
>
> In the last century it has cost us the potential of Abraham Lincoln, Mohandis [sic] Gandhi, John Kennedy, Martin Luther King and Robert Kennedy.
>
> But it was forty-four years before the crucifixion that the civilized world's first assassination was planned and executed.
>
> Its story is of such contemporary concern as to be required study in the psychology of power politics.

The narrative structures of Burge's *Julius Caesar* (1970), however, demonstrate stark inconsistencies. The opening cinematography suggests that this film adaptation of Shakespeare's tragedy will contain a critique of imperialism. In a precredit sequence without parallel in the play, an eagle soars through the sky and lands in a field littered with corpses and the detritus of the dictator's final civil war.[83] The camera roams over the battlefield before picking out a skeleton still clad in the uniform of a Roman soldier and zooms in on its skull. Spectators then hear, as if issuing from its grimacing mouth, hoarse shouts of "Caesar! Caesar!" before visually and aurally they are offered jarring shifts to the victorious general's triumphant procession through Rome and the celebratory cries from the assembled crowds of "Hail, Caesar!." Yet Shakespeare's assassination scene is performed cinematically so as to engage the sympathies of the film audience intimately with the imperialist (as the publicity equating political assassination with treachery requires). Played by John Gielgud up to this point as an urbane elderly statesman, Julius Caesar is suddenly under violent assault.[84] Discordant drumbeats, bangs, and whistles accompany the blows to his body. In disturbing close-up, blood issues from the dictator. Caesar's gaze, which briefly becomes one with an out-of-focus camera, picks out imprecisely a lunging dagger, a conspirator's face, the back of Brutus. Spectators are forced further to identify with Caesar's point of view as the camera moves shakily to seek Brutus out and bring within arm's reach the friend who will turn only to complete the kill. Then, shot from overhead fully to display their seemingly sacred choreography, and supported by a musical crescendo, the conspirators encircle their victim's corpse and bathe their hands in his blood.[85] When Mark Antony arrives (played by the film's biggest American star, Charlton Heston), he grasps each of the bloody hands in a slow ritual that gesturally denounces the conspirators' deed as unholy, messy murder.[86]

Even before the film's release in the United States, a lengthy account of the day-to-day activities of the production was published in the United Kingdom in the *Daily Telegraph Magazine* (6 February 1970). There the reporter observed that Jason Robards was attempting to play Brutus as a man haunted by the immorality of political assassination because the American actor had been a close friend of Robert Kennedy before his murder.[87] American newspaper reviews, however, generally dismissed Robards's low-key, suppressed performance as unsatisfying and labeled as superficial the film's pitch as a study in the tragic psychology of assassination. The *New York Post* (4 February 1971) commended it only as an educational tool of limited use—an adaptation to screen of a Shakespearean set text in attractive "super-gore," elegant color, and a conventionally executed melodramatic style.[88]

Revivals of Shakespeare's *Julius Caesar* on the American stage in the 1970s regularly sought to establish a variety of political parallels between the Roman past and the American present or future. Yet sampling the evidence suggests that few, if any, attempted a sustained analogy with the assassinations of the 1960s or Richard Nixon's "Imperial Presidency" in the systematic manner of Orson Welles's celebrated anti-Fascist production of the 1930s.[89] On 18 November 1971, New York's *Village Voice* published a muted review of a revival by the Classic Stage Company (an off-Broadway theater whose mission was and is to reimagine the classical repertory for a contemporary American audience). The reviewer described the Fascist-dress production directed by Christopher Martin as more fun than staying home to read current strategic analyses of the emerging Republican majority in American national politics.[90] But this passage from the Roman past and its Elizabethan representation to an American future hinges on a small point of Realpolitik thought to issue from the play: Brutus should have agreed to bring down Mark Antony along with Caesar; opponents of Richard Nixon should attack Vice President Agnew first. In 1976, the year in which the United States celebrated its bicentennial, the off-off-Broadway Impossible Ragtime Theatre staged the modern-dress flannel-suited adaptation *Caesar* set largely in a smoke-filled poker room. A theater critic for the *East Side Express* (3 June 1976) claimed that George Ferencz's powerful modernization had "flung the story bodily into the miasmic world of American politics in the seventies" because the conspirators looked and acted like slick Washington lawyers huddled together during the Watergate hearings. Similarly, according to an enthusiastic review broadcast on the New York public radio station WNYC on 25 May, under the direction of Ferencz the tale "of political and personal disintegration and the loss of values" had been relocated to Washington. Yet, for the same reviewer, Julius Caesar is played as an amalgam of several presidents (possessing the Irish twinkle of John Kennedy, the determined stride of Lyndon Johnson, and the thin, worried spouse of Richard Nixon), while Decius has the grin of Jimmy Carter, and Brutus the declamatory style of Ted Kennedy.[91] As Roman analogy faded from the rhetoric of American political discourse during the course of the 1970s, so imaginative theater directors began to see in Shakespeare's tragedy a platform on which to play out rather different, but no less vital, contemporary concerns.

A CAESAREAN CULTURE WAR AND A MULTIMEDIA CAESAR

At 8:00 p.m. on Wednesday, 14 February 1979, a made-for-television version of Shakespeare's *Julius Caesar* was broadcast in the United States on some of the channels utilized by the Public Broadcasting Service (PBS) in order to launch a hugely ambitious cultural project—the adaptation expressly for television of the entire canon of Shakespeare's plays, to be broadcast at a rate of approximately six per year over the course of six years.[92] The series was developed and made at the television studios of the British Broadcasting Corporation in London and produced in association with Time-Life Television. A highly elaborate publicity campaign claimed that now, for the first time, Shakespeare's plays would arrive on American television screens in plain terms for the benefit of a mass audience. Advertisements in newspapers and magazines, radio interviews, television spots, and press packs also drew attention to the educational potential of the series and the teaching aids that were being targeted at high schools and colleges. These included videotapes and records of the shows, study guides, and special editions of the play scripts illustrated with television stills, cumulatively designed to instate the BBC-TV programs as the canonical versions of Shakespeare in performance.[93] Although this televisual Shakespeare was partly financed by three large American corporations (Exxon, Morgan Guaranty Trust, and Metropolitan Life Insurance), many reviewers understood it to be fundamentally and flamboyantly British in its execution.[94] *Julius Caesar*, as the first of the series and under the direction of Herbert Wise (who was well known for his earlier adaptation for television of Robert Graves's novels *I, Claudius* and *Claudius the God*), was subjected on broadcast to very close scrutiny by American critics. Some lauded the program for a text only lightly trimmed, superb enunciation, faithful period detail, a traditional rendering of the Roman tragedy, and the use of a mobile camera, tight close-ups, and voice-overs to express soliloquies. In contrast, others found it to be relatively unimaginative television, dismally conventional Shakespearean drama, pure rhetoric, and no emotion; its British players were said to simper and orate while strutting through a papier-mâché Rome wearing bedsheet costumes.[95] Writing in one of New York's alternative newspapers, the *Soho Weekly News* (1 March 1979), Maurice Charney, professor of English at Rutgers University, protested against such overt nationalism but, after comparing an American revival of Shakespeare's *Julius Caesar* then on stage, felt forced to admit that—at least as far as Shakespeare and his Caesar were concerned—"Britannia still rules."

Julius Caesar as both Roman person and Elizabethan play had held an important place in the formation of an American national identity set against that of the British Empire. As this book seeks to demonstrate, in the course of the twentieth century the Roman dictator achieved wide diffusion in American education, political and social discourse, and mass cultural production and had become thoroughly Americanized. Thus American executive producers selected Shakespeare's *Julius Caesar* for the first television broadcast of the BBC-TV series that began in 1979 precisely because, for domestic audiences, it was the most familiar of all the Elizabethan plays. Yet, for those same audiences, Shakespeare and Caesar were now being fed back to them as the cultural property of Great Britain. At the outset of the television project, the head of the New York Shakespeare Festival, Joseph Papp, had protested against the use of American public funds (through the agency of PBS) to support such British cultural colonialism. The outcome, he argued, would be to alienate young Americans from Shakespeare as both too foreign and too highbrow.[96] In the context of this renewed cultural war of independence, it was to Papp's own revival of *Julius Caesar* (staged from 16 January to 1 April 1979) that Professor Charney had looked for a distinctively American Shakespeare but found it wanting. Papp had pioneered free open-air performances of the Bard in New York, color-blind casting, and uniracial minority companies. Papp's *Julius Caesar*, directed by Michael Langham, was the first production for a new black and Hispanic Shakespeare repertory troupe the theatrical producer had formed and housed in his Public Theater (see fig. 31). Disappointed reviewers, such as Charney, found the major players insufficiently trained in Shakespeare's iambic pentameters by comparison with the British television cast, and their mix of African-American and Hispanic regional accents a severe obstacle to maintaining the dramatic illusion that they were all members of ancient Rome's senatorial elite.[97] For the more outspoken drama critic of the magazine *Saturday Review* (31 March 1979), only white liberals were capable of enjoying the bizarre aural clash between a "super-black" Caesar (played by Sonny Jim Gaines) and a "super-Hispanic" Antony (played by Jaime Sanchez).[98] Such criticism, however, misunderstood the mission of Papp and his minority theater actors at a time of rising political and cultural conservatism: to bring diverse ethnicities to an original avant-garde performance, better to illuminate Shakespeare and to display a more radical and inclusive conception of American cultural appropriation and, thus, of national identity.[99] On seeing the production, the American playwright and black feminist Ntozake Shange wrote enthusiastically to Joseph Papp:

> i cant quite explain the great pride i felt at curtain/when so many black and latin artists took their bows in the arena that had known so few of us except as moors/sprites/& sword carriers/maybe since i am one of that generation of afro-americans who did in fact experience the 'last segregated childhood' i waz able to have an unadulterated commitment to shakespeare for the first time in my life.[100]

It is not a peculiarly British privilege, nor a white Anglo-American one, to give fresh meaning to (and draw in new audiences for) such celebrated Shakespearean tags as "But I am constant as the northern star" (*JC* 3.1.60).

A second major staging of Shakespeare's *Julius Caesar* during the

FIGURE 31. Roscoe Orman (Brutus), Sonny Jim Gaines (Caesar), and Gylan Kain (Cassius), in a scene from Shakespeare's *Julius Caesar,* Public Theater, New York (1979). Photograph by Bert Andrews. Courtesy of the Billy Rose Theatre Division, The New York Public Library for the Performing Arts, Astor, Lenox and Tilden Foundations.

1979 theater season also sought to cast fresh illumination on the play for American audiences without invoking sustained Roman analogy for the future (or the present) of American government. In a press release dated 11 June 1979, Gerald Freedman declared that his revival at the American Shakespeare Theater in Stratford, Connecticut, would not mirror any one current event but place in sharper focus an aspect of "the play's truth for today." As the director conceived it, that truth consisted in the conflict between the "honourable" motives publicly professed by political leaders, and their private self-interest.[101] Under Freedman's direction, the Roman tragedy then became in sum "a kind of anthology of modern political disintegration,"[102] abroad as well as at home: actors' rehearsals were inspired by the daily perusal of newspaper clippings that recounted the outbreak of the Iranian revolution, the deposition of the shah, and the subsequent struggle between factions;[103] Caesar was costumed like a Latin American caudillo (in military uniform decorated with gold braid and rows of service medals), the conspirators like dissenting academics or Unitarian ministers (with surplices draped over their three-piece suits); while the mise-en-scène included screens above the stage on which was played videotaped footage of a Kennedy-style cavalcade before the assassination scene and, after it, guerrilla fighting in the manner of battles in the Korean and Vietnam wars.[104] Holding together this political collage, and engaging theater audiences with it, was the consistent organization of the dramatic acts as a modern, multimedia experience. In order to give ancient Rome the feel of a technological society, a three-dimensional grid of long, thin silver rods stood in for the pillars of the Senate. As Julius Caesar proceeded to the Capitol in act 3, scene 1, video screens dropped from above the stage to display crowds watching a presidential motorcade, while, on arrival, the Roman dictator was surrounded by Secret Service agents and press photographers with cameras whose flashbulbs popped. After the assassination, during the Forum scene, first Brutus and then Antony faced a battery of microphones while a camera hidden in the theater pit telecast their faces onto large screens arrayed high above their heads, as if they were delivering their speeches at a political rally for broadcast on the television evening news. The speakers were separated from and dwarfed by their speaking images (a separation emphasized by the slightly different angle at which each image was projected, its black-and-white tones, and its relatively poor resolution). Stratford audiences were thus compelled disconcertingly to keep switching their gaze between the two and to judge what constituted the aesthetic and the ethical difference between them. Many reviewers were disturbed by such novel strategies, as well as by the liberties taken with Shakespeare's text, the intrusive, noisy modernity of the production, and the mutability of its "Everycaesar."[105] Yet others lauded Freedman's modern-dress revival as an innovative, controversial vision of the tragedy that simultaneously clarified the political rhetoric pronounced by Shakespeare's Romans and exposed how late twentieth-century politicians manipulate the mass media but are also made and betrayed by them.

WARNING AGAINST DEMOCRATIC IDEALISM'S ERADICATORS

Thirty years after the bimillennium of Julius Caesar's death, an attempt was made to reclaim the Roman dictator for the American Left and to rescue him from his dominant function in postwar, conservative political discourse as a reliable paradigm for the excesses of democratic liberalism and its alleged propensity to descend into dictatorship. In 1986, the History Book Club published as its selection for July a lively blend of scholarly biography and historical fiction entitled *The Education of Julius Caesar: A Biography, A Reconstruction.* Its author, Arthur D. Kahn, had come late to academic life and a professorship in classics after a long career of military service in World War II and, subsequently, radical activism in peace organizations and the civil rights movement. Across the course of the 450 pages of his book, Caesar is represented as an adherent of an enlightened Epicureanism (here treated as if it were a form of Socialist doctrine),[106] and as a lifelong principled reformer who confronts and overthrows the senatorial oligarchy in order to improve the conditions of the exploited provinces and the urban poor.[107] The honorable features of a New Dealer are retrojected onto the Roman dictator, while those of contemptible, McCarthyite witch-hunters are attributed to his opponents Cato and Cicero:[108] "Caesar recognized and warned that civil war would ravage the empire if he was killed, but the self-proclaimed champions of liberty and defenders of the constitution, the subversive-hunters, the praters of piety, of patriotism and of the ancestral virtues were prepared to pull down the world if their outmoded privileges were not restored" (Kahn 2000, 450–51). In this revision of Roman republican history, it is not the dictator's radicalism that brings down the world but the repressive conservatism of those who conspire against him. Consequently, Kahn is able to conclude that "Caesar is the greatest personality of the thousand years of Roman history. Rightfully do we continue to commemorate him in the seventh month of the year" (453).

In an impassioned preface, the author made clear that his historical biography would delineate not only the education *of,* but also an education *by,* Julius Caesar. Investigation of the Roman experience, he there argues, has long been a recognized mechanism to illuminate the contemporary experience of the United States. His own generation, which suffered the Depression and the Second World War and saw its postwar hopes wither along with the nation's democratic idealism, understands the poignancy of the end of the Roman republic and of Caesar. America's youth, in contrast, are indifferent to the past and thus stand numb and helpless before impending political catastrophe (Kahn 2000, ix). By implication, reading *The Education of Julius Caesar* might yet empower them.

Not all classical historians were impressed by the manipulations and elisions required to redesign the assassination of Julius Caesar (against the grain of conservative political discourse) as a lesson for young Americans about tragic assaults on democratic values. In the *New York*

Review of Books for 12 May 1988, the British scholar Jasper Griffin argued that Kahn was losing sight of the moral facts: the violence of Caesar's consulship, the ruthlessness with which he conducted war in Gaul, the personal pique that motivated his initiation of civil war, his unconstitutional honors and powers, his complete abandonment of republican principles. In the early twenty-first century, however, the Roman dictator would reenter American political debate (and international debate about America's foreign policy) far more forcefully as a weapon of the Left, but this time as an adverse exemplar for presidential autocracy and imperial aggression to be wielded against conservative advocates of American empire. Within American mass culture, Julius Caesar has more often achieved effect politically (if not pedagogically or commercially) as pure villain rather than flawed hero.

CHAPTER 7

Empire

1989–2008

During the last quarter of the twentieth century, from the administration of President Nixon's successor (Gerald Ford) to that of George W. Bush's predecessor (Bill Clinton), political commentators in the United States continued to explore questions of military interventionism abroad and executive predominance at home with little recourse to the vocabulary of Roman empire or Caesarism.[1] Until 1989, even apocalyptic anxieties about American expansion were often partly assuaged by the assumption that U.S. military growth and the creation of a colossal bureaucratic machinery at home were merely temporary departures from the nation's republican origins, part of a Cold War strategy of containment rather than conquest, and held in check by the opposition of the Eastern empire of the USSR.[2] A passing remark made by President George H.W. Bush seems to have inspired an opportunistic exception to the general absence of analogy to ancient Rome in the last quarter of the twentieth century. On 30 December 1990, an article published in the New York daily *Newsday* carried the headline "A New Caesar Tests the Republic." In it Jonathan Schell, a critic of nuclear armament, took as his starting point a comment that the then president Bush had recently made to a group of congressmen about his decision to go to war in the Persian Gulf: "I have crossed the Rubicon." What for George H.W. Bush formed a pleasingly impressive metaphor for a momentous and irrevocable military decision became for the columnist the president's unconscious revelation of a disturbing threat to the integrity of republican government—an unauthorized declaration of war:

> When Caesar crossed the Rubicon, he stood at the head of a legion. Bush has so far only declared an unconstitutional power. He has only placed a toe in the Rubicon. The die is not yet cast. He can still acknowledge the need to obtain a congressional declaration of war before he sends the troops into battle. If he does not volunteer to do this, Congress should require him to do it. The United States needs no Julius Caesar in the White House.[3]

At the start of the twenty-first century, however, analogies from Roman history and this type of Caesarean imagery began to appear frequently and at length in both national and international debate about American foreign policy.

On 27 March 2003, for example, the Italian newspaper *Il Messaggero* asked: "Is the President of the United States of America the Caesar of the twenty-first century?"[4] On that same day in March, just days after the invasion of Iraq, the magazine of the Italian newspaper *Corriere della Sera* carried a similar question on its front cover: "But is the American empire like that of Rome?"[5] In the course of an extensive interview within the pages of the magazine, the classical scholar Luca Canali was asked whether he saw any parallel between George W. Bush and Gaius Julius Caesar, given that (according to the reporter) they were both the supreme head of a superpower. The professor scornfully dismissed such historical analogies: Caesar was the greatest man in history ("il più grande uomo della storia"), how could he be compared with Bush? In private, Caesar was extremely cultivated and friend to the greatest intellectuals of his time (Canali continued), whereas Bush didn't know his Slovenia from his Slovakia (the interviewer conceded). In public, Caesar was a great political leader, who relied on the justice of his efforts in both peace and war to win the goodwill of all the people. He was an unconquerable general, who had the courage to enter the field of battle and fight on the front line. He was assassinated only because he preferred not to live guarded day and night. A great man indeed. Confronted by such a catalogue of extraordinary virtues, the interviewer gave up any further attempt at comparison between Bush and Caesar and, instead, tried out other Roman analogies for American empire until they are pushed playfully beyond the limits of credibility (Saddam Hussein as Hasdrubal, Osama bin Laden as Mithridates, Dick Cheney as Agrippa, Donald Rumsfeld as Cato).

Many political scientists and historians of the United States have also questioned the validity of comparing America with ancient Rome and its president with Julius Caesar. Their arguments include the following: the international power of the United States is hegemonic not imperial; the power of the United States consists in preeminence and leadership not domination; U.S. rule is informal or indirect; "empire," as administered by the United States, is by invitation and, to date, of short duration; U.S. hegemony does not involve the exercise of formal sovereignty overseas; the international power of the United States is driven by an economy of abundance and supported by the most highly advanced technology, including nuclear weaponry; the power of the United States does not rely on slave labor; the U.S. president is neither a dictator nor an emperor; the president is an impermanent magistrate who administers rather than enacts the law; the president does not rule, nor does he command the power to declare war.[6] Yet outright rebuttals like that of Professor Canali form an obstacle to the examination of why, in the first decade of the new millennium, such comparisons were made so often, were taken so seriously, and became so influential both in the United States and across the world.

In the lead-up to the invasion of Iraq in March 2003, and continuing in its aftermath, one common rhetorical strategy that emerged in the popular media to facilitate and embellish comment on American foreign policy consisted in finding multiple parallels between the empire of ancient Rome and modern American imperialism, and (on occasion) between Julius Caesar and a resurgent "imperial presidency."[7] Newspaper articles, political cartoons, and editorials, both in the United States and abroad, carried such resonant headlines as "All Roads Lead to D.C.," "Rome, AD ... Rome, DC?," "The Last Emperor," "Hail Caesar!" "Forget the Romans, U.S. Rules the World: Emperor Bush."[8] The deployment of such historical analogy became entrenched in popular political discourse about the Bush presidency and continued to emerge across the two terms of the administration in book-length studies by authors who were either nostalgic for or (far more often) critical of empire. Such studies included, among others, Andrew J. Bacevich's *American Empire* (2002) and contributed volume *The Imperial Tense: Prospects and Problems of American Empire* (2003); Senator Robert C. Byrd's *Losing America: Confronting a Reckless and Arrogant Presidency* (2004); Niall Ferguson's *Colossus: The Rise and Fall of the American Empire* (2004); Chalmers Johnson's *The Sorrows of Empire: Militarism, Secrecy, and the End of the Republic* (2004) and *Nemesis: The Last Days of the American Republic* (2007); and Cullen Murphy's *Are We Rome? The Fall of an Empire and the Fate of America* (2007).[9]

Some historians of ancient Rome and of the United States may well flinch at such attempts to make past events speak directly to the present, to make ancient Rome the prism through which to perceive more clearly contemporary global politics. Yet, soon after the invasion of Iraq, and in pointed contrast, the director of the Center for Strategic Studies at Johns Hopkins University, Eliot A. Cohen, argued that practitioners and pundits have the last word over scholars in this regard. Precisely because politicians and policymakers are frequently finding lessons in history, taking them to heart, and even acting on them, academics have an obligation to examine how history is informing, and how it should inform, current understanding of the United States of America as a "hyperpower."[10] Quite a number of scholars and political commentators have since shouldered that obligation. American global dominance in the twenty-first century can better be understood (they maintain) through comparison with empires of the past. Rome has provided the terminology of "empire"—the word derives from *imperium*, the Latin for "command" or "authority" (especially military). Rome also provides the paradigm of imperial structures in relation to which modern empires have even been modeled, as well as understood.[11] Analogy with the Roman republic and empire dominated American political debate during the originary revolt against British imperial rule, exercised exemplary authority in the establishment of the structures of American government, and has shaped much policy and political discourse in the centuries since. Thus, comparison with the Roman Empire is a legitimate strategy by which to think through the new place of the United States in the world. And (they further claim) it is also highly productive, because ancient Rome can open up to modern political debate a raised vantage point, an altered perspective, a new vocabulary, greater candor, heightened seriousness, and, even, a wider audience of "ordinary" Americans.[12]

The first decade of the twenty-first century thus witnessed a reinvigorated debate about seemingly close correspondences between Roman and American empire, and between their abuses (or, occasionally, their benevolences) of power. The catalogue of correspondences variously embraces rapid expansion from small republic to world power; the status of most powerful political actor in the world; overwhelming military strength and reach; strategic bases across vast territories; the centrality of technology to power; the exercise of not only hard (military) but also soft (linguistic, cultural, economic) dominance; multiethnic and hierarchical social structures; corruption, sybaritic excess, and a messianic sense of self-importance at the center; rapid aggrandizement of executive authority; and demagogic leadership.[13] This fresh debate differs from that sparked during the Cold War by the publication of Amaury de Riencourt's *The Coming Caesars* (1957).[14] It differs in its multiple points of origin (various monographs as well as political commentary on television and radio, in newspapers, and across the Internet), its duration (across the two terms of the Bush administration, and beyond, looking at it in retrospect), its "imperial tense" (the diagnostic present and perfect rather than the prognostic future), and its global reach (even, according to some, penetrating into the jihadist rhetoric of al-Qaeda).[15] Yet if a major political question at the start of the twenty-first century has been "Is the United States of America the New Rome?" then a further question for some commentators has been "Is George W. Bush the New Caesar?"—invading territories, centralizing executive powers, destroying the republic.

THE RISE TO EMPIRE OF NEW ROME

The fall of the Berlin Wall in 1989 constituted a turning point for the United States of America with regard to its stature in the world. From that date, if not before, an influential neoconservative foreign policy group started to articulate a grand strategy for the United States now that it was understood to have emerged as the world's only superpower. The old Cold War orthodoxies of multilateral containment and deterrence of the Soviet Union could no longer apply in a new, unipolar world. Raised to transcendent status, the United States should accept its transcendent mission.[16]

In 1997, the group launched the Project for the New American Century (PNAC) at www.newamericancentury.org and began to advocate aggressive intervention abroad, expressed as a doctrine of military might conjoined with "diplomatic energy and commitment to moral principle." Signatories to PNAC included a number of individuals who were to become key members of George W. Bush's administration, such as Paul Wolfowitz, Dick Cheney, and Donald Rumsfeld. By the following year, "empire" entered their vocabulary—if only figuratively—when Robert Kagan (then a senior associate of the strategic planning institute Carnegie Endowment for International Peace) argued in the pages of the journal *Foreign Policy* that the hegemony now being exercised by the United States preserved international security and prosperity and was, therefore, good for most of the world. His article, which was to become highly influential, bore the simple yet provocative title "The Benevolent Empire."[17] By the time of the presidential elections in 2000, a report commissioned by PNAC presented America's new strategic foreign policy goal as the establishment of permanent global hegemony, and better to characterize that hegemony drew on the old slogan *pax Americana*[18]—in a bold Latinate echo of Edward Gibbon's celebrated depiction of the *pax Romana* as a sustained period in the history of the Roman Empire when "the condition of the human race was most happy and prosperous."[19]

Yet, at that same time, George W. Bush found it necessary while campaigning for the presidency to assert: "America has never been an empire. We may be the only great power in history that had the chance, and refused—preferring greatness to power, and justice to glory."[20] At first, New Right circles were careful in the main to dismiss the idea that their doctrine constituted an outright call to empire.[21] It was a founding myth of the United States that it had been born out of struggle against imperial rule, despite the expansionist ambitions the nation had demonstrated at the time of its foundation and continuously thereafter.[22] Empire was commonly associated with a fatal historical sequence, thought, erroneously, to have been initiated by Julius Caesar when he crossed the river Rubicon: loss of republican liberty, domestic tyranny, foreign expansion, imperial overstretch, and final fall.[23] And, from the late nineteenth century and throughout the twentieth, the language of empire had become a weapon frequently deployed by the Left to critique American interventionism aboard.[24] Thus "imperial denial" was still in evidence in October 2002, when Donald Kagan, professor of classics and history at Yale University, declared vehemently in an article in the *Atlanta Journal–Constitution*:

> All comparisons between America's current place in the world and anything legitimately called an empire in the past reveal ignorance and confusion about any reasonable meaning of the concept empire, especially the comparison with the Roman empire. . . . The Romans acquired the greatest part of their empire by direct military conquest, subjected their people to Roman law, and imposed taxes and compulsory military service under Roman command. They deprived their subjects of freedom and autonomy. . . . To compare the United States with any such empire is ludicrous.[25]

Such neoconservative distaste for the concept of American empire became radically diluted, however, after 11 September 2001 and the terrorist attacks on the World Trade Center and the Pentagon. That day and its outcomes spurred more hawkish neoconservative intellectuals, politicians, and pundits to appropriate, even to revel in, both the concept of empire and historical comparison with ancient Rome. Now, enthusiastic assertions about the second coming of the Roman Empire began to surface in the national press, and were then disseminated in local newspapers, foreign policy magazines, bulletins of think tanks, conferences, monographs, and the digital media.

The events of 9/11 prompted the Bush administration to adopt a far more abrasive grand strategy—a revolutionary reorientation of American foreign policy toward a global war on terrorism. The new "National Security Strategy of the United States of America," formally published a year later in September 2002, declared an intention vigorously to sustain the worldwide military sovereignty of the United States against any potential rivals, and an exclusive entitlement to wage preemptive war in order to achieve that end.[26] In addition, the terrorist attacks profoundly altered the character of the presidency. George W. Bush now fully embraced the responsibility of commander in chief and both sought and found popular support for a strong style of leadership that restored to the chief executive (and even enhanced) the prerogatives the office had lost after Watergate.[27] Critics subsequently interpreted this unprecedented "Bush Doctrine" as authoritarian, nationalistic, militarist, unilateral, and decisively imperialist. Looking back at this period, for example, the historian and political scientist Chalmers Johnson observed that 9/11 "produced a dangerous change in the thinking of some of our leaders, who began to see our republic as a genuine empire, a new Rome, the greatest colossus in history, no longer bound by international law, the concerns of allies, or any constraints on its use of military force."[28]

The New York Times reported in March 2002 a striking statement made by the conservative columnist for the Washington Post Charles Krauthammer: "People are now coming out of the closet on the word 'empire'. . . . The fact is no country has been as dominant culturally, economically, technologically and militarily in the history of the world since the Roman Empire." Krauthammer's comments then reappeared in multiple newspaper articles and books produced at the time, and to this day they continue to be recycled and analyzed on numerous websites about American imperialism.[29] Similarly, a special "Empire" edition of the conservative foreign policy magazine the National Interest was issued in spring 2003, explicitly setting out its aim in its opening pages as an exploration of the needs of America's "imperial vocation." By May 2003, political debate about American empire had thoroughly saturated both the national and the international press. Bandied between neoconservatives and their critics, the vocabulary of "empire" and, specifically, of ancient Rome was regularly utilized better to articulate a new world order in which the United States held the exceptional status of a hyperpower, uniquely exercising direct, enduring control over other states from an imperial center.[30]

Use of the discourse of empire among its modern-day advocates, however, clearly came with rules attached. It was never spoken—indeed, it was modestly rejected—in the most official contexts. During a speech at a White House reception for veterans on 11 November 2002, for example, President Bush himself declared categorically: "We have no territorial ambitions, we don't seek an empire."[31] And in order to disassociate American-style empire from distasteful suggestions of economic dominance, loss of liberty, tyranny, and inexorable decline and fall, careful attempts were always made to picture its *imperium* as premised on a uniquely beneficial, civilizing mission. Writing in the *New York Times* in January 2003, Michael Ignatieff, professor of human rights policy at Harvard University, confidently differentiated this twenty-first century *imperium* from earlier types, as "an invention in the annals of political science, an empire lite, a global hegemony whose grace notes are free markets, human rights and democracy, enforced by the most awesome military power the world has ever known."[32]

NEW CAESAR CROSSING THE RUBICON

With the extreme (and fleeting) exception noted toward the end of this chapter, no advocate of a brand-new twenty-first-century American empire seems to have been so bold as to take up the conventional duality of Roman imperial analogy and suggest also that the president of the United States should take up the mantle of Julius Caesar.[33] Such a rhetorical strategy would have required extremely careful expression (however tentatively undertaken), not least because in the political history of the United States the Roman dictator had commenced his career as the quintessential enemy, symbolic of British tyranny, against which a whole nation of American Brutuses had so bravely fought the War of Independence, and most recently had been deployed by the Right to critique the Democratic presidencies of the Cold War era as demagogic, dictatorial, and dangerously imperialist.[34] On 2 February 2002, however, a columnist for the *Washington Post* reported:

George W. Bush delivered such a stunning State of the Union speech, during which he dazzled Congress with a mix of Julius Caesar and Billy Graham, that it left the opposition virtually speechless. Who is going to argue with the scourge of evil, the conqueror of Afghanistan? . . . Richard Gephardt, House Democratic leader, was reduced, in his reply to the president, to complaining that Bush did not mention campaign reform. Can you imagine that Caesar, addressing the Senate, would be faced with the effrontery of a query about the state of Rome's sewers?[35]

In her passing references to Caesar, the journalist Mary McGrory appears to bestow on President Bush by association the character of an eloquent orator, a high-minded statesman above trivial questions of domestic reform, a popular and resolute decision-maker and, most importantly of all in the heated context of the war on terror and the invasion of Afghanistan, a triumphant wartime commander in chief and principled conqueror. Any possible hint of dictatorship or brutality is seemingly offset by the additional association of Bush with Christian fundamentalism. Only later in the article does it emerge more clearly that here historical analogy may have an ironic purpose, that McGrory is trying to fling the Roman metaphor back at those whom she regards to be deploying it so pretentiously, perhaps even perniciously, as a cloak for domestic (and foreign) wrongdoings. Indeed, she goes on to argue that the gravity and high-mindedness of the president's oratory worked conveniently to render vulgar any questions from his audience about the Enron scandal. A commander in chief has no need to make mention of such matters: "When you are briefing the country on survival and revival, you have no time for such trifles."[36]

Subsequently, the lead-up to the invasion of Iraq prompted a whole spate of articles on both sides of the Atlantic that made sustained and unfavorable comparison between the president of the United States and Julius Caesar (or Roman emperors more generally). Such critiques gained their momentum specifically from the address George W. Bush delivered to the United Nations on 12 September 2002 (the day after the first anniversary of 9/11), in which he effectively declared that, if the UN were not going to act against Iraq, the United States would do so alone.[37] The day after that momentous address, Robert Fisk (Middle East correspondent for the British newspaper *The Independent*) observed that, seated in the United Nations General Assembly, surrounded by green marble fittings and a backcloth of burnished gold, the president was able to enjoy the furnishings of an emperor, "albeit a diminutive one." Suggesting that the

FIGURE 32. Cartoon by JAS (James A. Sillaman) to accompany the article "The Last Emperor," *The Guardian*, 13 September 2002. Reproduced by kind permission of the cartoonist.

president's menacing speech was tantamount to a declaration of war against Iraq, the journalist concluded his newspaper article dramatically: "What was the name of that river which Julius Caesar crossed? Was it not called the Rubicon? Yesterday, Mr Bush may have crossed the very same river."[38] The same day, another British newspaper, *The Guardian*, carried a lead comment by its columnist Polly Toynbee, in which she described President Bush as "this unlikely emperor of the world," telling the UN in effect to pass a resolution on war or be bypassed: "What the US wants, the UN had better solemnise with a suitable resolution—very like the Roman senate and one of its lesser god-emperors."[39] The accom-

FIGURE 33. "Hail, Bush."
Photomontage by Steve
Caplin, front cover of G2,
The Guardian, 18 September
2002. Reproduced by kind
permission of the cartoonist.

panying political cartoon by JAS (James A. Sillavan) showed a wreathed
and togate emperor incongruously waving a small Stars and Stripes pen-
nant triumphantly in his hand as he stands in an advancing armored
personnel carrier (fig. 32). Similarly, a photomontage by Steve Caplin of
President Bush as a wreathed and breastplated Roman general, gesturing
thumbs-down for death (fig. 33), appeared a few days later on the cover
of a tabloid insert of the same British newspaper above the legend "Hail,
Bush. Is America the New Rome?" Although the enclosed article was
concerned with the historical analogy of empire rather than emperor,
the image that illustrated it strongly suggested a critique of the American
presidency as an imperial, arbitrary, and bloody mode of leadership.[40]

Across just a few days in September 2002, these three examples from
the British press between them worked to construct George W. Bush
as simultaneously Julius Caesar and emperor of Rome. By means of
these manipulations of Roman history, the president becomes an imperial leader who is making an irrevocable and momentous decision to go
to war. When Julius Caesar ruthlessly expanded Roman dominion west
and north from his province of Gallia Narbonensis, he operated as one
of a number of aristocrats holding *imperium* who were working in competition with each other to obtain the highest military glory. The Roman

general was not head of state when he decided to cross the river Rubicon into Italy with his legionnaires, and, in so doing, he launched a civil not a foreign war. After crossing the Rubicon, Caesar scarcely altered the territorial expanse of the Roman Empire and was assassinated just before he was due to embark on further ambitious campaigns of conquest in the East. He was murdered because of his *aspirations* to divinity and monarchy; he was never king or emperor of Rome. Nevertheless, in September 2002, dressing George Bush up as an imperial Caesar became a seemingly credible and appealing device by which to attack American unilateralism.

The image of "Emperor Bush" advancing across his Rubicon gained credibility and force from its neat fit with the reemerging rhetorical strategy that indicted American intervention abroad through the vocabulary of "empire" and, in particular, through alarmist parallels with the period of the fall of the Roman republic and the extension of Roman empire under monarchic rule.[41] Above all other actions, the invasion of Iraq would brand the United States an imperial power.[42] Such an empire might be thought (however erroneously) to require an emperor for it to be criticized effectively. In American culture, Julius Caesar had long been both index and embodiment of a devastating turning point in Roman history: the collapse of the republic and the rise of an imperial monarchy to replace it. From this perspective, Caesar alone is the republic's ruin. His self-interested ambition leads him to usurp senatorial authority by arms. His designs on monarchy lead to the establishment of the rule of emperors, of whom he is positioned as the first. His expansion of empire and the centralization of power it entails lead ultimately to Rome's decline and fall. It is the figure of imperial Caesar who demonstrates (as he did before for Amaury de Riencourt or Theodore H. White) that external aggrandizement breeds internal tyranny, that empire will ruin the American republic.[43]

Additionally, in September 2002, representing the threatened invasion of Iraq as an advance across another Rubicon positioned the act as unlawful and its agent as defiant. The modern presidential Caesar is made to cross both a geographic boundary (advancing American troops across the border river Tigris into Iraq) and a metaphoric one (exceeding the military powers invested in him as commander in chief of the United States and flouting the authority of the United Nations). Roman history dictates that disaster lies on the other side. Caesarean analogy also suggestively linked son back to father. As we saw at the opening of this chapter, in late 1990 Bush Senior was accused of dipping his toe in the waters of the Rubicon when he appeared at first to be threatening war in the Persian Gulf without the approval of Congress or the sanction of the United Nations. Now Bush Junior could be presented as about to advance beyond the footsteps of his father, deep into unconstitutionality.

By the end of 2002, elements of the American press had also begun to condemn George W. Bush as an imperial Julius Caesar. In the December issue of the progressive monthly *Harper's Magazine,* under the title "Hail Caesar," the current editor, Lewis H. Lapham, contrasted his personal experience of fierce, nationwide opposition to the invasion of Iraq with the perceived sycophancy of most of the national news media and the subservience of both Senate and Congress:

> After the pretense of a debate that lasted less than a week, Congress on October 11 invested President George W. Bush with the power to order an American invasion of Iraq whenever it occurred to him to do so, for whatever reason he might deem glorious or convenient. Akin to the ancient Roman practice of enthroning a dictator at moments of severe crisis, the joint resolution was hurried into law by servile majorities in both a Senate (77–23) and a House of Representatives (296–133) much relieved to escape the chore—tiresome, unpopular, time-consuming, poorly paid—of republican self-government. The sergeants-at-arms didn't take the trouble to dress up the occasion with a slaughter of sacrificial goats or the presentation of a bull to Apollo, but the subtext of the vote could be understood as a submissive prayer: "Our President is a Great General; he will blast Saddam Hussein and rescue us from doom. To achieve this extraordinary mission he needs extraordinary powers, so extraordinary that they don't exist in law . . . Great is Caesar; God must be with him."[44]

Here again Caesar appears as a natural consequence of and ready counter to the New Right's embrace of empire. Merging President Bush with Julius Caesar creates a striking and extreme narrative. Traditional democratic institutions abdicate their power. An untrustworthy and bellicose leader usurps their authority. In a time of crisis, the country turns to dictatorship. A single individual amasses extraordinary powers.[45] War is declared illegally. Troops march blindly across forbidden borders into an invasion that will bring with it historic, and undoubtedly disastrous, consequences.

The imperial form of Caesarean analogy thus stimulates, naturalizes, and gives a semblance of plausibility to an especially vivid representation of contemporary American politics. It paints a portrait of its foreign policy in the bright reds of a bloody empire, its president in the deep purples of its ruthless emperor. It constructs this moment in

2002, on the eve of the invasion of Iraq, as equal in historical significance to the moment when the Roman republic collapsed. And it provides some protection for American commentators and politicians who
utilize it against the charge of lack of patriotism levied at them by their
Republican opponents.[46] Decrying an American Caesar at his Rubicon
might seem to ennoble them with the *gravitas* of a brave Cicero or Cato
and link them to their own nation's Founding Fathers as new guardians
of that glorious republican legacy.[47]

Finally, placing the president of the United States at the Rubicon
provides contemporary political commentary with a strongly teleologi-
cal narrative. It propels him on a journey that will lead directly to his
nation's destruction. Thus two months after the British journalist Robert
Fisk had first utilized the metaphor, he turned to it again to report a new
stage in George W. Bush's war on terror. Under the headline "George
Bush Crosses Rubicon—But What Lies Beyond?" he pronounced:

> Just after 5 p.m. yesterday, when the United Nations Security Council voted
> 15–0 to disarm Iraq, the US President George Bush crossed the Rubicon.
> "The world must insist that judgment must be enforced", he told us.
> 　The Rubicon is a wide river. It was deep for Caesar's legions. The Tigris
> river will be more shallow—my guess is that the first American tanks will be
> across it within one week of war—but what lies beyond?
> 　For Rome, civil war followed. And, be assured, civil war will follow any
> American invasion of Iraq. (*The Independent*, 11 November 2002)

Newspaper editors and their readers were so persuaded by Fisk's twin
accounts of the imminence of a damaging war that those accounts
became as popular as Krauthammer's neoconservative praise of imperial peace. Fisk's Rubicon articles were immediately posted on online
political magazines and discussion boards and reprinted in foreign
newspapers across the globe, including Pakistan's *Daily Times*.

Once American troops began to fight on Iraqi soil, the Rubicon metaphor advanced in popular political discourse to the other bank in order
to confront the endings that the history of the Roman republic predicted
would be in store for either the American president or the United States,
or both. Only twelve days after the invasion, for example, a journalist
from South Carolina reflected on the disturbingly impermanent leadership of the American commander in chief, given that his military gamble was likely to generate long-term challenges. In an article released on
31 March 2003 by *Knight Ridder / Tribune News Information Services*
(a leading information provider to American print, television, and elec-
tronic media), Brad Warthen observed: "George W. Bush has crossed

his Rubicon, and he has taken us with him. Julius Caesar set world history on a new course when he took his legion into Italy in defiance of the Senate. President Bush has taken an equally irrevocable step by entering the Tigris and Euphrates basin to wage war in spite of U.N. objections."[48] Warthen welcomed this development on the grounds that with great power comes the responsibility to act, and, in his view, only President Bush would be single-minded enough to pull the gamble off. Yet Bush could not last (he acknowledged with concern), for as a result of the presidential elections either in 2004 or certainly four years later, there would be a new president. One columnist's tragedy, however, was another's justice. In an editorial featured in the *Charleston Gazette* on 12 May 2003, the historical novelist Denise Giardina declared forthrightly that Bush had "assumed the mantle of Julius Caesar. He is in the process of ruining the American republic and establishing an American/corporate empire."

Avoiding the stance of a latter-day Cassius justifying conspiracy and assassination, and adopting instead that of a Cato attacking Julius Caesar for violations of the codes of war in his Gallic campaigns,[49] Giardina then called for the president's impeachment and trial for war crimes.[50] The Caesarean analogy might be pressed into predicting the commander in chief's downfall but not his bloody end.

While some American commentators looked beyond the banks of the river Rubicon to discern the end of the Bush presidency, others caught a glimpse of the end of the American republic and the escalation of empire. As a simple and striking example, the cartoonist Garry Trudeau launched a satirical new look for President Bush in his widely syndicated comic strip Doonesbury just a few weeks after the invasion of Iraq. Trudeau had regularly caricatured politicians and presidents by reducing them, in his strips, to inanimate objects as single index of their perceived failings. On Sunday, 13 April 2003 (and, therefore, in weekend color), over the asterisk that marked this presidency as won in a contested election, the customary Stetson hat was replaced with a plumed Roman helmet.[51] The bitterly critical significance of the new icon had already been set out in the comic strips that had been syndicated between 17 and 22 March (simultaneously with the launch of military operations), where an American aspirant to the role of manager of any postinvasion settlement was represented as already attempting ostentatiously to take on some of the props of Roman imperialism (the title of proconsul, the toga, the fasces, the Latin language), while failing arrogantly to understand any consequent responsibilities.[52] The

FIGURE 34. Doonesbury's first representation of George W. Bush as a Roman soldier's helmet (13 April 2003). DOONESBURY ©2003 G. B. Trudeau. Reprinted with permission of UNIVERSAL UCLICK. All rights reserved.

charge of militaristic, imperial arrogance was reinforced comically in the later strip, where President Bush is made to boast ignorantly "*Pox Americus!*" at the same time as he is first caricatured as the headdress of a conquering Roman general (fig. 34). By garbling the traditional Latinate slogan *pax Americana,* Doonesbury's comic-strip president is made unwittingly to ridicule his own foreign policy as a contagious disease that sickens those it touches. Across the first term of the Bush administration, by presenting an increasingly battered Roman helmet as the cartoon index for the President, Trudeau continued to design his political critique in terms of the gradually failing imperial ambitions of a Caesarean pretender.

George W. Bush was particularly vulnerable to criticism in an election year for the lack of closure to American military intervention in Afghanistan and Iraq, and for the abuse of prisoners at the Guantánamo Bay military base in Cuba and the Abu Ghraib prison in Iraq.[53] As if in anticipation of the imminent scandal, in April 2004 he felt moved to declare during a televised White House press conference: "We are not an imperial power . . . We are a liberating power." But, in contrast and in the same election year, Chalmers Johnson argued in his monograph

The Sorrows of Empire: Militarism, Secrecy, and the End of the Republic (2004) that the legacy of this Bush administration would be, precisely, an irreversible and damaging transformation of the American republic into full-blown empire. According to Johnson, Roman history teaches that imperial republics are prone to autocratic takeovers, and democracy is supplanted by military dictatorship and more urgent imperial expansion. In the wake of empire, four sorrows will flow over the United States: endless war abroad, loss of liberty at home, governmental secrecy and surveillance, and national bankruptcy. The introductory chapter that sets the scene for Johnson's exploration of American militarism opens with a quotation from Robert Fisk's first Rubicon article, and it closes with a depiction of Julius Caesar's troops first lured to the river's bank by the sweet sound of pipers and then triggered by a mysterious trumpet blast into an advance to the other side. For Johnson, the American people, like Caesar's soldiers, have been equally misled: "Post-Cold War American militarists have cast the die and the American people have blindly marched across their own Rubicon to become an empire with global pretensions."[54] Despite all these Caesarean critiques, however, the year 2004 would end with a close but clear election victory for the incumbent president and the launch of George W. Bush's second term of office.[55]

NEW CAESAR IN PERFORMANCE

During the first (and into the second) term of the Bush administration, further authority for the Romanization of American politics in the news media and the monographs of commentators could be found in the Americanization of the Roman dictator's representations elsewhere in the cultural practice of the United States.[56] At the start of the twenty-first century, as in much of the twentieth, Shakespeare's study of the assassination of Julius Caesar and the downfall of the Roman republic was staged for American audiences as a challenging performance of a political crisis now besetting their country.[57]

The Elizabethan tragedy was revived, for example, at the Chicago Shakespeare Theater in December 2002 and closed in February 2003, only one month before the invasion of Iraq. In interviews reported in the local press, the theater's artistic director, Barbara Gaines, gave an account of the preparations for her production of *Julius Caesar* designed, through the vocabulary of political topicality, to attract intrigued readers to attend a performance. In the months leading up to the opening, the director explained, when international doubt was mounting over whether it was either necessary or legitimate to depose the president of Iraq, and when Congress was investing in the president of the United States the power to declare war and initiate an invasion, she would first read the *Chicago Tribune* and the *New York Times* before arriving at the theater for rehearsal. Always, at that moment, she felt that she was slipping effortlessly from the world of international affairs into the world of ancient Rome. On the stage the names might have been Brutus, Julius Caesar, and Antony; yet, to Gaines, they could easily have been replaced by those of Colin Powell, Saddam Hussein, and George Bush. Like many other Americans, the director had been required to study the text of the Elizabethan play at school, but, as a child, she had found it incomprehensibly full of "too many togas, too many windy politicians." Now, however, that she was an adult, the tragedy of toppling a tyrant and dealing with the consequences had become all too clear to her:

> But now I understand—thanks to the horrible situation in the world today— what it's about. The conspirators all end up dead, end up hurting their country. The questions asked are, "Is the assassination of a world leader really the answer to complex questions? If this person is assassinated, how does it change the assassinated leader and the people around the assassinated leader? Does violence itself do good? Does it heal? How has history changed?" Shakespeare just asks the questions. He doesn't moralize. He just asks. The time couldn't be more right [to stage *Julius Caesar*].

Through this interview in the Arts & Entertainment section of the *Chicago Tribune* for 15 December 2002, Gaines represented her production to its potential audience variously as a mode of political interrogation, a challenge to the existing international order, or a patriotic stimulus to national debate. Her goal, she concluded, was for people to leave the theater in Chicago needing to ask questions of their government and of themselves.

As in the New York revival staged by Orson Welles in 1937, the use of contemporary dress and props in the performances at the Chicago Shakespeare Theater laid out a strong visual invitation to see the Elizabethan drama of Roman tyrannicide and its failures as a warning for the American present, while the disposition of the commoners at all three levels of the auditorium was designed to heighten audience engagement with the play's crowd scenes. A stage shining with ultramodern metal and glass swarms with armed police officers in black uniforms and flak jackets when Julius Caesar (Jack Ryland) arrives in act 1, scene 2, while most of his entourage are formally dressed in tuxedoes, business suits, or evening gowns. Brutus (Kevin Gudahl) is played as a brooding politician and agonized intellectual (coded here by his sweater and wire-rimmed glasses), Antony (Scott Jaeck) as a hungover playboy. Cinna is beaten to death, and his corpse stripped of jacket and shoes in act 3, scene 3, while in act 5, scene 5 Brutus impales himself on his knife to the sound of heavy gunfire offstage. Near both the opening and the close of the performance, extras costumed as newspaper reporters, photographers, and television crews mill around the Roman characters further to alert audiences that this representation of the assassination of Julius Caesar anticipates (in, perhaps, only modestly more extravagant terms) the news that might soon appear in American and international media of the overthrow of the president of Iraq.[58] Although the director took care publicly to express political neutrality (stating explicitly that she did not blame the Republican Party for the current desire in the United States to topple Saddam Hussein), her production graphically displayed a sense that on such tyrannicide there would inevitably follow catastrophic and bloody consequences. Grim, swirling clouds and dark storms were projected over the performance space, and the face of Caesar lit up red skies. Hostile reviewers were quick to spot the despised liberal credentials this seemed to bring to Shakespeare's *Julius Caesar*: "To the extent that the production has a political message . . . it's that of the holier-than-the-Democrats Left, insisting that because even the heroes are flawed there's no difference between them and villains."[59]

Another notable modern-dress production of the play was staged some two years later in spring 2005 in New York's Belasco Theater, coinciding roughly with the Ides of March and with the second anniversary of the invasion of Iraq. It too injected an American flavor into Roman (and, of course, Renaissance) politics, and it too was criticised in right-wing quarters as another example of Shakespeare distorted by knee-jerk liberalism. Notably the first major revival of *Julius Caesar* on Broadway since that of Orson Welles almost seventy years earlier, mise-en-scène and the presentation of Brutus together supported most of the weight of the production's political conception. The director, Daniel Sullivan, set the play in a ravaged state, a city of crumbling grandeur strewn with scaffolding and rubble. One of the banners that flew over it bore the face of Caesar (William Sadler)—a face that, for some reviewers, seemed to recall that of Saddam Hussein. In the first half, Roman politicians wore business suits; commoners carried security passes around their necks. The assassination took place in a boardroom inside the Senate, access to which required passage through metal detectors. In the second half, among the headless statues and the ruined facades, Brutus and Cassius, Octavius and Antony, wore camouflage fatigues and berets and carried assault rifles. The conflict and the suicides were bloody and noisy, accompanied by the sounds of explosive gunfire and helicopters overhead.[60]

Most press coverage of the production was devoted to an evaluation of the acting style of the Hollywood film star Denzel Washington, who had been cast as Brutus. For some critics, his self-questioning timbre and tired, doubting look marked the anxieties of an actor insufficiently experienced for the complex Shakespearean role. For others, his demeanor belonged wholly appropriately to a Brutus who should indeed exude the unsettled air of "someone who hears the world as a symphony of mixed signals." In at least one of his many publicity interviews, however, the star of this *Julius Caesar* attempted overtly to fix a more provocative analogy for its potential audiences than concern with the morality of killing a dictator and its aftermath. According to the *New York Times* for 3 April 2005, when interviewed in his Belasco dressing room, Washington pulled out a magazine photograph of President George W. Bush surrounded by his inner circle, and then asked who would lead the rebellion "if he decided he wanted to make himself King, like Julius Caesar." Asked by the journalist, in turn, who would be Brutus, "the conflicted honorable man," the actor replied: "You know, the obvious one is Colin Powell. But I don't know. Condoleezza might be Brutus. You just don't know."[61] The comparison here of George W. Bush with Julius Caesar is no passing fancy. Its use interlocks the New York production with the widespread left-liberal critiques of the Bush administration that had begun to escalate after the invasion of Iraq and continued through the course of Bush's second term—a critique often couched in terms of an increasingly imperialist, authoritarian, and secretive presidency.[62] Readers of the interview were thus invited by the star of the production to see its decayed marble city differently. No longer now a reflection of Iraq in the troubled conditions of an uncertain post-invasion present, but, even more disturbingly, of the neoclassical capital of the United States in the near future: an imperial center governed by a Caesarean executive that is riddled with decay and corruption and in need of radical purification and renewal.[63] Perhaps only within the relative safety—the pastness, the theatricality, the tradition, the cultural authority—of performances of Shakespeare's *Julius Caesar* was it possible to touch on the murder of the Roman general as a metaphor for contemporary opposition to the government of George W. Bush, for fear of appearing literally to advocate the president's assassination.[64]

The regular invocation of Julius Caesar as an interpretative tool in American political discourse partly results from the significant role he has been made to play on the stage and in the classrooms of the United States; yet, in turn, his political utility has had an impact on how he has been performed and how he has been taught.[65] In the first years of the twenty-first century, enrollments to study Latin in American high schools have continued to swell steadily from their lowest ebb in the late 1970s; nonetheless the vast majority of students graduating from college have never studied Latin.[66] In March 2011, for example, a staff writer for the *Gettysburg Times* noted wistfully that in years past Adams County Latin classes used to commemorate the assassination of Julius Caesar every Ides of March with a parade. School students would dress in togas, wield cardboard swords, and carry a Caesar imperson-ator on a stretcher through the streets of their hometowns. Under the headline "Once Caesar of Languages," the reporter notes that the last such parade was held in 2005 at Biglerville High. Like Julius Caesar, he implies, Latin is no longer celebrated, because it is no longer on the syl-labus at most local high schools.[67]

Where Latin continues to be taught in the United States (whether at high school or in college), it is not bound so closely to the Roman general and his war commentaries as it was at the start of the twen-tieth century. Nor are students undertaking secondary-level study of the Latin language addressed as if they were soldiers in Caesar's army being training linguistically and ethically into an ideal American iden-tity.[68] For example, *Latin for the New Millennium*, published in 2009 and designed by Milena Minkova and Terence Tunberg, directors of the Institute for Latin Studies at the University of Kentucky, deliberately breaks from more traditional curricula. Better to motivate enrollments, the course books embrace an extensive array of Latin authors from clas-sical antiquity to the early modern period, from Plautus to Antonius de Leeuwenhoek. In the student textbook for Level 1, an adapted passage from Caesar's *De bello Gallico* appears within the sixth of twenty-one chapters, which demonstrates uses of the present tense and the infinitive. At Level 2, roughly equivalent to what was once known as "the Caesar year," the student textbook threads through its chapters unabridged selections from a single classical text—Nepos's *Life of Atticus*. The life of Julius Caesar is reduced to a description in Latin of his assassination, which is presented in a chapter concerning the ablative absolute con-struction and different types of pronoun. The Latin language here (as in other twenty-first-century curricula) escapes Caesar's iron grip and the traditionally narrow conception of it as masculine, military, nationalist, and imperial.[69]

If, however, Caesar's *Gallic War* has been largely absent from most American high-school classrooms in the earliest years of the twenty-first century, Shakespeare's *Julius Caesar* has continued to exercise a strong presence as a regularly required set text.[70] But, for teachers of English, the challenge of engaging their students with the Roman tragedy has grown all the greater, because its study is no longer buttressed by parallel study in Latin classes of the writings of the tragedy's protagonist and his role in Roman republican history.[71] One convenient strategy for demonstrating to students the value and interest of the Elizabethan drama, therefore, is to present it as a heightened performance of political concerns that are of the utmost relevance to twenty-first-century Americans. At a time when teachers of Shakespeare's plays in American public schools rely fundamentally on performance-based instruction,[72] productions on the professional stage often offer handy guidance on how best to Americanize *Julius Caesar*.

Thus in 2002 the Chicago Shakespeare Theater, in support of its educational mission and the staging of Barbara Gaines's modern-dress revival, published a sixty-two-page illustrated handbook for teachers on Shakespeare's *Julius Caesar*, containing (besides information on Caesar, Shakespeare, republican Rome, and Renaissance theater, interpretative essays, and suggestions for classroom activities) an interview with the play's director.[73] To one of the questions posed by the theater's education staff, "What would you hope that our student audiences take away from seeing our production?" Gaines responded:

> If they leave with two or three really important questions about the nature of government, and about the role of government in all of our lives, I'd feel like we'd succeeded. If our country goes to war, what happens if you don't support it? Is it right under any circumstance for anyone to take another person's life, and if so, when? I don't mean that they should have answers to these questions. I would love the fact that they would just be asking. It's the questioning of our government that is essential. (35)

Hints as to the more precise kind of questioning in which school students might choose to engage were provided by the layout of the handbook. Several sections, including the act-by-act synopses, were illustrated with photomontages of the play's Roman characters dressed in the contemporary costume of paparazzi, senators, and soldiers and were also over- or underlaid with cuttings from recent press reports. The first such fragment, from the *New York Times*, 10 October 2002, and written by Senator Robert C. Byrd, carried the headline "Congress Must Resist the Rush to War." A significant number of the others were concerned with speeches made by the same senator against the passage of a proposed homeland security bill, speeches whose rhetorical flourishes conveniently included reference to the senator's political heroes from the days of the Roman republic.[74] Suggestions for classroom activities addressed directly to school students included the following:

> Pretend you are reporters at a press conference following Caesar's funeral. Some of you work for the Republican newspaper, some of you work for the Caesarian newspaper. Devise questions to ask Antony and Brutus. How would a Republican-friendly reporter phrase questions to Brutus? To Antony? How might a Caesarian reporter? Appoint a Brutus and Antony to answer your questions in character. What headlines might the differing newspapers print the next morning? (47)

American high-school students are explicitly invited by the handbook to adopt the voices of (or to "ventriloquate") Brutus, Antony, or Roman reporters contemporary with the action of Shakespeare's tragedy, and to shape a political position for themselves in the past that is either pro- or anti-Caesarean. But, implicitly, they are invited to position themselves in the present with one of the Democratic Party's most senior spokesmen, resisting the foreign and domestic policies of the Bush administration.[75] Political, theatrical, and educational discourses concerning Julius Caesar thus converge and feed off each other either for historical and cultural authority or for the most urgent contemporary relevance.

It is not only high-school students who have been invited to ventriloquate characters from Shakespeare's *Julius Caesar* and, on that basis, to position themselves ethically and politically. At the start of the twenty-first century, political, theatrical, and educational discourses concerning the Roman dictator have also converged with those of Anglo-American corporate culture. From the late 1990s, Shakespeare's plays began to be appropriated by both American and British business consultants and trade-book writers in order to find innovative and stimulating ways of delivering management guidance to readers imagined as established or aspiring CEOs.[76] The publishing subgenre that emerged treated Shakespeare's dramatic characters as portraits of a common human nature and the plots of his plays as a demonstration of management techniques in action. *Shakespeare in Charge: The Bard's Guide to Leading and Succeeding on the Business Stage* (New York, 1999) by

Norman Augustine and Kenneth Adelman was structured like a five-act play script. "Act 3"—entitled "Making Your Play in Business"—utilized scenes from *Julius Caesar* to stipulate the skills needed to get jobs done in business, such as goal setting, recruitment, team building, operations, and corporate communications. Such management manuals dressed up their rules for profit-oriented corporate success in the cultural authority of the Bard and cast themselves as forms of elevated literature on a par with Renaissance drama.[77] In addition, the management training company Movers & Shakespeares, established in 1997 by Adelman and his wife, began to run executive training seminars and leadership development programs (each focused on a single play) for a broad range of clients that included U.S. government agencies and the U.S. military, as well as multinational corporations, health-care providers, and law firms.[78] Attempts to translate Shakespeare's *Julius Caesar* into the vocabulary and the values of corporate capitalism could not, however, eliminate entirely the tragedy's oppositional potential.[79]

An article by Bruce Weber in the *New York Times* for 31 January 2005, entitled "Power Play: Friends, Generals and Captains of Industry, Lend Me Your Ears," reported on one such leadership seminar run at the Aspen Institute by Movers & Shakespeares for about twenty senior United States Air Force generals and executives. For the military clients, the day included watching film clips of Marlon Brando and Charlton Heston delivering Antony's Forum speech, interactive discussion of the relevant lessons to be learned from individual scenes, and role play and readings from the text while dressed in Roman helmets and breastplates. Participants liked particularly to explore the play in terms that were relevant to their military lives: while recognizing the arrogance of Caesar, they labeled Brutus a traitor because he fatally attacked a superior. The reporter also observed:

> It did not escape the notice of those in the room that the conspirators' hasty act of revolt failed to consider its aftermath, the lesson being that thorough planning, for any leader, is paramount. Those who would depose Caesar had, in effect, no exit strategy. . . .
>
> This was about as close as the discussion ever got to current events, though at one point, a parallel between Brutus and the conspirators and the Bush administration was raised. If the conspirators were in the wrong for taking violent action without hard evidence, but only on suspicion of the tyrant Caesar might become—in effect making a pre-emptive strike—couldn't the same argument be applied to the Bush administration's invasion of Iraq and the absence of weapons of mass destruction?
>
> "The president had more evidence than Brutus did," replied Adelman.

Here Adelman, a former chief adviser to the Reagan administration on U.S. arms control, a member of George W. Bush's Defense Policy Board, an early champion of the war on terror, advocate for the invasion of Iraq, and neoconservative activist, is forced to silence the voices of criticism that Shakespeare's Roman tragedy is momentarily encouraging members of the U.S. military to adopt.[80]

NEW CAESAR IN TELEVISUAL *ROME*

For some newspapers in the autumn of 2005, the political rhetoric of the United States as a New Rome appeared also to converge with the representation of Julius Caesar on television.[81] A month before the lavishly produced series *Rome* began in the United Kingdom, the British newspaper *The Observer* (23 October 2005) carried a full-page preview headlined "Quo Vadis America?"[82] Written by a lecturer in history, it argued that the BBC-HBO coproduction was painting on the historical canvas of ancient Rome a revelatory picture of "today's superpower," showing on the small screen how imperial ambition can co-exist with extreme domestic inequality. At the same time the *Economist* (22 October 2005) found in it a warning contrast rather than similarity: "This autumn's most gripping television series, HBO's 'Rome', tells the story, in deliciously graphic detail, of how Julius Caesar tightened his grip on power in the capital of the world's greatest empire. In the new Rome, on the banks of the Potomac, exactly the opposite is happening: George Bush's iron grip on power is loosening, as more and more Washingtonians join the revolt against the imperial presidency." Now that the war in Iraq had been so prolonged, and its pacification proven so difficult, now that the details of illegal torture, secret prisons, and substantial domestic surveillance had emerged, when financial costs had become so high and the loss of personnel so substantial, when domestic support for the president and the war was diminishing significantly, and the Senate, House, and Supreme Court were all beginning to reassert their political authority over and against the administration, the chilling efficiency of a televisual Caesar could be interpreted as criticism of the competence of a shadow Caesar in the White House.[83] When season 1 of *Rome* launched three months earlier in the United States on the premium cable network HBO, the review of episode 1 in the *LA Weekly* (28 August 2005) likewise argued that Cato's denunciation in the Senate of Caesar's illegal Gallic war and the general's subsequent concern over his army's war-ravaged morale called to mind contemporary headlines.[84] The *Los Angeles Times*

(12 January 2007) was a little more considered, when at the start of season 2 it described in retrospect how the series had cleverly engaged its audiences with the Roman past by recreating a world both familiar and remote.[85] Since that world's rules are not ours, the reviewer observed, it resonates for us without providing an exact contemporary moral.

At any rate, the narrative arc of season 1 (from the surrender of Vercingetorix in episode 1 and the crossing of the Rubicon in 2 to the assassination of the Roman dictator in episode 12) traversed the same political space as the rhetoric of New Rome currently being deployed by political commentators: the slow and painful death of an imperial republic. The first episode opens with a voice-over that declares: "The Republic of Rome rules many nations, but cannot rule itself." Across subsequent episodes, that imperial republic is repeatedly described as sick, dying, or dead by the agents in its demise. The conqueror Julius Caesar (Ciarán Hinds) equates the good of the republic with his own self-interest, grows progressively more ambitious and menacing, and combats aristocratic privilege with populist tyranny. The opposing republicans are priggish, weary, or incompetent. Brutus (Tobias Menzies) is appalled by the butchery in which he is reluctantly pressed to participate.[86] *Rome* thus appears to invite television audiences to compare the literal and metaphorical squalor of the ancient city it so graphically displays with Washington as the modern capital of empire, and to understand as a dismal lie the first season's closing claim (made by Caesar's spurned mistress) that "the republic has been restored."[87]

Most American press reports in 2005, however, were more concerned about whether the series would match up to HBO's signature brand of programming, which has come to be known as "para-television"—that is, a knowing play with the medium's genres.[88] After a significant drop in ratings in the preceding two years, and pitted against strong competition from the broadcast and basic cable networks, HBO was considered in desperate need of another dramatic success on the scale of *The Sopranos* (1999–2007), *Six Feet Under* (2001–5), or *Deadwood* (2004–6). *Rome* was therefore scrutinized for similar pay-cable features, its ancient setting understood as historical license for especially graphic sex and violence and extreme family intrigue. Reviewers commended its visually gritty and richly detailed reconstructions of the "otherness" of everyday life in the ancient city, and its original use of a class-conscious perspective, as camera and dramatic narrative centered not on Caesar but on two soldiers claimed to have come from his Thirteenth Legion. In the balance, the work of Bruno Heller as executive producer, writer,

FIGURE 35. Screenshot of Julius Caesar (Ciarán Hinds) accepting the surrender of Vercingetorix, in HBO's *Rome*, season 1, ep. 1 (2005).

and director was judged to be not as iconoclastic as HBO's previous and current products nor as psychologically probing, but imitative of the BBC historical soap opera *I, Claudius* (1977–78)—this time "on steroids and Viagra."[89] In its claims to historical authenticity and everyday realism, however, the television series *Rome* does play in interesting ways against the received histories of Julius Caesar in the United States with which this book has been concerned.

Near the start of the first episode of *Rome*, season 1, television viewers are offered the opportunity to witness Caesar as arrogant imperialist accept the surrender of the Gallic chieftain Vercingetorix, only to strip him of all dignity. The somber scene is choreographed as a kind of dynamic collage of nineteenth-century nationalist paintings by French artists such as Henri-Paul Motte or Lionel Royer that had once graced the pages of American high-school commentaries on Julius Caesar's *De bello Gallico* (fig. 35).[90] Within the narrative terms of HBO's *Rome*, this surrender has been achieved in part thanks to the military valor of two fictitious characters, whose actions are regularly made to encase and even shape crucial historical events like this. Across the twelve episodes of *Rome*, season 1, and into season 2, the dying moments of the Roman republic are narrated from the perspective of Titus Pullo (Ray Stevenson) and Lucius Vorenus (Kevin McKidd)—the only two legionaries to be given names in Julius Caesar's war commentary. Describing how one of his legions was besieged by the ferocious Belgic tribe the Nervii toward the end of the fifth book of *De bello Gallico*, the Roman general picks out and honors two of its bravest men (*fortissimi uiri*,

5.44) by the act of naming them. On this occasion, when their bitter rivalry has led Pullo and Vorenus to jump into the enemy and fight outside the entrenchments with the utmost glory and equal bravery, they each save the other from death.[91] This core narrative stratagem of *Rome* parallels and perverts that of the historical novels that (a century before) had been designed for juvenile readers to excite their interest in studying Caesar's text in their high-school Latin classes. One of the most popular of such novels was that published by A. C. Whitehead in 1914, *The Standard Bearer: A Story of Army Life in the Time of Caesar.*[92] The author, himself a high-school Latin instructor, had based the novel's fictitious young hero Caius on a passage in *De bello Gallico* (4.25) where Caesar had described the impetuous bravery of an unnamed standard-bearer who had led the landing on the shores of Britain. Caius joins Caesar's army in Gaul, meets his commander from time to time, and gradually rises through the ranks to become himself a witness to the surrender of Vercingetorix and, ultimately, the governor of Gaul. In *Rome,* season 1, the fictive protagonist Vorenus also rises up the ranks—both military and civilian—to become a senator and bodyguard for his commander, but association with Julius Caesar strips him of his political innocence and his honest republican values. By the end of the final episode, he has also lost his wife and his closest friend. While the twentieth-century juvenile novel offered its young readers an edifying story of a boy's rite of passage into and up society's ranks, achieved by virtue of his training in Caesar's army, the twenty-first-century television drama displays for its adult audience a mode of instruction that is much darker, more tragic, and more suited to twenty-first-century estimations of Caesar and of empire.[93]

That other key text for the circulation of the Roman dictator in American culture—Shakespeare's *Julius Caesar*—undergoes equally intriguing adjustments and distortions in the final episode of *Rome*'s first season. The series is haunted by Shakespeare's Roman plays in, for example, the precise enunciation of its largely British cast and its meta-theatrical self-consciousness (as when embedded Roman spectators watch pantomimers acting out events to which television viewers have previously been witness).[94] Yet an explicit preoccupation of the television series was to circumvent Shakespeare and thus alleviate the ossification of famed Roman events caused, the makers claimed, by the chronic study and performance of their Elizabethan depictions in high schools and colleges throughout the United States.[95] Thus the last episode of *Rome,* season 1, directed by Alan Taylor and scripted by Bruno Heller, is

FIGURE 36. Screenshot of the conspirators encircling Brutus and
Cassius after the assassination, in HBO's *Rome*, season 1, ep. 12 (2005).

entitled unexpectedly "Kalends of February." No soothsayer warns the
dictator to beware the Ides of March. Brutus is seduced into conspiracy
primarily by his mother and only secondarily by Cassius, and he has no
wife to berate him for secrecy in an orchard scene. Caesar is not delayed
at home on the Ides by his wife's fears, and, in the Senate, it is the fictive
Vorenus (like Shakespeare's Mark Antony) who is called away in order
that great Caesar might be left unprotected. To spite Shakespeare and the
long-standing tradition that Americanized the assassination as an act of
noble patriotism undertaken to preserve a suffering republic,[96] the lead-
up to the murder of the Roman general, and its aftermath, are conducted
on the television screen almost wordlessly. This televisual Caesar does
not utter the celebrated tag "*Et tu Brute?*" (*JC* 3.1.77) when he falls, and
no conspirator then cries out: "Liberty! Freedom! Tyranny is dead!" (*JC*
3.1.78). Instead Brutus physically rebuffs Cassius (Guy Henry) when the
latter grabs his arm, raises it high, and shouts an English translation of
the originary American motto engraved on Virginia's state seal: "Thus
ever for tyrants!" (fig. 36).[97] Overhead camera shots of chaotic and frenzied stabbings, shifts to slow motion, the heightened sound of Brutus's
dagger penetrating flesh, and close-ups of his distraught expression as
he confronts the father figure he has betrayed also direct television viewers to reinterpret the opening of Shakespeare's third act as a scene of
unqualified butchery and personal betrayal.[98] Finally, within the overall
narrative arc of HBO's *Rome,* the historic event is subordinated in dramatic importance to intercut scenes of a fictive domestic suicide—that
of Vorenus's wife when he finally confronts her over her past adultery.

In addition to the games HBO's *Rome* plays with the Julius Caesar that American television audiences were most likely to have known from their schooling, at various points the series also humorously undermines received understanding of the causes of the Roman republic's fall—whether that understanding has been derived from classical scholarship or cinematic histories such as Joseph Mankiewicz's *Cleopatra* (1963). As some media scholars have observed, *Rome* interestingly fractures the conventional "Great Man" narration of history (in which agency is located within individuals like Julius Caesar) by inserting a series of accidents into its televisual account of the last days of the Roman republic.[99] The dictator's customary responsibility for the republic's demise is almost comically undercut by the inadvertent interventions of one of the fictive protagonists. The title of episode 2, "How Titus Pullo Brought Down the Republic," draws audience attention to one significant example of the device that *Time* (22 August 2005) criticized as "all a bit too *Forrestus Gumpus.*" There the loutish legionary accidently triggers an apparent attack on the tribune Mark Antony that will provide Caesar with righteous cause to cross the Rubicon.[100] Class also combines with gender to shift traditional history (conceived as aristocratic, masculine, public, and destined) to the margins and to bring out of their shadows and before the eye of the television camera a private history that is driven by plebeians, women, and luck.[101] At the end of season 1, it is Atia (not the conspirators) who must flee Rome for Greece, and Servilia (not Caesar's heirs) who will be in hot pursuit. Such a revisionist transformation of the Roman historical record has implications also for the twenty-first-century political rhetoric of New Rome. Absence of overarching agency, multiple and shifting causation, a history driven by plebeians and women, and a world that does not conform to "our" rules all might work temporarily—at the point of consumption of this televisual Rome—to take some of the force out of the terrible warning the story of the Roman republic's fall was supposed to proffer the United States of America in the first decade of the twenty-first century.

THE FALL OF NEW CAESAR

Nevertheless, the rhetoric of New Rome appeared to amplify rather than reduce its prognostic utility, and to spread ever more widely into American culture, as political commentators critical of the Bush administration began to look forward to the presidential elections of 2008 and to predict a bleak future for the United States if it carried on along its present imperial path. Thus, under the title "Roman Candles: Wrapped in the Star-Spangled Toga," an article written by journalist and historian Adam Goodheart in the *New York Times* for 1 July 2007 claimed that everyone who had watched HBO's *Rome* possessed "a pet theory on which ancient warlord resembles which modern pol (Pompey as Al Gore, anyone?)." The journalist also argued that ancient Rome—or, more specifically, comparison of modern America to the Roman Empire—was now being discussed ubiquitously across all segments of the political spectrum, "left and right, Christian fundamentalists and Islamic radicals, Ivy League professors and renegade bloggers." One such sustained example was the work that Goodheart was here placing under review: Cullen Murphy's *Are We Rome? The Fall of an Empire and the Fate of America* (2007). Murphy (formerly editor of the *Atlantic Monthly* and subsequently editor at large of *Vanity Fair*) observed both the contemporary ubiquity and, even, the seeming naturalness of the Roman comparison in the opening pages of his book:

> President and emperor, America and Rome—the comparison is by now so familiar, so natural, that you just can't help yourself: it comes to mind unbidden, in the reflexive way that the behavior of chimps reminds you of the behavior of people. . . . When a reference is made to an "imperial presidency", or to the president's aides as a "Praetorian Guard", or to the deployment abroad of "American legions", no one quizzically raises an eyebrow and wonders what you could possibly be talking about. To American eyes, Rome is the eagle in the mirror. (2007, 5–6)

Murphy, like his reviewer, acknowledges that ancient Rome has been a point of reference for the United States in the struggle leading up to the nation's foundation and through the centuries ever since, and that Rome's efficacy lies in the way that America appears to trace the path it has already taken to consequences that are, therefore, foreseeable. But he also recognizes that ancient Rome has not always been drawn on in the same way or with the same degree of intensity throughout America's history—to extend Murphy's metaphor, the Roman eagle America sees in the mirror of history takes on different outlines at different times and fades in and out of view.[102]

During the Bush administration, the Roman eagle came into sharpest focus near the beginning and the end of the president's two terms. In 2002, just before the invasion of Iraq, liberal critics were most concerned to scrutinize parallels for the United States in the demise of the Roman republic—a demise situated in the period 49 to 44 B.C.E. and imputed to the agency of Julius Caesar when he crossed the Rubicon and compelled the Roman Senate to submit to his "perpetual dictatorship." By 2007, the object of scrutiny had changed to the fall of the Roman Empire, and comparisons were being found for the president in, for example, the emperors Nero, Diocletian, and Julian.[103] Roman history had been made to accelerate across anywhere from one hundred to four hundred years in order best to match perceived developments across five years of the American presidency and to provide an appropriately grander, Gibbonesque tone of impending decline and doom to predictions of America's imperial future.[104]

A few political commentators, however, continued to hold out for the rise of Julius Caesar and the purportedly consequent collapse of the Roman republic as the most germane combination for understanding and forecasting the consequences of America's imperial policies. In the third of his attacks on American militarism, *Nemesis: The Last Days of the American Republic* (2007), Chalmers Johnson again explored republican Rome as one of the most instructive "imperial pathologies" to draw on for comparison:

> The American republic has, of course, not yet collapsed; it is just under great strain as its imperial presidency and its increasingly powerful military legions undermine Congress and the courts. However, the Roman outcome—turning over power to a dictator backed by military force welcomed by ordinary citizens because it seems to bring stability—suggests what might well happen sometime in the future as a result of George Bush's contempt for the separation of powers. (59–60)

The startling prognosis for the sick American republic of a military, populist dictatorship is reiterated in Johnson's last chapter. There the political scientist enumerates all the respects in which he considers President George W. Bush to have implemented a deliberate policy to undermine constitutional government (especially the traditional separation of executive, legislative, and judicial powers). In particular, Johnson argues, Bush treats his role as commander in chief as above the law; he can define causes for war as he chooses and remain at war as long as he sees fit. Congress has abdicated its responsibility to prevent this presidential monopoly of power: "Corrupt and indifferent, the Congress, which the Founders believed would be the leading branch of government, is simply not up to the task of confronting a modern Julius Caesar" (267–68).

Despite the historical record that centuries of rampant imperial expansion preceded the Roman republic's collapse into dictatorship and monarchy,[105] and that the fall of the republic was caused by fundamental

and complex changes to its economic, military, political, and social institutions, as well as prolonged civil war between a number of pretenders
to power,[106] Johnson summons up the specter of a revolutionary Caesar
of old to support his argument that militarism is a disease that destroys
republican bodies politic with rapidity. The rhetorical deployment of
the Roman general (thus characteristically simplified) appears to give
historical credibility, physical substance, and a strong sense of urgency
to Johnson's claims. It implies that the chief cause of the nation's present sickness lies in an individual, not in broader and more fundamental problems with its institutions. And it pushes President Bush further
along the analogical path on which he was placed by journalists when,
in September 2002, he was described as crossing his own Rubicon into
an aggressively imperial presidency. Utilizing the vocabulary of new
Rome and new Caesar, the terrible prospect of American dictatorship
can be articulated and thus, Johnson hopes, averted.[107] Only the nastiest
and most extreme bigot might then embrace Johnson's dark depiction
of impending Caesarean rule as the true cure for (rather than the termi-
nal disease of) the ailing democratic governance of the United States of
America.[108]

By the end of the first decade of the twenty–first century, one other
discursive field for the articulation of Julius Caesar began to demonstrate a noticeable convergence with the political, theatrical, pedagogic,
corporate, and televisual fields—namely popular and academic historiography. When the British novelist Tom Holland published his first
work of history, *Rubicon: The Triumph and Tragedy of the Roman
Republic* (2003), he acknowledged in the preface that, during the time
he had been writing, comparisons of ancient Rome with the modern-
day United States had become something of a cliché (xxiii). Although
he proceeded to argue that ostensible parallels can be deceptive because
the circumstances of the Romans were so profoundly different from
our own, he nevertheless agreed that in the mirror of Roman history
it is possible to glimpse (however faint and distorted) modern geopolitics, globalization, and the *pax Americana,* as well as some of our more
quirky social habits (xxiv-xxv). No wonder then that it was largely on
Holland's stylish and engaging narrative (rather than academic scholarship) that Chalmers Johnson drew for his account of late republican Rome,[109] for the narrative of *Rubicon* was deeply infused with an
implicit invitation to make comparisons between the Roman past and
the American present.[110] Consequently, on Johnson's reading, the British
author "draws a picture of the late Republic that seems a model of the

modern United States with its flamboyant excesses of wealth, bad taste, and arrogance, as well as its impulse toward militarism. His social history of republican decadence, highlighting a puerile Roman vision of politics and war, sounds very much like the second Bush administration and the shop-until-you-drop world of American consumerism" (2007, 57). Some academics have seen advantage in such convergence and in the ways, more broadly, that the historiography of Roman antiquity has been transformed at the start of the new millennium by popular comparisons between the Roman Empire and imperial America.[111] Such convergence requires historiographers of the Roman Empire to confront the edifying purpose to which many of them once aspired (Edward Gibbon included), namely to record the Roman past as instruction for an imperial present.[112] It thus pushes to the surface of historical narration and renders self-conscious the extent to which, from the eighteenth to the twentieth century and beyond, scholarship on classical empires has been built up on the ideological platform of modern imperialism.[113] Furthermore, if the past is capable of speaking to the present, so the present can be utilized better to interpret the past. Situated in a new imperial context, engaging with modern models of empire and colonialism, and the modern vocabulary of hegemony and superpowers, historians, archaeologists, political philosophers, and political scientists have the opportunity to reevaluate the political, economic, and social structures of the Roman Empire and to reassess its imperial Caesars.[114]

By the time President George W. Bush completed his two terms of office, he had achieved the lowest approval rating of any sitting president. He was derided for foreign, economic, and social policy failures and criticized for having radically expanded the powers of the presidency.[115] Thus, even before he officially left office on 20 January 2009, the man about to succeed him as president, Barack Obama, was hailed in the British press as a new Cicero.[116] The use of such a descriptor constituted a convenient means not only to eulogize Obama's extraordinary powers of public speaking but also to identify the modern politician with the ancient as two fierce defenders of republican constitutions. In a moment of relief, left-liberal journalism could find a neat counter to its earlier rhetoric of the new Caesar who had crossed his Rubicon into the dangers of an imperial presidency. Instead, it implied, new Rome could reverse that trajectory, rewrite ancient history, revive a moribund republic, and establish a new American politics: Caesar is dead; long live Cicero.

After that brief respite, however, President Obama continued, and even escalated, some of the activities for which President Bush was charged with Caesarism (most notably wars abroad), and criticism of him also occasionally sharpened its barbs with Roman analogy. Writing in the *Washington Times* for 16 June 2011, for example, the conservative commentator Jeffrey T. Kuhner remarked, under the caption "Obama, the New Caesar," that, in authorizing military intervention in Libya, the president had crossed the Rubicon, acting as if untouched by the Constitution and above the law.[117] One reason such comparisons appear to be rather infrequent and superficial, however, is because New Rome has generally been recognized (at least temporarily) as a broken metaphor or a prophecy that has failed to come true.[118] Despite the passionate anger with which George W. Bush was compared to Julius Caesar, he did not fulfill the most startling of the Caesarean predictions that he would overthrow the Constitution, destroy the republic, usurp power, and establish a dictatorship. An American Caesar did not take over the White House at the start of the new millennium. Toward the end of its first decade, therefore, Julius Caesar's importance—at least to popular political debate—has radically diminished.

The presence of Julius Caesar in the culture of the United States waxes and wanes. Yet the story of the Roman dictator's reception in the United States of America across the last one hundred years that this book has attempted, in part, to tell would suggest that he will return. Wars and political crises summon him back, as does the study of his key texts. Shakespeare's *Julius Caesar* continues to be taught as part of the English curriculum in American high schools, to be performed on the American stage, and thus to stimulate the circulation of the Roman dictator in other discursive fields of American culture. Enrollments in high-school Latin classes are once again increasing significantly, as are the number of students taking college board examinations in the language.[119] As of 2012, Julius Caesar's war commentary *De bello Gallico* joins Virgil's *Aeneid* in the curriculum of the College Board's Advanced Placement Latin course in order to complement some consummate Latin poetry with some lucid Latin prose.[120] Advanced Placement courses are officially promoted as designed to provide students in high schools across the nation with "the skills and habits to be successful at college," and students expect to gain college credit, advanced placement in college courses, or both on the basis of high scores on the AP examinations.[121] Now that the College Board and AP teachers look once again for ways to make study of Caesar's *Gallic War* of interest to American high-school students (as Latin teachers did at the beginning of the twentieth century), they will have an even richer tradition of American receptions of the Roman general on which to draw.[122] As villain (or, less often, as hero), Caesar will always be a part of American culture.

Notes

INTRODUCTION

1. On the early history of the Virginia state seal, see Tyler 1894.

2. Cf. Cole 2009, 421. The tradition is pseudoclassical, but I have not been able to pinpoint its origins.

3. The place of classics in American colonial and revolutionary life has received considerable attention. See, for example, Shero 1966, 18–21; Reinhold 1984; Richard 1994, 12–38; Waquet 2001, 22; Dyson 2001, 57–63; Pearcy 2005, 43–83; Briggs 2007, 279–82; Shalev 2009.

4. Matthews 1978, 302; Richard 1994, 90–93; Wyke 2007, 218–20; Shalev 2009, esp. 219 on Julius Caesar.

5. On the popularity of Addison's *Cato* in eighteenth-century America, see Litto 1966; Wills 1985, 133–38; Richard 1994, 57–58; Winterer 2007, 2; Murphy 2007, 36–39; Shalev 2009, 151–87. See Edwards 2005 on the original political context of British performances.

6. For rhetorical appeal to the assassins of Caesar as models for revolutionary action such as Patrick Henry's celebrated "liberty or death" speech delivered on 23 March 1775, see Matthews 1978; Litto 1966, 444–45; Richard 1994, 65–66; Shalev 2009, 144–47.

7. Dunn 1939, 92–93, 95–96; Ripley 1980, 100. Cf., on Abigail Adams's adoption of the persona of "Portia" in her letters, Winterer 2007, 46–47.

8. Ripley 1980, 100; Sinfield 1996, 50–51; Daniell 1998, 105; Wyke 2007, 218–21.

9. Wyke 2007, 222. For the constitutional debates of 1787–88 and subsequent accusations of Caesarism against, or in turn by, statesmen like Alexander Hamilton and Thomas Jefferson, see Adair 1955; Govan 1975, 476–79; Richard 1994, 39–42, 92, 119–20; Cole 2009, 418–24; Shalev 2009, 223–25. Cf.

Malamud 2009, 18–25 and Richard 2009, 62–66 on similar criticisms about President Andrew Jackson.

10. Furtwangler 1991 explores the family history of John Wilkes Booth and the expression of its republican sentiments in both Roman and Shakespearean terms.

11. On the assassination of President Lincoln and its supposed replay of Roman history, see Rogin 1987, 86–88; Furtwangler 1991; Derrick 1998, 107–31; Wyke 2007, 221–26; Shalev 2009, 219.

12. On this and other caricatures of President Lincoln, see Wilson 1945, esp. viii–xi and 326–27.

13. For the place of classics and of Caesar in American cultural life before the twentieth century, see esp. Reinhold 1984; Richard 1994, 2009; Winterer 2002, 2007; Pearcy 2005; and Shalev 2009.

14. I am most grateful to Carl J. Richard for drawing my attention to this quotation from Professor William Hooper of the University of North Carolina, which Richard cites in his monograph *The Founders and the Classics* (1994, 17).

15. Dodge 1892.

16. Those that I have found most useful in my studies on the reception of ancient Rome in America include the broad survey contained in Reinhold 1984; Richard 1994 on the Founders; Winterer 2002 on nineteenth-century intellectual life; Pearcy 2005 on classical education; Malamud 2009 on the intersections between "highbrow" and "lowbrow" cultural receptions.

17. Most works that explore Julius Caesar's reception in some depth have concentrated on his place in the high culture of classical scholarship, political thought, historiography, and/or European literature and art; these include Yavetz 1983, 10–57; Christ 1994; Baehr 1998; Baehr and Richter 2004; Gentili 2008; M. Griffin 2009; Moreno Hernández 2010. For some discussion of popular culture and the United States, see Wyke 2007 and some of the essays in Chevallier 1985 and Wyke 2006b.

18. See, in particular, Baehr 1998, esp. 29–33; Wyke 2007, 1–21; M. Griffin 2009, 1–8.

19. In Spencer 2002, where the author is concerned with Alexander's reception in ancient Rome.

20. See, for example, Wyke 1997; Joshel, Malamud, and McGuire 2001; Winkler 2004, 2009; Cyrino 2005; Malamud 2009; Lowe and Shahabudin 2009; Kovacs and Marshall 2011.

21. For Shakespeare's challenge to cultural hierarchies, see, for example, Levine 1988, 11–81; Lanier 2002b; Abele 2004.

22. For a useful discussion of variations in (and problems attached to) definitions of popular culture, see Oswell 2006, 74–102.

23. Leonard and Prins 2010, 2, in their editorial foreword to a special issue of *Cultural Critique* dedicated to "classical reception and the political."

1. MATURATION

1. Kelsey 1927, 1–5; Shero 1966, 17–39; Church and Sedlak 1976, 184; Winterer 2002, 102–3; Wyke 2006b, 182; Tompkins 2006, 100–101. Church

and Sedlak 1976, 301, however, caution against too much enthusiasm for these statistics, because by 1910 high schools were still only catering to 15 percent of children who were of high-school age.

2. Students studied Cicero and, sometimes, Sallust in their third year of Latin, and only in their fourth did they embark on Virgil and other Latin poets such as Ovid. See, for example, Mierow 1915 for data collected on the basis of a questionnaire sent out to schools in the Midwest in February 1915. Cf. Gray 1929, 1–6; Shero 1966, 30; Kennedy 1992, 226–27.

3. Mierow 1915, 87.

4. See Mierow 1915, 87–88; Shero 1966, 30; Kennedy 1984, 223–31. For contemporary discussion of the *Gallic War* in second-year Latin, see, for example, G. Lodge et al., *Teachers College Record* 3 (1902); W. Dennison, *Classical Journal* 1.5 (1906); W.M. Gardner Hale, *School Review* 18.5 (1910).

5. For the role of Shakespeare's *Julius Caesar* (both in the classroom and on the stage) in the American understanding of the Roman dictator, see below and Wyke 2007, 218–38 with further bibliography there.

6. See, for example, Donald (1992, 17–47), who bases his arguments on changes to the British education system in the nineteenth century. On classical education in turn-of-the-century America, see, usefully, Akenson 1966.

7. Kelsey 1927, 9–13; Akenson 1966, 7–8. Cf. Winterer 2002, 99 on the social background to developments in classical education at American universities in the late nineteenth century.

8. In contrast, Farrell (2001, 100–105) notes that with the emergence of comparative linguistics in the nineteenth century and the consequent division of the European nations linguistically into Germanic and Latin, Protestant Anglo-Saxons often conceived Latin as a mark of the racial difference and inferiority of the Catholic speakers of Romance languages.

9. Colvin 1998, esp. 47 and 65–66; Farrell 2001, xi–xii, 2, 7; Waquet 2001.

10. Shero 1966, 18, 25; Reinhold 1984, esp. 116–41; Waquet 2001, 176, 179–206; Winterer 2002, 103–10, 179–83; Meckler 2006b, 70; Briggs 2007, 279–94.

11. See Game 1925, 19.

12. Game 1925, 12.

13. Published in *Classical Journal* 21 (1925–26).

14. Thompson 2002, 35–39.

15. Veysey 1963, esp. 622.

16. Harwood 1909.

17. Pearcy 2005, 55–56, citing an anthropological study from the 1950s on Latin teaching in the Renaissance. Cf. Waquet 2001, 30–40, 145–51; Ball and Ellsworth 1989. At the beginning of the twentieth century, Owen Johnson published a series of novels about the fictional schoolboy John Humperdink ("Dink") Stover, who comes of age while at Lawrenceville preparatory school in New Jersey. The Latin master—alias "The Roman"—routinely and terrifyingly tests his class on their gerunds and gerundives in the novel in this series titled *The Varmint* (1910). Reflecting on the popularity of these stories when they were reprinted in the 1960s, an alumnus of the school recalls that, as one of Dink's major antagonists, it is "The Roman" who acknowledges in the end that

out of the boy has been born a man (Frederick Buechner, *Life*, 22 September 1967, p. 12).

18. On the campaign against the Helvetii, see, for example, Gelzer 1968, 102–7; Meier 1996, 235–41; Canfora 1999, 110–15; Goldsworthy 2006, 205–23.

19. Janes and Jenks 1906, 3. On this use of Caesar in first-year Latin, see also Gray 1929, 73, 108.

20. See, for example, the comments of Krebs (2006, 111–12) and Kraus (2009).

21. Ferrero 1907, 336–47.

22. Janes and Jenks 1906, 13, on the characterization of Caesar as general and founder.

23. Game 1925, 93–94. There are many such examples throughout the period under discussion.

24. For the common pedagogical conception of Latin (and its study) as masculine, see Farrell 2001, xi-xii, 52–58. Cf. Colvin 1998 on the constraints applied for centuries to girls' education in Latin and Greek within the German system of schooling.

25. Harwood 1909, 98–99.

26. Harwood 1909, 99.

27. On the increasing feminization of Latin (though running in tandem with a decline in its prestige), see Farrell 2001, 98; Winterer 2002, 119–21; 2007, esp. 142–64, 191–206.

28. Harwood 1909, 100. Cf. *Classical Review* 16 (1902): 29–34. Twenty years later, in the pages of another professional publication, a teacher of boys was still advocating the construction of a small-scale version of the Rhine bridge, as well as model catapults, ballistae, and other weaponry. See *Classical Journal* 24 (1928–29).

29. Game 1925, 93–94 and 127–28.

30. See, for example, the edition of the *Gallic War* by Riess and Janes published in 1914. Already by then the New York State Education Department had recommended limiting second-year study of Latin to the first two books, and Riess and Janes follow that directive.

31. On the controversy surrounding Caesar's actions against the Germanic tribes and the frankness or otherwise of his account, see, for example, Lee 1969; Meier 1996, 278–79; Canfora 1999, 118–20; Goldsworthy 2006, 272–77.

32. I am indebted to Victoria Pagán of the University of Florida for the suggestion that prose composition handbooks deserve scrutiny as instruments for structuring students' understanding of Caesar.

33. W.M. Gardner Hale, *School Review* 18.5 (1910): 297–318; Hale 1910.

34. For a more recent critique of prose composition as a pedagogical tool that works to humiliate and marginalize students, see Ball and Ellsworth 1989.

35. Baker and Inglis's course in Latin composition was still being reprinted some fifty years later.

36. Walker 1907, 4.

37. Dennison 1906, 134. Much of the following evaluation of *Caesar's Conquest of Gaul* comes from Dennison's article in the *Classical Journal*, but similar praise is rendered elsewhere.

38. Holmes 1903, x.

39. Holmes 1903, vii.

40. Dennison 1906, 136.

41. Dennison 1906, 135.

42. Dennison 1906, 142.

43. Dennison 1906, 135–36. Critics of Julius Caesar might suggest, rather, that any "lessons" from the *Gallic War* consist of the utility of recklessness and cruelty, and the strategic advantage of genocide.

44. Clarke was also author of a version of the story of Troy and the story of Aeneas in a series of "eclectic school readings."

45. On Shakespeare's Antony as "a cunning demagogue," see Zander 2005, 9.

46. See my introduction for discussion of the various ways in which Abraham Lincoln had been linked for good or ill with Julius Caesar: in his centralizing powers, his conduct of the Civil War, his assassination, and in the public mourning that followed.

47. The full text of the eulogy for Clay can be found, conveniently, in Fornieri 2004, 128–40.

48. See, for example, the sermon delivered by Reverend Pliny H. White in Coventry, Vermont (and printed by the Vermont Record Office), on the occasion of the president's assassination in April 1865, or the eulogy delivered by G.W. Briggs in Salem, Massachusetts. Both are accessible via the "Internet Archive" at www.archive.org.

49. See Dunn 1911; Wilson 1932.

50. As late as 1932, *The Standard Bearer* was still described as probably the best-known and most widely used work of historical fiction for Latin classes; see Wilson 1932. Compare, in the pages of *Classical Weekly*, 8 May 1915, and *Classical Journal* 24 (1928–29), the enthusiasm of teachers for *A Friend of Caesar: A Tale of the Fall of the Roman Republic* (1900) by William Steams Davis.

51. Atque nostris militibus cunctantibus, maxime propter altitudinem maris, qui decimae legionis aquilam ferebat, contestatus deos, ut ea res legioni feliciter eveniret, "Desilite," inquit, "milites, nisi vultis aquilam hostibus prodere: ego certe meum rei publicae atque imperatori officium praestitero." Hoc cum voce magna dixisset, se ex navi proiecit atque in hostes aquilam ferre coepit. Tum nostri cohortati inter se, ne tantum dedecus admitteretur, universi ex navi desiluerunt.

52. For which, see Hunt 2006, 5.

53. Hale 2008.

54. Similarly, the *History of Julius Caesar* (1900) by Jacob Abbott was published by Altemus in its popular series the Young People's Library. Abbott begins by describing Caesar as Rome's hero (14) and concludes that, when a comet appeared after his death, the people recognized their mighty hero's soul was reposing in heaven, 278. Yet, in between, Abbott acknowledges the hero's debts, his exploitation of the mob, his violence, his political selfishness, and his aspirations to sovereignty.

55. The extract is taken from a footnote to the final pages of the last volume of a five-volume study titled *The Decline of the Roman Republic* (1864–74) by George Long (English classical scholar and former professor of Greek and Latin at University College London).

56. Taken from the *History of the Later Roman Commonwealth,* which was published posthumously in 1845. For the severe splintering of judgments on Julius Caesar (both as a whole person, and between his military, political, sexual, social, and ethical manifestations) in nineteenth-century historiography, see the introduction, discussions and bibliography in Wyke 2007 and M. Griffin 2009.

57. Waddell 1907, 7.

58. For the association, in the United States, of admiration for Caesar with the nation's political and social decline, see also chapters 6 and 7 below.

2. AMERICANIZATION

1. See Zander 2005b, 4 on the influence of Shakespeare's play.

2. See Simon 1989; Dietler 1994, 587–93; Goudineau 2001; Pucci 2006; Hemmerle 2006; Wyke 2007, 41–65; and chapter 3 below.

3. Raymond 1881, 143. For the nationalistic appropriation of Shakespeare into American culture more generally, see Levine 1988, 13–81; Buchanan 2009, 114–15 and references there. On *Julius Caesar* as Shakespeare's most American play, see Ripley 1980; Charney 1979, 433–34; Sinfield 1996, 50–52.

4. On time out of sync in *Julius Caesar,* see Wyke 2007, 213.

5. Dunn 1939, 247–48, quoted in Frey 1984, 541. For this tendency to "co-opt" Shakespeare, see Levine 1990, 36; and, on *Julius Caesar* in particular, Sinfield 1996, 50–53.

6. According to Frey 1984, 543.

7. See Wyke 2007, 214, 218–21; and the introduction to this book.

8. Andrews 1990, 26. For a late twentieth-century student handbook that continues to look for resonances with modern American political culture in Shakespeare's *Julius Caesar,* see Derrick 1998, esp. questions 7–9 on pp. 130–31.

9. On Cassius's envy, see, for example, Humphreys 1984, 35; Girard 1991, 187; Zander 2005b, 9.

10. See Wyke 2007, 221–26; and the introduction.

11. Note Waddell's complaints above. For the late nineteenth-century turn to Caesarism, see Baehr 1998; Wyke 2007, 79–82, 156–72; and the introduction.

12. See Malamud 2009, 150–85.

13. In a study of current practice during the 1930s, Van Cleve (1938, 344) reports that *Julius Caesar* is still in the top nine most frequently taught plays, that 71 percent of schools investigated taught *Julius Caesar,* and that the majority favored a ninth- or tenth-grade placement (348). Sklar (2002) states that, even at the beginning of the twenty-first century, *Julius Caesar* is a required text in most American school curricula, and speculates on how best to teach the play in high school, and Zander (2005b, 4) observes that *Julius Caesar* is part of the school syllabus in many countries.

14. On the teaching of Shakespeare in American schools during the nineteenth century and into the early twentieth, see Van Cleve 1938, 334–44; Ripley 1980, 102–3; Frey 1984, 541–46; Levine 1990, 37–40; Pearson and Uricchio 1990, 251–52.

15. On the mechanisms by which Hudson captured Shakespeare for American conservatism, see Stafford 1951.

16. Levine 1990, 39–40.

17. Raymond 1881, 143.

18. Jones (1891) expresses his debt explicitly on p. 7. For the history of ISNU, see McCurrie 2004.

19. For the role of Illinois in the Civil War, see Hicken 1991.

20. Jones (1891, 25–26) draws attention to the eulogy of Lee offered at the dedication of a memorial to him in Virginia the year before publication of his own work, only to challenge its judgment of the general. For the mythological dimensions that accrued to Robert E. Lee after the Civil War, see Reid (2007, esp. pp. 25–44), who charts their growth from sectional to national.

21. See the introduction and Malamud 2009, 89–92.

22. For the growth of support for American *imperium* in the 1890s, see Malamud 2009, 150–85.

23. For the importance of anarchism to public understanding of McKinley's assassination, see Fine 1955 and Rauchway 2003, 83–111.

24. Lewis 1914, 284. For this development, see Van Cleve 1938, 334–37 and Frey 1984, 546–52. For recent emphasis on performance of *Julius Caesar* as an essential pedagogic strategy, see Sklar 2002.

25. Abbott 1913, 93–94. Compare Van Cleve (1938, 347–48), who, on the basis of his investigation of teaching Shakespeare in schools in the 1930s, reports that having pupils attend a theatrical performance ranked sixteenth out of the forty most favored teaching techniques.

26. Wilstach 1908, 400; Winter 1910, 270; Ripley 1980, 215.

27. Levine 1988, 16–21.

28. Ripley 1980, 115.

29. Pinkston 1980, 297, 299–300; Ripley 1980, 215.

30. The scene descriptions that follow are collated from the *Chicago Tribune* (15 October 1902), the *Evening Journal,* Chicago (15 October 1902), the *New York Sun* (2 December 1902), and the *Baltimore Herald* (24 February 1903). Other reviews are also cited in Ripley 1980, 216 and Pinkston 1980, 273–311.

31. Winter 1910, 270.

32. For turn-of-the-century changes to Shakespearean acting styles, see Levine 1988, 46, 48–49. For Mansfield's influential role in the transition, see Wilson 1962; Pinkston 1980, 298, 301–2; Ripley 1980, 216–17, 220.

33. On the twin performance, see Winter 1910, 35–46. My thanks to David Mayer for pointing out the importance of those preceding roles.

34. Again here, my scene descriptions utilize the phraseology of the contemporary reviews listed in note 30 above and discussed in Ripley 1980, 217 and Pinkston 1980, 301–2.

35. In addition to the reviews cited in note 30 above, see Winter 1910, 270; Ripley 1980, 219; Pinkston 1980, 304.

36. Pinkston 1980, 292.

37. Wilstach 1908, 399.

38. So Wilstach 1908, 397–99; Pinkston 1980, 274, 281; Ripley 1980, 215.

39. For the public debate about the political fanaticism or the insanity of Czolgosz, see Rauchway 2003.

40. For example, Waddell (1907), in his campaign against the idolaters of Caesar and Napoleon, draws on Shakespeare's tragedy as an anti-Caesar play.

41. For more of her comments and further analysis of them, see chapter 1.

42. Useful discussion of *Julius Caesar* as a Vitagraph product and an example of "transitional" cinema—that is, film made between 1907 and 1913—can be found in Pearson and Uricchio 1990 and Buchanan 2009, 115–26. Throughout the following account, I am particularly indebted to those two works.

43. Buchanan 2009, 112–13. Cf. Rothwell 2004, 9.

44. Buchanan 2009, 18–19, 105–12. Cf. Wyke 1997, 76 on Vitagraph's *Antony and Cleopatra,* also released in 1908.

45. Buchanan 2009, 114–19.

46. Vitagraph's description in its publicity release of the fifteen scenes is quoted, conveniently, in Pearson and Uricchio 1990, 258, as well as appearing in the trade paper *Moving Picture World* 3.23 (1908): 462. The copy of *Julius Caesar* (1908) that survives in the British National Film Archive has German intertitles and is missing the opening scene.

47. For this standard narrative format, see Pearson and Uricchio 1990, 257–58; Rothwell 2004, 9; Buchanan 2009, 16, 74–104. Cf., on the Italian films *Gli ultimi giorni di Pompei* (1908) and *Nerone* (1909), Wyke 1997, 158–59, 119.

48. As noted by Rothwell 2004, 9 and Buchanan 2009, 118.

49. *Contra:* Buchanan 2009, 118–19.

50. Contrast the savagery of the assassination scene in the painting by Rochegrosse, which was used to illustrate a late nineteenth-century juvenile biography of Caesar (see chapter 1). For animation of famous paintings as a common filmic strategy in this period, see Dunant 1994 and Buchanan 2009, 52–55. For the use of Gérôme in Roman history films, see Wyke 1997, 119–22; Winkler 2004, 98; Cyrino 2005, 225–26.

51. Buchanan 2009, 121–26 discusses in some detail this "divertingly comic touch."

52. So Pearson and Uricchio 1990, 258–59; Buchanan 2009, 17, 42–56.

53. See Miller 2002 on the civil persuasion of the first four acts of Shakespeare's *Julius Caesar* overriding the limited military violence contained in the last.

54. The phrase is not found in the scene-by-scene synopsis released by Vitagraph but appears as "Worte vor Taten" in the intertitles of the surviving German print.

55. On W. Stephen Bush, see Rothwell 2004, 9 and Buchanan 2009, xxi.

56. Pearson and Uricchio 1990, 243–44; Butsch 2000, 158–62; Buchanan 2009, 17–18.

57. Pearson and Uricchio 1990, 248–49, 254–56; Buchanan 2009, 75.

58. The descriptions come from an article in the *New York Herald* for 24 December 1908, quoted in Pearson and Uricchio 1990, 245.

59. From the same article in the *New York Herald,* quoted in Pearson and Uricchio 1990, 245.

60. Czitrom 1982, 50; Pearson and Uricchio 1990, 248–49 and 254–56; Buchanan 2009, 75.

61. Pearson and Uricchio 1990, 250; Buchanan 2009, 10–16.

62. Butsch 2000, 139, 151–57.

63. Czitrom 1982, 47; Pearson and Uricchio 1990, 246–48.

64. *The Film Index*, 12 November 1910, 1, quoted in Pearson and Uricchio 1990, 260.

65. Pearson and Uricchio 1990, 248.

66. Pearson and Uricchio 1990, 260–61. It would be another six years before a film about Julius Caesar became widely accepted as an educational tool, on which see chapter 3.

67. Pearson and Uricchio 1990, 258. Cf. Buchanan 2009, 5–6 and 55, more generally, on the homage early Shakespeare films pay to both high and popular culture.

68. See, most notably, Levine 1988, 13–81. And, for a more recent and broader analysis of Shakespeare in popular culture, see Shaughnessy 2007.

69. The term was coined by Lanier 2002a. See the introduction by Elizabeth Abele to the 2004 special issue of *College Literature* for recent speculation on the question of whether "Shakespop" should be used as a tool in teaching Shakespeare's plays.

70. On Shakespeare in general, see Levine 1988, 13–45. On Shakespeare's Caesar in particular, Pearson and Uricchio 1990, 250–57. For more recent examples of Shakespeare's Caesar in high and low culture, see Derrick 1998, 195–237.

71. Pearson and Uricchio 1990, 258.

72. Bush's remarks are conveniently reproduced in Buchanan 2009, 15.

73. As I have not seen the trade cards of either Fairbanks or Libby, I am indebted to Pearson and Uricchio 1990, 253 for this description of them. Cf. Levine 1988, 54.

74. So Levine 1988, 45–81.

75. On the use of classical imagery in early cigar and tobacco advertising, see Okell 2007, esp. 55–58.

76. For Julius Caesar as an advertising sign, see Wyke 2007, 119–21.

3. MILITARISM

1. See, for example, Zacher 2008, 146–49.

2. On the treatment of Kaiser Wilhelm II in the British press in particular, see Reinermann 2008.

3. The British journal *Truth*, 21 June 1888, 1065, quoted in Reinermann 2008, 473.

4. The article "The Germans and Their Kaiser" in *The Eclectic Magazine of Foreign Literature* 66.5 (November 1897): 704 is written under the pen name Germanicus and reprinted from the *Contemporary Review*.

5. *New York Times*, 7 August 1914.

6. Fanny Cannon, "Belgian Resistance to Caesar," *New York Times*, 8 November 1914.

7. Cf., on parallels claimed between ancient and modern warfare, Kent 1914, 69–70; Claflin 1915, 208.

8. For the thoroughgoing demonization of Wilhelm II in the Anglo-American press after the German attack on Belgium, see Reinermann 2008, 480–84.

9. Game 1925, 12; and see chapter 1 above.

10. On Flexner's attempts at educational reform, see Wheatley 1988.

11. Flexner 1916. The quote comes from p. 18 of the original pamphlet. Cf., from the same period and perspective, John Dewey's *Democracy and Education: An Introduction to the Philosophy of Education* (1916). He too distrusts the traditional curriculum, because he regards it as inappropriate for a democratic society. Latin is suspect, and the modern curriculum should, instead, contain subjects of more instrumental value (284).

12. On *Value of the Classics,* see Kelsey 1927, 300–302; Shore 1927; Kennedy 1984; Waquet 2001, 202–3; Meckler 2006a, 10, 73.

13. Game 1925, 12–13.

14. Shero (1966, 30–31) states that enrollments had dropped from 50 percent in 1910 to 39 percent in 1915, although they rose again for a short while after the war was over.

15. D'Ooge and Eastman 1917.

16. McKinlay (1918, 103–4) inserts evidence in support of this claim of Caesar's in the form of statistics from a grammar test conducted in the high schools of Portland. Of the Latin pupils in the author's own school, 81 percent achieved results above the average.

17. So Powell 2003, esp. 19–26 and Meckler 2006b, 69–71.

18. Linton 1995.

19. Powell 2003, 23–24; Meckler 2006b, 71.

20. On which, see Griese 2001, 44–49, 58–59.

21. On Finley in this period, see Hedrick 2004, 392–400.

22. Cf. the similar argument of C.B. Hudson in the *New York Times* for 17 March 1918, entitled "Persistence of Teuton's Traits from Caesar's Time."

23. On lobbying in support of the Fatherland by many German Americans, see Thompson 2002, 100, 107.

24. For Woodrow Wilson's changing responses to war in Europe during the years 1914 to 1917, see Thompson 2002, 96–187.

25. So Thompson 2002, esp. 114–58.

26. See Simon 1989; Dietler 1994, 587–93; Goudineau 2001; Pucci 2006; Hemmerle 2006; Wyke 2007, 41–65.

27. Wyke 2007, 59–61.

28. See *Vercingétorix et Alésia* 1994, 366–67, nos. 342–43; Dietler 1994, 584, 588–90.

29. Englar 1919, 99.

30. Englar 1919, 99.

31. Englar 1919, 101.

32. See, for example, Shipley 1909 on the Saalburg collection of Roman models, its display as an educational exhibit of the German Empire at the St. Louis Exposition of 1904, and the subsequent purchase and display of some of its pieces by the University of Washington.

33. Rich and Fisher 1955, 381. Cf. Cecil 1996, 116.

34. Cf. above, the description of the young German emperor as a schoolboy who masquerades as the god Mars.

35. Today the website of the society dedicated to the conservation and inter-

pretation of the statue in Minnesota describes "Hermann the German" as "an official symbol recognizing the great achievements of Germanic-Americans" (www.hermannmonument.com). I am most grateful to Oliver Hemmerle for drawing my attention to the monument as a possible model for the caricature in the *New York Times*.

36. See above, chapters 1 and 2.

37. The following discussion of Enrico Guazzoni's film *Cajus Julius Caesar* borrows from, adapts, and adds to a discussion contained in Wyke 2006a.

38. Ferrero 1933, 9–13.

39. See Thayer 1964, 192–270; Seton-Watson 1967, 351–52, 362–81; Doumanis 2001, 107–31; Isnenghi and Rochat 2000, 85–122; Wyke 2006a, 172–73.

40. In 1913, for example, the same director and the same production house (Cines) had released *Marcantonio e Cleopatra*, containing documentary footage of Egypt shot during the Libyan campaign and ending with Octavian celebrating his African triumph through the streets of Rome. The production house Cines was controlled by leading figures in Italian industry and finance and was closely associated with the Vatican and the state. On the nationalistic ideology of Cine's historical films, see Redi 1991, 9, 37–38; Wyke 1997, 1999b; Bertellini 1999a; 1999b, 32–36; 1999c, 48–49; Rhodes 2000, 318; Tomadjoglou 2000, 262–63.

41. See Redi (1991, 44–45), who notes that the opening, almost modern, middle-class drama distinguishes this film from other Cines historical epics, like *Marcantonio e Cleopatra*. The plotline of Guazzoni's *Caesar* draws on ancient rumors about the dictator's multiple affairs with Roman matrons that survive in some of the sources. Historians of the late republic, however, concede that Caesar may have had an affair with Servilia, but point out that chronology prohibits him from fathering her son Brutus; see Syme 1960, 326.

42. These English translations of the original Italian intertitles can be found among the papers in the George Kleine Collection, Library of Congress, Motion Picture Archive.

43. Francesco Giuffrida in *L'Alba Cinematografica* (Catania) for 1 April 1915, quoted in Martinelli 1992, 81. The translation is my own.

44. My thanks are due to Giorgio Bertellini for pointing out the importance to my investigations of the Italian-American consumption of Italy's historical epic films. For that consumption, see Bertellini 1999b, 1999c, and 2003.

45. As in a *PIA* review of Guazzoni's earlier film, *Marcantonio e Cleopatra*, published on 27 November 1913 and cited in Bertellini 1999b, 41.

46. So Bertellini 1999b, 30–31; 1999c, 48; 2003, 48.

47. A review of the film in the *New York Dramatic Mirror* for 11 November 1914 refers to the invited viewing at the Candler.

48. On Kleine's interest in Italian historical epics, see Bertellini 1999a, 251 n. 49.

49. The documents can now be found in the George Kleine Collection, Library of Congress (esp. Subject Files 1886–1946). Similar Kleine documents are available in the New York Public Library for Performing Arts, Theatre Collection. A copy of the version of the film exhibited in the United States is also available for viewing in the Motion Picture Archive of the Library of Congress.

50. Hansen 1994, 15. For the "reform-driven" climate in which Kleine distributed his films, see Tomadjoglou 2000, 267–69.

51. Curiously the very last Italian intertitle that epitomizes Caesar as the embodiment of Rome's imperial dominion has, in the American version, been replaced by "Mount, mount, O soul of Caesar, Thy seat is up on high!" The latter is an adaptation of the dying words of Richard II in another Shakespeare play: "Mount, mount, my soul! Thy seat is up on high" (*Richard II* 5.5.111–12). Of course, nothing suitable can be supplied from the concluding scenes of *Julius Caesar* because it ends with preparations for the last rites of Brutus and the celebrated acknowledgment of his nobility.

52. A sheet of "musical cues and suggestions" for *Julius Caesar* compiled by the well-known exponent of silent-film music Max Winkler survives in the Kleine collection of materials on this film.

53. A clipping in Kleine's scrapbooks from the *Atlanta Constitution* for 13 December 1914 expresses surprise at this nationwide interest. See Bertellini 1999b, 36 more generally for the ways in which imported Italian historical films were singled out for their educational benefits.

54. The event was reported in the *San Francisco Examiner* and the *San Francisco Bulletin,* both for 28 November 1914.

55. The *Milwaukee Free Press,* 6 January 1915, for example, announces that the Shakespeare scholar Professor F.P. Cleaves has been engaged to lecture for George Kleine's *Julius Caesar* at the Rex Theatre in San Jose.

56. According to a newsletter produced by the Kleine distribution company that year.

57. Bertellini 1999a, 232–34; Alovisio 2000, 256–58. Cf. *Motion Picture World,* 21 November 1914, which describes Guazzoni's film as the kind of "high-class production that would strengthen the hold of the motion picture upon American society."

58. Lindvall 2007, 179–202; Nichols 2006, 7.

59. Cf. Bertellini 1999a, 263–64 n. 74.

60. Details of the special distribution and exhibition strategies employed for *Julius Caesar* can be found in the papers of the Kleine Collection. Prize competitions were also organized by newspapers during the film's initial run. See, for example, the *Madison Democrat,* 26 November 1914.

61. According to an exchange of letters between the Kleine company and the MacMillan Company Educational Editorial Department in November 1926.

62. Harvey M. Dann to Superintendent A.G. Balcom, 25 April 1922, George Kleine Collection.

63. See, for example, the *Boston Morning Globe* for 3 November 1914 and the *New York Dramatic Mirror* for 11 November 1914.

64. For the international disarmament talks held in this period, see Steiner 2005, 372–83.

65. See chapter 4 below.

66. Winterer 2002, 102–3.

67. For contemporary discussion of the "Report of the Classical Investigation," see, for example, Game 1925, 85–86 and Gray 1929.

68. See chapter 1 above.

69. I am very grateful to Peter Rose and his colleagues at Miami University, Oxford, Ohio, for loaning me one of their department's copies of Scudder.

70. See, for example, Sklar 2002.

4. DICTATORSHIP

1. Howell 1929, 509.

2. Cf. the account of second-year Latin in an article decrying the removal of the classical languages as requirements for entry into Yale: the teacher's students "are part of Caesar's army. One week they will conduct a campaign against the Helvetians; next month they will march against the blond German barbarians." "Dead Languages Revived as a Live Issue," *New York Times,* 24 May 1931.

3. See, for example, Erisman 2006, 105–64 for the immediate cult of Lindbergh and the marketing of his story specifically to American boys.

4. On the exponential growth in the production of aviation materials and model-making kits for boys as a result of Lindbergh's flight, see Erisman 2006, 125.

5. Branch and Hirst 1981, 114–15.

6. Branch and Hirst 1981, 108–9.

7. Minio-Paluello 1946; Koon 1985; Williams 1994.

8. E.g., teacher Fanny Howell (above).

9. See the anonymous article in the *New York Times,* 24 May 1931, headed "Dead Languages Revived as a Live Issue: Greek and Latin, Now to Be Dropped from Yale's Requirements, as They Linger in the Memory of the Former Schoolboy."

10. Koon 1985, 19–21; Williams 1994, 37–38, 65–134. On the Fascist myth of *romanità,* see Visser 1992; Quartermaine 1995; Berezin 1997, esp. 70–140; Wyke 1999a; Laurence 1999; Stone 1999; Dunnett 2006; Nelis 2007; Wyke 2007, 82–88, 172–84; Fleming 2007, 343–46.

11. See Kliebard 2004, 224.

12. The term comes from Waquet 2001, 29.

13. Canfora 1980, 101–4.

14. Quoted in Koon 1985, 81.

15. Koon 1985, 21; Williams 1994, 215. Cf. Thomas and Thomas 1940, 292 for contemporary recognition in the United States that Mussolini "wants to bring up fighters instead of thinkers."

16. *Capo centuria* n.d., 245 (published by the Partito Nazionale Fascista, Gioventù Italiana del Littorio, sometime after 1936), quoted in Koon 1985, 21.

17. See Wyke 1999a; 2007, 82–88, 172–84; Nelis 2007, 405–7.

18. Translation from Dorfles 1969, 113.

19. Nelis (2007, 406) observes that Julius Caesar continued to be Mussolini's favorite Roman even after Augustus came to be deployed by the Fascist regime as a model for Italian empire and a more enduring rule.

20. On American pro-Fascism and the importance of the press, see, for example, Diggins 1972, 46–77; Block 1994, 141–43; Bertellini 2005, 692–701; Iorizzo and Mondello 2006, 248–62; Nelis 2007, 395.

21. Mussolini 1936, 8.

22. Diggins 1972, 46–53; De Felice 1974, 578; Cohn 1990, 165–217; Block 1994, 141; Falasca-Zamponi 1997, 52; Alpers 2003, 17–21; Iorizzo and Mondello 2006, 253.

23. Other reproductions or discussions of Lady Drummond Hay's interview appeared in the *Los Angeles Times* (11 September 1925), the *New York Times* (30 August 1925), and *Time* (31 August 1925).

24. So Diggins 1972, 28–29.

25. The full interview was then reproduced, again without adverse comment, on 30 August 1925 under the headline "Mussolini Takes Caesar as His Ideal."

26. Wyke 1999a; 2007, 82–88, 172–84; Nelis 2007, 405–7.

27. The article was republished in the *Urbana Daily Courier* for 17 October 1935.

28. Cf. P.W. Wilson's argument in "It Is Not Yet the Rome the Caesars Ruled," *New York Times*, 7 June 1936.

29. For aural innovation in the newsreels of the early 1930s, see Doherty 1999, 197–99.

30. For the event and its militarism, see Berezin 1997, 116–21.

31. The newsreel can be found in the Hearst Movietone News Collection of the Film & Television Archive at UCLA, vol. 2.226.

32. On anti-Fascism in the United States during this period, see Diggins 1972; Ceplair 1987, 181–241; Alpers 2003.

33. Diggins 1972, 44–46; Alpers 2003, 24.

34. The description is that of Diggins 1972, 53.

35. The cartoon is reproduced in Gianeri 1945, 43.

36. On what came to be known as the Abyssinian crisis, see, for example, Mallett 2003, 6–9, 32–82; Rose 2007, 92–100.

37. I am most grateful to Chiara Thumiger for suggesting this translation of "Squagliamoci e più che in fretta!!"

38. The following account of Welles's *Caesar* borrows, adapts, and adds to material in Wyke 1999a, 176–79; 2007, 226–32.

39. In both Houseman 1973, 298–99 and Houseman 1986, 149. Houseman's memoirs provide substantial details on the preparation of the production. The promptbook survives in the Folger Shakespeare Library, Washington, D.C. The playscript is reproduced in France 1990. Other original materials can be found in the Billy Rose Theatre Collection, New York Public Library for the Performing Arts. Public interest in this anti-Fascist version of Shakespeare's *Julius Caesar* has been reignited recently with the release of the Hollywood film *Me and Orson Welles* 2009. Directed by Richard Linklater, it stars Zac Efron as a teenager who bluffs his way into the production.

40. Ripley 1980, 223. Cf. France 1977, 109; 1990, 104.

41. So Houseman 1973, 298; France 1977, 106; 1990, 2; Higham 1985, 131, 134; Anderegg 1999, 19; Chothia 2003, 130.

42. Welles and Houseman managed to advertise this "declaration of principles" on the front page of the *New York Times* Sunday drama section for 29 August 1937. See also the comments in Naremore 1978, 16–18; Leaming 1985, 139; Valentinetti 1981, 17–21; France 1990, 1–17; Axline 2001, 35; Casale 2001, 125..

43. France 1977, 107–8; Ripley 1980, 223–25; Spevack 1988, 38; Brady 1990, 121–22; Casale 2001, 131–34; Axline 2001, 35–36; Chothia 2003, 119; Anderegg 2005, 296.

44. Houseman 1973, 296–97; France 1977, 107; Brady 1990, 120–25; Axline 2001, 38–39.

45. Houseman 1973, 97; France 1977, 112, 120; Ripley 1980, 226; Casale 2001, 136–37; Axline 2001, 39.

46. Houseman 1973, 306–7.

47. Houseman 1986, 156; Ripley 1980, 226; Brady 1990, 124; Axline 2001, 39–40.

48. Welles's production was not, however, the first modern-dress version. The Delaware Federal Theatre had already staged a modern-dress, anti-Fascist version of the Roman tragedy earlier that year, as noted by Chothia 2003, 118–19, Anderegg 2005, 298, and others.

49. France 1977, 109; 1990, 104; Houseman 1986, 149.

50. Noted and quoted in Brady 1990, 123–24.

51. On this opening scene, see, for example, Ripley 1980, 226–27; Valentinetti 1981, 19; Higham 1985, 132; Brady 1990, 123; Chothia 2003, 119; Anderegg 2005, 300–301.

52. See the *New York Times,* 12 November 1937; the *New York Sun,* 12 November 1937; *Variety,* 17 November 1937; the *New Republic,* 1 December 1937 and 29 December 1937.

53. Welles 1998, 301.

54. France 1977, 112, 116; Ripley 1980, 228–31; Chothia 2003, 120–23.

55. These evocations of city life in 1930s America are taken up in France 1977, 109; Ripley 1980, 227; Higham 1985, 132. The date of the *Washington Times* review is obscured in the NYPL Billy Rose Theatre Collection clippings file of dramatic criticism for 1937–38.

56. For Salvatore "Little Caesar" Maranzano, see Reppetto 2004, 135–40; DeStefano 2006, 20–26; Raab 2006, 26–32; DeVico 2007, 21–27. My thanks are due to Suzanne Dixon, who, some years ago, pointed out to me the curious connections and disconnections between Mussolini, Caesar, and American gangsterism.

57. DeStefano 2006, 23.

58. Gardaphé 2006, 3; Iorizzo and Mondello 2006, 184–215.

59. Horsley 2005, 119–24; Mason 2002, 1–30. Gili (1981, 48–49) notes that the film *Little Caesar* (1930) was prohibited in Italy because of the perceived evocation of Mussolini in the lead character played by Edward G. Robinson.

60. For brief discussion of the film, see Dennis 2006, 44–46. Subsequently, the name was used to designate the African-American gangster who breaks away from service to "the mob" in the blaxploitation film *Black Caesar* (1973). The figure of the gangster was then taken up and celebrated in "gangsta rap," where the name 'Caesar' continues to circulate. An album released in 2001 by the Chicano artist C-Blunt is entitled *Julius Ceasar* [*sic*]. One version of its cover art displays a representation of the singer sporting a laurel wreath and Roman breastplate and greaves seated magisterially on a throne.

61. Reppetto 2004, 114.

62. For the genre, see Cassuto 2009.

63. See the introduction to this book and Wyke 2007, 222–26.

64. See, for example, Edsforth 2000, 99–109 on such concerns around the period 1932–33. The references in Irwin's novel to the Fusionists and the Fresh Air Fund would seem to pinpoint the mayoralty of Fiorello La Guardia in New York as the modern parallel readers are invited to see in the administration of "CJC," but the only model explicitly mentioned by the author is Adolf Hitler 22. For the "dictatorship" of La Guardia, see, for example, Jeffers 2002. For Franklin D. Roosevelt as Caesarean, see chapters 5 and 6 below.

65. According to Williams 1981, 4. For the perception of a drift toward dictatorship in Huey Long's governance of Louisiana, and its consequences nationally, see Hair 1991, 276–326.

66. See esp. Perry 2004, 44–81. Cf., for example, Alpers 2003, 51–56.

67. Quoted in Leaming 1985, 140.

68. Stark Young, *New Republic,* 1 December 1937, 101.

69. For the political radicalism of the production, see Houseman 1973, 313–19; France 1977, 112–16; Leaming 1985, 140–41; Brady 1990, 123–25; Callow 1996, 336–40.

70. *The Mercury: A Weekly Bulletin of Information Concerning the Mercury Theatre,* n.d., quoted in Ripley 1980, 222–23.

71. As noted by, e.g., Brady 1990, 124; Sinfield 1996, 52.

72. Although not to the excessive degree of Richard Mansfield's mad, fanatical Brutus of 1902, on which see chapter 2 above.

73. Houseman (1973, 318) remarks on the consistency with which many reviewers understood this to be the point of how Brutus was played. Cf. Ripley 1980, 222–23.

74. Holland 1960, 441, 443.

75. So Ripley 1980, 224. Furthermore, as France (1990, 105) points out, even in Shakespeare's play the scene is short on dialogue, lacks significant action, and contains none of the play's major characters.

76. My account of this crucial scene is based on France 1977, 112–16; 1990, 105; Ripley 1980, 224; Higham 1985, 133; Brady 1990, 124–25; Casale 2001, 135–36; Chothia 2003, 123–25; Anderegg 2005, 296.

77. So Houseman 1973, 309–10; Ripley 1980, 222–23; Sinfield 1996, 52.

78. In an interview with the *New York Post* (24 November 1937) conducted by Michael Mok, quoted in, for example, Brady 1990, 125.

79. Compare similar comments on the difference between this production and the teaching of *Julius Caesar* in school in the *Daily Mirror* and the *New York Herald Tribune,* both for 12 November 1937.

80. For the crucial pedagogic component of Welles's production and its enormous impact on students, see Brady 1990, 127–28; Anderegg 1999, 27–28.

81. So Chothia 2003, 129 and Anderegg 2005, 301–2.

82. See the beginning of this chapter.

83. Tolman 1940, 831.

84. See, conveniently, Reynolds 1990 for the importance of 1940—and the fall of France in particular—in the international politics of the twentieth century. Similarly, in 1940, the advertising poster for a modern-dress production of

Shakespeare's *Julius Caesar* at the Little Theatre of Dallas included a caricature of Stalin as well as of Mussolini and Hitler.

85. See the opening of this chapter.

86. Armstrong 1938.

87. In the following year, in the same journal, Armstrong elaborates on the greatness of Caesar's art of war through an analysis of his campaign against Vercingetorix (Armstrong 1939).

88. Thomas and Thomas also wrote "living biographies" of philosophers, scientists, novelists, and composers targeted at high-school and college students. Thomas and Thomas's *Living Biographies of Famous Rulers* condenses twenty lives into easily digestible portions of about ten pages apiece. Oddly, the work was released as an audiobook in 1995, aimed explicitly at grades 9–12.

89. The sequence appears in Hearst's News of the Day for 27 July 1943 after the captions MUSSOLINI OUT! RISE AND FALL OF A DICTATOR! It can still be viewed in the Film & Television Archive of UCLA. The name of the series was changed from Hearst Metrotone News to News of the Day in 1936 because of increased public criticism of Hearst as a bigot or a Fascist, on which see Nasaw 2001, 506–7.

90. Diggins 1972, 366–67.

91. Armstrong 1939, 291.

92. On Patton's identification with Julius Caesar, see Ayer 1964, 2, 9, 94–95; Essame 1974, 25; Farago 1981, 31–32; D'Este 1995, 40, 257, 708, 735.

5. TOTALITARIANISM

1. I have consulted clippings and production files for MGM's *Julius Caesar* (1953) in the Margaret Herrick Library, the USC Cinematic Arts Library (including its MGM special collection), and the UCLA John Houseman special collection (no. 816), all in Los Angeles; the Folger Shakespeare Library in Washington D.C.; the Museum of Modern Art and the New York Public Library for the Performing Arts; and the British Film Institute Library in London. Discussion of the MGM film in this chapter utilizes but also adapts, extends, and provides a broader historical context for an earlier consideration of its style in Wyke 2004.

2. A strategy commented on by Lower and Palmer 2001, 147.

3. As noted in the *New York Times* for 21 September 1952, when the film was in production.

4. On the theatricality of Mankiewicz's film style, see Dick 1983 and La Polla 1987.

5. As did Roy Walker in the *Twentieth Century* for December 1953. On the relation between Houseman's filmed *Julius Caesar* and Welles's staged production, see also Geist 1978, 223; Sinyard 1986, 13; Miller 2000, 95; Chothia 2003.

6. See, for example, the review in the *New York Herald Tribune* (n.d.). Cf. *This Week*, 1 March 1953; *Motion Picture Herald*, 6 June 1953; *Twentieth Century* 154.922 (1953); *Quarterly of Film, Radio and Television* 8.2 (1953): 125.

7. See, for example, *Time*, 1 June 1953; *Variety*, 3 June 1953.

8. See, conveniently, Malamud 2009, passim.

9. An article in the *Los Angeles Times* for 20 October 1937, for example, noted that Alf M. Landon (who had failed to win the presidency for the Republican Party in the elections of 1936) was now inferentially comparing the victorious President Roosevelt to Julius Caesar "feeding on power," through his accusation that Roosevelt was violating the Constitution and his call for a fight to preserve the Republic. In the year before the elections, in counterpoint, an article in the *New York Times* for 26 March 1936, entitled "Power Feeds on Power," attempted to reassure readers (and voters) that President Roosevelt did not, like Julius Caesar, feed on the meat of power.

10. See Renshaw 2004, 3, 136.

11. See also chapter 6. For concerns about Roosevelt's expansion of executive prerogative more generally, see, for example, Jones 1995, 476.

12. Koelb (1998, 89) observes that the genre of the historical novel set in antiquity was fostered from the 1930s to the 1950s by an ambition to challenge Fascism's claimed relationship to the past.

13. I use here the page numbers of the Penguin Books edition of 1961.

14. Burbank 1961, 97; Goldstein 1965, 138; Goldstone 1975, 212; Harrison 1983, 254; Koelb 1998, 89–90.

15. For the distance between Wilder's Caesar and modern dictators, see Burbank 1961, 97; Goldstein 1965, 131; Goldstone 1975, 217; Koelb 1998, 90–91.

16. Koelb (1998, 91–93) presents a strong case for Wilder's novel as itself an "assassination" of the Caesar who had been constructed as a model for Mussolini.

17. Burbank 1961, 102, 105; Goldstein 1965, 132–33; Goldstone 1975, 212; Castronovo 1986, 126; Wiseman 1987, 235.

18. On the novel's deliberate anachronisms as well as its historical manipulations, see Goldstein 1965, 132–33; Harrison 1983, 251; Castronovo 1986, 131; Wiseman 1987, 234–41.

19. Goldstein 1965, 132–33; Goldstone 1975, 212; Castronovo 1986, 126; Borgmeier 2001, 356.

20. Against Fascism's definitive histories of Caesar, as Koelb (1998, 91) would argue.

21. As noted by Goldstein (1965, 134) and Koelb (1998, 92, 94).

22. Quoted in Harrison 1983, 254.

23. A contrast Koelb (1998, 93) observes.

24. See esp. Burbank 1961, 97–99 for this generalizing function of Caesar in Wilder's novel.

25. See Cotkin 2003 for existentialism in the United States, and 79–83 for Wilder's Kierkegaardian version of it. For Wilder's Caesar as existentialist hero, see Burbank 1961, 97–106; Goldstein 1961, 141–43; Goldstone 1975, 213–14; Harrison 1983, 251–55; Christensen 1995, 297; Koelb 1998, 92.

26. So Castronovo 1986, 129. Cf. Burbank 1961, 102–4.

27. Burbank 1961, 99–100. Cf. Goldstein 1961, 141; Castronovo 1986, 127; Borgmeier 2001, 358.

28. Harrison 1986, 255.

29. Wilder's Caesar is characterized in this way in the review by the classicist MacKendrick (1948, 66).

30. Atkinson 1948.

31. Lucas 1999, 6–10.

32. So Goldstone (1975, 218–21) describes Wilder's vision of a charming Caesar.

33. On early American television, see Butsch 2000, 235–51; Doherty 2003, 1–18.

34. Based on the data provided in Butsch 2000, 236.

35. See Raw 2009 for a brief history of the *Studio One* drama series, to which I am indebted for some of the details of the production provided here.

36. So Jack Gould in his review for the *New York Times*, 13 March 1949. For the role of Shakespeare and Caesar in raising the cultural status of early film, see chapter 2 above.

37. On Miner's critique of the power of the state, see Raw 2009, 92.

38. Lucas (1999, 53–73) describes how in this period the U.S. government developed and disseminated its menacing depiction of Communism as part of a crusading "war for Freedom" against the Soviet Union.

39. See Jones 2002, 89 for discussion of the *New York Times* review. I am very grateful to William B. Jones Jr. for his advice on locating the copyright holders of *Classics Illustrated,* and for other useful information about the comic-book editions of *Julius Caesar* in particular.

40. Jones (2002, 220; 2009) notes that this comic-strip version of *Julius Caesar,* with artwork by Henry C. Kiefer, had originally been published between 11 October and 1 November 1947 in four installments as a newspaper supplement distributed by the New York Post Syndicate.

41. For the history of *Classics Illustrated,* see Jones 2002; and, more briefly, Rasula 1990, 51, 56–57 and Jensen 2006.

42. A copy of the original sixty-eighth edition of *Classics Illustrated* can be found, for example, in the Folger Shakespeare Library in Washington D.C. (Sh. Misc. 1705). Numerous copies are also available for purchase from comic-book collectors advertising on the Internet. The Kiefer edition was reprinted in 1951 and 1953, and then again in 1960 with a new cover design. A new edition, with artwork by George Evans and Reed Crandall, appeared in 1962 and was itself reprinted a number of times in the 1960s. Another new edition, retaining the artwork of Evans and Crandall, was published as recently as 2009. Details from Jones 2002, 220; 2009.

43. On which, see Jones 2002, 223 n. 130; and chapter 6 below.

44. See Rasula 1990, 57 and Heuman and Burt 2002, 158 for this unusual publishing strategy.

45. For Vitagraph's film *Julius Caesar* (1908) and the term "uplift," see chapter 2 above.

46. Heuman and Burt (2002, 156–57) discuss the educational ambitions of Gilberton's series.

47. So Rasula 1990, 56, on Shakespeare's Caesar in comic-book form.

48. See Perret 2004 for the interpretative strategies of comic-book Shakespeare.

49. Perret (2004, 74–75) discusses this distinction between caption blocks and speech balloons.

50. The evocation of Eisenhower is noted by Halpern 1997, 67.

51. As the general was termed by William Manchester in the title of his 1978 biography. For MacArthur, see also Mayer 1982 and Perret 1996.

52. For the tradition of Shakespeare's Brutus as an American hero, see chapter 2 above. Jones (2002, 89) notes that the *New York Times* review likened this Brutus in his features to Superman and in his words to Captain Marvel.

53. Halpern (1997, 67) observes a connection between the comic-book representation of the conspirators and contemporary anti-Communist hysteria.

54. On the impact of the Cold War on comic books, see Wright 2001, 109–53.

55. Lucas (1999, 74–77) discusses the rising fear in the United States in 1949 and early 1950 that it might lose the Cold War.

56. Jones (2002, 51) observes that Kiefer employs a deliberately antiquated design and reproduces the formal poses of nineteenth-century Shakespearean theater.

57. On reading the cover art of comic books, see Perret 2004, 77–80.

58. The argument is made by Halpern (1997, 67).

59. For this summation, I am indebted particularly to Rasula 1990 and Heuman and Burt 2002, 155–59.

60. Jones 2002, 90.

61. *Newsweek* (n.d.). For the significance of the monochrome photography, see Chothia 2003, 120–21.

62. Compare similar justifications for monochrome in *Time*, 27 October 1952; *Christian Science Monitor*, 18 December 1953; *Sight & Sound* 23.1 (1953); Houseman 1979, 393–94; 1988, 324.

63. For such school exercises that require students to turn the death of Julius Caesar into a journalistic report, see chapter 4 above.

64. Contrast Chothia (2003, 126–27), who argues that the film contains little sense of the climate of 1953 and is largely retrospective in its political tone. Lower and Palmer (2001, 149) are less circumspect about the contemporary political dimension of the film. My earlier discussion in Wyke 2004 focuses largely on the film's stylistic vocabulary as backward-looking (and anti-Fascist). Here I am more concerned with its additional, contemporary expressions.

65. See esp. Miller 2000, 96.

66. For the kind of ideological guidance these titles provided to spectators, see Lenihan 1992, 48.

67. Further discussion of these opening sequences and their sinister, quasi-Fascist style can be found in Wyke 2004, 61–63. See also the secondary literature collated there.

68. See, for example, Ades et al. 1995.

69. So Miller 2000, 96.

70. See Wyke 2004, 61.

71. Thirty-seven typed pages of Pasinetti's background notes for Mankiewicz's *Julius Caesar* survive in the MGM collection of USC's Cinematic Arts Library. They are dated 23 June 1952.

72. Page references here are to the 1968 edition of *Party Politics;* the work was originally delivered as a series of lectures when Taylor was Sather Profes-

sor of Classics at University of California, Berkeley. For Taylor's significance in American classical scholarship, see Saller 1998, 225–26.

73. Specifically, Taylor (1968, 162) bases her arguments on the work of Ronald Syme and Anton von Premerstein.

74. For the concept of totalitarianism in postwar political thought, see Baehr and Richter 2004; Canovan 2004; Geyer 2009, 1–13. See Arendt (1966, originally published in 1949), 460–79 for its description as a novel form of government.

75. For the implied contrast of the Soviet Union with the United States, see Hendershot 2003, 3–4 and Geyer 2009, 1–2. And for the U.S. crusade against the USSR more broadly, see Schrecker 1998, 119–53 and Lucas 1999.

76. So Lucas 1999, 107–27.

77. Henry A. Grunwald, "The Mapping of a Great Mind," *Life,* 29 November 1954, 87–98.

78. "Toynbee and the Future," *Life,* 8 November 1954, 36.

79. Malamud (2009, 209) argues that all Hollywood films representing ancient Rome in this early postwar period systematically projected onto antiquity an American Cold-War discourse that collapsed Fascism and Communism into one overriding totalitarianism that would be defeated.

80. Recalled in Houseman 1988, 325.

81. Quoted, for example, in a preview published in the *New York Times,* 21 September 1952.

82. For further discussion of the Forum sequence, see Wyke 2004 and the literature cited there.

83. Cf., in December 1940, an American student's understanding of act 4, scene 1 of the Shakespeare set text as playing out the division of the world between the three dictators Mussolini, Hitler, and Stalin. See chapter 4 above.

84. The importance of this sequence for the film's characterization of Antony is discussed by Jorgens (1977, 100), Geist (1978, 229), and Lenihan (1992, 49–50).

85. The educational guide can be found in the Houseman special collection at UCLA, (no. 816, box 119) in a scrapbook of materials the producer collated about the film. It is dated only by the month of February but clearly belongs to a period after the film's release.

86. As noted by Belsey (1983, 152–54) and Buchman (1991, 64–83). See Holderness 2002, 53–56 and Wyke 2004, 63–65 for further discussion.

87. For the political ambivalence of Shakespeare's play, see Zander 2005a and the summaries in Wyke 2007, 211–18 and J. Griffin 2009, 381–86. See also chapter 2 above.

88. For the neoclassical architecture designed to celebrate the European dictatorships, see Ades et al. 1995; Murphy 2007, 26–27.

89. See Allen 2001 for an architectural history of the Capitol, also available from an official government website: http://www.access.gpo.gov/congress/senate/capitol/index.html.

90. See, for example, the popular history of Hollywood's "cheap tricks" by Johnson (1996, 339–40).

91. Houseman (1979, 399–40) so describes the sequence. Cf. *Twentieth*

Century, December 1953, 471; Geist 1978, 230; Dick 1983, 134–35; Belsey 1983, 152–53.

92. Cf. *Rochester Times-Union,* 19 March 1954. And see, further, Manvell 1971, 87–88; Geist 1978, 228; Willson 1995, 37; Sinyard 1996, 14.

93. For the importance of genre in understanding how films are produced, consumed, and analyzed (and for the provisionality of the concept of film genre), see Langford 2005.

94. The evocation of film noir is observed by Jorgens (1977, 102 and n. 21) and discussed more hesitantly by Anderegg (2004, 93–94). The correlation of Shakespeare's Roman senators with American gangsters was further naturalized by the strong bond long established in American popular culture between Julius Caesar, Italian Americans, and gangsterism—a bond exploited by Orson Welles in his 1937 modern-dress revival (for which see chapter 4 above).

95. For the link made in Hollywood cinema between domestic Communism and organized crime, see Hendershot 2003, 22–24 and Wilson 2005, esp. 85–87. Wilson also discusses the especially strong contemporary relevance of the postwar gangster genre: between 1950 and 1951, the hearings of a Senate special committee into interstate organized crime were constantly in the headlines of newspapers, newsreels, and radio and television broadcasts and directly stimulated the production of multiple postwar films about American gangster syndicates.

96. The term "intertextual relay" was formulated by Gregory Lukow and Steve Ricci (1984) to describe the industrial strategies by which a narrative image is advanced and disseminated for a film, and the expectations of viewers channeled. Neale (2000) then elaborated the term especially with regard to genre.

97. The specific political context for understanding MGM's *Julius Caesar* is discussed in Lenihan 1992, 48; Crowl 1994, 149; Willson 1995, 37; Miller 2000, 95–96. For analysis of the broad political and social changes that occurred in the United States after the war, see Abrams 2006, esp. 62–91.

98. I can trace this anecdote about Mankiewicz's analogy no further than Geist 1978, 224. It does not appear within the interviews collated by Dauth (2008) but is taken up in Willson 1995, 38; Sinyard 1996, 14; Miller 2000, 96–97. On Adlai Stevenson and the 1952 presidential campaign, see Martin 1977, 605–765.

99. Cited in Martin 1977, 655.

100. See esp. Murphy 1999, 9–34 for the impact of the HUAC hearings and of McCarthyism on the production of American drama, film, and television between 1947 and 1960. For the impact of both specifically on Hollywood, see Ceplair and Englund 1979. Cf. Schrecker 1998, 240–65, 317–33; Doherty 2003.

101. For the experience and the stance of Mankiewicz and Houseman, see also Navasky 1980, 179–81; Houseman 1979, 253, 414–17; Dauth 2008, 139, 140, 156–57.

102. For this biographical reading of Brutus, see Lenihan 1992, 49–50; Crowl 1994, 149–51; Willson 1995, 37; Sinfield 1996, 52–53; Miller 2000, 98; Eldridge 2006, 82–83. Cf. Malamud (2009, 208–28), who discusses the novelis-

tic and cinematic representation of Spartacus in the Cold War as an example of how Roman dress could cloak otherwise forbidden political expression.

103. Anderegg (2004, 92) usefully catalogues the televisual (rather than the more usually acknowledged newsreel) aesthetics of MGM's monochrome *Julius Caesar*.

104. The program can be viewed at the UCLA Film & Television Archive. On the series, see Ceplair 1982; Horowitz 1983; Schultheiss 1996; Bernstein 1996, 216–37; Cronkite 1996, 308–10; Murphy 1999.

105. Doherty 2003, 81–104.

106. So Monoson 2007. And for the perspective of Cronkite himself, see Cronkite 1996, 173–98. For Cronkite's later celebrity as the journalist who, on 22 November 1963, cried on air when reporting the assassination of President Kennedy, see Zelizer 1992, 146–49.

107. Interestingly, the American classical scholar Lily Ross Taylor had recently argued that the best modern analogy for Roman election campaigning lay in the organization and maneuvering of American nominating conventions. See Taylor 1949, 8 and chapter 6 below.

108. See Murphy 1999 for historical analogy as a common ploy in American cultural production during the Cold War.

109. Note, however, that "The Assassination of Julius Caesar" was scripted by Arnold Schulman, who was not one of the three blacklisted. His teleplay is not as direct a critique of McCarthyist repressions as, say, "The Death of Socrates," which was broadcast two months later (on the latter, see Monoson 2007), or Arthur Miller's play *The Crucible*, which ran on Broadway the same year and dealt with literal witch-hunts.

110. On the series, and this program in particular, see Leab 1983; Rosteck 1994; Ranville 1996; Doherty 2003, 161–88. As with the *You are There* series, the program can be viewed at the UCLA Film & Television Archive.

111. On Clooney's reconstruction, see Richter 2007, 144–46. And, as a sample review of its contemporary significance, see that by Neal Ascherson posted on the openDemocracy website on 17 February 2006 (http://www.opendemocracy .net/democracy-Film/good_night_3280.jsp). Also in 2005, the New Video group included the broadcast in a commercial DVD, "The Edward R. Murrow Television Collection: The McCarthy Years," hosted by Walter Cronkite. On the cover of the DVD the telecast is described as "one of the finest and proudest moments of broadcast journalism."

112. See Doherty 2003, 176–77 for the possibility that MGM's film might have influenced the use of Shakespeare's *Julius Caesar* in the *See It Now* report. Contrast Miller 2000, 98 on the television program's relevance for understanding MGM's film; another critic interprets a later screen Brutus in the light of Murrow: Manvell 1971, 94 on the 1969 film adaptation of *Julius Caesar* starring Jason Robards as Brutus (on which, see chapter 6 below).

113. For the fall of McCarthy, see, for example, Schrecker 1998, 260–65; Doherty 2003, 189–214.

114. As noted by Doherty 2003, vii.

115. On the casting of Brando, see Geist 1978, 225; Houseman 1979, 388–89; Manso 1994, 323; Dauth 2008, 163–64.

116. For Brando's star persona and its reinforcement in *Julius Caesar*, see Geist 1978, 226–28; Miller 2000, 98; Lower and Palmer 2001, 151–52.

117. Cf., for example, *This Week*, 1 March 1953, and *Hollywood Reporter*, n.d.

118. Houseman 1973, 308n. For discussion of this perceived miscasting of Brando, see also Geist 1978, 227.

119. Lenihan (1992, 48) discusses the poster, a copy of which can be seen in the USC Cinematic Arts Library. Cf. Miller 2000, 97 on its Cold War vocabulary.

120. Here I am much indebted to Miller 2000, 95 and 97 for the argument that the "divided Caesar" of MGM's film sits well with the ambivalences of Shakespeare's play and the contradictions of American political ideology in the 1950s.

6. PRESIDENTIAL POWER

1. For the battle of Zela, see, for example, Canfora 1999, 252–54 and Goldsworthy 2006, 446–47.

2. Siedler 1956, 31.

3. For the phenomenally successful Marlboro Man campaign, see Lohof 1969. On the use of classical images in earlier tobacco advertising, see OKell 2007.

4. Russell's talk was published alongside Siedler's and a number of others on 19 October 1956 in a special issue of the *Classical Weekly* dedicated to Caesar.

5. Russell 1956, 18–19.

6. For this contemporary view of Eisenhower, see, for example, Boyle 2005, passim and esp. 150–51. On the foreign policy of Eisenhower's presidency, see also Bowie and Immerman 1998.

7. See chapter 5 above and elsewhere in this chapter for some of the associations made in popular culture between Dwight Eisenhower and Julius Caesar.

8. Compare Malamud 2006 and 2009, 18–25 on claims that General Andrew Jackson had become America's Caesar after he became president in 1829.

9. Gerber 1956, 19. She makes no overt reference to the status of her university as one historically dominated by African-American enrollment.

10. See above, chapter 1, for talk of "the Caesar grade" or "the Caesar year" in the 1910s and an era when the text of the *Gallic War* was even used to teach beginners in the first year of high school.

11. For the history of *Classics Illustrated* and its strategies for comic-strip abridgment, see Jones 2002 and, more briefly, Rasula 1990, 51 and 56–57, and Jensen 2006, as well as the discussion in chapter 5 above.

12. For the important distinction between caption blocks and speech balloons in the creation of comic-book meaning, see Perret 2004, 74–75.

13. For other examples, directed at young American readers, where the text of the *Gallic War* is taken at face value, see chapter 1 above. In contrast, for the *Tendenz* of Caesar's commentaries, see, for example, Krebs 2006, 111–12 and Kraus 2009, especially 163–64, where she discusses the narrative strategies of a more recent comic-strip *Gallic War* directed at students of Latin.

14. Dictatorship and violent death are only mentioned in the barest terms toward the end of a separate one-page biography within the back pages of the comic book. The biography itself begins with a bold proclamation: "Julius Caesar was one of the most remarkable men in all history" (45).

15. On the success of which, see, for example, Ambrose 2003, 238–41 and Boyle 2005, 11–12.

16. Boyle (2005, 150–51) describes the public image of President Eisenhower as a soldier who had adopted civilian dress, and as a leader thought capable of offering political stability precisely because of his earlier success as wartime commander. See chapter 5 above and Halpern 1997, 67, for echoes of General Eisenhower in the early pages of *CI*'s abridgment of Shakespeare's *Julius Caesar*.

17. On Gilberton's educational ambitions for the *Classics Illustrated* series, see Heuman and Burt 2002, 156–57 and chapter 5 above.

18. For reprinting as a distinctive feature of the *Classics Illustrated* series, see Rasula 1990, 57; Heuman and Burt 2002, 158; chapter 5 above. For reprints of *Caesar's Conquests* specifically, see Jones 2002, 223 n. 130.

19. In Lewin and Frazier 1957, 122–31. See chapter 3 above for the earlier exploitation of an Italian silent film (Enrico Guazzoni's *Cajus Julius Caesar*, 1914) as a vehicle for enriching study of Shakespeare's play.

20. On Lewin's activities to support photoplay appreciation in schools, see Selby 1978, 72–83.

21. Cf. Smoodin 2001, 352–54 on the rhetoric of a photoplay guide to the film *Mr. Smith*.

22. Lewin 1957, 123–24.

23. Mack's lecture was published in 1960 and reproduced in Derrick 1998, 144–58. Page numbers here refer to the reprint in Derrick.

24. Mack 1998, 158.

25. Mack 1998, 144–45.

26. See, for example, Henry 2003, xi–xxv. For the resurgence in the early twenty-first century of such concerns (and the analogical topos of ancient Rome's decline), see chapter 7 below.

27. The article was headlined "Europe's Culture, America's Civilization" and appeared in *National Review* 3.22 (1 June 1957): 521–24.

28. See Brantlinger 1983, esp. 35–37 for similar examples of the argument that America is the new Rome.

29. As the editors of the *National Review* noted in their preface to de Riencourt's summary of his startling thesis. Baehr (1998, 257–65) provides further comment on and criticism of de Riencourt's use of Spengler. See chapter 5 above for Toynbee on Caesar.

30. With respect to the analogical strategies adopted by critics of Andrew Jackson, Miles (1968, 362) noted that Americans are inclined to attribute the loss of Roman liberty to causes they consider menacing to their own.

31. For the importance of Mommsen and Ferrero in the twentieth-century reception (and understanding) of Julius Caesar, see chapter 1 above and Yavetz 1983, 10–57.

32. In contrast on Eisenhower, Boyle (2005, 47–48, 81–82) notes the signifi-

cance of the Formosa Resolution passed by Congress in 1955, which gave to an American president—for the first time—discretionary powers to engage U.S. troops in combat abroad.

33. For Roosevelt's leadership as a turning point in the modern American presidency, see Greenstein 2001, 3.

34. On the Caesarean rhetoric of Jackson's opponents, see Malamud 2009, 18–25. De Riencourt (1957, 77) utilizes that tradition to claim that the American president was metamorphosed "into a powerful tribune of the people" from the time of Jackson onward.

35. Charles Poore, a contemporary reviewer of *The Coming Caesars*, notes that the parallels between America and ancient Rome have grown in vogue as America's international stature has grown (*New York Times*, 1 June 1957).

36. For this postwar recognition of an emerging American empire, see Liska 1978 and Miller 1981, 123–41. Cf. Johnson 2004, 193 and see chapter 7 below.

37. As observed by Miles 1968 and Miller 1990.

38. In *World Affairs Quarterly* 29.1 (1958): 82, one contemporary critic of *The Coming Caesars* observes dryly of its author: "An unwonted modesty prevents him from likening himself to Greek Polybius."

39. Meyer 1957, on which see the libertarian commentator Stromberg (2001). Cf. the review by Richard M. Weaver in *The Freeman* 7.10 (1957): 61–63.

40. Miller (1981, 123–41) noted the problem about the number of hats but was otherwise fairly well disposed toward de Riencourt's thesis, believing the Caesars to have finally arrived in Washington. For contemporary criticism of the book's historical shortcomings, see the reviews in *World Affairs Quarterly* 29.1 (1958) and *Political Quarterly* 30 (1959).

41. Chambon 1958, 14. On the significance of involving army paratroopers in the restoration of order in Little Rock, see, for example, Boyle 2005, 98–100 and Wagner 2006, 81–85.

42. Chambon 1958, 11.

43. So Baehr 1998, 264.

44. On this trend in postwar American conservatism, see Piper 1997, 183–98 and Henry 2003, xi-xxv. The latter constitutes an introduction to James Burnham's *Congress and the American Tradition*. Originally published in 1959, the book is disturbed by the prospect of the death of Congress and the dictatorship of the executive. See also, more generally, Abrams 2006, 199–218.

45. Molnar 1966, 409–10. On Molnar (as on Frank Meyer above), see the more recent libertarian commentator Stromberg (2001).

46. Molnar 1966, 411.

47. See Dallek 2005, 190–271. And, more broadly, Grantham 1988, 253–305; Greenstein 2001, 75–89; Chafe 2003, 266–93.

48. By a sleight of hand, Sulzberger draws for support of his thesis on de Riencourt and fails to observe that *The Coming Caesars* describes the situation of the United States and not of Western democracy as a whole. Sulzberger makes pretty much the same case seven months earlier in an article entitled "Great Caesar's Ghost Arises" (*New York Times*, 27 August 1965), where de Riencourt's focus on the United States is acknowledged.

49. I am grateful to Don Board, who, in e-mail correspondence, pointed out the pun in "Ev."

50. As in "The Commander in Chief," a Radio-TV Weekly Report issued by Dirksen in the week 21–27 February 1966 and archived at http://www.dirksen center.org/Vietnam/February211966.htm.

51. On Dirksen's questioning of White House foreign policy, see LaFeber 2005, 11–12.

52. On the rapid rise to affluence of many Americans in the third quarter of the twentieth century, see Abrams 2006, 27–52.

53. For a history of this form of "negative classicism," where dark predictions are based on perceived parallels between the Roman Empire's bread and circuses and modern society's mass culture, see Brantlinger 1983, esp. 35–37.

54. Mumford's work was originally published in 1961; page references are to the Penguin edition of 1966.

55. For such modern constructions of the ancient city of Rome as an exemplary metropolitan dystopia, see Laurence 1997. On Mumford's advocacy of small-scale, low-density garden cities, and developments in his conception of social organism, see Casillo 1992.

56. Cf. Malamud 2009, 230–31.

57. On the Roman-themed casino, see Martin 1985; Malamud 1998; Malamud and McGuire 2001; Malamud 2009, 229–52. Cf. Wyke 2007, 117–18.

58. See discussion of the Marlboro cigarettes campaign at the beginning of this chapter and Wyke 2007, 118–19 for a late twentieth-century British advertisement for bedroom furniture. For Julius Caesar's role in earlier American advertising, see chapter 2 above.

59. White 1978, 35. See, further, Hoffman 1995, 151, and the discussion of Julius Caesar in American education throughout this book.

60. White 1978, 497.

61. White notes the comparison between the three acts of his Roman play, which lead Caesar across the Rubicon, and the three acts of Kennedy's ascent to the presidency in his *New York Times* interview with George Gent (12 February 1971).

62. According to White's autobiography (1978, 474).

63. In the epilogue to *Caesar at the Rubicon* (1968, 160).

64. Balbus is described thus in White's cast of characters (1968, 17–18).

65. See Zelizer 1992, 146–49 and esp. Hoffmann 1995, 107–44. Hoffmann suggests that White bestowed on John F. Kennedy the grandeur of a Roman emperor and records that, in a letter to JFK's brother Robert one month after the assassination, White declared: "I feel the modern world can neither understand Christ nor Democratic politics unless we understand Caesar first" (151).

66. White in *Life*, 29 November 1963, 32E.

67. White signs off his prologue with the places where and the dates when he worked on his play: Villa Serbelloni in Como, Italy, in June 1966; Fair Harbour on Fire Island, New York, in October 1967 (16).

68. See, for example, White 1969, 396–97.

69. For the collapse of support for President Johnson, the decline in popularity of the Democratic Party, and the consequent election of Richard Nixon

late in 1968, see LaFeber 2005. Cf. White's own analysis in *The Making of the President, 1968*.

70. Dudley Fitts, "Now and Then," *New York Times*, 14 April 1968. Other reviews of the play's publication in 1968 and its performance in 1971 noted its contemporary relevance. See, for example, *Chicago Tribune*, 14 July 1968; *Hartford Courant*, 17 March 1968; *Time*, 29 March 1968; *New York Times*, 12 February 1971; *Tuscaloosa News*, 6 March 1971. In an article entitled "America: Toward a Decline and Fall?' in the *Wall Street Journal* for 11 December 1968, the reporter observed that White's play seemed to be part of a current trend in monitory comparisons between the United States and Rome exploited by everyone from governors and liberal columnists to social commentators.

71. Hoffmann (1995, 149, 174) argues that thanks to White's commentary many Americans expected their president to have a regal presence and a touch of omnipotence.

72. White 1968, 171.

73. Taylor 1949, 8, and 1966, ix, respectively.

74. As noted in Foster 2002.

75. Schlesinger 2004, xv–xvi. He argues there for the revitalization of the "Imperial Presidency" in the twenty-first century, on which compare Rudalevige 2005 and see chapter 7 below. For a convenient synopsis of Schlesinger's conception of the "Imperial Presidency," see Strine 2009, 55–56 and Morris 2010, 123–25. On Schlesinger's history, see also Theoharis (1979), who locates the origins of the "Imperial Presidency" in the years when Truman held office.

76. Contrast Liska (1978), who employs an explicitly "analogico-historical method" to understand American imperial expansion but argues (unlike de Riencourt) that the Roman Empire is just one past empire that might illuminate the American, and one whose differences, as well as similarities, should be acknowledged. In his analysis of an emerging "democratic dictatorship" in the United States, Miller (1981, 123–41) characterizes the president as both a Caesar and a secular pope.

77. On the controversial presidency of Richard Nixon, see, for example, Morgan 2002, esp. 155–89.

78. A letter endorsing that depiction of the presidency and citing de Riencourt in support follows on 27 May 1972.

79. For those traditions, see esp. chapters 23 and 4 above as well as earlier in this chapter.

80. Cotham 1968, 21.

81. I am most grateful to Madeline Matz of the Motion Picture, Broadcast and Recorded Sound Division of the Library of Congress (Washington, D.C.) and Ned Comstock of the Cinematic Arts Library at the University of Southern California (Los Angeles) for drawing my attention to various clippings associated with Burge's *Julius Caesar*. Exploitation materials can also be found in the Margaret Herrick Library of the Academy of Motion Picture Arts and Sciences (Beverly Hills).

82. The reconstruction of Caesar's assassination in the language of newspaper reporting was both a commonly used assignment for American students of

English literature and a long-standing strategy for marketing the play's modernity and that of its screen adaptation (see chapters 4 and 5 above).

83. For discussion of this inserted scene, shot on location in Spain, see Crowl 1994, 151.

84. Crowl (1994, 151) notes the discrepancy between the opening scene of carnage and the subsequent performance of Caesar by Gielgud.

85. So Manvell 1971, 94.

86. See Keyishian 2003, 100–101 for the film's utilization of blood imagery to repudiate the conspirators' deed.

87. The report was written by Sharmini Tiruchelvam and was spread across nine pages of the magazine. On Robards's performance of Brutus, see Manvell 1971, 93–94.

88. Cf. *Daily Variety*, 9 June 1970, and the comments in Crowl 1994, 151.

89. Contrast the director of the Shakespeare Theater in Ontario, Michael Kahn, who in 1972 publicized his production of *Julius Caesar* as motivated by the Nixon-McGovern presidential race; on which, see Sinfield 1996, 53.

90. The political studies referred to are Kevin Phillips's *The Emerging Republican Majority* (1969) and R.M. Scammon and B.J. Wattenberg's *The Real Majority* (1970).

91. Clippings for these productions and the script for the WNYC radio broadcast can be found in the New York Public Library.

92. For the BBC-TV Shakespeare plays, see esp. Willis 1991.

93. On the intensity of the educational outreach activities that accompanied the broadcast of the BBC-TV plays in the United States, see esp. Mullin 1984 and Willis 1991, 47–50.

94. See, for example, Maurice Charney in the *Soho Weekly News*, 1 March 1979. Cf. Willis 1991, 75.

95. These judgments are culled from press reviews published on 14 February 1979 in *Daily Variety*, the *New York Times*, the *Los Angeles Times*, and the *Hollywood Reporter*. See also the preview in the *Christian Science Monitor*, 12 February 1979; Maurice Charney in the *Soho Weekly News*, 1 March 1979; and Jorgens 1979, 411–12. Cf. Rothwell 2004, 107.

96. So Mullin 1984, 584 and Willis 1991, 14, 58.

97. For discussion of the Papp revival in the context of African-American theater history, see briefly Hill and Hatch 2003, 424–25.

98. Martin Gottfried, quoted in Widener 2006, 161. For another review, see *Shakespeare Quarterly* 31.2 (Summer 1980): 192–93; and, very briefly, *Jet*, 15 February 1979, 26.

99. On the history of Papp's support for color-blind and uniracial theater, see Widener 2006, 145–81.

100. Quoted in Widener 2006, 171; the lowercase letters, punctuation, and spelling all belong to Shange.

101. The press release can be found among the materials on the production archived in the Folger Shakespeare Library (Washington, D.C.).

102. According to a review of the production in the *New York Times*, 10 July 1970.

103. So Freedman states in a radio documentary entitled "Shakespeare

Becomes American," which was commissioned by the Folger Shakespeare Library and aired on Public Radio International (PRI) stations in 2007. The transcript is available at http://www.shakespeareinamericanlife.org/transcripts/freedman4.cfm.

104. My description of Freedman's *Caesar* is based on the following press reports: *Westport News,* 27 June 1979; *Daily News,* 7 July 1979; *Women's Wear Daily,* 9 July 1979; *New York Times,* 10 July 1979; *Wall Street Journal,* 10 July 1979; *Christian Science Monitor,* 13 July 1979; *Harvard Crimson,* 17 July 1979; *Our Town,* 22 July 1979; *New York Amsterdam News,* 18 August 1979; *New York Theatre Review,* August 1979; and *Shakespeare Quarterly* 31.2 (Summer 1980): 189–90.

105. The term was coined by Jeremy Gerard in *Our Town,* 22 July 1979.

106. As noted in a review by Elizabeth Rawson in *American Historical Review* 93.1 (1988): 129. And compare Kahn's own comments in the *New York Review of Books,* 16 June 1988.

107. So Jasper Griffin in the *New York Review of Books,* 12 May 1988.

108. In the *History Teacher* 21.1 (1987): 144–45, a reviewer from California State University, Long Beach, noted that the jacket provided for the version published later in 1986 by Schocken Books carried notice of Kahn's own experience of persecution during the McCarthy era, thus encouraging an autobiographical reading of the author's account of Caesar's education. Tellingly, Kahn's own multivolume autobiography is entitled *The Education of a 20th Century Political Animal.*

7. EMPIRE

1. This chapter utilizes but also significantly extends and updates (and situates in the context of this book as a whole) earlier considerations of George W. Bush as a twenty-first-century Caesar in Wyke 2006c and 2007, 191–95, 237–38.

2. See, for example, Stromberg 2001; Bacevich 2002, esp. vii–ix; Foster 2002; Ferguson 2005, esp. 3–7; Henrickson 2009, 4–5.

3. For the journalistic exploitation of this remark by President George H.W. Bush, cf. the article "For Bush, Die Is Cast in Mideast," *Tulsa World,* 26 December 1990. There the author utilizes the Rubicon reference to suggest that the president, like Julius Caesar before him, is taking a great gamble with his political future: "impeachment, or total triumph." One other significant exception I have come across occurs in 1993, at the start of the Clinton administration. During that year, in a series of speeches in the U.S. Senate, Robert C. Byrd placed before his colleagues the monitory example of Julius Caesar's rise to power better to urge them not to cede yet further powers to the presidency. For Byrd's anti-Caesarist interventions, see Maddox 2006, 146–51 and Malamud 2009, 1–4, 256–58.

4. Roberto Livi, "Il presidente Usa sarà il Cesare del XXI secolo?" *Il Messaggero,* 27 March 2003, 9.

5. Edoardo Vigna, "Ma l'impero Americano è come quello Romano?" *Sette, Corriere della Sera* 13, 27 March 2003, 33–43. I am most grateful to Jan Nelis for drawing the magazine to my attention that day when we were both in Rome.

6. For discussion of such claims, see, for example, Bacevich 2003b, 94; Walker 2003; Ferguson 2005, 8–13; Maier 2006, 62–63; Murphy 2007, 11–12, 16–17; Burton 2011. The latter claims about the limited powers of the president belong to the early part of George W. Bush's first term and may seem somewhat quaint in retrospect.

7. As noted in Hendrickson 2009, 5. For earlier concerns about the rise of an "imperial presidency," see chapter 6 above.

8. These articles and others like them are discussed further below. Most were found through ProQuest newspaper database searches in U.S. libraries for the combination of names "Caesar" and "Bush," undertaken in March 2004 and again in April 2010, which revealed a clustering of such critical comment during the course of 2002–3.

9. On these works (and others like them), see Burton 2011. For an example of the far less frequent analogies with Athenian empire, see Hendrickson 2009.

10. So Cohen 2004. The term "hyperpuissance" was coined in 1999 by the then French foreign minister Hubert Védrine to signal that the United States had now exceeded the status of one among several superpowers, as noted by Bacevich (2003a, xi), among others.

11. It is this paradigmatic status that, for some critics, makes the Roman Empire a superior comparandum to the British or any other empire.

12. I here summarize the terms in which the legitimacy and value of the Roman imperial analogy are expressed in Bacevich 2003a, xiii–xiv; Ferguson 2005, vi; James 2006, 2–3, 6–23; Maier 2006, 3; Meckler 2006a, 3, 8, 11; Murphy 2007, 2–23; Johnson 2007, 59. For the frequent superficiality and historical inaccuracy of many of these analogies, see Burton 2011.

13. Convenient catalogues of perceived correspondence between Roman and American empire are contained in, for example, Ferguson 2005; Maier 2006, 24–77; Murphy 2007, vi, 2–23; Kellow 2009, 158–59; Mattingly 2011, 3–42.

14. For responses to de Riencourt's use of the Roman analogy, see chapter 6 above.

15. In the *New York Times* for 1 July 2007, for example, the reviewer of Cullen Murphy's book *Are We Rome?* noted that leaders of al-Qaeda were referring to the goal of their jihad as the destruction of Rumieh (Arabic for "the Roman Empire").

16. On the significance of the fall of the Berlin Wall for America's status in the world, see Bacevich 2002, esp. vii–ix; Kagan 2003, 26–27; Kraus 2004a, 176; Ferguson 2005, 27; Johnson 2004, 18–21; Hendrickson 2009, 7–8.

17. On the neoconservative network and the development of the Project for the New American Century, see, for example, Rilling 2003; Keller and Mills 2003; Johnson 2004, 227–30; Robertson 2006, 160–61.

18. In "Rebuilding America's Defenses: Strategies, Forces, and Resources for a New Century," published on the PNAC website in September 2002.

19. In the first volume of *The Decline and Fall of the Roman Empire*, published in 1776; see Gibbon 1900, 90. On the long history of the deployment of the term *pax Americana* in echo of Gibbon's *pax Romana* (itself a term borrowed from ancient sources), see Parchami 2009.

20. In a speech in Simi Valley, California, on 19 November 1999; noted, for example, in Bacevich 2003a, x and Ferguson 2005, 6–7.

21. On neoconservative reluctance to use the term "empire," see Freedland 2002; Ferguson 2005, passim; Johnson 2004, 3; James 2006, 29. More favored terms include "hegemon," "liberal imperialism," and "humanitarian intervention."

22. The Founders of the new nation held to a vision of a continental American empire as one that, in direct contrast to the British, would extend liberty rather than remove it; see, for example, Onuf 2000.

23. Burton (2011, 70–76) clarifies the nature of the historical error: the Roman republic possessed a territorial empire for several centuries before the dictatorship of Julius Caesar; the greatest imperial expansion occurred during the republic; "the Roman empire" (or the "imperial period") refers to the domestic structuring of Roman government under its emperors and begins with Augustus c. 27 B.C.E.; the imperial period witnessed in the main territorial consolidation.

24. On the history of "empire" as an indictment of American expansionism, see Bacevich 2003a, ix–x; Ferguson 2005, 3–4, 33–60; James 2006, 28–29; Hendrickson 2009, 4–5, 9–14.

25. Kagan 2002. For the term "imperial denial," see Ferguson 2005.

26. On the terrorist attacks of 2001 and their significance for debates about American empire, see, for example, Kagan 2003, 93–94; Bacevich 2003a, xi–xiii; Rilling 2003; Johnson 2004, 3; 2007, 72; Kraus 2004a; Robertson 2006, 154–55; Wroe and Herbert 2009, 8; Hendrickson 2009, 4, 7–9; O'Reilly 2009, 152; Hook 2009.

27. Kraus 2004b; Singh 2009, 17; Wroe and Herbert 2009, 8.

28. Johnson 2004, 3. Cf. Johnson 2007, 72. For the passionate advocacy of American empire and the twinned interest in Roman analogy after 9/11, see also Eakin 2002; Foster 2002; Freedland 2002; Ignatieff 2003, 22; Keller and Mills 2003; Prestowitz 2003; Smith 2003, 252; Cyrino 2004, 145; Ferguson 2005, 4–5; Murphy 2007; Hendrickson 2009, 9–14; Burton 2011.

29. Krauthammer's comments are quoted in a *New York Times* article of 31 March 2002 entitled "All Roads Lead to DC"; see Eakin 2002. Recently, for example, they featured in the Wikipedia entry "American imperialism."

30. On the perceived utility of "empire" as a discourse within which to understand American unilateralism, see usefully Rilling 2003.

31. As noted by Bacevich 2003a, ix–x and Hendrickson 2009, 4–5, and available for access from the website http://georgewbush-whitehouse.archives. gov. Cf. the president's comment "America has no empire to extend or utopia to establish," made in a graduation speech at West Point on 1 June 2002.

32. Ignatieff 2003, 24. On his conception of "empire lite," see Tønnesson 2004, 334–35.

33. On the awkwardness of Caesar for American imperial analogy, cf. James 2006, 29. Miles (1968, 373–74) notes that some supporters of President Andrew Jackson attempted to describe him favorably as Caesarean but more often rejected the comparison as too dangerous. Compare on Jackson, Malamud 2006 and 2009, 18–25.

34. See esp. chapter 6 above.

35. McGrory 2002.

36. My thanks to Tim Whitmarsh for first drawing to my attention the potential ironies in McGrory's Caesarean comparison.

37. On the significance of this moment, see Johnson 2004, 73, 90; Byrd 2004, 159–61; O'Reilly 2009, 153.

38. Fisk 2002.

39. Toynbee 2002.

40. Cf. Burton 2011, 81 n. 73 on caricatures of George W. Bush as a Roman emperor or legionary.

41. For this return to the language of empire to critique American foreign policy, see James 2006, 28–29; Murphy 2007, 7–8; Hendrickson 2009, 5; Burton 2011.

42. So Hendrickson 2009, 8.

43. On Caesar in the traditions of American republicanism, see the previous chapters in this book and, for example, Baehr 1998, esp. 4–5; Johnson 2004, 15; Hendrickson 2009, 9–14.

44. Lapham 2002, 9.

45. For such criticism of quasi-dictatorial powers accrued by the president, compare the account by Senator Byrd (2004) of the president's persistent assault on the separation of powers after 9/11, and the acquiescence of Congress in handing over to him even their constitutional power to declare war. See also Warshaw 2004; Johnson 2004, esp. 256, 284, 291–98; 2007, 241–79; Malamud 2009, 256–58; Strine 2009.

46. See Beachler 2004, 42 and Rankin 2004 for the Republican accusation.

47. For explicit example, in a review of Senator Byrd's condemnation of President Bush that was quoted on his book's back cover, Arthur Schlesinger declared that the senator "speaks with the voice of a Founding Father defending the traditional ideals of the old republic against the ideological radicals who have seized Washington, today an occupied city." See also Malamud 2009, 257–59.

48. Warthen 2003.

49. On Cato's attack against Caesar's tactics in Gaul, see chapter 1 above.

50. Giardina 2003.

51. On the bitter critique of President Bush's foreign policy that was regularly put on display in the Doonesbury strip in terms of a new Roman empire, see Soper 2008, 137; Shalev 2009, 234–35; Freedman 2009, 25–32; Dittmer 2010, 64–65.

52. As noted in Wyke 2006c, 322 n. 29. I am very grateful to one of the readers for the University of California Press who drew my attention to the relevance of the Doonesbury strip and "*Pox Americus*" in particular.

53. On the prisoner abuse scandals, and the damage they did to the reputation of the Bush administration, see Long 2009, 52–54; Ralph 2009, 85–88; Herbert and Wroe 2009, 261–62.

54. Johnson 2004, 37. Contrast Niall Ferguson's *Colossus*, published in the same year, which argues for the benefits to the world if only the United States were self-consciously to embrace its imperial status and pursue an agenda of

liberal imperialism. On these different visions of American empire, see Murphy 2007, 7–8.

55. On the 2004 presidential elections, see, for example, Singh 2009, 14.

56. For the purposes of this chapter, I am concerned with cultural practices that engage closely with the discourse of America as "the new Rome" and George W. Bush as "the new Caesar." I have not had space to include here analysis of the representation of Julius Caesar in digital strategy games and its evident focus on warmongering and empire building. For a sample analysis of a scenario in *The Rise of Rome* expansion to *Age of Empires* (Microsoft 1998), see Wyke 2007, 36–40.

57. For some examples of the Americanization of Shakespeare's *Julius Caesar* in the twentieth century, see the previous chapters in this book.

58. For a description of the contemporary features of Gaines's production, see Shaltz 2003.

59. Aislesay Chicago (an Internet magazine of stage reviews and opinions), at www.aislesay.com/CHI-JULIUS.html.

60. For details of the New York production, see reviews such as those in the *New York Times,* 4 April 2005; the *Hollywood Reporter,* 2 April 2005; *Newsweek,* 18 April 2005; and *United Press International,* 8 May 2005.

61. Cf. the actor's recollection in the *Sunday Express* for 19 March 2006 that he used to keep the photo of Bush and his inner circle stuck to the front of his script throughout rehearsals, and ask those around him who might lead a rebellion against Bush should one prove necessary. Washington draws on the common perception of General Colin Powell at the time as strongly at odds with the policymakers of the Bush administration. For Powell's position, see Kraus 2004a, 181.

62. On the Bush administration's adverse impact on the institution of the presidency, see, for example, Grossman and Matthews 2009, 4; Strine 2009.

63. Compare the strategies for critiquing the Bush administration deployed by Deborah Warner in the sell-out modern-dress *Julius Caesar* she directed for London's Barbican Theatre around the same time, and then took on European tour. See a joint review of the two productions in the British Sunday newspaper *The Observer* for 10 April 2005. On Warner's production, see also Wyke 2006c, 319 and Rutter 2006.

64. Compare Miles (1968, 370–71), who argues that opponents of Andrew Jackson found scant consolation in reflection on Caesar's bloody death for what that might imply, especially after an attempt was made on the president's life in 1835.

65. See esp. chapters 1 and 2 of this book for Caesar's *Gallic War* and Shakespeare's *Julius Caesar* as key drivers of the Roman general's circulation in American culture. On the importance of education for the place of classical antiquity more broadly in American culture, see Meckler 2006a, 5.

66. As noted, for example, by Swope 1993, vii; Meckler 2006a, 10, 176; Levine 2006, 50.

67. The article by Scot Andrew Pitzer was posted on www.gettysburgtimes.com on 14 March 2011. Contrast an article in the *Taunton Daily Gazette* for 15 March 2011 that simultaneously celebrates the vibrant Latin program at

Taunton High School and the continuation of the traditional parade for Caesar on the Ides of March.

68. For the centrality of Caesar's *De bello Gallico* to the teaching of Latin in the 1900s and 1910s and for his role in shaping the identity of young people as future American citizens, see chapters 1 and 3 above.

69. Compare, for example, the atypical *Wheelock's Latin,* revised by Richard LaFleur and in its seventh edition in 2011. As far back as its original publication in 1956, Frederic M. Wheelock was advising Latin teachers in its preface that, thanks to the linguistic skills students could acquire from use of this new introductory text, it would be possible for those wishing to carry on to a second year of study to skip the traditional course in Caesar and proceed directly on to Cicero and other Latin authors. In 1967, Wheelock produced his own course for this intermediate level (revised in 2001 also by LaFleur as *Wheelock's Latin Reader*), whose core classical authors were duly Cicero, Livy, Ovid, and Pliny.

70. See, for example, a discussion with four high-school teachers of English in McDonald 1995, esp. 150 and Sklar 2002, 36.

71. As noted by Swope 1993, vii.

72. For the pedagogic importance of performance, see McDonald 1995, 146 and Sklar 2002, 37–39.

73. The handbook was published online at http://www.chicagoshakes.com/res/TeacherHandbooks/TH_CAES_02–03_sm.pdf.

74. On Robert Byrd's critiques of the Bush administration couched in the vocabulary of Roman republicanism, see Maddox 2006, 146–51 and Malamud 2009, 1–4, 256–58.

75. On the concept of "ventriloquating" Shakespeare's *Julius Caesar* in the classroom and its consequences for the positioning of students socially, ethically, and politically, see Wortham 2001. The Chicago theater's handbook invites students to position themselves in terms of personal ethics through reflection on an occasion when they had to choose between a friend's wish and doing what they thought was right. On this use of Shakespeare's play as a mode of psychotherapy, see chapter 6 above.

76. On this particular type of accommodation of Shakespeare to mainstream capitalist culture, see Lanier 2002a, 157–61 and Hedrick 2002.

77. See Lanier 2002a, 160–61.

78. Compare, in the United Kingdom, the training courses organized between Cranfield School of Management and the Shakespeare Globe Theatre, or the management course based around *Julius Caesar* held at the Said Business School in 2006.

79. Contrast Lanier 2002a, 167.

80. In 2006, however, Adelman himself began to accuse President Bush of incompetence over Iraq and in late 2008 publicly declared his support for Senator Barack Obama in the coming election.

81. Murphy (2007, 6) regards the launch in 2005 of both HBO's *Rome* and ABC's miniseries *Empire* as related to the current political obsession with ancient Rome. On ABC's *Empire,* see Futrell 2008, 106–8.

82. The preview was written by Tristram Hunt. *Rome* began broadcasting on BBC2 at 9:00 p.m. on 9 November 2005.

83. On the escalating denigration of the Bush administration from shortly after the start of the president's second term, see, for example, O'Reilly 2009, 153–54; Singh 2009, 26; Grossman and Matthews 2009, 4; Wroe and Herbert 2009, 1–2, 274.

84. On *Rome,* season 1, see Cyrino 2008, passim.

85. Pittman (2011, 209) discusses the series' processes of familiarization and estrangement, while Haynes (2008) compares its strategies for constructing both a realistically quotidian and an exotic Roman world.

86. On the political narrative of *Rome,* season 1, see Toscano 2008, 162–63 and Futrell 2008, 109–11.

87. Lockett (2010, 104) argues for the significance of a collective rather than an individual as the title of the series.

88. On HBO's distinctive programming mode of "para-television," see Pittman 2011, 209, citing Avi Santo.

89. The quote is from *Newsweek,* 22 August 2005. Otherwise I summarize from previews or reviews in *Daily Variety,* 16 and 31 August 2005; the *New York Times,* 21 August 2005; *Time,* 22 August 2005; the *Los Angeles Times,* 24 and 26 August 2005; the *Hollywood Reporter,* 26–28 August 2005; the *Wall Street Journal,* 26 August 2005; *LA Weekly,* 28 August–1 September 2005.

90. For the illustrative role of such paintings and the equivocal connotations they add to the Latin text, see chapter 3 above. Boyd (2008, 91) notes the presence elsewhere in *Rome* of painterly evocations of Lawrence Alma-Tadema's domestic depictions of Roman lovers and poetic recitals.

91. The clever creation of *Rome*'s fictive protagonists out of a short passage in *De bello Gallico* is noted by Bataille 2008, 220; Cyrino 2008, 4–5; and Cooke 2008, 78–79.

92. For discussion of the novel, see chapter 1 above.

93. Cyrino (2008, 5) observes that the rise and fall of Vorenus across the twelve episodes of season 1 stands as a metaphor for Rome. Compare Boyd 2008 on the perverse education of the young Octavian in *Rome,* season 1. In Caesar's shadow, he is initiated into the corruptions of Roman manhood by intercourse with prostitutes, incest, torture, and killing.

94. On play with Shakespeare in HBO's *Rome,* see Bataille 2008 and Pittman 2011, 207–34.

95. Pittman (2011, 209, 214) and Bataille (2008) analyze the implications for the series of the declaration of intent to avoid Shakespeare made, for example, in the online blog for season 2 written by the historical consultant Jonathan Stamp. Cf. Lockett 2010, 107.

96. For the traditional methods of Americanizing Shakespeare's *Julius Caesar,* see, in particular, chapter 2 above.

97. For the significance of *Sic semper tyrannis* to the history of Julius Caesar's reception in the United States, see the introduction to this book.

98. See Futrell 2008, 111–13 for how this televisual assassination of Julius Caesar undermines the traditional script.

99. On *Rome*'s fracturing of conventional historical narration, see esp. Lockett 2010, 102.

100. Cf. Cyrino 2008, 5–6.

101. See Toscano 2008, 153–54 for a very useful discussion of the kind of history HBO's *Rome* puts before the television camera. Cf. Pittman 2011, 227.

102. On Murphy's exploration of Rome/America parallels, see Burton 2011, 82–84.

103. President Bush was compared with Diocletian in Murphy 2007, 1–5 and with Julian in Ferguson 2006. He appeared as Nero on the front cover of the *New Yorker* on 22 January 2007, playing the lyre while his country burned.

104. On the shift of interest among political commentators away from the end of the Roman republic to the fall of the Roman Empire, compare Murphy 2007, 6 and Ferguson 2006. For the intimations of loss and renunciation that Roman imperial historiography provided, see Maier 2006, 75–77.

105. For an exploration of Johnson's distortions of Roman history, see Burton 2011, 70–76.

106. For a convenient overview of the long history of debates about why the Roman republic fell, see Morstein-Marx and Rosenstein 2010.

107. Burton (2011, 98) discusses the discursive mechanisms for articulating the fate of Rome in American political commentary in order to deflect it away from the United States.

108. A few months after the publication of Johnson's *Nemesis,* on 3 August 2007, an article of extreme bigotry by Philip Atkinson was briefly uploaded to a mothers' Internet group called *Family Security Matters* (a site sponsored by the neoconservative think tank Center for Security Policy). In an extraordinarily perverse distortion of Johnson's rhetoric of new Rome, the article advocated that beleaguered President Bush *copy* and even *exceed* Julius Caesar: undertaking mass slaughter of his nation's enemies through the use of nuclear weaponry; utilizing military support to become "President-for-Life"; "conquering the drawbacks of democracy." Although the article was swiftly removed, it was subsequently pasted back up on a number of sites such as RationalWiki) to enable bloggers to criticize its appalling views.

109. On Johnson's reliance on Holland's *Rubicon* for his Roman history, see Burton 2011, 77.

110. As noted by the reviewer for *The Independent,* 24 August 2003.

111. See Burton 2011, 69–70 and Mattingly 2011, xvii for intersections between political commentary on imperial America and recent historiography on the Roman Empire. Compare the mutual reinforcements discussed in chapter 6 above between the scholarship on Roman party politics of Lily Ross Taylor and the political commentary on American presidential elections by Theodore H. White.

112. On Gibbon's choice of the Roman Empire as his historical subject in order to challenge eighteenth-century worldviews and, in particular, to shed light on the British Empire's dealings with its North American colonies, see James 2006, esp. 6–23. On James, see Burton 2011, 81–82.

113. The observation is made by Mattingly 2011, 10–13.

114. Cf., for example, Tabachnick and Koivukoski 2009, vii.

115. See, for example, the various chapters in the two collections edited by Grossman and Matthews (2009), and Wroe and Herbert (2009).

116. See Charlotte Higgins in *The Guardian,* 26 November 2008.

117. Compare the radically conservative website Canada Free Press, where Kelly O'Connell claimed, in an article posted on 28 February 2010, that President Obama started out with the same goal as Julius Caesar: "to take a functioning democratic republic and move it closer towards statist, one-man rule."

118. Another reason may be that some commentators regard accusations of Caesarism as now the exclusive property of the Left.

119. Meckler 2006a, 176.

120. The new curriculum, beginning in the academic year 2012–13, is detailed at http://advancesinap.collegeboard.org/world-languages/latin/reading-list. I am most grateful to Judith Hallett for her generous advice on how to find details of the current Latin curricula for schools and colleges in the United States, and to her colleagues in the American Classical League, Sherwin Little and Peter Howard, for supplying additional information.

121. For the official promise of college advancement through the AP program, see the official website http://www.collegeboard.com/student/testing/ap/about.html.

122. Compare Boyd 2006 on questions of how to teach Virgil's *Aeneid* within the context of the AP program.

References

Abbott, A. 1913. "A High-School Course in Drama." *English Journal* 2.2: 93–98.

Abele, E. 2004. "Introduction: Whither Shakespop? Taking Stock of Shakespeare in Popular Culture." *College Literature* 31.4: 1–11.

Abrams, R. M. 2006. *America Transformed: Sixty Years of Revolutionary Change, 1941–2001.* Cambridge.

Adair, D. 1955. "A Note on Certain of Hamilton's Pseudonyms." *William and Mary Quarterly* 12.2: 282–97.

Ades, D., T. Benton, D. Elliott, and I. B. Whyte, eds. 1995. *Art and Power: Europe under the Dictators, 1930–45.* London. Exhibition catalogue.

Akenson, D. H. 1966. "The English and the American School Systems." In *Classics in the USA,* edited by M. P. O. Morford, 5–16. London.

Allen, W. C. 2001. *History of the U.S. Capitol: A Chronicle of Design, Construction, and Politics.* Washington, D.C.

Alovisio, A. 2000. "The 'Pastrone System': Itala Film from the Origins to World War 1." *Film History* 12: 250–61.

Alpers, B. L. 2003. *Dictators, Democracy, and American Public Culture: Envisioning the Totalitarian Enemy, 1920s–1950s.* Chapel Hill, NC.

Ambrose, S. E. 2003. *Eisenhower: Soldier and President.* London.

Anderegg, M. 1999. *Orson Welles, Shakespeare, and Popular Culture.* New York.

———. 2004. *Cinematic Shakespeare.* Lanham, MD.

———. 2005. "Orson Welles and After: *Julius Caesar* and Twentieth-Century Totalitarianism." In *Julius Caesar: New Critical Essays,* edited by H. Zander, 295–305. New York.

Andrews, J. F. 1990. "Was the Bard behind It? Old Light on the Lincoln Assassination." *Atlantic Monthly* 266.4: 26–32. Also printed in the *Washington Post,* 9 October 1990.

Arendt, H. 1966. *The Origins of Totalitarianism*. New York. First published in 1949.

Armstrong, D. 1938. "In the Classroom: A New Approach to Caesar." *Classical Weekly* 31.22: 222–23.

———. 1939. "Caesar's Art of War." *Classical Weekly* 32.25: 291–93.

Atkinson, B. 1948. "Mr. Wilder's Roman Fantasia: An Urbane Appraisal of Julius Caesar and the Last Busy Months of His Rule." *New York Times Book Review*, 22 February, 1.

Axline, K. 2001. "A 'New Deal' and a New Direction: Welles' and Houseman's Depression-Era Productions of *Macbeth, Doctor Faustus,* and *Julius Caesar.*" *Theatre Studies* 45: 16–47.

Bacevich, A.J. 2002. *American Empire*. Cambridge, MA.

———, ed. 2003a. *The Imperial Tense: Prospects and Problems of American Empire.*. Chicago.

———. 2003b. "New Rome, New Jerusalem." In Bacevich, *The Imperial Tense*, 93–101.

Baehr, P. 1998. *Caesar and the Fading of the Roman World: A Study in Republicanism and Caesarism*. New Brunswick, NJ.

Baehr, P., and M. Richter, eds. 2004a. *Dictatorship in History and Theory: Bonapartism, Caesarism, and Totalitarianism*. Cambridge.

———. 2004b. Introduction to Baehr and Richter 2004a, 1–29.

Baker, C.M., and A.J. Inglis. 1909. *High School Course in Latin Composition*. New York.

Ball, R.J., and J.D. Ellsworth. 1989. "Against Teaching Prose Composition in Classical Languages." *Classical Journal* 85.1: 54–62.

Bataille, S. 2008. "Haunted by Shakespeare: HBO's *Rome.*" In *Television Shakespeare: Essays in Honor of Michèle Willems*, edited by S. Hatchuel and N. Vienne-Guerrin, 219–250. Rouen.

Beachler, D. 2004. "Ordinary Events and Extraordinary Times: The 2002 Congressional Elections." In *Transformed by Crisis: The Presidency of George W. Bush and American Politics*, edited by J. Kraus, K.J. McMahon, and D.M. Rankin, 29–50. New York.

Belsey, C. 1983. "Shakespeare and Film: A Question of Perspective." *Film Literature Quarterly* 11.3: 152–58.

Berezin, M. 1997. *Making the Fascist Self: The Political Culture of Interwar Italy*. Ithaca, NY.

Bernstein, W. 1996. *Inside Out: A Memoir of the Blacklist*. New York.

Bertellini, G. 1999a. "Epica spettacolare e splendore del vero: L'influenza del cinema storico italiano in America 1908–15." In *Storia del cinema mondiale*, vol. 2, *Gli Stati Uniti*, edited by G.P. Brunetta, 227–65. Turin.

———. 1999b. "Italian Imageries, Historical Feature Films, and the Fabrication of Italy's Spectators in Early 1900s New York." In *American Movie Audiences: From the Turn of the Century to the Early Sound Era*, edited by M. Stokes and R. Maltby, 29–45. London.

———. 1999c. "Shipwrecked Spectators: Italy's Immigrants at the Movies in New York, 1906–1916." *The Velvet Light Trap* 44: 39–52.

———. 2003. "Ethnic Self-Fashioning at the Café-Chantant: Southern Italian Immigrants, Vernacular Theater, and Films in Pre-World War One New York." In *Public Space/Private Lives: Race, Gender, Class, and Citizenship in New York, 1890–1929*, edited by W. Boelhower and A. Scacchi, 39–66. Amsterdam.

———. 2005. "DUCE/DIVO: Masculinity, Racial Identity, and Politics among Italian Americans in 1920s New York City." *Journal of Urban History* 31.5: 685–726.

Block, A.A. 1994. *Space, Time, and Organized Crime.* 2nd ed. New Brunswick. 1st ed., 1991.

Bolenius, E.M. 1915. *Teaching Literature in the Grammar Grades and High School.* Boston.

Borgmeier, R. 2001. "'The Gods' Messenger and Secretary'?—Thornton Wilder and the Classical Tradition." *International Journal of the Classical Tradition* 7.3: 344–65.

Bowie, R.R., and R.H. Immerman. 1998. *Waging Peace: How Eisenhower Shaped an Enduring Cold War Strategy.* New York.

Boyd, B. 2006. "Textbook and Context: 'The Next Aeneid.'" *Classical World* 99.2: 166–69.

———. 2008. "Becoming Augustus: The Education of Octavian." In *Rome, Season One: History Makes Television,* edited by M.S. Cyrino, 87–99. Malden, MA.

Boyle, P.G. 2005. *Eisenhower.* Harlow, UK.

Brady, F. 1990. *Citizen Welles: A Biography of Orson Welles.* London.

Branch, E.M., and R.H. Hirst, eds. 1981. *The Works of Mark Twain: Early Tales and Sketches.* Vol. 2, *1864–1865.* Berkeley.

Brantlinger, P. 1983. *Bread and Circuses: Theories of Mass Culture as Social Decay.* Ithaca, NY.

Briggs, W. 2007. "United States." In *A Companion to the Classical Tradition,* edited by C.W. Kallendorf, 279–94. Oxford.

Buchanan, J. 2009. *Shakespeare on Silent Film: An Excellent Dumb Discourse.* Cambridge.

Buchman, L.M. 1991. *Still in Movement: Shakespeare on Screen.* Oxford.

Burbank, R. 1961. *Thornton Wilder.* 2nd ed. Boston.

Burton, P. 2011. "*Pax Romana/Pax Americana*: Perceptions of Rome in American Political Culture, 2000–2010." *International Journal of the Classical Tradition* 18.1: 66–104.

Butsch, R. 2000. *The Making of American Audiences: From Stage to Television, 1750–1990.* Cambridge.

Callow, S. 1996. *Orson Welles: The Road to Xanadu.* London.

Canfora, L. 1980. *Ideologie del classicismo.* Turin.

———. 1999. *Giulio Cesare: Il dittatore democratico.* Rome and Bari.

Canovan, M. 2004. "The Leader and the Masses: Hannah Arendt on Totalitarianism and Dictatorship." In *Dictatorship in History and Theory: Bonapartism, Caesarism, and Totalitarianism,* edited by P. Baehr and M. Richter, 241–60. Cambridge.

Casale, G. 2001. *L'incantesimo è compiuto: Shakespeare secondo Orson Welles.* Turin.

Casillo, R. 1992. "Lewis Mumford and the Organicist Concept of Social Thought." *Journal of the History of Ideas* 53.1: 91–116.

Cassuto, L. 2009. *Hard-Boiled Sentimentality: The Secret History of American Crime Stories.* New York.

Castronovo, D. 1986. *Thornton Wilder.* New York.

Cecil, L. 1996. *Wilhelm II: Prince and Emperor, 1859–1900.* Chapel Hill, NC.

Ceplair, L. 1982. "Great Shows: You are There." *Emmy Magazine* 4.1: 43–47.

———. 1987. *Under the Shadow of War: Fascism, Anti-Fascism, and Marxists, 1918–1939.* New York.

Ceplair, L., and S. Englund. 1979. *The Inquisition in Hollywood: Politics in the Film Community, 1930–1960.* Berkeley.

Chafe, W.H. 2003. *The Unfinished Journey: America since World War II.* New York.

Chambon, C. 1958. "Les pouvoirs césariens du président des États-Unis." *Écrits de Paris* 166: 11–15.

Charney, M. 1979. "On Mankiewicz's *Julius Caesar.*" *Literary Review* 22.4: 433–59.

Chevallier, R., ed. 1985. *Présence de César: Hommage au Doyen M. Rambaud.* Paris.

Chothia, J. 2003. "*Julius Caesar* in Interesting Times." In *Remaking Shakespeare: Performance across Media, Genres, and Cultures,* edited by P. Aebischer, E.J. Esche, and N. Wheale, 115–33. Houndmills, Basingstoke, UK.

Christ, K. 1994. *Caesar: Annäherungen an einen Diktator.* Munich.

Church, R.L., and M.W. Sedlak. 1976. *Education in the United States: An Interpretive History.* New York.

Claflin, E.F. 1915. "Caesar's Bridge and the Modern Offensive-Defensive Strategy." *Classical Weekly* 8.26: 208.

Clarke, M. 1898. *Story of Caesar.* New York.

Cohen, E.A. 2004. "History and the Hyperpower." *Foreign Affairs,* July/August. www.foreignaffairs.org.

Cohn, J. 1990. *Creating America: George Horace Lorimer and the Saturday Evening Post.* Pittsburgh.

Cole, N. 2009. "Republicanism, Caesarism, and Political Change." In *Blackwell Companion to Julius Caesar,* edited by M. Griffin, 418–30. Chichester, UK.

Colvin, S. 1998. "'"Die Zung" ist dieses Schwert': Classical Tongues and Gendered Curricula in German Schooling to 1908." In *Pedagogy and Power: Rhetorics of Classical Learning,* edited by Y.L. Too and N. Livingstone, 47–66. Cambridge.

Cooke, B. 2008. "Caesar's Soldiers: The *pietas* of Vorenus and Pullo." In *Rome, Season One: History Makes Television,* edited by M.S. Cyrino, 78–86. Malden, MA.

Cotham, H.C. 1968. "The Modernity of *Julius Caesar.*" *Interpretations* 1.1: 11–21.

Cotkin, G. 2003. *Existential America.* Baltimore.

Cronkite, W. 1996. *A Reporter's Life.* New York.

Crowl, S. 1994. "A World Elsewhere: The Roman Plays on Film and Television."

In *Shakespeare and the Moving Image: The Plays on Film and Television,* edited by A. Davies and S. Wells, 146–62. Cambridge.

Cyrino, M.S. 2005. *Big Screen Rome.* Malden, MA.

———, ed. 2008. Rome, *Season One: History Makes Television.* Malden, MA.

Czitrom, D. 1982. *Media and the American Mind: From Morse to McLuhan.* Chapel Hill, NC.

Dallek, R. 2004. *Lyndon B. Johnson: Portrait of a President.* London.

Daniell, D., ed. 1998. *The Arden Shakespeare: Julius Caesar.* Walton-on-Thames.

Dauth, B., ed. 2008. *Joseph L. Mankiewicz: Interviews.* Jackson, MS.

De Felice, R. 1974. *Mussolini il duce.* Vol. 1, *Gli anni del consenso, 1929–1936.* Turin.

Dennis, J.D. 2006. *Queering Teen Culture: All-American Boys and Same Sex Desire in Film and Television.* Binghamton, NY.

Dennison, W. 1906. "Recent Caesar Literature." *Classical Journal* 1.5: 131–45.

Derrick, T.J. 1998. *Understanding Shakespeare's* Julius Caesar: *A Student Casebook to Issues, Sources, and Historical Documents.* Westport, CT.

DeStefano, A.M. 2006. *King of the Godfathers: "Big Joey" Massino and the Fall of the Bonanno Crime Family.* New York.

DeVico, P.J. 2007. *The Mafia Made Easy: The Anatomy and Culture of La Cosa Nostra.* Mustang, OK.

Dick, B.F. 1983. *Joseph L. Mankiewicz.* Boston.

Dietler, M. 1994. "'Our Ancestors the Gauls': Archaeology, Ethnic Nationalism, and the Manipulation of Celtic Identity in Modern Europe." *American Anthropologist* n.s. 96.3: 584–605.

Diggins, J.P. 1972. *Mussolini and Fascism: The View from America.* Princeton, NJ.

Dittmer, J. 2010. *Popular Culture, Geopolitics, and Identity.* Lanham, MD.

Dodge, T.A. 1892. *Caesar: A History of the Art of War among the Romans down to the End of the Roman Empire, with a Detailed Account of the Campaigns of Caius Julius Caesar.* Boston.

Doherty, T.P. 1999. *Pre-Code Hollywood: Sex, Immorality, and Insurrection in American Cinema.* New York.

———. 2003. *Cold War, Cool Medium: Television, McCarthyism, and American Culture.* New York.

Donald, J. 1992. *Sentimental Education: Schooling, Popular Culture, and the Regulation of Liberty.* London.

D'Ooge, B.L., and F.C. Eastman. 1917. *Caesar in Gaul: With Introduction, Review of First-Year Syntax, Notes, Grammar, Prose Composition, and Vocabularies.* Boston.

Dorfles, G., et al. 1969. *Kitsch: The World of Bad Taste.* New York.

Doumanis, N. 2001. *Italy: Inventing the Nation.* London.

Dunant, C. 1994. "Olympian Dreamscapes: The Photographic Canvas; The Wide-Screen Paintings of Leighton, Poynter, and Alma-Tadema." In *Melodrama: Stage Picture Screen,* edited by J. Bratton, J. Cook, and C. Gledhill, 82–93. London.

Dunn, E.C. 1939. *Shakespeare in America.* New York.

Dunn, F.S. 1911. "The Historical Novel in the Classroom." *Classical Journal* 6.7: 296–304.

Dunnett, J. 2006. "The Rhetoric of *Romanità*: Representations of Caesar in Fascist Theatre." In *Julius Caesar in Western Culture,* edited by M. Wyke, 244–65. Oxford.

Durant, W. 1944. *The Story of Civilization.* Vol. 3, *Caesar and Christ: A History of Roman Civilization and of Christianity from Their Beginnings to A.D. 325.* New York.

Dyson, S.L. 2001. "Rome in America." In *Images of Rome: Perceptions of Ancient Rome in Europe and the United States in the Modern Age,* edited by R. Hingley, 57–69. Portsmouth, RI.

Eakin, E. 2002. "All Roads Lead to DC." *New York Times,* March 31.

Edsforth, R. 2000. *The New Deal: America's Response to the Great Depression.* Malden, MA.

Edwards, C. 2005. "Modelling Roman Suicide? The Afterlife of Cato." *Economy and Society* 34.2: 200–22.

Eldridge, D. 2006. *Hollywood's History Films.* London.

Englar, M.T. 1919. "Second Year Latin and Some Aspects of the World War." *Classical Weekly* 12.13: 99–102.

Erisman, F. 2006. *Boys' Books, Boys' Dreams, and the Mystique of Flight.* Fort Worth, TX.

Falasca-Zamponi, S. 1997. *Fascist Spectacle: The Aesthetics of Power in Mussolini's Italy.* Berkeley.

Farrell, J. 2001. *Latin Language and Latin Culture.* Cambridge.

Ferguson, Niall. 2005. *Colossus: The Rise and Fall of the American Empire.* London. 1st ed., 2004.

———. 2006. "Lessons Unlearned: Empire Falls." *Vanity Fair,* October.

Ferrero, G. 1907. *The Greatness and Decline of Rome.* Vol. 2, *Julius Caesar.* Translated by A.E. Zimmern. New York.

———. 1933. *The Life of Caesar.* Translated by A.E. Zimmern. Abr. ed. London. First published in English as the first two volumes of the five-volume *The Greatness and Decline of Rome* (1907).

Fine, S. 1955. "Anarchism and the Assassination of McKinley." *American Historical Review* 60.4: 777–99.

Finley, J.H. 1917. "France, Battleground of Civilization." *The World's Work,* October: 629–35.

Fisk, R. 2002. "The Mantra That Means This Time It's Serious." *The Independent,* 13 September.

Fleming, K. 2007. "Fascism." In *A Companion to the Classical Tradition,* edited by C.W. Kallendorf, 342–54. Oxford.

Flexner, A. 1916. "A Modern School." *American Review of Reviews* 53: 465–74. http://historymatters.gmu.edu/d/4995.

Fornieri, J.R., ed. 2004. *The Language of Liberty: The Political Speeches and Writings of Abraham Lincoln.* Washington, DC.

Foster, J.B. 2002. "The Rediscovery of Imperialism." *Monthly Review* 54.6: 1–16.

France, R. 1977. *The Theatre of Orson Welles.* Lewisburg, PA.

———, ed. 1990. *Orson Welles on Shakespeare: The W.P.A. and Mercury Theatre Playscripts.* New York.

Freedland, J. 2002. "Rome, AD . . . Rome, DC?" *The Guardian,* 18 September.

Freedman, L. 2009. *The Offensive Art: Political Satire and Its Censorship around the World from Beerbohm to Borat.* Westport, CT.

Frey, C.H. 1984. "Teaching Shakespeare in America." *Shakespeare Quarterly* 35.5: 541–59. Reprinted in Frey, *Experiencing Shakespeare: Essays on Text, Classroom, and Performance.* (Columbia, MO, 1988), 122–43.

Furtwangler, A. 1991. *Assassin on the Stage: Brutus, Hamlet, and the Death of Lincoln.* Urbana, IL.

Futrell, A. 2008. "'Not Some Cheap Murder': Caesar's Assassination." In Rome, *Season One: History Makes Television,* edited by M.S. Cyrino, 100–16. Malden, MA.

Game, J.B. 1925. *Teaching High-School Latin: A Handbook.* Chicago.

Gardaphé, F.L. 2006. *From Wiseguys to Wise Men: The Gangster and Italian American Masculinities.* New York.

Geist, K.L. 1978. *Pictures Will Talk: The Life and Films of Joseph L. Mankiewicz.* New York.

Gelzer, M. 1968. *Caesar: Politician and Statesman.* Translated by P. Needham. Cambridge, MA.

Gentili, G., ed. 2008. *Giulio Cesare: L'uomo, le imprese, il mito.* Milan.

Gerber, S.W. 1956. "The Importance of the Caesar Semester." *Classical Weekly* 50.2: 19–20.

Geyer, M. 2009. "Introduction: After Totalitarianism—Stalinism and Nazism Compared." In *Beyond Totalitarianism: Stalinism and Nazism Compared,* edited by M. Geyer and S. Fitzpatrick, 1–37. Cambridge.

Gianeri, E. 1945. *Il cesare di cartapesta: Mussolini nella caricatura.* Turin.

Giardina, D. 2003. "Iraq: Bush Should Be Impeached and Tried for War Crimes." *Charleston Gazette,* 12 May.

Gibbon, E. 1900. *The Decline and Fall of the Roman Empire.* Vol. 1. With notes by the Rev. H.H. Milman. New York. First published in multiple volumes from 1776 to 1788.

Gili, J.A. 1981. *Stato fascista e cinematografia: Repression e promozione.* Rome.

Girard, R. 1991. *The Theatre of Envy: William Shakespeare.* New York.

Goldstein, M. 1961. *The Art of Thornton Wilder.* Lincoln, NE.

Goldstone, R.H. 1975. *Thornton Wilder: An Intimate Portrait.* New York.

Goldsworthy, A. 2006. *Caesar: The Life of a Colossus.* London.

Goudineau, C. 2001. *Le dossier Vercingétorix.* Arles.

Govan, T.P. 1975. "Alexander Hamilton and Julius Caesar: A Note on the Use of Historical Evidence." *William and Mary Quarterly* 32.3: 475–80.

Grantham, D.W. 1988. *Recent America: The United States since 1945.* Wheeling, IL.

Gray, M.D. 1927. *Teachers' Manual to Accompany Latin for Today: A First-Year Course.* Boston.

———. 1929. *The Teaching of Latin.* New York.

Greenstein, F.I. 2001. *The Presidential Difference: Leadership Style from FDR to Clinton.* New York.

Griese, N.L. 2001. *Arthur W. Page: Publisher, Public Relations Pioneer, Patriot.* Tucker, GA.

Griffin, J. 2009. "Shakespeare's *Julius Caesar* and the Dramatic Tradition." In *Blackwell Companion to Julius Caesar,* edited by M. Griffin, 371–98. Chichester, UK.

Griffin, M., ed. 2009. *Blackwell Companion to Julius Caesar.* Chichester, UK.

Grossman, M.O., and R.E. Matthews, eds. 2009. *Perspectives on the Legacy of George W. Bush.* Newcastle, UK.

Guérif, F. 1977. "Jules Cesar." *Lumière du cinema* 3: 59–64.

Hair, W.I. 1991. *The Kingfish and His Realm: The Life and Times of Huey P. Long.* Baton Rouge.

Hale, E. 2008. "Classics as a Test of Character in Victorian Public School Stories." *New Voices in Classical Reception Studies* 3. www.2.open.ac.uk/classicalreceptions.

Hale, W.G. 1910. *Latin Prose Composition: Pt. 1, Based on Caesar.* Boston.

Halpern, R. 1997. *Shakespeare among the Moderns.* Ithaca, NY.

Hammond, C. 1996. *Caesar: The Gallic War.* Oxford.

Hansen, M. 1991. *Babel and Babylon: Spectatorship in American Silent Film.* Cambridge, MA.

Harrison, G.A. 1983. *The Enthusiast: A Life of Thornton Wilder.* New Haven, CT.

Harwood, M.E. 1909. "Aids in Teaching Caesar." *Classical Weekly* 2.13 (23 January): 98–100.

Haynes, H. 2008. "*Rome*'s Opening Titles: Triumph, Spectacle, and Desire." In *Rome, Season One: History Makes Television,* edited by M.S. Cyrino, 49–60. Malden, MA.

Hedrick, C.W. 2004. "The American Ephebe: The Ephebic Oath, U.S. Education, and Nationalism." *Classical World* 97.4: 384–407.

Hedrick, D.K. 2002. "Bard Guides of the New Universe: Niche Marketing and the Cultural Logic of Late Shakespeare." In *Shakespeare after Mass Media,* edited by R. Burt, 35–58. New York.

Hemmerle, O.B. 2006. "Crossing the Rubicon into Paris: Caesarian Comparisons from Napoleon to de Gaulle." In *Julius Caesar in Western Culture,* edited by M. Wyke, 285–302. Oxford.

Hendershot, C. 2003. *Anti-Communism and Popular Culture in Mid-Century America.* Jefferson, NC.

Hendrickson, D.C. 2009. "In the Mirror of Antiquity: The Problem of American Empire." In *Enduring Empire: Ancient Lessons for Global Politics,* edited by D.E. Tabachnick and T. Koivukoski, 3–19. Toronto.

Henry, M. 2003. "Introduction to the Transaction Edition." In James Burnham, *Congress and the American Tradition,* xi-xxv. New Brunswick, NJ.

Heuman, J., and R. Burt. 2002. "Suggested for Mature Readers? Deconstructing Shakespeare's Value in Comic Books." In *Shakespeare after Mass Media,* edited by R. Burt, 151–72. New York.

Hicken, V. 1991. *Illinois in the Civil War.* Urbana, IL.

Higham, C. 1985. *Orson Welles: The Rise and Fall of an American Genius.* London.

Hill, F., and J.V. Hatch. 2003. *A History of African American Theatre.* Cambridge.

Hoffmann, J. 1995. *Theodore H. White and Journalism as Illusion.* Columbia, MO.

Holderness, G. 2002. *Visual Shakespeare: Essays in Film and Television.* Hatfield, UK.

Holland, N.N. 1960. "The 'Cinna' and 'Cynicke' Episodes in *Julius Caesar.*" *Shakespeare Quarterly* 11/1: 439–44.

Holmes, T. Rice 1903. *Caesar's Conquest of Gaul: Part 1.* London.

Hook, S.W. 2009. "Beyond the Bush Doctrine." In *Perspectives on the Legacy of George W. Bush,* edited by M.O. Grossman and R.E. Matthews, 161–77. Newcastle.

Horowitz, R.F. 1983. "History Comes to Life and *You Are There.*" In *American History/American Television,* edited by J.E. O'Connor, 79–94. New York.

Horsley, L. 2005. *Twentieth-Century Crime Fiction.* Oxford.

Houseman, J. 1973. *Run-Through: A Memoir.* London.

———. 1979. *Front and Center.* New York.

———. 1988. *Unfinished Business: Memoirs, 1902–1988.* New York.

Howell, F. 1929. "Caesar and the Boy of Today." *Classical Journal* 24.7: 509–14.

Hudson, H.N. 1874. *Shakespeare's Julius Caesar for Use in Schools and Classes.* Boston.

Humphreys, A., ed. 1984. *The Oxford Shakespeare: Julius Caesar.* Oxford.

Hunt, P. 2001. *Children's Literature.* Malden, MA.

Ignatieff, M. 2003. "The Burden." *New York Times Magazine,* 5 January.

Iorizzo, L.J., and S. Mondello. 2006. *The Italian Americans.* 3rd ed. Youngstown, NY. First published in 1971.

Irwin, W. 1935. *The Julius Caesar Murder Case.* New York.

Isnenghi, M., and G. Rochat. 2000. *La grande guerra, 1914–1918.* Milan.

James, H. 2006. *The Roman Predicament: How the Rules of International Order Create the Politics of Empire.* Princeton, NJ.

Janes, A.L., and P.R. Jenks. 1906. *Bellum Helveticum: A Beginner's Book In Latin.* Chicago.

Jeffers, H.P. 2002. *The Napoleon of New York: Mayor Fiorello La Guardia.* New York.

Jensen, M.P. 2006. "The Comic Book Shakespeare, Part I." *Shakespeare Newsletter* 56.3: 81–87.

Johnson, C. 2004. *The Sorrows of Empire: Militarism, Secrecy, and the End of the Republic.* New York.

———. 2007. *Nemesis: The Last Days of the American Republic.* New York.

Johnson, J. 1996. *Cheap Tricks and Class Acts: Special Effects, Makeup, and Stunts for the Films of the Fantastic Fifties.* Jefferson, NC.

Jones, M.A. 1995. *The Limits of Liberty: American History, 1607–1992.* 2nd ed. Oxford. 1st ed., 1983.

Jones, R.D. 1891. *The Ethical Element in Literature: Being an Attempt to Promote a Method of Teaching Literature, Illustrated by an Interpretation of the In Memoriam, and by Comments on the Tragedy of Julius Caesar, including the Text of Julius Caesar with Notes.* Bloomington, IL.

Jones, W.B.J. 2002. *Classics Illustrated: A Cultural History with Illustrations.* Jefferson, NC.

———. 2009. "Introduction." *Classics Illustrated* No. 68: *Julius Caesar*. Reprint, 1962 adaptation. Jake Lake Productions, Inc. Toronto.

Jorgens, J.J. 1977. *Shakespeare on Film*. Bloomington, IN.

———. 1979. "The BBC-TV Shakespeare Series." *Shakespeare Quarterly* 30.3: 411–15.

Joshel, S.R., M. Malamud, and D. McGuire, eds. 2001. *Imperial Projections: Ancient Rome in Modern Popular Culture*. Baltimore.

Kagan, D. 2002. "Reaction to 'Bush's real goal in Iraq': Comparing American to Ancient Empires Is Ludicrous." *Atlanta Journal-Constitution*, 6 October.

Kagan, R. 1998. "The Benevolent Empire." *Foreign Policy* 111: 24–35.

———. 2003. *Paradise and Power: America and Europe in the New World Order*. London.

Kahn, A.D. 2000. *The Education of Julius Caesar: A Biography, A Reconstruction*. Lincoln, NE. First published in 1986.

Kallendorf, C.W., ed. 2007. *A Companion to the Classical Tradition*. Oxford.

Keith, A.L. 1914. "Two Wars in Gaul." *Classical Weekly* 8: 42–43.

Keller, J., and M. Mills. 2003. "'Empire' Losing Evil Associations." *Deseret News*, 27 April.

Kellow, G. 2009. "The Rise of Global Power and the Music of the Spheres: Philosophy and History in Cicero's *De re publica*." In *Enduring Empire: Ancient Lessons for Global Politics*, edited by D.E. Tabachnick and T. Koivukoski, 147–63. Toronto.

Kelsey, F.W. 1918. *C. Iulii Commentarii rerum gestarum: Caesar's Commentaries; The Gallic War Books I–IV, with Selections from Books V–VII and from the Civil War*. Boston.

———. 1927. *Latin and Greek in American Education*. 2nd ed. New York. 1st ed., 1911.

Kennedy, G.A. 1984. Afterword to *Classica Americana: The Greek and Roman Heritage in the United States*, by M. Reinhold, 338–41. Detroit.

———. 1992. "Classics and Canons." In *The Politics of Liberal Education*, edited by D.J. Gless and B.H. Smith, 223–31. Durham, NC.

Kent, R.G. 1914. "The Military Tactics of Caesar and of To-day." *Classical Weekly* 8: 69–70.

Keyishian, H. 2003. "Storm, Fire, and Blood: Patterns of Imagery in Stuart Burge's *Julius Caesar*." In *Shakespeare in Performance: A Collection of Essays*, edited by F. Occhiogrosso, 93–103. Newark.

Kliebard, H.M. 2004. *The Struggle for the American Curriculum, 1893–1958*. 3rd ed. New York. 1st ed., 1987.

Koelb, C. 1998. *Legendary Figures: Ancient History in Modern Novels*. Lincoln, NE.

Koon, T.H. 1985. *Believe, Obey, Fight: Political Socialization of Youth in Fascist Italy, 1922–1943*. Chapel Hill, NC.

Kovacs, G., and C.W. Marshall, eds. 2011. *Classics and Comics*. Oxford.

Kraus, C.S. 2009. "*Bellum Gallicum*." In *Blackwell Companion to Julius Caesar*, edited by M. Griffin, 159–74. Chichester, UK.

Kraus, J. 2004a. "Acting a Colossus: Bush's Foreign Policy, Unilateralism, and the Pursuit of Primacy." In *Transformed by Crisis: The Presidency of George W.*

Bush and American Politics, edited by J. Kraus, K.J. McMahon, and D.M. Rankin, 167–97. New York.

———. 2004b. "September 11th and Bush's Presidency." In Kraus et al., *Transformed by Crisis,* 1–7.

Kraus, J., K.J. McMahon, and D.M. Rankin, eds. 2004. *Transformed by Crisis: The Presidency of George W. Bush and American Politics.* New York.

Krebs, C.B. 2006. "'Imaginary Geography' in Caesar's *Bellum Gallicum.*" *American Journal of Philology* 127: 111–36.

LaFeber, W. 2005. *The Deadly Bet: LBJ, Vietnam, and the 1968 Election.* Lanham, MD.

Langford, B. 2005. *Film Genre: Hollywood and Beyond.* Edinburgh.

Lanier, D. 2002a. "Shakescorp Noir." *Shakespeare Quarterly* 53.2: 157–80.

———. 2002b. *Shakespeare and Modern Popular Culture.* Oxford.

Lapham, L.H. 2002. "Hail Caesar!" *Harper's Magazine* 305/1831: 9–11.

La Polla, F., ed. 1987. *L'insospettabile Joseph Leo Mankiewicz.* Venice.

Laurence, R. 1997. "Writing the Roman Metropolis." in *Roman Urbanism: Beyond the Consumer City,* edited by H.M. Parkins, 1–19. London.

———. 1999. "Tourism, Townplanning and *Romanitas:* Rimini's Roman Heritage." In *The Uses and Abuses of Antiquity,* edited by M. Wyke and M. Biddiss, 187–205. Bern.

Leab, D.J. 1983. *"See it Now:* A Legend Reassessed." In *American History/American Television,* edited by J.E. O'Connor, 1–32. New York.

Leaming, B. 1985. *Orson Welles: A Biography.* London.

Lee, K.H. 1969. "Caesar's Encounter with the Usipetes and the Tencteri." *Greece & Rome* 16.1: 100–103.

Lenihan, J.H. 1992. "English Classics for Cold War America." *Journal of Popular Film & Television* 20.3: 42–52.

Leonard, M., and Y. Prins. 2010. "Foreword: Classical Reception and the Political." *Cultural Critique* 74: 1–13.

Levine, L.W. 1988. *Highbrow/Lowbrow: The Emergence of Cultural Hierarchy in America.* Cambridge, MA.

Levine, M. 2006. "Oracles of a Quadragenarian Latin Teacher." *Classical World* 100.1: 49–53.

Lewin, W., and A. Frazier. 1957. *Standards of Photoplay Appreciation.* Summit, NJ.

Lewis, C.L. 1914. "The Neglected Side of English." *English Journal* 3.5: 282–89.

Lindvall, T. 2007. *Sanctuary Cinema: Origins of the Christian Film Industry.* New York.

Linton, D.S. 1995. "American Responses to German Continuation Schools during the Progressive Era." In *German Influences on Education in the United States to 1917,* edited by H. Geitz, J. Heideking, and J. Herbst, 69–84. Washington, DC.

Liska, G. 1978. *Career of Empire: America and Imperial Expansion over Land and Sea.* Baltimore.

Litto, F.M. 1966. "Addison's *Cato* in the Colonies." *William and Mary Quarterly* 23.3: 431–49.

Lockett, C. 2010. "Accidental History: Mass Culture and HBO's *Rome*." *Journal of Popular Film and Television* 38.3: 102–12.

Lohof, B. 1969. "The Higher Meaning of Marlboro Cigarettes." *Journal of Popular Culture* 3.3: 441–50.

Long, E. 2009. "George W. Bush and the US Supreme Court." In *Assessing the George W. Bush Presidency: A Tale of Two Terms,* edited by A. Wroe and J. Herbert, 44–58. Edinburgh.

Lowe, D., and K. Shahabudin, eds. 2009. *Classics for All: Reworking Antiquity in Mass Culture.* Newcastle upon Tyne.

Lower, C.B., and R.B. Palmer. 2001. *Joseph L. Mankiewicz: Critical Essays.* Jefferson, NC.

Lucas, S. 1999. *Freedom's War: The US Crusade against the Soviet Union, 1945–56.* Manchester.

Lukow, G., and S. Ricci. 1984. "The 'Audience' goes 'Public': Intertextuality, Genre, and the Responsibilities of Film Literacy." *On Film* 12: 29–36.

Mack, M. 1960. "Teaching Drama: *Julius Caesar*." In *Essays on the Teaching of English, Reports of the Yale Conferences,* edited by E.J. Gordon and E.S. Noyes, 320–36. New York. Reprinted in *Understanding Shakespeare's* Julius Caesar: *A Student Casebook to Issues, Sources, and Historical Documents,* ed. T.J. Derrick (Westport, CT, 1998), 144–58.

MacKendrick, P. 1948. Review of *The Ides of March*, by Thornton Wilder. *Classical Journal* 44.1: 65–67.

Maddox, R.F. 2006. "Senator Robert C. Byrd and the Wisdom of the Ancients." In *Classical Antiquity and the Politics of America: From George Washington to George W. Bush,* edited by M. Meckler, 141–51. Waco, TX.

Maier, C.S. 2006. *Among Empires: American Ascendancy and Its Predecessors.* Cambridge, MA.

Malamud, M. 1998. "As the Romans Did? Theming Ancient Rome in Contemporary Las Vegas." *Arion* 6.2: 11–38.

———. 2001. "Living like Romans in Las Vegas: The Roman World at Caesars Palace." In *Imperial Projections: Ancient Rome in Modern Popular Culture,* edited by S.R. Joshel, M. Malamud, and D.T. McGuire, 249–69. Baltimore.

———. 2006. "Manifest Destiny and the Eclipse of Julius Caesar." In *Julius Caesar in Western Culture,* edited by M. Wyke, 148–69. Oxford.

———. 2009. *Ancient Rome and Modern America.* Chichester, UK.

Mallett, R. 2003. *Mussolini and the Origins of the Second World War, 1933–40.* New York.

Manchester, W. 1978. *American Caesar: Douglas MacArthur, 1880–1964.* Boston.

Manso, P. 1994. *Brando.* London.

Manvell, R. 1971. *Shakespeare and the Film.* New York.

Martin, J.B. 1976. *Adlai Stevenson of Illinois: The Life of Adlai E. Stevenson.* New York.

Martin, M.R. 1985. "César à Las Vegas, ou les clefs d'un royaume." In *Présence de César: Hommage au Doyen M. Rambaud,* edited by R. Chevallier, 509–16. Paris.

Martinelli, V. 1992. "Il cinema muto italiano: 1914." *Bianco e Nero* 53.1–4.

Mason, F. 2002. *American Gangster Cinema: From* Little Caesar *to* Pulp Fiction. London.

Matthews, L.J. 1978. "Patrick Henry's 'Liberty or Death' Speech and Cassius's Speech in Shakespeare's *Julius Caesar.*" *Virginia Magazine* 86.3: 299–305.

Mattingly, D.J. 2011. *Imperialism, Power, and Identity: Experiencing the Roman Empire.* Princeton, NJ.

McCurrie, M.K. 2004. "From the Edges to the Center: Pedagogy's Role in Redefining English Departments." *Pedagogy* 4.1: 43–64.

McDonald, R. 1995. "Shakespeare Goes to High School: Some Current Practices in the American Classroom." *Shakespeare Quarterly* 46.2: 145–56.

McGrory, M. 2002. "That's Presidential." *Pittsburgh Post-Gazette,* 2 February.

McKinlay, A.P. 1918. "Caesar redivivus." *Classical Journal* 14.2: 103–10.

Meckler, M., ed. 2006a. *Classical Antiquity and the Politics of America: From George Washington to George W. Bush.* Waco, TX.

———. 2006b. "The Rise of Populism, the Decline of Classical Education, and the Seventeenth Amendment." In Meckler, *Classical Antiquity and the Politics of America,* 69–82.

Meier, C. 1996. *Caesar.* Translated by D. McLintock. London.

Meyer, F.S. 1957. "Principles and Heresies: America; No Imperial Rome." *National Review* 4.10: 233.

Mierow, C.C. 1915. "The College-Entrance Requirements in Latin and the Schools: An Investigation." *Classical Journal* 11.2: 85–94.

Miles, E.A. 1968. "The Whig Party and the Menace of Caesar." *Tennessee Historical Quarterly* 27: 361–79.

Miller, A. 2000. "*Julius Caesar* in the Cold War: The Houseman-Mankiewicz Film." *Literature/Film Quarterly* 28.2: 95–100.

———. 2002. "'Words before Blows': Civil and Military in *Julius Caesar.*" *Sydney Studies in English* 28: 124–35.

Miller, A.S. 1981. *Democratic Dictatorship: The Emergent Constitution of Control.* Westport, CT.

Minio-Paluello, L. 1946. *Education in Fascist Italy.* Oxford.

Molnar, T. 1966. "Imperial America." *National Review* 18.8: 409–11.

Monoson, S.S. 2007. "Socrates in American Life: WW II and the Cold War." *Reception of Classical Texts Project E-seminar 2007–8,* November 2007: Topic 2. www2.open.ac.uk/ClassicalStudies/GreekPlays/e_archive/2007/MonosonTopic2.pdf.

Moreno Hernández, A., ed. 2010. *Julio César: Textos, contextos y recepción; De la Roma clásica al mundo actual.* Madrid.

Morford, M.P.O., ed. 1966. *Classics in the USA.* Joint Association of Classical Teachers Pamphlet 3. London.

Morgan, I. 2002. *Nixon.* London.

Morris, I.L. 2010. *The American Presidency: An Analytical Approach.* Cambridge.

Morstein-Marx, R., and N. Rosenstein. 2010. "The Transformation of the Republic." In *A Companion to the Roman Republic,* edited by N. Rosenstein and R. Morstein-Marx, 625–37. Oxford.

Mullin, M. 1984. "Shakespeare USA: The BBC Plays and American Education." *Shakespeare Quarterly* 35.5: 582–89.

Mumford, L. 1966. *The City in History: Its Origins, Its Transformations, and Its Prospects.* Harmondsworth, UK. First published in 1961.

Murphy, B. 1999. *Congressional Theatre: Dramatizing McCarthyism on Stage, Film, and Television.* Cambridge.

Murphy, C. 2007. *Are We Rome? The Fall of an Empire and the Fate of America.* New York. Published in the United Kingdom as *The New Rome: The Fall of an Empire and the Fate of America,* Cambridge. Page numbers in notes refer to the UK edition.

Mussolini, B. 1928. *My Autobiography.* New York.

Naremore, J. 1978. *The Magic World of Orson Welles.* New York.

Nasaw, D. 2001. *The Chief: The Life of William Randolph Hearst.* New York.

Navasky, V.S. 1980. *Naming Names: The Social Cost of McCarthyism.* New York.

Neale, S. 2000. *Genre and Hollywood.* London.

Nelis, J. 2007. "Constructing Fascist Identity: Benito Mussolini and the Myth of *Romanità.*" *Classical World* 100.4: 391–415.

Nichols, J. 2006. "Countering Censorship: Edgar Dale and the Film Appreciation Movement." *Cinema Journal* 46.1: 3–22.

O'Connor, J.E., ed. 1983. *American History/American Television.* New York.

OKell, E. 2007. "The Anglo-American 'Tobacco Wars' and the Use of the Classics to Establish a Global Company." *New Voices in Classical Reception Studies* 2: 55–72.

Onuf, P.S. 2000. *Jefferson's Empire: The Language of American Nationhood.* Charlottesville, VA.

O'Reilly, M.J. 2009. "The Crusader: George W. Bush and the American Empire in the Persian Gulf." In *Perspectives on the Legacy of George W. Bush,* edited by M.O. Grossman and R.E. Matthews, 152–60. Newcastle.

Oswell, D. 2006. *Culture and Society: An Introduction to Cultural Studies.* London.

Parchami, A. 2009. *Hegemonic Peace and Empire: The Pax Romana, Britannica, and Americana.* Abingdon, UK.

Pearcy, L.T. 2005. *The Grammar of Our Civility: Classical Education in America.* Waco, TX.

Pearson, E.R., and W. Uricchio. 1990. "How Many Times Shall Caesar Bleed in Sport: Shakespeare and the Cultural Debate about Moving Pictures." *Screen* 31.3: 243–61.

Perret, G. 1996. *Old Soldiers Never Die: The Life of Douglas MacArthur.* London.

Perret, M.D. 2004. "Not Just Condensation: How Comic Books Interpret Shakespeare." *College Literature* 31.4: 72–93.

Perry, K. 2004. *The Kingfish in Fiction: Huey P. Long and the Modern American Novel.* Baton Rouge.

Pinkston, C.A. 1980. "Richard Mansfield's Shakespearean Productions." PhD diss., University of California, Los Angeles.

Piper, J.R. 1997. *Ideologies and Institutions: American Conservative and Liberal Governance.* Oxford.

Pittman, L.M. 2011. *Authorising Shakespeare on Film and Television: Gender, Class, and Ethnicity.* New York.

Powell, A.G. 2003. "American High Schools and the Liberal Arts Tradition." *Brookings Papers on Education Policy:* 7–37.

Prestowitz, D. 2003. "The New American Empire?" *Knight Ridder Tribune News Service,* 18 June.

Pucci, G. 2006. "Caesar the Foe: Roman Conquest and National Resistance in French Popular Culture." In *Julius Caesar in Western Culture,* edited by M. Wyke, 190–201. Oxford.

Quartermaine, L. 1995. "'Slouching towards Rome': Mussolini's Imperial Vision." In *Urban Society in Roman Italy,* edited by T.J. Cornell and L. Lomas, 203–15. London.

Raab, S. 2006. *Five Families: The Rise, Decline, and Resurgence of America's Most Powerful Mafia Empires.* London.

Ralph, J. "To Usher in a New Paradigm? President Bush's Foreign Policy Legacy." In *Assessing the George W. Bush Presidency: A Tale of Two Terms,* edited by A. Wroe and J. Herbert, 77–99. Edinburgh.

Rankin, D.M. 2004. "The Press, the Public, and the Two Presidencies of George W. Bush." In *Transformed by Crisis: The Presidency of George W. Bush and American Politics,* edited by J. Kraus, K.J. McMahon, and D.M. Rankin, 51–71. New York.

Ranville, M. 1996. *To Strike at a King: The Turning Point in the McCarthy Witch-Hunts.* Troy, MI.

Rasula, J. 1990. "Nietzsche in the Nursery: Naive Classics and Surrogate Parents in Postwar American Cultural Debates." *Representations* 29: 50–77.

Rauchway, E. 2003. *Murdering McKinley: The Making of Theodore Roosevelt's America.* New York.

Raw, L. 2009. "Form and Function in the 1950s Anthology Series: *Studio One.*" *Journal of Popular Film and Television* 37.2: 90–96.

Raymond, R.R., ed. 1881. *Shakespeare for the Young Folk: A Midsummer Night's Dream, As You Like It, Julius Caesar.* New York.

Redi, R. 1991. *La cines: Storia di una casa di produzione italiana.* Rome.

Reid, B.H. 2007. *Robert E. Lee: Icon for a Nation.* Amherst, NY.

Reinermann, L. 2008. "Fleet Street and the Kaiser: British Public Opinion and Wilhelm II." *German History* 26.4: 469–85.

Reinhold, M. 1984. *Classica Americana: The Greek and Roman Heritage in the United States.* Detroit.

Renshaw, P. 2004. *Franklin D. Roosevelt.* Harlow, UK.

Reppetto, T. 2004. *American Mafia: A History of Its Rise to Power.* New York.

Reynolds, D. 1990. "1940: Fulcrum of the Twentieth Century?" *International Affairs* 66.2: 325–50.

Rhodes, J.D. 2000. "'Our beautiful and glorious art lives': The Rhetoric of Nationalism in Early Italian Periodicals." *Film History* 12: 308–21.

Rich, N., and M.H. Fisher, eds. 1955. *The Holstein Papers.* Vol. 2, *The Diaries.* New York.

Richard, C.J. 1994. *The Founders and the Classics: Greece, Rome, and the American Enlightenment.* Cambridge, MA.

———. 2009. *The Golden Age of Classics in America: Greece, Rome, and the Antebellum United States.* Boston.

Richter, D.H. 2007. "Keeping Company in Hollywood: Ethical Issues in Nonfiction Film." *Narrative* 15.2: 140–66.

de Riencourt, A. de 1957. *The Coming Caesars.* New York.

———. 1968. *The American Empire.* New York.

Riess, E., and A.L. Janes. 1914. *Caesar Gallic War, Books I–II.* New York.

Rilling, R. 2003. "'American Empire' as Will and Idea: The New Grand Strategy of the Bush Administration." *Rosa-Luxemburg Stiftung Policy Paper.* www.rainer-rilling.de.

Ripley, J. 1980. *Julius Caesar on Stage in England and America, 1599–1973.* Cambridge, MA.

Robertson, N.G. 2006. "Platonism in High Places: Leo Strauss, George W. Bush, and the Response to 9/11." In *Classical Antiquity and the Politics of America: From George Washington to George W. Bush,* edited by M. Meckler, 153–74. Waco, TX.

Rogin, M. 1987. *Ronald Reagan, The Movie.* Berkeley.

Rolfe, W.J. 1903. *Shakespeare's Tragedy of Julius Caesar, Edited, with Notes.* New York.

Rose, L.A. 2007. *Power at Sea.* Vol. 2, *The Breaking Storm, 1919–1945.* Columbia, MO.

Rosteck, T. 1994. *See It Now Confronts McCarthyism: Television Documentary and the Politics of Representation.* Tuscaloosa, AL.

Rothwell, K.S. 2004. *A History of Shakespeare on Screen: A Century of Film and Television.* 2nd ed. Cambridge.

Rudalevige, A. 2005. *The New Imperial Presidency: Renewing Presidential Power after Watergate.* Ann Arbor, MI.

Russell, W.H. 1956. "Caesar, the General." *Classical Weekly* 50.2: 17–19.

Rutter, C.C. 2006. "Facing History, Facing Now: Deborah Warner's *Julius Caesar* at the Barbican Theatre." *Shakespeare Quarterly* 57.1: 71–85.

Saller, R. 1998. "American Classical Historiography." In *Imagined Histories: American Historians Interpret the Past,* edited by A. Molho and G.S. Wood, 222–37. Princeton, NJ.

Schlesinger, A.M. 1973. *The Imperial Presidency.* Boston.

———. 2004. *The Imperial Presidency.* New ed., with additional introduction and epilogue. New York.

Schrecker, E. 1998. *Many Are the Crimes: McCarthyism in America.* Princeton, NJ.

Schultheiss, J. 1996. "A Season of Fear: The Blacklisted Teleplays of Abraham Polonsky." *Literature Film Quarterly* 24.2: 148–64.

Scudder, J.W. 1927. *Second Year Latin.* New York. Reprinted in 1934.

Selby, S.A. 1978. *The Study of Film as an Art Form in American Secondary Schools.* New York.

Seldes, G. 1935. *Sawdust Caesar: The Untold History of Mussolini and Fascism.* New York.

Seton-Watson, C. 1967. *Italy from Liberalism to Fascism, 1870–1925.* London.

Shalev, E. 2009. *Rome Reborn on Western Shores: Historical Imagination and the Creation of the American Republic.* Charlottesville, VA.

Shaltz, J. 2003. "Julius Caesar." *Shakespeare Bulletin* 21.2: 37–38.

Shaughnessy, R., ed. 2007. *The Cambridge Companion to Shakespeare and Popular Culture.* Cambridge.

Shero, L.R. 1966. "A Historical Survey of the Classics in the Schools and Universities of the United States." In *Classics in the USA,* edited by M.P.O. Morford, 17–39. London.

Shipley, F.W. 1909. "The Saalburg Collection." *Classical Weekly* 2.13: 100–102.

Shore, P. 1927. "The Case for the Classics." In F.W. Kelsey, *Latin and Greek in American Education,* 249–314. New York.

Siedler, C.W. 1956. "Rhetorical Devices in Caesar's Commentaries." *Classical Weekly* 50.2: 28–31.

Simon, A. 1989. *Vercingétorix et l'idéologie française.* Paris.

Sinfield, A. 1996. "Theatres of War: Caesar and the Vandals." In *Shakespeare: The Roman Plays,* edited by B. Loughrey, A. Murphy, and G. Holderness, 45–65. London.

Singh, R. 2009. "George W. Bush and the US Congress." In *Assessing the George W. Bush Presidency: A Tale of Two Terms,* edited by A. Wroe and J. Herbert, 13–28. Edinburgh.

Sinyard, N. 1986. *Filming Literature: The Art of Screen Adaptation.* Beckenham, UK.

Sklar, S.M. 2002. "Shall We Bury *Caesar* or Praise Him? Ideas for the Revitalization of an Old Standard." *English Journal* 92.1: 36–40.

Smith, N. 2003. "After the American *Lebensraum:* 'Empire,' Empire, and Globalization." *Interventions* 5.2: 249–70.

Smoodin, E. 2001. "'Compulsory Viewing for Every Citizen': *Mr. Smith* and the Rhetoric of Reception." In *Keyframes: Popular Culture and Cultural Studies,* edited by M. Tinkcom and A. Villarejo, 343–58. London.

Soper, K. 2008. *Garry Trudeau: Doonesbury and the Aesthetics of Satire.* Jackson, MS.

Spencer, D. 2002. *The Roman Alexander: Reading a Cultural Myth.* Exeter.

Spevack, M., ed. 1988. *Julius Caesar.* Cambridge.

Stafford, J. 1951. "Henry Norman Hudson and the Whig Use of Shakespeare." *Proceedings of the Modern Language Association* 66.5: 649–61.

Steiner, Z. 2005. *The Lights That Failed: European International History, 1919–1933.* Oxford.

Stone, M. 1999. "A Flexible Rome: Fascism and the Cult of Romanità." In *Roman Presences: Receptions of Rome in European Culture, 1789–1945,* edited by C. Edwards, 205–20. Cambridge.

Strine, H.C.N. 2009. "George W. Bush's Signing Statements: Advancing the Imperial Presidency?" In *Perspectives on the Legacy of George W. Bush,* edited by M.O. Grossman and R.E. Matthews, 53–71. Newcastle.

Stromberg, J.R. 2001. "The Old Cause: Empire and Reaction." 13 March. http://antiwar.com/stromberg/?articleid=3401.

Swope, J.W. 1993. *Ready-to-Use Activities for Teaching Julius Caesar.* New York.

Syme, R. 1960. "Bastards in the Roman Aristocracy." *Proceedings of the American Philosophical Society* 104.3: 323–27.

Tabachnick, D.E., and T. Koivukoski, eds. 2009. *Enduring Empire: Ancient Lessons for Global Politics.* Toronto.

Taylor, L.R. 1966. *Roman Voting Assemblies.* Ann Arbor, MI.

———. 1968. *Party Politics in the Age of Caesar.* Berkeley. First published in 1949.

Thayer, J.A. 1964. *Italy and the Great War: Politics and Culture, 1870–1915.* Madison, WI.

Theoharis, A.G. 1979. *The Truman Presidency: The Origins of the Imperial Presidency and the National Security State.* Stanfordville, NY.

Thomas, H., and D.L. Thomas. 1940. *Living Biographies of Famous Rulers.* New York.

Thompson, J.A. 2002. *Woodrow Wilson: Profiles in Power.* London.

Tolman, H.L. 1940. "Julius Caesar Up to Date." *English Journal* 29.10: 830–32.

Tomadjoglou, K. 2000. "Rome's Premiere Film Studio: Società Italiana Cines." *Film History* 12: 262–75.

Tompkins, D.P. 2006. "The World of Moses Finkelstein: The Year 1939 in M.I. Finley's Development as a Historian." In *Classical Antiquity and the Politics of America: From George Washington to George W. Bush,* edited by M. Meckler, 95–125. Waco, TX.

Tønnesson, S. 2004. "Review Essay: The Imperial Temptation." *Security Dialogue* 35: 329–43.

Too, Y.L. 1998. Introduction to Too and Livingstone, *Pedagogy and Power,* 1–15.

Too, Y.L., and N. Livingstone, eds. 1998. *Pedagogy and Power: Rhetorics of Classical Learning.* Cambridge.

Toscano, M.M. 2008. "Gowns and Gossip: Gender and Class Struggle in Rome." In Rome, *Season One: History Makes Television,* edited by M.S. Cyrino, 153–67. Malden, MA.

Toynbee, P. 2002. "The Last Emperor." *The Guardian,* 13 September.

Tyler, L.G. 1894. "The Seal of Virginia." *William and Mary Quarterly* 3.2: 81–96.

Valentinetti, C.M. 1981. *Orson Welles.* Florence.

Van Cleve, C. 1938. "The Teaching of Shakespeare in American Secondary Schools." *Peabody Journal of Education* 15.6: 333–50.

Vercingétorix et Alésia. 1994. Catalogue de l'exposition au Musée des Antiquités Nationales de Saint-Germain-en-Laye. Paris.

Veysey, L.R. "The Academic Mind of Woodrow Wilson." *Mississippi Valley Historical Review* 49.4: 613–34.

Visser, R. 1992. "Fascist Doctrine and the Cult of *Romanità*." *Journal of Contemporary History* 27: 5–22.

Waddell, W. 1907. *Caesar's Character or In Defense of the Standard of Mankind.* New York.

Wagner, S. 2006. *Eisenhower Republicanism: Pursuing the Middle Way.* DeKalb, IL.

Walker, A.T. 1907. *Caesar's Gallic War: With Introduction, Notes, Vocabulary, and Grammatical Appendix.* Chicago.

Walker, M. 2003. "An Empire unlike Any Other." In *The Imperial Tense: Prospects and Problems of American Empire,* edited by A.J. Bacevich, 134–45. Chicago.

Waquet, F. 2001. *Latin or the Empire of the Sign: From the Sixteenth to the Twentieth Centuries.* Translated by J. Howe. London.

Warshaw, S.A. 2004. "Mastering Presidential Government: Executive Power and the Bush Administration." In *Transformed by Crisis: The Presidency of George W. Bush and American Politics,* edited by J. Kraus, K.J. McMahon, and D.M. Rankin, 101–17. New York.

Warthen, B. 2003. "The 'Long Haul' Will Last Longer Than Bush Presidency; So Then What?" *Knight Ridder Tribune News Service,* 31 March.

Welles, O., P. Bogdanovich, and J. Rosenbaum. 1998. *This Is Orson Welles.* New York.

West, A.F., ed. 1917. *Value of the Classics.* Conference on Classical Studies in Liberal Education. Princeton, NJ.

Wheatley, S.C. 1988. "Abraham Flexner and the Politics of Educational Reform." *History of Higher Education Annual* 8: 45–57.

White, T.H. 1968. *Caesar at the Rubicon: A Play about Politics.* New York.

———. 1969. *The Making of the President, 1968.* New York.

———. 1978. *In Search of History: A Personal Adventure.* New York.

Whitehead, A.C. 1972. *The Standard Bearer: A Story of Army Life in the Time of Caesar.* New York. First published in 1914.

Widener, C. 2006. "The Changing Face of American Theatre: Colorblind and Uni-Racial Casting at the New York Shakespeare Festival under the Direction of Joseph Papp." PhD diss., University of Missouri-Columbia.

Williams, G.L. 1994. *Fascist Thought and Totalitarianism in Italy's Secondary Schools: Theory and Practice, 1922–1943.* New York.

Williams, T.H. 1981. *Huey Long.* New York.

Willis, S. 1991. *The BBC Shakespeare Plays: Making the Televised Canon.* Jefferson, NC.

Wills, G. 1985. *Cincinnatus: George Washington and the Enlightenment.* London.

Willson, R.F. 1995. "The Populist *Julius Caesar.*" *Shakespeare Bulletin* 13.3: 37–38.

Wilson, C. 1932. "Historical Fiction for the High-School Latin Class." *Classical Journal* 28.2: 107–15.

Wilson, G.B. 1962. "Richard Mansfield: Actor of the Transition." *Educational Theatre Journal* 14.1: 38–43.

Wilson, R.R. 1945. *Lincoln in Caricature.* Elmira, NY.

Wilson, R.W. 2005. "Gang Busters: The Kefauver Crime Committee and the Syndicate Films of the 1950s." In *Mob Culture: Hidden Histories of the American Gangster Film,* edited by L. Grieveson, E. Sonnet, and P. Stanfield, 67–89. Oxford.

Wilstach, P. 1908. *Richard Mansfield: The Man and Actor.* New York.

Winkler, M.W. 2004. "*Gladiator* and the Colosseum: Ambiguities of Spectacle." In *Gladiator: Film and History,* edited by M.W. Winkler, 87–110. Malden, MA.

———. 2009. *Cinema and Classical Texts: Apollo's New Light.* Cambridge.

Winter, W. 1910. *Life and Art of Richard Mansfield with Selections from His Letters.* Vol. 2. New York.

Winterer, C. 2002. *The Culture of Classicism: Ancient Greece and Rome in American Intellectual Life, 1780–1910.* Baltimore.

———. 2007. *The Mirror of Antiquity: American Women and the Classical Tradition, 1750–1900.* Ithaca, NY.

Wiseman, T.P. 1987. *Catullus and His World: A Reappraisal.* Cambridge.

Wortham, S. 2001. "Ventriloquating Shakespeare: Ethical Positioning in Classroom Literature Discussions." *Working Papers in Educational Linguistics* 17.1/2: 47–64.

Wright, B.W. 2001. *Comic Book Nation: The Transformation of Youth Culture in America.* Baltimore.

Wroe, A., and J. Herbert, eds. 2009. *Assessing the George W. Bush Presidency: A Tale of Two Terms.* Edinburgh.

Wyke, M. 1997. *Projecting the Past: Ancient Rome, Cinema and History.* New York.

———. 1999a. "Sawdust Caesar: Mussolini, Julius Caesar, and the Drama of Dictatorship." In *The Uses and Abuses of Antiquity,* edited by M. Wyke and M. Biddiss, 167–86. Bern.

———. 1999b. "Screening Ancient Rome in the New Italy." In *Roman Presences: Receptions of Rome in European Culture, 1789–1945,* edited by C. Edwards, 188–204. Cambridge.

———. 2004. "Film Style and Fascism: *Julius Caesar.*" *Film Studies* 4: 58–74.

———. 2006a. "Caesar, Cinema, and National Identity in the 1910s." In Wyke, *Julius Caesar in Western Culture,* 170–89.

———, ed. 2006b. *Julius Caesar in Western Culture.* Oxford.

———. 2006c. "A Twenty-First-Century Caesar." In Wyke, *Julius Caesar in Western Culture,* 305–23.

———. 2007. *Caesar: A Life in Western Culture.* London.

Wyke, M., and M. Biddiss, eds. 1999. *The Uses and Abuses of Antiquity.* Bern.

Yavetz, Z. 1983. *Julius Caesar and His Public Image.* London. 1st ed., in German, 1979.

Zacher, D.E. 2008. *The Scripps Newspapers Go to War, 1914–18.* Chicago.

Zander, H., ed. 2005a. *Julius Caesar: New Critical Essays.* New York.

———. 2005b. "*Julius Caesar* and the Critical Legacy." In Zander, *Julius Caesar,* 3–55.

Zelizer, B. 1992. *Covering the Body: The Kennedy Assassination, the Media, and the Shaping of Collective Memory.* Chicago.

Index

Abbott, Allan, 55
Abu Ghraib prison, 218
Addison, Joseph, 2–3, 239n5
Adelman, Kenneth, 226–27
Advanced Placement courses, 237
advertisements, 16–17, 65–67, 66fig., 167–68, 185, 193fig.
Aeneid (Virgil), 237
Afghanistan, 211, 218
Africa, 2, 83, 109, 111–12, 134, 179–80
After Dark (magazine), 192
Agnew, Spiro, 196
Agrippa, Marcus, 204
Alesia, 76–78, 79fig., 84
Alexander the Great, 8
Alma-Tadema, Lawrence, 56
Alpert, Hollis, 166
American Book Company, 40
American Civil War, 9, 50, 52
American Classical League, 95
American Empire (Bacevich), 205
American Empire, The (de Riencourt), 190
American Historical Association, 90
American International Pictures (AIP), 192–94
Americanization, 23, 47–67, 76, 86, 122, 197, 219, 224, 231
American Philological Association, 23, 90, 150
American Revolution, 1–4, 7, 9, 48–49, 210
American Shakespeare Theater, 199

Amsterdam, 108
Andrew, John F., 48–49
Antony (Marcus, Antonius): 121, 137, 173, 187, 231–32; in Shakespeare's Julius Caesar, 40, 60, 62, 65–66, 89, 114–15, 117, 118fig., 124, 126, 139, 142–45, 142fig., 151–56, 153fig., 158, 164–66, 192, 195–96, 198, 200, 220–22, 225–26
architecture, 62, 148, 155, 184, 259nn88,89
Arendt, Hannah, 150
Are We Rome? The Fall of an Empire and the Fate of America (Murphy), 205, 233
Ariovistus, 38, 69, 75–76, 81, 170
Arkansas, 178
Armes, William Dallam, 90
Arminium, 112
Arminius. See Hermann
Armstrong, Donald, 127–28
Arnold, Thomas, 45
Asia, 143, 167, 179, 181
assassination: Caesar, Julius (see Caesar, Julius, murder); Garfield, James A., 53; Kennedy, John F., 188, 192–93, 200; Kennedy, Robert F., 189, 192–93, 195; King, Martin Luther, Jr., 189, 192–93; Lincoln, Abraham, 4–6, 5fig., 50–53, 121; Long, Huey P., 122; McKinley, William, 53, 58, 62, 245n23
Assassination of Caesar, 44 BC, The (painting; Rochegrosse), 39fig., 246n50
Atia, 232

Atlanta, Georgia, 40
Atlanta Journal-Constitution, 208
Atlantic Monthly, 233
Augustine, Norman, 226
Augustus, Emperor, 126, 143, 150, 153, 176, 184, 222

Bacevich, Andrew J., 205
Baker, Charles M., 36
Balbus, Lucius Cornelius, 187
Baltic states, 126
Baltimore, 26, 30, 32, 55, 59, 80, 83, 167
Bandello, Cesare, 120
Bankhead, Tallulah, 136
Bargellini, Piero, 105
BBC. *See* British Broadcasting Service
Belgium, 70, 73, 78–80, 179
Bellum Helveticum: A Beginner's Book in Latin (Janes and Jenks), 27–29
Better Films Movement, 92
Bin Laden, Osama, 204
Blackton, J. Stuart, 60
Bolenius, Emma Miller, 50, 54–55
Bolitho, William, 111
Bondurant, Alexander L., 91
Booth, John Wilkes, 4, 50–53, 121, 240n10
Boston, 48, 51, 90, 93–94, 185
Boston Morning Globe, 93–94
Boston Transcript, 90
Boxoffice Magazine, 165
Brady, Kathleen, 102–3
Brando, Marlon, 151–52, 164–66, 226
British Broadcasting Service (BBC), 196–97, 227, 229
Brown, James Mason, 125
Brutus, Lucius Junius (founder of Roman Republic), 4
Brutus, Marcus Junius (Caesar's assassin): as Booth's model, 4, 50; depictions of (non-Shakespearean), 121, 135, 160, 161fig., 181, 182fig., 225, 228, 231; political views through history of, 1–4, 49–65, 157–58, 181–82, 192, 196, 210, 220, 225–26; in Shakespeare's *Julius Caesar,* 49–51, 56–58, 57fig., 62, 65, 115–17, 116fig., 123–24, 139, 142fig., 143, 152, 156–58, 165, 176, 192, 195, 199fig., 200, 220–22, 226
Bryd, Robert C., 205, 225
Bryn Mawr College, 25, 150
Buffalo, Pan-American Exposition, 53
Bunn, Henry W., 108–9
Burdett, Winston, 168
Burge, Stuart, 192–94, 193fig.
Burnett, W.R., 120

Bush, George H.W., 203, 214–15
Bush, George W., 17, 162, 203–27, 232–37, 203–4, 207–22, 213fig., 218fig., 225–27, 232–37, 275n103
Bush, W. Stephen, 63–65

Caesar at the Rubicon: A Play about Politics (White), 185–90
Caesar (Impossible Ragtime Theatre), 196
Caesar in Gaul (D'Ooge and Eastman), 33, 34fig., 39fig., 72–73, 76–77, 83
Caesarism, 4, 13, 16, 46, 50, 108, 174–78, 181, 190, 203, 237, 239n9
Caesar, Julius
—murder: assassination, actual, 17, 214; assassination, depictions of, 8, 39fig., 61fig., 88–89, 103, 105, 109, 114, 121, 124, 132, 139, 141, 143, 152–54, 153fig., 159, 192–93, 200–201, 204, 223, 228, 231fig.
—overview, 8; clemency, 35; commentaries, see *Gallic Wars (de bello Gallico)* (Caesar) and *Civil War (de bello civili)* (Caesar); Rubicon crossing, 17, 105, 185–89, 214, 228, 232–33; sexual immorality, 87; writing style, 22, 41
—representations of: in advertisements, 16–17, 65–67, 66fig., 167–68, 185; in cartoons, political, 5fig., 81, 82fig., 108, 112, 113fig., 181, 182fig., 212fig., 213, 217–18; in comic books, 140–45, 142fig., 144fig., 148, 166, 170–71, 172fig.; in film, 13, 59–65, 61fig., 83–94, 85fig., 130–31, 145–59, 149fig., 153fig., 161–66, 171–73, 192–95, 193fig.; in novels, 40–45, 42fig., 43fig., 120–21, 134–39, 230; in paintings, 39fig., 62, 76, 77fig., 84, 229, 246n50; on statues, 81, 106fig., 112; on television, 138–39, 159–64, 161fig., 191, 196–97, 227–32, 229fig., 231fig.; in the theater, 55–59, 113–19, 116fig., 118fig., 195–98, 199fig., 219–22, 224
—in Shakespeare's *Julius Caesar,* 51–53, 56–57, 61fig., 62, 115–17, 116fig., 139, 149fig., 165, 173, 194–96, 199fig., 220–21, 226
Caesar's Character or In Defense of the Standard of Mankind (Waddell), 45–46
Caesar's Commentaries (Kelsey), 31fig., 78–80, 79fig.
Caesar's Conquest of Gaul (Holmes), 37–38
Caesar's Conquests (comic book), 140, 170–71, 172fig.
Caesars Palace, 184–85

Caius Volcatius Tullus, 41–45, 42*fig.*, 43*fig.*, 230
Cajus Julius Caesar (film), 83–94, 85*fig.*
Calhern, Louis, 147, 156, 165
California, University of, 90
Californian, 103
Calpurnia, 87, 92, 143
Canali, Luca, 204–5
Candler Theater, 86–87
Caplin, Steve, 213*fig.*
Capone, Al, 119–21
caricatures. *See* cartoons, political
Carnegie Endowment for International Peace, 207
Carter, Jimmy, 196
cartoons, political, 5*fig.*, 81, 82*fig.*, 108, 112, 113*fig.*, 181, 182*fig.*, 212*fig.*, 213, 217, 218*fig.*
Casca, 116, 143, 194
Cassius, 2–3, 121, 217, 231*fig.*; in Shakespeare's *Julius Caesar*, 49, 51, 58, 65–66, 88, 113, 139, 142*fig.*, 143, 162, 165–66, 199*fig.*, 222
Castro, Fidel, 192
Cato, 2, 3, 84, 87, 93, 177, 201, 204, 216–17, 227
Catullus, 134–35
CBS. *See* Columbia Broadcasting System
Centostelle, 105
Charleston Gazette, 217
Charney, Maurice, 197
Cheney, Dick, 204, 207
Chicago, 35, 55, 64, 89, 120, 186, 192, 219–20
Chicago Daily Sun-Times, 158–59
Chicago Defender, 109
Chicago Herald, 89–90
Chicago Shakespeare Theater, 219–20, 224
Chicago Tribune, 110, 220
Child, Richard Washburn, 107
China, 141
Chronicle, 108
Cicero, Marcus Tullius, 2, 3, 86, 177, 185, 201, 216, 236, 241n2
Cincinnatus, 133
cinema. *See* film
Cinna the Conspirator, 124, 143
Cinna the Poet, 124
City in History, The: Its Origins, Its Transformations, and Its Prospects, (Mumford), 183–84
Civil War (de bello civili) (Caesar) 6, 8, 22, 76, 101
Clarke, Michael, 38–40, 45
Classical Association, 91

Classical Association of the Atlantic States, 80, 167–69
Classical Journal, 73, 101, 126
Classical Weekly, 26, 30, 32, 59, 91, 127–28
Classic Comics. See Classics Illustrated
Classics Illustrated, 140–45, 142*fig.*, 144*fig.*, 148, 166, 170–71, 172*fig.*
Classic Stage Company, 195
Claudius the God (Graves), 197
Clay, Henry, 40
Clemens, Samuel L., 103
Cleopatra, 135, 137, 168, 184
Cleopatra (film), 184, 232
Cleveland, Grover, 72
Cleveland Press, 153
Clinton, Bill, 203
Clodia, 135–37
Clooney, George, 162
Cohen, Eliot A., 206
Cold War, 12, 15–16, 131, 138, 143, 150, 155–56, 158, 165–66, 168–69, 173–74, 190, 203, 207, 210
Colossus: The Rise and Fall of the American Empire (Ferguson), 205
Columbia Broadcasting System (CBS), 138, 159–64
comic books, 140–45, 142*fig.*, 144*fig.*, 148, 166, 170–71, 172*fig.*
Coming Caesars, The (de Riencourt), 174–78, 190, 207
Commonwealth United, 192
communism, 16, 108, 138–39, 141, 143, 147, 150–53, 156–58, 162, 165–66, 169, 181
Connecticut, 199–200
Cornelia, 87, 92
Corriere della Sera, 204
Cortes, Hernando, 37
Cotham, Harry C., 192
Coulouris, George, 118*fig.*
Crassus, 87
Cronkite, Walter, 159–61
Crusade in Europe (Eisenhower), 171
Cuba, 218
Cue Magazine, 164
Czechoslovakia, 138–39
Czolgosz, Leon, 58

Daily Chariot, 147, 156
Daily Evening Fasces, 103
Daily Express, 107
Daily Telegraph Magazine, 195
Daily Times, 216
Dallas, 188
Deadwood (television series), 228

Death of Caesar, The (painting; Gérôme), 62
de Bosis, Lauro, 134
DeMille, Cecil B., 158
Dennison, Walter, 38
Depression, The Great, 120, 122, 169, 201
De Quincey, Thomas, 45
de Riencourt, Amaury, 174–78, 190, 207, 214
dictatorships, 14–15, 80, 83, 101–34, 147–48, 150, 153, 155, 157, 171, 174, 186, 189, 192, 200, 211, 215, 219, 234–37
Diocletian, Emperor, 234, 275n103
Dirksen, Everett, 181–82
Dodge, Theodore Ayrault, 6–7
D'Ooge, Benjamin L., 33, 34*fig.*, 39*fig.*, 72, 76, 82
Doonesbury, 217, 218*fig.*
Dumnorix, 32
Dunn, Esther Cloudman, 48, 51
Durant, Will, 132–33

eagle imagery, 60, 84, 86, 88, 148, 152, 194, 233
Eastman, Barrett, 58–59
Eastman, Frederic C., 33, 34*fig.*, 39*fig.*, 72, 76, 83
East Side Express, 196
Eclectic Magazine of Foreign Literature, The, 70
Economist, 227
Écrits de Paris, 178
Education, 6, 12–15, 17, 21–97, 101–5, 125–27, 223–24, 237
Educational Consultants on Entertainment Films (ECEF), 154
Education of Julius Caesar, The: A Biography, A Reconstruction (Kahn), 201–2
Eisenhower, Dwight D., 141, 157, 159, 162, 169, 171, 176, 178
Encyclopaedia Britannica Films, 173
Englar, Margaret T., 80, 81
English Journal, 54–55, 102, 125–26
Enron scandal, 211
Ethical Element in Literature, The (Jones), 51–52
ethics and morality, 8, 13, 17, 24, 27, 35, 45, 49, 50–52, 80, 96–97, 127, 154, 166, 169, 174, 182–83
Ethiopia, invasion of, 107, 109, 112
Evening Journal, 59
Evening Standard, 108
Evening Tibur, 121
Exhibitors Trade Review, 92, 94
existentialism, 134–38
Exxon, 197

fascism, 14–15, 83, 104–19, 122–28, 131, 134–39, 195
Fascist League of North America, 107
Ferencz, George, 196
Ferguson, Niall, 205
Ferrero, Guglielmo, 28, 83, 175
film, 13, 59–65, 61*fig.*, 83–94, 85*fig.*, 120, 130–31, 145–59, 149*fig.*, 153*fig.*, 161–66, 171–73, 192–95, 193*fig.*
Films Incorporated, 173
Films in Review, 146–47
Finley, John H., 74, 75
Fisk, Robert, 211–12, 216, 219
Flavius, 148
Flexner, Abraham, 71, 74
Florida, State College for Women, 24, 29, 71, 95
Ford, Gerald, 203
Foreign Policy (journal), 207–8
France, 11, 47, 69, 74–77, 80, 81, 82, 95, 102, 126, 132, 129, 137, 179, 181; Vercingetorix, 14, 42, 47, 76, 77*fig.*, 80–84, 85*fig.*, 88, 101, 170, 228–30, 229*fig.*
Freedman, Gerald, 199
Froude, James Antony, 45

Gaines, Barbara, 219–21, 224
Gaines, Sonny Jim, 198, 199*fig.*
Gallic War (*de bello Gallico*) (Caesar): in the classroom, 9, 12–14, 17, 21–30, 32–39, 43–46, 54, 68, 71–73, 76, 80–81, 86, 95–97, 101, 105, 120, 127, 154, 169–71, 223–24, 237–38; and First World War, 14, 68–83, 79*fig.*, 102; and novels, 40–44, 42*fig.*, 230; school editions, 33–39, 34*fig.*, 39*fig.*, 72, 76–80, 79*fig.*, 83, 96, 120, 223
Gallic War (Walker) 33, 35
gambling, 184–85
Game, Josiah B., 24, 29, 32, 71–72, 74, 95–97
gangsterism, 119–21, 128, 156, 260nn94,95
Garfield, James A., 53
General Education Board, 71
George III, 2–3, 49
George Washington University, 127
Gerber, Sylvia W., 169–70
Germanic tribes, 32–33, 41–42, 37–38, 41, 44, 69–70, 73, 82*fig.*, 86, 93, 101, 229
Germany, 11, 14, 36, 69–70, 73–76, 80–81, 96, 115, 117, 126, 132, 147–48, 150, 157, 180, 207
Gérôme, Jean-Léon, 62
Gettysburg Times, 223
Giardina, Denise, 217

Gibbon, Edward, 236
Gielgud, John, 165, 194
Gilberton publishing company, 140, 170
Goodheart, Adam, 233
Good Night, and Good Luck (film), 162
Gould, Jack, 139
Gracchi, the, 175, 185
Grant, Ulysses, S., 52
Graves, Robert, 197
Great Britain and Britons, 2–4, 11, 33, 38,
    40–41, 47–48, 93, 95, 101, 112, 126,
    179, 181, 195–97, 206, 210–13, 225,
    227, 230
Great War. See Wars, First World War
Greece, 40, 175, 178, 232
Griffin, Jasper, 202
Guantánamo Bay, 218
Guardian, The, 212fig., 213fig.
Guazzoni, Enrico, 83–94, 85fig.
Gudahl, Kevin, 220

Hale, Nathan, 49
Hale, William, Gardner, 35
Halleck, Fitzgreene, 40
Hannibal, 6
Harper's Magazine, 215
Harrison S., 49
Harvard University, 210
Harwood, Mary, 26, 30–32, 59, 83, 97
Hasdrubal, 204
Hay, Lady Grace Drummond, 107–8
HBO, 227–33, 229fig., 231fig.
Hearst Corporation, 109–10, 114, 128
Heller, Bruno, 228, 230
Helvetii, 32, 33, 38, 44, 101
Henry, Guy, 231
Henry, Patrick, 3, 49, 239n6
Hermann, 82fig., 249n35
Heston, Charlton, 195, 226
High School Caesar (film), 120
High School Course in Latin Composition
    (Baker and Inglis), 36
Hindenburg, Paul von, 78
Hinds, Ciarán, 228, 229fig.
History Book Club, 200–201
Hitler, Adolf, 117, 122, 126, 132, 138, 147,
    192
Holland, Joseph, 116fig.
Holland, Tom, 235–36
Holmes, T.R. 37–38
Holstein, Friedrich August von, 81
Horace Mann School, 36, 55
Houseman, John, 113–14, 131, 146–47,
    152, 165–66
House of Representatives, 103

House Un-American Activities Committee
    (HUAC), 158
Howard University, 169
Howell, Fanny, 101–2
Hudson, Henry Norman, 51
Humphrey, Hubert, 192
Huneker, James, 58
Hussein, Saddam, 204, 220–21

I, Claudius (Graves), 197
I, Claudius (television series), 229
Ides of March, The (Wilder), 134–38
Ignatieff, Michael, 210
Illinois, 51–52
illustrations in textbooks, 29–30, 31fig., 33
imperialism, 69, 175, 177, 190–91, 194,
    205, 209, 210–19, 222, 236
Imperial Presidency, The (Schlesinger),
    190–91
Imperial Tense, The: Prospects and Prob-
    lems of American Empire (Bacevich),
    205
Impossible Ragtime Theatre, 196
Independent, The, 211–12, 216
Inglis, Alexander, J. 36
In Search of History: A Personal Adventure
    (White), 185–86
Interpretations (journal), 192
Iowa, 72, 91, 101, 126
Iran, 199
Iraq, 204–6, 211–22, 227, 233
Ireland, O'Dale, 120
Irwin, Wallace, 120–22
Italy, 11, 14–15, 81–85, 92, 94–95, 104–13,
    115, 117, 120, 132, 134–35, 147–49,
    181, 187–88, 214. See also Rome
It Can't Happen Here (Lewis), 122–23
Ivy League, 104

Jackson, Andrew, 177
Jaeck, Scott, 221
James I, 2
Janes, Arthur Lee, 27
Japan, 95, 141
Jenks, Paul Rockwell, 27
Joffre, Joseph, 78
John Hopkins University, 206
Johnson, Chalmers, 205, 209, 218–19,
    234–36
Johnson, Lyndon B., 16, 180–81, 185, 189,
    196
Jones, Richard D., 51–53
Julian, Emperor, 234, 275n103
Julius Caesar (comic book), 140–45, 148,
    166

Julius Caesar: Death of a Dictator (theater, dir. Welles), 14–15, 113–20, 116*fig.*, 118*fig.*, 123–26, 130–31, 139, 165, 195, 220
Julius Caesar (film, dir. Burge), 192–95
Julius Caesar (film, dir. Guazzoni), 87–94
Julius Caesar (film, dir. Mankiewicz), 130–31, 145–59, 149*fig.*, 153*fig.*, 161–66, 172–73
Julius Caesar (film, dir. Ranous), 60–65, 61*fig.*, 83, 88
Julius Caesar Murder Case, The (Irwin) 120–22
Julius Caesar (Shakespeare). *See* Shakespeare's *Julius Caesar*
Julius Caesar (television, dir. Nickell), 138–39
Julius Caesar (television, dir. Wise), 196–97
Julius Caesar (theater, dir. Freedman), 199–200
Julius Caesar (theater, dir. Gaines), 219–22, 224
Julius Caesar (theater, dir. Langham), 198, 199*fig.*
Julius Caesar (theater, dir. Mansfield), 55–59, 57*fig.*, 62, 64
Julius Caesar (theater, dir. Sullivan), 221

Kagan, Robert, 207–8
Kain, Gylan, 199*fig.*
Kaiser Wilhelm II, 69–70, 75, 80–81
Kansas, University of, 33, 35
Kanter, Albert L., 140
Keith, Arthur, L., 69–70, 81
Kelsey, Francis Willey, 23–24, 30, 31*fig.*, 77–80, 79*fig.*
Kennedy, John B., 128
Kennedy, John F., 16, 185–89, 192–93, 196, 200
Kenney, Robert F., 189, 192–93, 195
Kennedy, Ted, 196
Kentucky, 126, 223
Khan, Arthur D., 201–2
Kiefer, Henry C., 144
King, Martin Luther, 189, 192–93
Kleine, George, 87–94
Klu Klux Klan, 192
Knight Ridder / Tribune News Information Services, 216
Korea, 141, 200
Kowalski, Stanley, 165
Krauthammer, Charles, 209, 216
Kuhner, Jeffrey T., 237

Labienus, 32, 187

Lamb, Charles, 49
Lamb, Mary, 49
Langham, Michael, 198
Lapham, Lewis H., 215
Las Vegas, 182–85
Latin for the New Millennium (Minkova and Tunberg), 223
Lavisse, Ernest, 77
LA Weekly, 227
League of Nations, 112
Lee, Robert, E., 52
Leeuwenhoek, Antonius de, 223
Lepidus, 153
LeRoy, Mervyn, 120
Levy, Sol P., 89
Lewin, William, 171–73
Lewis, Sinclair, 122–23
Lexington Junior School, 126
Libby, McNeill and Libby, 66
liberalism, 123, 158, 179, 189, 192, 200, 221
Libya, 83, 237
Lictor Federation, 107
Life, 151–52, 188
Life of Atticus (Nepos), 223
Lincoln, Abraham, 4–6, 5*fig.*, 40, 50–53, 121, 243n46
Lindbergh, Charles A., 102
Literary Digest, 108
Little Caesar (novel, Burnett), 120
Little Caesar (film), 120
Living Biographies of Famous Rulers (Thomas and Thomas), 127
Long, Huey P., 122–23
Longworth, Nicholas, 103
Los Angeles Times, 227–28
Losing America: Confronting a Reckless and Arrogant Presidency (Bryd), 205
Louisiana, 122
Lupercal, the, 143, 148, 149*fig.*

MacArthur, Douglas, 141
Mack, Maynard, 173–74
Mafia, the, 119
Making of the President, 1960, The (White), 186
Maney, Richard, 146
Mankiewicz, Joseph L., 130–31, 148, 151, 153, 156–58, 166, 184, 232
Mansfield, Richard, 55–59, 57*fig.*, 62, 64
Maranzano, Salvatore, 119–20
Marathon Pictures, 120
March on Rome (Mussolini), 110–11
Marlboro cigarettes, 17, 167–68, 262n3
Martin, Christopher, 195

Mason, James, 158, 165
Massachusetts, Cambridge, 53
Matteotti, Giacomo, 110
McCarthy, Joseph R., 16, 158, 161–64, 173, 201
McCarthyism. *See* McCarthy, Joseph R.
McGrory, Mary, 211
McKidd, Kevin, 229
McKinlay, A.P., 73–74
McKinley, William, 53, 58, 62, 245n23
Memphis, 192
Menzies, Tobias, 228
Mercury Theater, 114, 116–18, 123–25
Messaggero, Il, 204
Metro-Goldwyn-Mayer (MGM), 130–31, 145–59, 149*fig.,* 153*fig.,* 161–66, 172–73
Metropolitan Life Insurance, 197
Meyer, Frank, 178
MGM. *See* Metro-Goldwyn-Mayer
Michigan, 23, 38, 72, 78
militarism, 68–97
military theory, 6–7, 14, 38, 68–70, 75, 78–80, 79*fig.,* 127, 203, 207
Millet, Aimé, 77
Miner, Worthington, 138–39
Minkova, Milena, 223
Minnesota, 69, 82
Mississippi, University of, 91
Missouri State Normal School, 24
Mithridates, 204
Modern School, A (Flexner), 71
Molnar, Thomas, 179–82, 184
Mommsen, Theodor, 37, 45, 133, 175
Montana, 93
Morgan Guaranty Trust, 197
Morris, Philip, 167
Motte, Henri-Paul, 229
Movers & Shakespeares, 226
movie theaters. *See* film
Moving Picture World, 63–65
Mülhausen, 69
Mumford, Lewis, 183–84
Murphy, Cullen, 205, 233
Murrow, Edward R., 162–64, 163*fig.*
Mussolini, Benito, 14–15, 95, 104–12, 106*fig.,* 113*fig.,* 116, 119, 122, 126–28, 132, 134–36, 138, 147, 192
My Autobiography (Mussolini), 107

Naples, 81
Napoleon I (Napoleon Bonaparte), 6, 37, 45, 46, 51, 59, 97, 129
Napoleon III (Louis Napoleon), 6, 77
National Better Films Committee, 93

National Education Association, 74
National Interest (magazine), 209
National Review, 174, 178–79, 182
National Socialism, 150
Nazism, 115, 117, 126, 150, 157
Nemesis: The Last Days of the American Republic (Johnson), 205, 234
Nepos, 223
Nero, Emperor, 184, 234, 275n103
Nervii, 32, 41–42, 70, 93, 101, 229
New Amsterdam Theatre, 66
Newark, 50, 54–55, 93, 172
New England, 173
Newman, Paul, 160, 161*fig.*
New Mexico, 90
New Orleans, 112
Newsday, 203
New York, 27, 36, 55, 62, 66, 74–75, 86–87, 91, 102, 113, 116, 119, 124–25, 132, 139–41, 146, 167, 195–98, 199*fig.,* 220–22
New York Daily News, 117
New York Herald Tribune, 128, 152, 154–56
New York Journal-American, 125
New York Post, 125, 195
New York Review of Books, 202
New York Shakespeare Festival, 197
New York Sun, 58
New York Times, 70, 81, 82*fig.,* 94, 95, 108–9, 114, 138–40, 146, 162, 164, 181, 186, 189, 191, 209–10, 220, 222, 225–26, 233
New York World, 111
nickelodeons. *See* film
Nixon, Richard, 189, 191–92, 195–96, 203
N.K. Fairbanks and Company, 65
Notenkraker, De, 108
novels, 40–45, 42*fig.,* 43*fig.,* 120–21, 134–39, 197, 230, 241n17

Obama, Barack, 236–37
Observer, The, 227
Octavian. *See* Augustus
Oklahoma City Advertiser, 163–64
Oregon, 73, 74
Orgetorix, 27–28, 32
Orlando, Joe, 170
Orman, Roscoe, 199*fig.*
Ottoman Empire, 83
Ovid, 241n2

paintings, 39*fig.,* 62, 76, 77*fig.,* 84, 229, 246n50
Pakistan, 216

Pan-American Exposition, 53
Papp, Joseph, 197–98
Parthia, 132
Party Politics in the Age of Caesar (Taylor), 150, 190
Pasinetti, Pier Maria, 149–50
Patton, George S., 129
PBS. See Public Broadcasting Service
Pharsalus, battle of, 85
Philadelphia, 49
Philippi, battle of, 62, 155
Philippines, 53
Photoplay Studies, 172
Plautus, 223
Plutarch, 93, 148
Poland, 126
Pollio, Asinius, 187–88
Polybius, 177
Pompey (Gnaeus Pompeius Magnus), 39, 116, 187
Portia, 143
Powell, Colin, 220
presidents of America, comparisons with Caesar, 133, 168, 176–77, 179–80, 186–87, 204–5
Princeton, University of, 25, 71, 95
Progresso Italo-Americano, Il, 86–107
Prohibition, 119
Project for the New American Century (PNAC), 207–8
Public Broadcasting Service (PBS), 196–97
Public Theater, New York, 198, 199fig.
Pullo, Titus, 229–30

Quo Vadis (film), 146

Ranous, William V., 60
Ravenna, 85, 186
Raymond, Robert R., 48, 51
Reagan, Ronald, 227
Reid, Albert T., 112, 113fig.
Reincarnazione di Cesare—Il predestinato (Rosavita), 106fig.
Reinhard, H. 31fig.
Renaissance, 21, 27
Rhine, Caesar's bridge across the, 32-35, 34fig., 38, 69, 101–2, 129
Rhode Island, 65
Rico. See Bandello, Cesare
Rimini, 112
Rochegrosse, George Antoine, 39fig., 246n50
Rockne, Knute, 103
Rolfe, William J., 53, 58
Romagna, 111

Roman Clarion, 193
Roman Herald, The, 103
romanità, 104–5, 119, 134
Roman Tribune, The, 103
Roman Voting Assemblies (Taylor), 190
Rome, 38, 90, 95–96, 101, 107–8, 110, 133–34, 136–37, 139, 148–49, 151–53, 155, 160, 175, 178–79, 183, 186, 188–89, 194, 197–98, 200, 205–6, 220, 232–33
Rome (television series), 227–33, 229fig., 231fig.
Roosevelt, Franklin D., 114, 133, 175–76, 180
Roosevelt, Theodore, 72
Rosavita, 106fig.
Royer, Lionel, 76, 77fig., 84, 229
Rubicon: Caesar's crossing, 17, 105, 185–89, 214, 228, 232–33; change of name under Mussolini, 111; proverbial meaning, 176, 210–19, 235–37
Rubicon: The Triumph and Tragedy of the Roman Republic (Holland), 235
Rubinstein, Annette, 170
Rugby school, 45
Rumsfeld, Donald, 204, 207
Russell, W.H., 168–69
Russia, 147–48, 188. See also Soviet Union
Rutgers University, 197
Ryland, Jack, 220

Saalburg, 81
Sabin, Francis E., 91
Sadler, William, 221
Sallust, 241n2
Sanchez, Jaime, 198–99
San Francisco, 90
Sarno, Jay, 184
Saturday Evening Post, 107
Saturday Review, 166, 198
Sawdust Caesar: The Untold History of Mussolini and Fascism (Seldes), 110–11, 122, 134
Schell, Jonathan, 203
Schlesinger, Arthur M., 190–91
School Review, 35
Scribo, Mannie, 121
Scudder, Jared W., 96–97
seals. See Virginia, seal
Second Year Latin (Scudder), 96–97
See It Now (television series), 162–64, 163fig.
Seldes, George, 110–12, 122, 126–28, 134
Selzer, Milton, 160
Servilia, 84, 87, 232

Shakespeare for the Young Folk (Raymond), 51
Shakespeare Guild, The, 48
Shakespeare in Charge: The Bard's Guide to Leading and Succeeding on the Business Stage (Augustine and Adelman), 225–26
Shakespeare's *Julius Caesar*: American resonance, 3–4, 9–10, 13–17, 48–53, 58–59, 119, 191–96, 193*fig.*, 199–200, 219–24; Antony in, 40, 60, 62, 65–66, 89, 114–15, 117, 118*fig.*, 124, 126, 139, 142–45, 142*fig.*, 151–56, 153*fig.*, 158, 164–66, 192, 195–96, 198, 200, 220–22, 225–26; Brutus in, 49–51, 56–58, 57*fig.*, 62, 65, 115–17, 116*fig.*, 123–24, 139, 142*fig.*, 143, 152, 156–58, 165, 176, 192, 195, 199*fig.*, 200, 220–22, 226; Caesar in, 51–53, 56–57, 61*fig.*, 62, 115–17, 116*fig.*, 139, 149*fig.*, 165, 173, 194–96, 199*fig.*, 220–21, 226; Cassius in, 49, 51, 58, 65–66, 88, 113, 139, 142*fig.*, 143, 162, 165–66, 199*fig.*, 222; in comic books, 140–45, 142*fig.*, 144*fig.*, 166, 170; on film, 13, 59–65, 61*fig.*, 83, 87–90, 130–31, 145–59, 149*fig.*, 153*fig.*, 163–66, 171–73, 192–95, 193*fig.*; literary variations, 49, 53, 39–40, 49, 121, 136, 225–26; modern dress, 15, 113–18, 116*fig.*, 118*fig.*, 123, 125, 196, 199–200, 220–21, 224, 253n48
—modern film, stage, & television productions: dir. Burge (1970), 192–95, 193*fig.*; dir. Freedman (1979) 199–200; dir. Gaines (2003), 219–22, 224; dir. Langham (1979), 198, 199*fig.*; dir. Mankiewicz (1953), 130–31, 145–59, 149*fig.*, 153*fig.*, 161–66, 172–73; dir. Mansfield (1902), 55–59, 57*fig.*, 62, 64; dir. Nickell (1949), 138–39; dir. Ranous (1908), 60–65, 61*fig.*, 83, 88; dir. Sullivan (2005), 221; dir. Welles (1937), 14–15, 113–20, 116*fig.*, 118*fig.*, 123–26, 130–31, 139, 165, 195, 220; dir. Wise (1979), 196–97
Shakespeare's Tragedy of Julius Caesar (Rolfe), 53, 58
Shange, Ntozake, 198
Sicily, 119
sic semper tyrannis, 1, 4, 121, 231
Siedler, Charles W., 167–68
Sillavan, James A., 213
Six Feet Under (television series), 228
Slovakia, 204
Slovenia, 204
Smith College, 48
Sobbicus, Vittoria, 157
Soho Weekly News, 197

Sopranos, The (television series), 228
Sorrows of Empire, The: Militarism, Secrecy, and the End of the Republic (Johnson), 205, 219
South Carolina, 216
South Dakota, 102–3, 125–26
Soviet Union, 126, 138–39, 147, 150–51, 155, 157, 203, 207
Spearing, James O., 94
Spengler, Oswald, 175
Stalinism. *See* Stalin, Joseph
Stalin, Joseph, 16, 126, 138, 147–53, 157, 192
Standard Bearer, The: A Story of Army Life in the Time of Caesar (Whitehead), 40–45, 42*fig.*, 43*fig.*, 230
State Foreign Relations Committee, 181
Stevens, Matt, 120
Stevenson, Adlai E., 157, 159
Stevenson, Ray, 229
Stone, Shepard, 109
Story of Caesar (Clarke), 38–40, 45
Story of Civilization, The (Durant), 132
Strange Case of Dr Jekyll and Mr Hyde (theater), 56
Streetcar Named Desire, A (theater and film), 165
Studio One (television series), 138
Study of History (Toynbee), 151
Suetonius, 135
Sulla, 133
Sullivan, Daniel, 221
Sulzberger, C. L., 181

Taft, William Howard, 72
Tales from Shakespeare (Lamb and Lamb; Morris) 49
Taylor, Alan, 230
Taylor, Lily Ross, 150, 190
Teaching Literature in the Grammar Grades and High School (Bolenius), 50, 54–55
television, 138–39, 159–64, 161*fig.*, 191, 196–97, 227–32, 229*fig.*, 231*fig.*
Tencteri, 33
terrorist attacks, 208–9
Tertulla, 87
Teutons, 37–38, 73, 82, 86
textbooks, 27–36, 31*fig.*, 39, 53, 72–73, 76–80, 83, 95–97, 105, 154, 224–25, 229. *See also* illustrations in textbooks
theater, 2–3, 55–59, 62, 66, 113–19, 116*fig.*, 123–25, 128, 138, 195–98, 199*fig.*, 219–22, 224
This Week, 64
Thomas, Dana Lee, 127
Thomas, Henry, 127

Three Musketeers, The (comic book), 140
Time, 133, 156, 232
Time-Life Television, 196
Tolman, H.L., 126
totalitarianism, 130–66
Toynbee, Arnold, 151, 175
Toynbee, Polly, 212
trade cards, 65–66
Travaso, 112, 113*fig.*
Trudeau, Garry, 217–18
Truman, Harry, 138, 162, 191
Tunberg, Terence, 223
Turrinus, 136
Twentieth Century, 155
tyranny, 13, 17, 48, 50, 58, 59, 62

United Cigar Stores, 66*fig.*, 67
United Nations, 141, 211–12, 214–15, 217
United States Naval Academy, 168–69
United States of America: colonial, 2–4, 49–
   50, 53, 239n3; constitution, 3–4, 37, 88,
   150, 154, 176, 181, 190, 215, 234, 236–
   37; economy, 23, 114, 133, 183, 189,
   205, 209–10; education, 6, 12–15, 17,
   21–97, 101–5, 125–27, 223–24, 237.
   See also presidents of America, compari-
   sons with Caesar; textbooks; wars
University of California, Los Angeles
   (UCLA), 149
Usipetes, 33, 37

Value of the Classics (West), 71–72
Vanity Fair, 233
Variety, 117, 165
Veneti, 32, 101
veni, vidi, vici, 167–68
Vercingetorix, 14, 42, 47, 76, 77*fig.*, 80–84,
   85*fig.*, 88, 101, 170, 228–30, 229*fig.*
*Vercingétorix jette ses armes aux pieds de
   César* (painting; Royer), 76, 77*fig.*, 84,
   229
Vietnam, 180–81, 189, 191, 200
Village Voice, 195
Virgil, 237, 241n2
Virginia: House of Burgesses, 3; and Lee,
   Robert E., 52; seal, 1, 3*fig.*, 4, 10, 231;
   sic semper tyrannis motto, 1, 4, 121, 231
visual art: architecture, 62, 148, 155, 184,
   259nn88,89; paintings, 39*fig.*, 62, 76,
   77*fig.*, 84, 229, 246n50; statues, 77, 81–

82, 106*fig.*, 112
Vitagraph, 60–65, 61*fig.*, 83, 88
Vorenus, Lucius, 229–31

Waddell, William, 45–46
Walker, Arthur Tappan, 33, 35
wars: American Civil War, 9, 50, 52; Ameri-
   can Revolution, 1–4, 7, 9, 48–49, 210;
   First World War, 14, 68–80, 78, 83,
   95,— and Gallic Wars, 14, 68–83,
   79*fig.*, 102; Iraq War, 204–6, 211–22,
   227, 233; Korean War, 141, 200; Persian
   Gulf, 203, 215; Second World War, 126–
   27, 131, 134, 137, 141, 169, 171, 177,
   183, 201; Vietnam War, 181, 189, 200
Warthen, Brad, 216–17
Washington, 23, 32, 95, 155, 196, 228
Washington, Denzel, 222
Washington Evening Post, 128
Washington, George, 2, 6, 45
Washington Post, 181, 182*fig.*, 209–11
Washington Times, 117, 237
Watergate scandal, 191, 196, 209
Weber, Bruce, 226
We (Lindbergh), 102
Welles, Orson, 15, 113–20, 116*fig.*, 118*fig.*,
   123–26, 130–31, 139, 165, 195, 220
West, Andrew F., 71
Westinghouse, 139
Whitehead, A.C., 40–45, 42*fig.*, 43*fig.*, 230
White House, the, 169, 171, 177–82, 186,
   188, 190, 210, 218, 227, 237
White, Theodore H., 185–90, 214
Wilder, Thornton, 134–38
Wilhelm II. *See* Kaiser Wilhelm II of
   Germany
Wilson, Woodrow, 25–26, 29, 72, 75
Windrup, Berzelius, 122
Wisconsin, 91, 158, 162
Wise, Herbert, 197
WNYC (radio station), 196
Wolfowitz, Paul, 207
World's Work, The (magazine), 74–76

Yale University, 173, 208, 251n2
You Are There (television series), 159–60,
   161*fig.*
Ypres, 78, 79*fig.*

Zela, battle of, 167